D1491857

Edge Hill University
WITHDRAWN

Crime and Authority in Victorian England

THE BLACK COUNTRY 1835–1860

DAVID PHILIPS

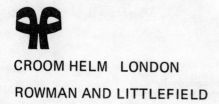

CROOM HELM   LONDON

ROWMAN AND LITTLEFIELD

© David Philips
Croom Helm Ltd, 2-10 St John's Road, London SW11

British Library Cataloguing in Publication Data

Philips, David
    Crime and authority in Victorian England.
    1. Crime and criminals — England — Black country
    I. Title
    364'.9424'9   HV6950.B/

    ISBN 0-85664-568-0

First published in the United States 1977
by Rowman and Littlefield, Totowa, N.J.

Library of Congress Cataloging in Publication Data
Philips, David.
    Crime and authority in Victorian England.

    Bibliography: p.302
    Includes index.
    1. Crime and criminals — England — History.
2. Police — England — History. I. Title.
HV6946.P48 1977   364'.942   77-8145
ISBN 0-87471-866-X

To my parents
with gratitude and affection

Edge Hill College Library
364·942
142314

Printed in Great Britain by offset lithography by
Billing & Sons Ltd, Guildford, London and Worcester

CONTENTS

Tables

Graphs and Map

Abbreviations

Preface

TABLES

GRAPHS

MAPS

ABBREVIATIONS

Ass.	Assizes
CC	Chief Constable
CJA	Criminal Justice Act 1855
DNB	Dictionary of National Biography
HC	Hatherton Correspondence
HO	Home Office
JOA	Juvenile Offenders Acts 1847 and 1850
JSSL	*Journal of the Statistical Society of London*
MC	*Morning Chronicle*
MDTC	Minutes of the Dudley Town Commissioners
MWWC	Minutes of the Wolverhampton Watch Committee
PP	Parliamentary Papers
PRO	Public Record Office
QS	Quarter Sessions
RC	Royal Commission
SA	*Staffordshire Advertiser*
Sal. RO	Shropshire County Record Office
SC	Select Committee
SRO	Staffordshire County Record Office
TLB	Talbot Letter Book
WC	*Wolverhampton Chronicle*
WCL	Wolverhampton Central Library
WH	*Worcester Herald*
Worc. Chron.	*Worcester Chronicle*
WRO	Worcestershire County Record Office
WSL	William Salt Library, Stafford

Specific Quarter Sessions are abbreviated as follows:

E.	Epiphany
Ea.	Easter
M.	Midsummer
Mich.	Michaelmas
Adj.	Adjourned

PREFACE

Crime is not an easy subject to define or to handle with precision. When examined historically, the normal problems of material to be examined and interpretation to be used, grow to enormous proportions. This book seeks to contribute to an understanding of the issues of lawbreaking and law enforcement in the England which was experiencing the effects of the first Industrial Revolution. Problems of material and interpretation have forced this study to concentrate on just one industrial area, the Black Country. The findings of this study can help to throw light on many of the issues of crime and law enforcement which faced all of industrial England in this period; and it is hoped that this book may stimulate comparable studies of other industrial areas in this period.

This book grows out of an Oxford D.Phil thesis. Two chapters of the thesis, dealing respectively with riots and public order measures, and with the magistracy of the area, have already been published, and their contents are largely omitted from this book. The relevant articles are: 'Riots and Public Order in the Black Country 1835-60' in Stevenson, J. and Quinault, R. (ed.), *Popular Protest and Public Order* (London 1974); and 'The Black Country Magistracy 1835-60; a changing local elite and the exercise of its power' in *Midland History* (spring 1976).

I am grateful to the Warden and Fellows of Nuffield College, Oxford, who supported my thesis research with three years of a College Studentship and one term of a Prize Studentship. The work of compiling, coding and analysing the data from more than 20,000 cases was made possible by the assistance of Clive Payne and his Research Services Unit at Nuffield; I received especial help from Mrs Jean Nichols and Mrs Kleri Smith.

The material for this study came from record offices and local libraries. I am grateful to the staffs of the Public Record Office in London and their depository in Ashridge; the British Museum Newspaper Library at Colindale; the Worcestershire and Shropshire County Record Offices; the reference sections of the Wolverhampton and Dudley Central Public Libraries; and to the Clerk of the Peace for the County Borough of Walsall for allowing me to consult the Quarter Sessions records of the Borough of Walsall for 1836-60 which are held in his office.

I owe a particular debt of gratitude to Mr F. Stitt, County Archivist, and his staff in the Staffordshire County Record Office and the William Salt Library in Stafford. Most of my material comes from these twin institutions, and during my long hours spent compiling it, I was shown unfailing kindness, friendliness and helpfulness by Mr Stitt and the Record Office staff, especially Mrs S. Pilmore and Dr D. Robinson.

Parts of this work were read and criticised in earlier drafts by Nigel Walker, now Professor of Criminology at Cambridge, and Jennifer Hart, of St Anne's College; their criticisms were very useful. I also benefited greatly from extended debates and mutual criticism sessions with Thomas Laqueur, now at the University of California at Berkeley, and from discussions with Alan Gilbert, John Stevenson, Mary Daly and Roland Quinault. I am very grateful to Brian Harrison, of Corpus Christi College, and Barry Smith, of the Australian National University, who read through the entire thesis and made valuable criticisms and suggestions for its revision. Needless to say, I alone bear responsibility for the final product.

My greatest personal debt is to my thesis supervisor, Max Hartwell, of Nuffield College. Despite our ideological disagreement on many points, he was of the greatest help to me in this work — encouraging my interest in this area, sustaining my confidence through bouts of depression, and vigorously criticising all my written drafts. I hope that he finds this book a worthwhile end-product of his invaluable encouragement and friendship.

Finally, I would like to thank: Charles Evans, of the Educational Technology section of the Centre for the Study of Higher Education at Melbourne University, for drawing the graphs and map; the Arts Faculty of Melbourne University for a grant from their Research Development Fund towards the cost of having this manuscript typed; and Miss Mary Holyoake for efficiently typing it.

Transcripts of Crown copyright records in the Staffordshire County Record Office appear by permission of the Controller of HM Stationery Office. Parts of the Hatherton and Talbot papers deposited in the Staffordshire County Record Office were consulted by kind permission of Lord Hatherton and the Earl of Shrewsbury.

Melbourne,
February 1977

1 INTRODUCTION

I

In 1844, Friedrich Engels returned from a twenty-month stay in England and wrote his classic study of *The Condition of the Working Class in England*. In this, he developed his account of how the Industrial Revolution and the concomitant urbanisation had called into being the English proletariat, who lived and worked in miserable conditions and who were rapidly becoming an alienated and demoralised class, set apart from their upper and middle class rulers. One of the effects of this development, said Engels, was a rapid growth in crime in industrial and urban England:

> The clearest indication of the unbounded contempt of the workers for the existing social order is the wholesale manner in which they break its laws. If the demoralisation of the worker passes beyond a certain point then it is just as natural that he will turn into a criminal — as inevitably as water turns into steam at boiling point. . . Consequently the incidence of crime has increased with the growth of the working-class population and there is more crime in Britain than in any other country in the world. . .There can be no doubt that in England the social war is already being waged. . .The criminal statistics prove that this social war is being waged more vigorously, more passionately and with greater bitterness every year. Social strife is gradually developing into combat between two great opposing camps — the middle classes and the proletariat.[1]

Engels' ideological viewpoint was not one shared by many observers of the workers' frustrations; they could be expected to continue to grow in number until the ultimate dissolution of English society in social war and revolution.

Engels' ideological viewpoint was not one shared by many observers of the nineteenth-century English scene; yet his view that industrialisation and urbanisation must inescapably be accompanied by growing crime and disorder was also held by men of a very different political complexion. For instance, the Tory Sheriff of Lanarkshire, Sir Archibald Alison, wrote in 1844:

13

If the past increase and present amount of crime in the British islands be alone considered, it must afford grounds for the most melancholy forebodings. [Since 1805, the population of England has increased 65 per cent and crime in England 700 per cent.] . . . It is difficult to say what is destined to be the ultimate fate of a country in which the progress of wickedness is so much more rapid than the increase of the numbers of people. . .Meanwhile, destitution, profligacy, sensuality and crime advance with unheard-of rapidity in the manufacturing districts, and the dangerous classes there massed together combine every three or four years in some general strike or alarming insurrection, which, while it lasts, excites universal terror. . .The vast preponderance of crime is to be found in the manufacturing or densely-populated districts.[2]

Alison's attitude towards the predicted developments is very different from Engels', and yet his prediction is a similar one of growing crime and disorder leading to social breakdown. (Note how he juxtaposes 'general strike' and 'insurrection' with 'crime', 'manufacturing districts', and 'dangerous classes' to link all these developments to a common root.)

Not all contemporary writers on this subject were as apocalyptic in their predictions of the ultimate outcome as Engels and Alison were, but many others shared this view that England's industrialisation and urbanisation were causing a dangerous increase in crime.[3] G.R. Porter's *The Progress of the Nation* is an exuberantly optimistic celebration of England's industrial and commercial expansion, filled with tables showing the great increase in every sphere; one of the few areas in which Porter allowed a possible qualification to enter his radiant optimism about the industrial future was in his discussion of English crime rates since the beginning of the nineteenth century. Here, tables showing a steady increase suggested that rising crime rates might be an unavoidable accompaniment to growing industrial prosperity. As Porter noted:

It would indeed be a heart-sickening prospect, if, in looking forward to the continued progress of our country in its economical relations, we must also contemplate the still greater multiplication of its criminals. The nature of the case does not indeed admit of our realising such a future as is here supposed, for, ere it could be reached, the whole physical frame-work of society must be broken up.

Porter was able to reassure himself and his readers that industrial and economic growth need *not* necessarily entail a growth in crime, provided the government took the necessary 'moral' measures; but the fear was still there.[4]

All these writers, especially those writing in the 1840s, could produce *prima facie* evidence to show that crime had increased in England and was likely to continue to increase. In 1810, the government had begun publishing annual figures of the numbers of persons tried for indictable (the more serious) offences, taking the series back as far as 1805. These figures show that, between 1805 and 1842, the number of committals to trial for indictable offences increased to nearly seven times their original amount, during a period when the total population had increased by only about 80 per cent.

Year	Total Committals for Trial England and Wales[5]
1805	4,605
1810	5,146
1815	7,818
1820	13,710
1825	14,437
1830	18,107
1832	20,829
1835	20,731
1840	27,187
1842	31,309
1845	24,303

The fact of this great increase in indictable committals to trial was indisputable. It was also apparent that the greatest increases in these figures were registered at times in which they coincided with periods of economic depression and political unrest — 1815-19, 1832, 1842. It is not surprising that Engels and Alison, writing in 1844, took the crime figures, together with the disturbances of the Chartist period from 1838 onwards, to suggest a general growth in violence, political unrest and threats to the stability of society. And they and other commentators linked both the growing crime figures and the political unrest to the development of industrialisation and the concentration of population in urban and industrial centres.

But how far is it true that there *was* a great 'growth in crime' in this period? Certainly the figures of persons brought to trial show a great increase, but some of this may reflect improvements in police and changes in the legal system. This study sets out to examine crime and law enforcement in one industrial area in this period, in order to try to answer some of the questions which this issue poses — for what sorts of offences were the committals increasing, how effective were the agencies of police and the judiciary, who were the offenders and their victims, and what motivation can one attribute to the offenders? What was the attitude of the growing industrial working class towards the law and its agents — did they accept the legitimacy and authority of the law; was there a clear distinction between the honest 'respectable poor' and the dishonest 'criminal class'?

Crime is a notoriously slippery subject to define and deal with; this is all the more true when it is studied historically. Of crucial importance is the question of what material can be used for such an historical study, and the equally important question of how such material should be approached and analysed. In the few recent historical studies of nineteenth-century English crime, the questions of material and type of analysis to be used have dictated the shape taken by those studies and their conclusions. Before proceeding any further, therefore, it is both useful and necessary to examine in some detail the sources and approach used in the three relevant recent historical studies — those of J.J. Tobias, K.K. Macnab, and V. Gatrell and T. Hadden.[6]

Tobias's is probably the best known of these works. Of the possible sources open to him for his study, he rejects entirely the official criminal and judicial statistics, whether of court appearances or of offences reported to the police, chiefly on the grounds that the police statistics were not kept with any consistency as between one place and another, or one period and another. Any statistics other than the police figures of reported offences (such as the numbers of persons appearing in court for particular offences, or the number convicted of offences) he rejects as too remote from the criminal act itself to give accurate information on the state of crime. The numbers of persons appearing in court charged with particular offences would depend, to a large extent, on the adequacy of police enforcement, and the uniformity and efficiency of prosecution, as well as on the number of offences committed. When the police services are weak and prosecution not uniformly and thoroughly carried out, as was the case in the nineteenth century, the figures of court appearances will be far removed from the numbers of offences being committed; and some of the changes in the levels of the statistics would be influenced more by changes in law-enforcement efficiency and practices, and changes in the administration of the law, than by changes in the numbers of criminal acts. Therefore, he concludes, 'criminal statistics have little to tell us about crime and criminals in the nineteenth century'.[7]

Having rejected the official statistics, Tobias uses as his sources: the evidence given to Parliamentary Commissions of Enquiry and Select Committees, of which there were many dealing with subjects concerning crime, the law and the police in the nineteenth century; books and articles written by law reformers, penal reformers, magistrates, prison chaplains, statistical investigators, policemen, journalists, civil servants, educationists, and the large number of contemporary commentators with a strong interest in crime and the criminal law, and in supplying remedies for crime. This, in Tobias's view, gives him a much fuller insight into the realities of 'the criminal class' (a phrase which he uses, and whose use he defends, throughout the book) at work and in the areas in which they lived.

This approach carries with it the advantage that much of the evidence can be about the normal life and *modus operandi* of the criminal rather than being restricted to looking only at those offenders whose offences have been detected and prosecuted. If one accepts that much 'real crime' never reaches the courts, but can be learned from the accounts of policemen about what really goes on, or from the confessions of ex-criminals, then one will obviously learn more about it from these sorts of sources than from the official figures — a Mayhew will tell one more about the typical method of operation of a pickpocket than can be learned in the official figures. And there is much useful information contained within Tobias's book, in which he distils the fruits of his very wide reading in this type of source.

However, exclusive reliance on this type of source carries with it disadvantages of which Tobias seems too little aware. First, the only view which is obtained is the official view of crime — one might say the police view. The magistrates, prison chaplains, social reformers, police officers, etc. who gave evidence to the Commissions or wrote articles for the *Journal of the Statistical Society of London* were all people of similar social backgrounds, from the upper or middle classes, who viewed crime and the criminal as social problems which must be contained, and for which remedies must be sought; generally, increased education and religion for the lower classes was the remedy which they recommended. Consciously or unconsciously, they slanted much of the evidence which they gave to committees, or published in articles or books, to this end. There is nothing very surprising about this — it is now generally accepted that some of the most influential Parliamentary enquiries of the mid-nineteenth century were packed and manipulated towards a favourable verdict by those with a cause to advance.[8] But Tobias does not seem to allow for the possibility that such a bias may be operating, and has no adequate checks on the evidence. It is not enough to cite, as he often does, the views of five, six, or even ten such witnesses, and take the fact that they agree with each other as proof that that point of view is correct. This is an important point since Tobias uses this method to 'establish' some of his important conclusions (such as 'the view that crime was not as a rule the result of want appears to have been generally correct' and 'it thus seems certain that a marked decline in the level of juvenile crime took place in the 1850s and 1860s').[9] These statements may be correct, but the supporting evidence is in no sense convincing.

Secondly, even if one accepted that all evidence given to Parliamentary enquiries was automatically correct (and certainly they contain a great deal of useful information if cautiously handled), it would still not be enough simply to quote such judgements as fact, since the same enquiry generally contains witnesses who will state diametrically opposed views about the same topics. For instance, in the evidence given to the Select Committee on Criminal Commitments (1828), a number of witnesses said that the increase in commitments to trial *did* mean an increase in the actual number of criminal acts which had been committed, while a number of others denied this and attributed the increase entirely to increased prosecution owing to an extension of the reimbursement of expenses available to prosecutors; a number expressed it as their opinion that crime was directly caused by poverty and distress, while a number of others stated that crime was definitely not caused by want.[10] Similarly, to support his own contention that crime was not caused by economic hardship, Tobias quotes a statement by the magistrate and prison reformer M.D. Hill, made in the 1850s, to the effect that crime was produced not by economic depressions but by increased prosperity which led to greater drunkenness and hence to greater crime. But Tobias ignores the fact that in 1861 Hill stated that: 'as a general rule. . .every increase of crime that was common to the whole country, and that lasted more than a short period, was evidently due to a depression in the pecuniary circumstances of the country'.[11] If treated as statements of opinion, these statements can be useful; if taken as statements of fact, and checked only against similar statements, they are likely to prove unreliable. Which of the sets of quotations one would choose to cite would depend on which point of view one wished to establish – no bad thing if one has other types of evidence as well, on which the conclusions can be based, but dangerous if this is the sole type of evidence. As Tobias himself notes, when trying, by this method, to establish whether there was or was not an increase of crime in the first half of the nineteenth century: 'This game of matching quotation to quotation could go on for a long time',[12] but he does not seem to feel that use of this method, unchecked by any other form of evidence, renders any of his conclusions at all suspect.

Thirdly, Tobias feels the need, as anyone writing on crime must do, to venture some generalisations about the subject and make some statements which, if only implicitly, are essentially quantitative in nature. No particular point is established about crime in general by concentrating on a few individual offences or offenders, if no indication is given of how typical such events or people are, and how they relate to the overall picture. But the use of such essentially impressionistic sources does not lend itself easily to the drawing of quantitative conclusions, and Tobias has explicitly rejected the quantitative statistics as evidence. The result is that he has the worst of both worlds, and draws quantitative conclusions from his impressionistic sources, which turn out, on closer examination, to be derived from the use of the criminal statistics at secondhand.

The defect in the statistics of appearances in court, conviction and imprisonment, Tobias has said, is that they only tell us about those offenders who were detected, prosecuted, found guilty, and imprisoned; not about what was happening among the 'criminal class' themselves. Yet he can make a categorical statement such as: 'There was a marked drop in juvenile crime, and in the number of juvenile criminals, in the 1850s and 1860s'. On examination, this statement turns out to be based on the expressed opinions of Rev. John Clay, chaplain of Preston Gaol, T.B.L. Baker, a Gloucestershire magistrate and an important figure in the movement to establish reformatories for juvenile offenders, Mary Carpenter, also a writer and prominent member of the Reformatory movement, Rev. W.L. Clay, also a prison chaplain, and Rev. S. Turner, Inspector of Reformatory Schools.[13] But from what had these people derived their estimates of the numbers of juvenile criminals, but from the *numbers of juvenile offenders who passed through the courts, prisons or reformatories;* and if Tobias wanted these figures, he could get them direct from the criminal statistics, and not refracted through the opinions of Rev. John Clay or

T.B.L. Baker.

Tobias is aware of the difficulties here — 'It must be admitted that (Baker) was relying, in part at any rate, on the criminal statistics, as indeed other people may have been' — but hopes to avoid this by stating: 'but some of the names on the list of those who shared his opinions are impressive'; he then cites the names listed above, and concludes: 'These are powerful authorities'.[14] But this is to evade the point at issue — if the criminal statistics really are misleading and useless in what they tell us about nineteenth-century crime, then it makes no difference to the soundness of the conclusion whether they are being analysed by T.B.L. Baker in the 1850s, or by an historian in the 1960s — the conclusion they yield will be false and useless. The fact that Baker, Clay *et al.* are 'powerful authorities' will not make the conclusions any more correct if the data on which they are based are essentially faulty; after all, Edwin Chadwick and many powerful medical authorities in the 1840s believed in the miasmatic theory of the diffusion of disease, and based much of official health policy on this theory,[15] but this does not mean that historians of the subject must accept that belief as valid, simply because it emanates from these 'powerful authorities'. If, on the other hand, the conclusions of Baker, Clay *et al.* have validity, then there is no reason why the data on which they are based — the criminal statistics themselves — cannot be analysed directly. If Tobias can cite with approval the opinions of Clay and Baker that the numbers of juveniles in court and prison had decreased, why can he not go direct to the statistics and set out the national figures for juveniles being prosecuted and imprisoned in this period? Nor is this example of juvenile crime an isolated one. Tobias has to use similar methods when dealing with the question of whether 'the level of crime' increased or decreased; whether the number of crimes committed had any connection with the cyclical movements of the economy; and whether crime was in any sense caused by poverty or by 'the temptations of the profit of a career of depredation, as compared with the profits of honest and even well paid industry'.[16] He cites a number of opinions on these subjects, from similar sorts of people to those listed for the question of juvenile crime, and takes these as establishing the facts relating to these difficult questions which essentially require some form of quantitative statement to be made. These statements are useful and instructive in showing what people thought about these subjects; they do not establish the truth on these questions.

Fourthly, the official 'policeman' view of the book comes out strongly in its concentration on professional criminals and the 'criminal class', as if these were the only people concerned in the questions of rising crime rate, reform of the police, changes in prosecution and the administration of the criminal law. It implicitly seems to make a distinction between 'real crime', which is committed on a regular basis by professional criminals who have no other occupation, and 'other crime' which is offences for which people who are not professional criminals are prosecuted. Even if this distinction is a valid one (and it is argued in the following chapter that it is not), it is, nonetheless, the case that the majority of persons prosecuted in the courts were prosecuted for small thefts, not for large professional crimes (see chapters 5 and 6). If the study of 'crime' is really the study of professional crime only, then these cases must somehow be excluded from the definition of 'crime'; but if they are accepted as a valid part of 'crime', then a study of professional crime gives only a partial picture. It leaves out the social dimension from a study of lawbreaking; by concentrating on a single entity called 'crime', committed by 'criminals', it blurs the fact that 'crime' is in fact made up of a number of different sorts of acts (including murder, rape, riot, theft, illegal picketing, robbery, using seditious language, burglary, etc.) which contravene a number of statutes of criminal law; and it ignores the role of lawmaking and law enforcement in creating and defining crime. (This point is developed in chapter 2.)

So Tobias's whole approach to the problem is unsatisfactory. He has pointed out some of the pitfalls for the unwary to be found in the criminal statistics; I agree with this point and indeed in the following chapters I develop a much fuller analysis of the adequacy and meaning of the official figures of crime. But because the figures are deficient, it does not follow that the historian must not use them at all. Rather, he must use them with a great deal of caution and a clear understanding of their limitations — the temptation must be resisted to perform complex statistical analyses on data essentially too 'soft' to support such analysis. Within these limits, the figures *can* provide a clear quantitative framework in which to set the discussion. Even Tobias, as we have seen, has to resort to the figures at secondhand for his quantitative judgements; if one is going to do this, it is better to confront the figures directly, and set out what they can and cannot show, and what forces influence changes in them, than to claim to have nothing to do with them because of their defects, and then make use of conclusions drawn from those faulty figures.

The studies of Macnab, and of Gatrell and Hadden, differ

fundamentally from Tobias's book in that both are based firmly on the official criminal statistics. Both studies consider movements in the official figures in relation to social and economic developments in England and Wales at the time, particularly the movements of the trade cycle with its crucial effects on employment. Both show that the figures moved in inverse correlation with the trade cycle — when cyclical depressions were at their trough the criminal figures reached their peak, and when the cycle moved upwards again the figures fell. Macnab's is the earlier, and more flawed, work; it deals with the period 1805-60, and deals with only indictable committals[17] for this period. It is marred by an overemphatic statement of the extent to which changes in the national figures of indictable committals to trial can be relied on to reflect directly changes in the level of lawbreaking; and by an overstated denial of the role which changes in the law and in the behaviour of prosecutors could play in artificially inflating the figures. It also completely overlooks the effect on the figures of the Juvenile Offenders Acts (1847 and 1850) and Criminal Justice Act (1855) which transferred a large number of indictable larcenies to summary trial — and therefore removed a very large number of such cases from the statistics of indictable committals, although there had been no fall in the number of such larcenies taking place; Macnab takes this artificial fall as a real fall in the level of crime. But, on the whole, the thesis is a good attempt to relate changes in the amount and nature of crime (in so far as these can be determined from the national statistics) to social and economic changes flowing from the Industrial Revolution, stressing the fact that changes in economic conditions seem to have made up one of the key factors in determining changes in the level of criminal activity.

Gatrell and Hadden's is a later, and much more thorough, reworking of this ground; they deal with the longer period 1805-1900, and they use not only the figures for indictable committals, but also all available figures for summary offences; this prevents the error into which Macnab fell for the 1850s. They also make a very thorough and sound analysis of the limitations and possibilities of the uses of the criminal statistics and of the possible external factors which may have influenced them — indeed, Part 1 of their article is the best account which exists of the availability and potential for use of the nineteenth-century criminal statistics.[18] Basically, they show a clear *inverse* correlation between the swings of the trade cycle and the figures for *all* offences and for *all property* offences; on the other hand, there is a *direct* correlation between offences of *drunkenness and assault* and the trade cycle swings. In other words, in times of depression, property offences tended to rise, and offences of drunkenness and assault to fall; in times of prosperity, property offences tended to fall, and offences of drunkenness and assault to rise — suggesting that distress was likely to drive more people to theft and prosperity to lessen their numbers, but that prosperity also meant more money spent on drink, and hence more drunkenness and more assaults. This correlation breaks down at about the 1880s, and on the whole it is more convincingly established for the first half of the century than for the second, particularly since the trade cycle which they use for 1850-1900 is much sketchier than the one they use for 1800-50.

However, Gatrell and Hadden have taken this form of analysis about as far as it can be taken. The criminal statistics are inherently likely to have flaws in their local components — one police force will be more conscientious than another in recording offences, and the introduction, or increase in strength, of a force in one area will affect the figures of that area for the next few years, etc. The larger the scale on which such figures are used, the less chance there is that arbitrary differences in the local components will distort the overall total; if the statistics are used for the whole country, over a long period of years, one could expect the over-recording in one area to be balanced by under-recording in another, etc., and besides, small distortions at the local level will not significantly distort the *trends* which emerge from the overall national figures. But it is only at this level, of national figures and trends over time, that they can be safely used; to use the criminal statistics on a smaller scale, for a shorter time period, to find out about actual specific offences, is to run a much larger risk of distortion — the smaller the scale, the greater the possibility that these distortions will significantly affect the figures.

And yet, all that one can get from the large-scale analysis is the outline of national trends. As Gatrell and Hadden point out:

> As in the case of any average, however, national and county crime rates may mask important and perhaps contradictory movements in the incidence of criminal activity, often of a very localised character.[19]

The national average lumps together agricultural and industrial, rural and urban, rich and poor areas, areas badly affected by swings in the trade cycle and areas hardly affected at all, areas of industrial militancy and areas of docile agricultural labour. If one wants to see how patterns of criminal activity and law enforcement might relate to the pattern of employment in an area, to its social, economic and industrial structure, to its degree of urbanisation, to the makeup of its population in terms of age, sex, education, political and industrial activities, then it is necessary to go beneath the surface of the national statistics, and concentrate on one town or area. A county is unlikely to be satisfactory for this purpose; industrial and urban development was no respecter of county boundaries, so that, for instance, the Manchester cotton complex straddled the Lancashire-Cheshire border, while a county like Warwickshire contained within it an industrialised and urbanised northern half, together with a rural and agricultural southern half. Redgrave, the Criminal Registrar, expressed well the masking effect which could come from giving figures broken down only to the county level:

> The county is a useful, and for some purposes, an inevitable unit. But within the same county may be the most diverse conditions: a high rate of criminality and a low; a population very dense in some parts, sparse in others, and very different rates of marriages and births, mortality, and amount of school accommodation. Certain towns affect the returns for the whole county; outside them or their zone of influence the criminal returns may be very different.[20]

It is therefore necessary to go below the county level, and look at a town or area which comprises a reasonable economic and social unit. The criminal statistics collected by the Home Office offer no help for studying an area of this size, and in any case they can at best provide no more than the bare bones of the totals for six broad categories of offence. To obtain more information and detail on the pattern of lawbreaking in the area, the sorts of offences committed, the sorts of offenders prosecuted, the working of the forces of law enforcement, it is necessary to go to the original court records themselves and the newspaper reports of court proceedings. These court records form the basis of this study; details of their compilation are set out in Appendix I. In chapter 2 I discuss fully the theoretical approach towards this material on which this study is based. The industrial area which was chosen for study is the Black Country, for the period 1835-60.

II

The Black Country, black by day and red by night, cannot be matched for vast and varied production, by any other space of equal radius on the surface of the globe. It is a section of Titanic industry, kept in murky perspiration by a sturdy set of Tubal Cains and

Vulcans, week in week out, and often seven days to the week.[21]

So ran the enthusiastic description by Elihu Burritt, American Consul in Birmingham in the 1860s, of the area known since the 1830s as 'the Black Country'. The Black Country is the area of about 100 square miles immediately to the north-west of Birmingham. Its exact boundaries are not rigidly defined, and most works on the area differ slightly on the question of which of the outlying towns are included in the area. But all accounts are agreed that the area is basically defined by the South Staffordshire coalfield and the mining and manufacturing industries which developed around it and gave the area its name in the 1830s. In this study, the Black Country is taken to be the roughly oblong area whose corners are Wolverhampton in the north-west, Stourbridge in the south-west, West Bromwich and Handsworth in the south-east, and Walsall and Bloxwich in the north-east (see Map).[22]

Most of the area fell into South Staffordshire, but the towns of the south-west corner were in Worcestershire, while Dudley, though in the centre of the Black Country and surrounded by Staffordshire on all sides, formed a detached part of Worcestershire. The parish of Halesowen, in the south, formed a detached part of Shropshire until 1844, when it was transferred to the contiguous county of Worcestershire. These county boundaries affected the policing and prosecution of offences in the area. Dudley, though surrounded by Staffordshire, had to send its prisoners to Worcester, not Stafford, to be tried, and the Staffordshire county police force, when it came into existence, had no jurisdiction in Dudley. Halesowen, even more inconveniently, had to send its prisoners to Shrewsbury for trial, though it was policed by the Worcestershire force once that force came into existence.

The population of the area increased from 211,323 in 1831 to 473,946 in 1861, and was to be found in a number of different-sized units, ranging from large towns like Wolverhampton, Dudley, Walsall, West Bromwich and Bilston, through smaller industrial towns, to small industrial and mining villages.[23] The area had many of the characteristics of an unevenly sprawling conurbation, as was noted by the commissioner sent to the area in 1843:

In traversing much of the country included within the [South Staffordshire coalfield], the traveller appears never to get out of an interminable village, composed of cottages and very ordinary houses. In some directions he may travel for miles and never be out of sight

Map I   Map of Birmingham and the Black Country showing chief industrial towns and villages.

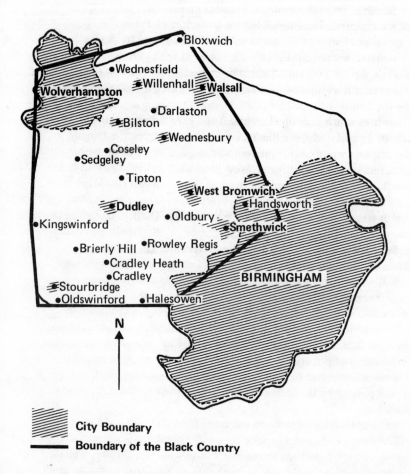

of numerous two-storied houses; so that the area covered by bricks and mortar must be immense. These houses, for the most part, are not arranged in continuous streets, but are interspersed with blazing furnaces, heaps of burning coal in the process of coking, piles of ironstone calcining, forges, pit-banks and engine chimneys; the country being besides intersected with canals, crossing each other at various levels; and the small remaining patches of the surface soil occupied with irregular fields of grass and corn, intermingled with heaps of the refuse of mines or of slag from the blast furnaces.[24]

This disfigurement of the Black Country landscape gave it its name; it derived from the fact that the Black Country drew almost all its wealth and employment from the mining of coal and iron, the manufacture of iron in all its forms, and the manufacture of a large variety of iron articles. It had been an area of ironworking and some coal mining as early as the seventeenth century; but its real prominence as a centre of coal and iron production began in the 1780s, with the use of coke and the puddling process for iron smelting, and the application of the steam engine to iron furnaces, mills and forges. By 1800, the Black Country had become established as a leading producer of iron and coal and an important centre of iron manufactures. From then on until the 1860s, there was no basic change in the industrial structure of the area. By 1830, it was rivalling South Wales as a coal and iron producing area, and it experienced its greatest period of industrial and population expansion between 1830 and the 1860s. By the 1860s, coal production was falling off, as many of the older mines became exhausted or waterlogged, and iron production was declining relative to production in Britain as a whole; the depression of the 1870s completed the decline of the old Black Country iron and coal industries — coal mining never recovered, and the old iron industry was replaced in the 1880s and 1890s by heavy engineering, and new industries such as the manufacture of bicycles (and later motor cars) and of electrical apparatus.[25] So the period of the Black Country's first great industrial expansion, based on iron and coal, was between about 1800 and 1860, with the greatest expansion being between 1830 and 1860.

In its coalmining heyday, the Black Country was famous for its 'ten yard' seam of 'thick' coal, mined in the areas around Dudley, Wednesbury and Sedgley, but 'thin' coal was also mined, so that there were coal mines in virtually every part of the area. During the period 1830-60, a large number of mines were opened up in places away from the traditional 'ten yard' seam, especially in the area around West

Bromwich. Black Country coal occurred very near the surface, and the pits were therefore of a small and primitive nature. Most pits were run on the 'butty' system, whereby the proprietor did not work his mines himself, but subcontracted them to a 'butty' or 'chartermaster' who would be paid a fixed price per ton for the coal he raised, and in turn would have to hire and pay the miners himself. Iron was mined in the same way, the ironstone being found among the layers of coal. Limestone was also quarried in the area around Dudley. Taken together, the coal, iron and limestone miners were the largest single employed group in the Black Country, numbering about 19,000 in 1851 and about 28,000 in 1861.[26]

In the iron industry, the Black Country firms produced both pig-iron and finished iron on a large scale. Unlike the production of ironmongery articles (see below), the manufacture of iron was conducted in relatively large-scale units; Allen describes the typical ironworks as consisting of 10-20 puddling furnaces, a 'balling-up' furnace, a steam-hammer, a 'forge train', 2-3 reheating furnaces and two sets of rolling mills — employing about 250 men. Furthermore, the Black Country coal and iron trades were very closely linked, with most Black Country coal being locally consumed by the iron industry. From the early 1800s, firms had developed which utilised this point by becoming integrated concerns, owning their own coal and iron mines as well as blast furnaces, puddling furnaces, forges and mills; this became more common during the period 1830-60, and by 1860 the coal and iron trades were dominated by the coal and iron masters of about twenty integrated concerns. These were the really large employers and entrepreneurs of the Black Country, men with large amounts of capital invested in the industry and employing hundreds, sometimes thousands, of men in their integrated concerns.[27] The large coal and iron masters maintained a powerful control over the coal and iron industries of the area, by meeting quarterly to fix among themselves the local prices of coal and iron and the wages to be paid in the local coal and iron industries.[28] The numbers employed in the manufacture of pig-iron and finished-iron are estimated at about 17,000 in 1851 and 26,000 in 1861.[29] Iron manufacture, like coalmining, was found in virtually every part of the Black Country.

The remaining Black Country industries were more localised within the area. Other forms of heavy iron manufacture were: the production of tubes at Wednesbury (employing about 2,000); springs and railway axles and wheels at Wednesbury and West Bromwich (employing, together, about another 2,000); and cast-iron hollow-ware, chiefly at

West Bromwich (employing about 3,000 by 1860).

The only other industry which was organised into large factories of a scale comparable to the ironworks, was the glass industry, which was located in and around Stourbridge, and in Smethwick. Chance Brothers, in Smethwick, had a large factory manufacturing crown-glass and sheet-glass, employing 1,200 hands in 1852. Flint-glass was made in Stourbridge by about twelve smaller firms, employing about another 1,000 hands between them, almost all of them in factories. It was also made in Dudley, though on a small scale, and the Dudley glass industry collapsed in the 1850s. Tinplate, japanned iron, and papier-mâché articles were also produced in factories, in Wolverhampton and Bilston, and employed about 2,000 by 1861.[30]

The other Black Country industries were marked by the absence of large-scale factory production. Of these, the most important was nailmaking, which was carried on as a domestic outwork industry in the tiny forges attached to the nailers' houses. This had been a traditional industry in the Black Country for centuries, and it experienced a great expansion between 1800 and 1830. The rods of nail iron were distributed weekly to the nailers by nailmasters, the nails being made by hand by the nailers, using simply a forge, bellows, hammer, anvil and heading tool. However, in 1830, they began to experience for the first time the competition of machine-made nails, which gradually undercut the hand-working nailers. The two factories making these nails by steam-powered machine were in Wolverhampton. In 1830, there were about 40,000 nailers, found throughout the Black Country; by 1860, there were only about 18,000, found mainly in the western half of the area (Sedgley parish, Tipton parish, Halesowen, Stourbridge and the Lye, Dudley and the surrounding area), living and working mainly in small villages. From 1830 onwards, nailing wages and prices were continually falling, and the nailers are continually described, in this period, as living in conditions of desperate poverty and squalor.[31] Similar to the nailers in much of their work, but not in their desperate conditions, were the chainmakers, making chains, cables and anchors by hammering by hand on small forges. This industry only began in the 1820s, and was found in the south-west corner of the Black Country, chiefly in the villages of Cradley and Netherton, around Dudley, and in Sedgley parish. They were nowhere near as numerous as the nailers, with only about 2,500 of them in 1861.[32]

The numerous ironmongery articles produced in the Black Country were produced in small workshops mostly by small masters working with 1-6 apprentices. The articles produced were locks and keys

(Willenhall and Wolverhampton), keys (Wednesfield and Sedgley), iron and steel traps (Wednesfield), nuts and bolts, screws, latches, hinges, gunlocks (Darlaston), saddlers' ironmongery (Walsall), edge-tools (Wolverhampton, Stourbridge, Oldbury, Halesowen). In all, these iron trades employed about 21,000 people by 1861. Leather manufacture and saddlery was carried on in Walsall, employing about 1,500 in 1861; and chemical factories employed about another 1,000 persons at Oldbury, Smethwick and Tipton.[33]

The smaller ironmongery trades were marked by a high degree of localisation – thus Willenhall dominated the manufacture of locks, Darlaston the manufacture of gunlocks and nuts and bolts, and Walsall the manufacture of saddlers' ironmongery, while Cradley was predominant in chainmaking. In the case of the smaller industrial towns or large villages, most of the employment, and the character, of the town was determined by their local industry. Thus the people of Willenhall, the town of lock manufacture, to take what was probably the extreme example, formed a group regarded by themselves and the other towns as distinct from the inhabitants of the other towns – they generally married only other Willenhall people; they were even physically distinct, and Willenhall was known within the Black Country as 'Humpshire' because of the prevalence of deformities among the population caused by working long hours at lock-filing.[34] The larger towns – Wolverhampton, West Bromwich, Dudley, Walsall, Bilston – had a greater variety of industries within them. But virtually all of them were dependent in some way on the iron and coal industries of the area.[35]

Coal and iron were the economic mainstay of the area, and the large coal and iron masters were the dominant entrepreneurial group. Because coal and iron were so closely tied together, they can virtually be considered a single industry in terms of their effect on the economic life of the area. Since most of the coal was consumed locally, the demand for coal depended on the state of demand for iron – when the demand for iron was low, coal prices dropped, and coalminers, as well as ironworkers, would have their wages cut, or be laid off, until conditions improved; when the demand for iron was high, coal prices went up, and miners and ironworkers were kept in full-time work. This was implemented through the coal and iron masters meeting quarterly to agree on common prices for coal and iron, and common wages to be paid to miners and ironworkers throughout the area, in accordance with the current state of the market for iron. It meant that a slump in the demand for iron would hit a large number of miners and ironworkers throughout the area very quickly, and that wage cuts were generally enforced by all or most of the masters simultaneously. So the state of prosperity and employment in the Black Country at any given time would depend on the state of the iron trade, and the decision of the important coal and iron masters.[36]

The industrial structure of the area affected the social structure of its towns. Towns like Willenhall and Darlaston, which relied on a few workshop trades, were characterised by having only one or two large masters, and a very large number of small masters, employing 1-3 apprentices in their workshops; towns like Sedgley and the Lye were dominated by nailers and chainmakers. Such towns also contained a number of miners and ironworkers, a small number of retail traders, and a minuscule number of upper or middle class people; these latter might comprise a few clergymen, a few teachers, and perhaps one or two of the local ironmasters – though the successful ones, as a rule, bought estates outside the towns though still near their works. The French observer Faucher commented on Sedgley and Willenhall in 1844 that they had no mixture of classes such as would be found in a large city, but were inhabited exclusively by one class of workers. Willenhall, said Faucher, possessed no civilisation, even though it was only six miles from Wolverhampton – it had no magistrates or police, no merchants or large shops, only workers living from day to day.[37] Even the much larger town of Bilston, a number of commentators noted, had no middle or upper class to speak of. Bilston was the Black Country town with the greatest concentration of, and dependence on, coalmining and ironworks, with the mines extending to very close to the centre of the town. The Children's Employment Sub-Commissioner pointed out, in 1843, that Bilston (1841 population 20,181) had 3,783 inhabited houses and dwellings of some sort; only 600-700 of those paid rent of more than £10 a year. 'You will perceive, therefore, that the 3,000 dwellings are inhabited by the working classes, who are chiefly ironworkers, miners, and pitmen.' The *Morning Chronicle* correspondent, in 1850, noted: 'Bilston is almost exclusively inhabited by colliers and ironworkers.'[38]

Only Wolverhampton, Dudley and Walsall, of the towns of the Black Country, were urban in the full sense, with proper town centres and a considerable number of professional, commercial and financial men working and living in them. Wolverhampton was the chief town of the area, its population easily outstripping that of the other towns, and possessing a considerable wealthy class of coal and iron masters, manufacturers, merchants and bankers. Dudley was the next most important town of the area, an old town which experienced considerable industrial development of the town and its surrounding area in the first half of the nineteenth century. Walsall was also an old town, which developed industrially, though not as rapidly as Wolverhampton or Dudley. But a town like West Bromwich, which, thanks to the expansion of ironworks and coalmines, grew very rapidly during the period 1801-61 to overtake Walsall in terms of population, remained more an aggregation of villages connected by the main turnpike roads than a proper town.[39]

The absence from a number of the towns and areas of a substantial middle class was matched by the virtual absence of the landed upper class from the Black Country. Staffordshire and Worcestershire were both counties well supplied with aristocracy and gentry, and there were some prominent men of this sort in the Black Country vicinity. But as the industrialisation of the area proceeded apace, many of them began to move out of the area, retaining property but residing elsewhere, or turning their estates to industrial or housing purposes, and buying themselves estates further out from the industrial areas.[40]

It is not surprising that the upper classes found the Black Country an unattractive area in which to live; industrialisation had blackened and disfigured its landscape, and filled its air with smoke. All visitors to the area remarked on its grim, polluted appearance. The towns and villages extended in unplanned, straggling roads of brick houses, many of them hastily thrown up after 1800 to cope with the sudden population increase, and lacking adequate sanitary facilities; in a period in which sanitary facilities in the industrial towns were generally poor, the Black Country housing and sanitary facilities were rated as among the very worst.[41] The 1832 cholera epidemic hit the Black Country towns very badly, and Bilston had the unpleasant distinction of suffering the highest number of cholera deaths per capita of any town in Britain.

Between the towns, the landscape was scarred by thousands of pits and slag heaps, the air blackened from the furnaces and chimneys, and the ground undermined by mine-workings. An observer in 1850 noted that

> for dozens of miles together, the country is literally a waste of cinders and refuse coal dust, studded with flaming ironworks, countless engine-houses, and thickly clustered groups of dismal, squalid villages. . .The appearance of the country around Wolverhampton, Willenhall, and Bilston. . .is strange in the extreme. For miles and miles the eye ranges over wide-spreading masses of black rubbish, hills on hills of shale, and mashed and mudded coal

dust, extracted from beneath, and masking, as it were, the whole face of nature. . .This uninviting-looking region is honeycombed with pit-shafts, and many of the surface undulations which catch the eye are the result of the earth having fallen in and collapsed on insufficiently propped workings. . .Engine-houses lean this way and that — great cracks and rents opening in their walls; and the visitor is sometimes shown spots where rows of houses have been engulfed altogether in the earth.

A German visitor, in 1835, described how, in his journey,

about Wolverhampton, trees, grass, and every trace of verdure disappear. As far as the eye can reach all is black, with coal mines and iron works; and from this gloomy desert rise countless pyramidal chimneys, whose flames illumine the earth, while their smoke darkens the heavens.[42]

This atmosphere and landscape ensured that the landed upper classes, on the whole, kept out of the area: 'It would indeed be a bold man and indifferent to dirt who could venture to settle himself among these cloud-compelling furnaces', said Edward Scott, a landowning gentleman who had asked to be made a Deputy Lieutenant of Staffordshire, but who withdrew his request when told that it would necessitate his living in South Staffordshire.[43] So the towns and villages of the Black Country were left predominantly to the working class together with the retail traders, and the relatively small entrepreneurial and commercial classes.

As well as the bad housing and sanitary conditions of its towns, all investigators stressed the bad social and 'moral' conditions of the Black Country working class — 'Black, in truth, it now is, alike in its appearance, and in the character of a large section of its inhabitants'.[44] The area had a standard of literacy well below the average for England as a whole, and below that of a number of other industrial areas; it was short of day schools, and the colliers and workers in the metal crafts were reported to show little interest in procuring an education for their children. Large sections of the colliers, ironworkers and metalworkers never attended church. The men and women of the area were notorious for their heavy drinking, and 'St Monday' was observed by the colliers, metal craftsmen and nailers. The colliers and ironworkers were reported to be much dirtier in the condition of their houses and clothing than colliers in Northumberland or Durham, or cotton operatives in

Manchester.[45]

These 'moral' criticisms were made by middle-class observers coming from outside the area, with little knowledge of, and feeling for, the local community. It is easy to point out the factors which these criticisms miss. The hot and exhausting work of the colliers, ironworkers and glassworkers required them to replace the moisture sweated out with some liquid, and beer was the easiest, safest and most pleasant way of doing so. The taking of 'St Monday' as a leisure day, followed by days of hectic overtime working to make up for it, can be seen as a rational allocation of their time by the workers concerned, preferring a period of full leisure followed by strenuous overtime working, to a steady pattern of twelve hours' work a day.[46] But these were the typical criticisms which investigators of the time tended to make of the industrial areas; and usually heading the list of 'moral' criticisms was the one with which this study is concerned — that the bad moral conditions of the industrial areas bred crime. The *Morning Chronicle* correspondent began his two articles on the Black Country by linking the list of its bad moral conditions to the fact that it had a crime rate above the national average; and he stressed that it had a particularly high proportion of female offences, linking this to the fact that

> the women work at rude and unsexing labour at the pit mouth,
> partly assuming the habiliments and altogether adopting the
> coarseness of the men.[47]

The general connection assumed to exist between areas of industrialisation and rapid population growth, and a growing level of lawlessness, was assumed for the Black Country as for other industrial areas. For instance, the Assize Judge who came on circuit to the Worcester Assizes in March 1858 observed, in his address to the Grand Jury, that

> although in the county of Worcester generally the state of morals
> and the small amount of crime evinced the good conduct of the
> population, yet in one district of the county — the coal and mining
> neighbourhood of Dudley — a very large proportion of the offences
> against the laws occurred.

And another Assize Judge noted, in addressing the Grand Jury at the Staffordshire Assizes in March 1859, that Staffordshire had recently had a Winter Assize added to the existing Assizes, which

is not a matter of surprise considering the population of this
country, its extensive mines and pottery manufacture, and other
circumstances, *which make it natural that a greater amount of
offences should be committed in it than in some other counties.* [48]

The Black Country, then, was a significant industrial area, within which
the issues of lawbreaking and law enforcement are examined in this
study, for the period 1835-60. Since the method used to assemble the
data of committals to trial (compilation of the totals from the individual
cases in the court records — see Appendix I) required a large expenditure
of time and effort for each additional year covered, this imposed limits
on the number of years for which the data could be compiled. (As it is,
the data were compiled for over 20,000 cases.) The years 1835-60 were
chosen to cover the period of the Black Country's greatest industrial
and population expansion. They include the years in which the first
paid 'New Police' forces were established for the area, enabling an
examination of law enforcement in the years both before and after their
establishment. The period also coincides with the time when the
magistracy of the area was undergoing an important change in its
composition, with effects on the administration of justice in the area.
It covers a number of alternating spells of depression and prosperity
for the area, including the severe depression of 1840-3, which saw
serious rioting in the area. The initial and terminal dates also owe
something to the availability of the material: information on the
occupation of persons tried in Staffordshire is not available before
1854; information on the standard of literacy of the persons tried is
not available before 1835; the Criminal Justice Act (with its important
effects on the conduct of prosecutions) did not come into force until
1855. Generally, the initial and terminal dates have no great significance
in themselves; but they are chosen as the best period for the analysis, in
the Black Country, of the issues raised by this study.

Finally, the structure of local government of the area must be
briefly described. Unusually for an industrial area, only one of the
Black Country towns had powers of municipal government at the
beginning of this period — Walsall had been granted a municipal charter
in the seventeenth century, and was regranted a charter by the
Municipal Corporations Act of 1835. This gave Walsall a ratepayer-
elected Mayor and Corporation for the local government of the town,
empowered them to have magistrates appointed for the borough,
enabled them to hold their own Borough Quarter Sessions under a
Recorder appointed and paid by the Corporation, and required them to

set up a paid Borough Police Force. Wolverhampton, Dudley, West
Bromwich and Bilston, despite their size and importance, were not
granted charters by the Act. It was not until 1848 that Wolverhampton
was granted a charter, and even then it did not gain the right to hold
its own Quarter Sessions until after 1860. So, all the towns of the area —
with the exception of Walsall, and of Wolverhampton after 1848 — fell
under the local government of County Quarter Sessions. As far as the
jurisdiction of the courts was concerned, all the towns except Walsall
sent those persons committed for indictable offences for trial at the
County Quarter Sessions; the more serious indictable offences were
sent for trial at the County Assizes, and this applied to all the towns
without exception, no Assize rights being granted to any Black Country
town.[49]

The counties concerned were Staffordshire and Worcestershire (and
Shropshire, for Assize and Quarter Sessions trials of offences from
Halesowen parish 1835-44; Halesowen parish will be treated here as a
part of Worcestershire, which it formally became in 1844). By far the
largest part of the Black Country came under the authority of
Staffordshire. About 23 per cent of the population (the south-western
corner of the area plus Dudley) came under Worcestershire; the Borough
of Walsall (in Staffordshire, and therefore under Staffordshire for Assize
purposes, but not for local government or for Quarter Sessions) made
up another 7 per cent; and the remaining 70 per cent of the Black
Country population fell under the local government and legal
jurisdiction of the Staffordshire Quarter Sessions.[50] South Staffordshire
was an important part of the county of Staffordshire, comprising about
one-tenth of its area, and 40 per cent of its population. Staffordshire
was divided into three clear sections: in the south was the Black
Country; in the north was the other Staffordshire industrial
agglomeration of the Potteries and the silk factories of Leek; between
these two came a large, primarily agricultural area. The County Quarter
Sessions comprised the magistrates from all three of these areas, meeting
in the county town of Stafford in the centre of the county, to pass local
ordinances, levy rates and hear criminal cases. The Worcestershire parts
of the Black Country made up a relatively less important part of
Worcestershire, being only its north-eastern corner, about 3 per cent
of its area and about 21 per cent of its population; Worcestershire was
a predominantly agricultural county, and the Black Country parts made
up most of its industrial area. Since Staffordshire county was the local
authority controlling 70 per cent of the Black Country population,
more attention is paid in this study to the actions of the Staffordshire

than to the Worcestershire authorities, but the Worcestershire authorities, and those of Walsall and of Wolverhampton after 1848, are discussed where relevant.

Notes

1. F. Engels, *The Condition of the Working Class in England* (1844; trans. and ed. W.O. Henderson and W.H. Chaloner, Oxford 1958), pp.145-6, 149.
2. Anon. [A. Alison] 'Causes of the Increase of Crime', *Blackwood's Edinburgh Magazine,* LVI (1844), pp.1-14, at pp.1-3. Identification of Alison as author by the *Wellesley Index to Victorian Periodicals 1824-1900,* vol.1 (Canada 1966), p.74.
3. For instance, John Wade, *History and Political Philosophy of the Middle and Working Classes* (Edinburgh 1842); L. Faucher, *Etudes sur l'Angleterre* (Brussels 1845); R.W. Rawson, 'An Inquiry into the Statistics of Crime in England and Wales', *JSSL* 2, (1839), pp.316-44; J. Fletcher, 'Moral and Educational Statistics of England and Wales', *JSSL* 10 (1847), pp.193-233. See also *Select Committee on Criminal Commitments and Convictions* (2nd Report) P.P. 1828, VI − evidence of Francis Maude, p.484, and of James Morris, p.499.
4. G.R. Porter, *The Progress of the Nation* (3 vols., London 1836-43; revised edn. 1847), Section VII, quotation at p.641. See M.J. Cullen, *The Statistical Movement in Early Victorian Britain* (Hassocks, Sussex 1975), for a full discussion of Porter's views and activities as a statistical investigator into crime and education.
5. A table of the committal figures for each year 1805-45 is reproduced in Porter, *Progress of the Nation,* p.642.
6. J.J. Tobias, *Crime and Industrial Society in the Nineteenth Century* (London, Batsford 1967; Pelican 1972 − page references to Pelican edn.); K.K. Macnab, 'Aspects of the History of Crime in England and Wales between 1805-60' (Sussex Univ. D.Phil thesis 1965); V.A.C. Gatrell and T.B. Hadden, 'Criminal Statistics and their Interpretation' in E.A. Wrigley (ed.), *Nineteenth Century Society: essays in the use of quantitative methods for the study of social data* (Cambridge 1972), pp.336-96. It is not necessary to deal with the numerous popular books on Victorian crime, which have little historical worth − e.g. Kellow Chesney, *The Victorian Underworld* (London 1970), which is not a systematic study of what its title promises, but a disorganised series of anecdotes and pieces of information on criminals, vagrants, the non-respectable poor, the world of illegal prize-fighting etc. It contains some useful information, and a few passages of sustained analysis, but is not a coherent whole. Most of its information on the lives and methods of operation of criminals is taken direct from H. Mayhew, *London Labour and the London Poor,* 4 vols. (London 1861-2; reprinted New York 1968), especially from vol.4, which might as well be consulted directly, rather than via Chesney's selections.
7. Tobias, *Crime,* p.25; also pp.23-4, 296-308.
8. e.g. *Report from the Select Committee on Import Duties,* P.P. 1840, V − see L. Brown, *The Board of Trade and the Free Trade Movement 1830-42* (Oxford 1958); *Report of the Royal Commission on the Poor Laws,* P.P. 1834, XXVII − see M. Blaug, 'The Myth of the Old Poor Law and the Making of the New' and 'The Poor Law Report Re-examined', *Journal of Economic History,* XXIII (1963) and XXIV (1964), and S.E. Finer, *The Life and Times of Sir*

Edwin Chadwick (London 1970), pp.69-95.

9. Tobias, *Crime*, pp.181, 142.

10. *SC on Criminal Commitments* (1828).

11. Tobias, *Crime,* pp.180-1; Hill quotation in *Aris's Birmingham Gazette,*
26 October 1861. I owe this reference to Dr Susan Eade of the Australian
National University; see Appendix to her thesis 'The Reclaimers: A Study
of the Reformatory Movement in England and Wales 1846-1893' (A.N.U.
Ph.D thesis 1976), pp.419-20, 423.

12. Tobias, *Crime*, p.139.

13. Ibid., pp.140-1.

14. Ibid.

15. See M. Flinn's introduction to E. Chadwick, *Report on the Sanitary
Condition of the Labouring Population of Great Britain* (1842; ed. M. Flinn,
Edinburgh 1965), pp.62-4.

16. Tobias, *Crime*, pp.134-43, 179-87; (quotation is from *First Report of the
Commissioners appointed to inquire as to the Best Means of establishing an
efficient Constabulary Force in the Counties of England and Wales,* P.P. 1839,
XIX, p.73 – cited with approval by Tobias, *Crime,* p.179).

17. For the distinction between indictable and summary offences, see
Appendix II.

18. Gatrell and Hadden, 'Criminal Statistics', pp.336-62.

19. Ibid., pp.361-2.

20. Introduction to the Annual Criminal Statistics, PP. 1901, LXXXIX, p.68,
quoted in ibid., p.429, footnote 31.

21. Elihu Burritt, *Walks in the Black Country and its Green Borderland*
(London 1868), p.1.

22. The best works on the Black Country, its geography, towns, and social and
economic development in the nineteenth century, are: G.C. Allen, *The
Industrial Development of Birmingham and the Black Country* (London 1929);
W.H.B. Court, *The Rise of the Midland Industries 1600-1838* (London 1953);
G.J. Barnsby, 'Social Conditions in the Black Country in the Nineteenth
Century' (Birmingham Univ. Ph.D thesis 1969); D.B.M. Huffer, 'The Economic
Development of Wolverhampton 1750-1850' (London Univ. MA thesis 1957);
V.L. Davies and H. Hyde, *Dudley and the Black Country 1760-1860* (Dudley
1970); T.J. Raybould, *The Economic Emergence of the Black Country*
(Newton Abbot 1973); J.F. Ede, *History of Wednesbury* (Birmingham 1962);
F.W. Willmore, *A History of Walsall and its Neighbourhood* (London 1887).
Very good descriptions of the area, its industries, and industrial and social
conditions are to be found in *Appendix to the Second Report of the Children's
Employment Commission (Trades and Manufactures),* Part II, P.P. 1843, XV
(432), pp.561-738; *Appendix to First Report of the Children's Employment
Commission (Mines),* P.P. 1842, XVI (381), pp.1-88; *First Report of the
Midland Mining Commission (South Staffordshire),* P.P. 1843, XIII (508).
There is a rambling but vivid description of working-class life in Bilston in the
1830s and 1840s, in J. Freeman, *Black Country Stories and Sketches* (Bilston
1930); this relies on a mixture of oral evidence, gathered for some time before
1930 from old local inhabitants, personal diaries, newspaper reports, local
stories, traditions, songs.

23. See list of Black Country towns and parishes and their populations in
Appendix III.

24. *First Report of Midland Mining Commission* (hereafter cited as *Midland
Mining Commission),* p.iv.

25. Court, *Midland Industries;* Allen, *Industrial Development.*

26. Allen, *Industrial Development,* pp.142-4, 97-8; Census 1851 and 1861.

27. Allen, *Industrial Development*, pp.147-50.
28. S. Griffiths, *Guide to the Iron Trade of Great Britain* (London 1873), pp.51-2.
29. These have to be estimates because the Census categories of 'Iron manufacture' and 'Other workers in Iron and Steel' are too vague to be used with precision. See estimates in Allen, *Industrial Development*, p.91, and Census 1851 and 1861.
30. Allen, *Industrial Development*, pp.68-72, 91-3, 132-5; S.J. Langley, 'The Wednesbury Tube Trade', *Univ. of Birmingham Historical Journal* (1949-50), pp.163-77; R.A. Church, *Kenricks in Hardware* (Newton Abbot 1969); H.J. Haden, *The Stourbridge Glass Industry in the 19th Century* (Tipton 1971); Davies and Hyde, *Dudley and the Black Country*, pp.68-75.
31. Allen, *Industrial Development*, pp.39, 75-7, 125-8. See descriptions of the miserable conditions in the nailmaking villages of Lower Gornal, Coseley, and the Lye in *Children's Employment Commission* (1843), pp.635, 647, and in *Midland Mining Commission* (1843), p.vi.
32. Allen, *Industrial Development*, pp.94-5.
33. Ibid., pp.78-83, 97-8; *Children's Employment Commission* (1843).
34. *Children's Employment Commission* (1843); P. Drabble, *Black Country* (London 1952), p.1. Disraeli used the Children's Employment Commission evidence on Willenhall to produce his picture of the horrific conditions of children working in the lockmaking workshops of 'Wodgate' in his novel *Sybil* (1845).
35. Allen, *Industrial Development*, pp.65-110.
36. Barnsby, 'Social Conditions'; Huffer, 'Economic Development'.
37. Faucher, *Etudes*, pp.103-5.
38. *Children's Employment Commission* (1843), p.624; *Morning Chronicle* (henceforth *MC*), 'Labour and the Poor', 7 January 1850. Barnsby, 'Social Conditions', p.20, shows that, of Bilston's 5,656 male workers of all ages in 1841, 2,475 were miners and 955 ironworkers.
39. *Midland Mining Commission* (1843), pp.cxliv-cxlv, cxlvii-cli; Faucher, *Etudes*, pp.95-100; Huffer, 'Economic Development'.
40. For instance, the Earl of Dartmouth, in the 1850s, turned his Sandwell estate into urban housing for West Bromwich and bought another estate in a more rural setting some miles away (R.W. Sturgess, 'Landowners, Mining and Urban Development in 19th Century Staffordshire' in J.T. Ward and R.G. Wilson (ed.), *Land and Industry* (Newton Abbot 1971), pp.175-6. See also *Midland Mining Commission* (1843), pp.cxlvii-cli; Appendix, pp.36, 52.
41. *Children's Employment Commission* (1843); *Report of Commissioners for Inquiring into the State of Large Towns* (1st Report 1844; 2nd Report 1845).
42. *MC*, 'Labour and the Poor', 3 January 1850; F. von Raumer, *England in 1835* (London 1836), vol.3, pp.232-3. See similar descriptions in Burritt, *Walks in the Black Country;* W. White, *All Round the Wrekin* (London 1860), p.6; [Anon], 'The Black Country', *Edinburgh Review*, 117 (1863), pp.406-43.
43. HC 5/5/3, Scott to Hatherton, 21 May 1855.
44. Rev. W.F. Vance, *A Voice from the Mines and Furnaces* (Wolverhampton and London 1853).
45. Registrar-General's annual reports P.P. 1839 onwards; *Children's Employment Commission* (1843); *Midland Mining Commission* (1843); 'Report on the State of Education among the Working Classes in West Bromwich', *JSSL*, 2 (1839), pp.375-7; 'Education in the Mining and Manufacturing District of South Staffordshire', *JSSL*, 10 (1847), pp.232-42; *MC*, 'Labour and the Poor', 3 and 7 January 1850.
46. See B. Harrison, *Drink and the Victorians* (London 1971), pp.37-9; E.P. Thompson, 'Time, Work-Discipline, and Industrial Capitalism', *Past and*

Present, 38 (1967), pp.56-97; Douglas A. Reid, 'The Decline of Saint Monday 1766-1876', *Past and Present,* 71 (1976), pp.76-101.

47. *MC,* 'Labour and the Poor', 3 January 1850.

48. *Worcester Herald* (henceforth *WH),* 6 March 1858, report of Ass.; *Staffordshire Advertiser* (henceforth *SA*), 12 March 1859, report of Ass. (italics added). Similar points were made in grand jury charges to Worcs. Ass., December 1856 and December 1859, and to Staffs. Ass., July 1858.

49. For more detail on these different jurisdictions, see Appendix I. The larger towns also had Improvement Commissioners, appointed under local Acts, with powers to make regulations for the watching, lighting, cleansing of the town, care of the streets, control of the markets, etc. The Walsall Corporation received such powers by local Act in 1824, which remained in force until Walsall's incorporation in 1835; Wolverhampton had Improvement Commissioners from 1777 until incorporation in 1848; Dudley had them from 1791 until 1853 when they were superseded by a Local Board of Health. Improvement Commissioners were set up, by local Act, for Bilston in 1850, and for West Bromwich in 1854.

50. Census 1831, 1841, 1851, 1861.

2 CRIME AND THE CRIME FIGURES

The tables cannot show the amount of actual crime, but only of such as has been detected, and become the subject of legal cognizance. Several causes have been in operation which must necessarily have increased the proportion of detected crime to that actually committed. Amongst these the following may be enumerated; — a better organised, more numerous, and more active police; the mitigation of the criminal law, and the consequent increase of prosecutions; an improved prison discipline, and therefore a greater willingness on the part of the public to prefer charges; vast facilities for rapid communication, inevitably leading to a greater amount of detection.
(Rev. W. Russell, 'Abstract of the Statistics of Crime in England and Wales from 1839 to 1843', *JSSL*, 10 (1847), p.39.)

Crime can most usefully be considered, for our purposes, in terms of Sutherland and Cressey's definition:

Criminal behaviour is behaviour in violation of the criminal law. No matter what the degree of immorality, reprehensibility, or indecency of an act, it is not a crime unless it is prohibited by the criminal law. The criminal law, in turn, is defined conventionally as a body of specific rules regarding human conduct which have been promulgated by political authority, which apply uniformly to all members of classes to which the rules refer, and which are enforced by punishment administered by the state.[1]

The crucial elements in this definition are: the body of rules laid down by political authority, the enforcement of those rules by the state and its agencies of authority by means of punishment, and the acts which violate the body of rules. No attempt is made in this study to draw distinctions between degrees of moral turpitude involved in different types of offence — to claim to distinguish 'real crimes' from 'quasi-criminal offences', or good 'social crimes' from bad 'antisocial crimes'. If an act was prohibited by law, and was treated as such by the agencies of law enforcement and the courts of law, then it is of concern to this study.

The emphasis on enforcement of the rules by the agencies of police, prosecution and the courts is important. What is normally spoken of, in everyday language, as 'crime' is usually either serious criminal acts against victims (robberies, thefts of large amounts, serious assaults, homicides, sexual assaults, etc.), or less serious criminal acts which have been processed by the machinery of the law. Acts which are *technical* violations of the law, but which are not processed as such, are not usually regarded as crimes. For instance, most people have, at some time or another, probably committed acts which were technically assaults and which, if prosecuted, would have been treated as crimes; because they are not prosecuted, they are not popularly looked on as crimes, even though they *are technically* violations of the law, as strictly construed. Modern surveys have shown that large numbers of people have, at some time or another, committed acts which were breaches of the law but which had not been detected or punished. Much will depend on the attitude which the authorities and the public take to a particular type of offence, whether they choose to treat it as a crime and prosecute accordingly. A Select Committee reported in 1828:

> The sons of persons of the highest rank in this country, when at school, often commit offences out of the exuberance of spirits and activity, which the law, if it visited them at all, must visit by sentences of great severity. Offences of a similar kind, passed over as frolics in the sons of the rich, are treated in the children of the poor as crimes of magnitude.

Similarly, Lord Eldon, the Lord Chancellor, told an amused House of Lords that as a boy he had stolen fruit and gone poaching — offences which Eldon himself was now insisting must be rigorously punished when committed by members of the lower classes. Had he been similarly prosecuted and punished, he could never have become Lord Chancellor, and might well have ended up a convict in Australia. And employers might choose to treat pilfering by employees either as the normal taking of 'perks' to be expected and tolerated, or as crimes to be rigorously prosecuted.[2]

So one can see that a very strict construction of 'crime' as meaning all acts which violate the criminal law — what one might call 'total crime' — would have to include all acts committed by anyone in violation of the criminal law, which would be so broad a category that it would probably include virtually every citizen in a society. It is unlikely that this figure of 'total crime' could ever be known;[3] even if it could be known, the numbers of acts which in some way infringed a criminal law would be so large that (except perhaps for very serious crimes such as murder and robberies) they would not tell anything very informative about what society regards as normal lawbreaking and the normal process of law enforcement.

For everyday purposes, a state will be concerned not with 'total crime' but with those offences and offenders who are felt to pose some sort of threat to the society, and who therefore come to the attention of the police and the courts. The regular functioning of a state's machinery of criminal justice is dependent on the number of people dealt with as criminals being a small fraction of the population; otherwise, it would become very difficult to enforce the law, and legal order in the society would tend to break down. A state cannot prosecute and imprison a majority or a large proportion of its population — hence, when a law is widely disobeyed by a large section of the population, there will be a tendency in most states to repeal or change that law (such as Prohibition in the United States, or the laws on homosexuality and abortion — perhaps also the recent Industrial Relations Act — in Britain) or if it remains on the statute book, for it not to be rigorously enforced against every violation (such as some of the drug laws). The police may well enforce a law or a number of laws selectively, concentrating on those people and offences which they see as constituting 'the real danger'; those offences, and those people who break the law, which do not obviously and urgently come to the attention of the authorities as a danger, will on the whole be left alone.[4]

So as well as 'total crime', one can talk of the existence of official rates which one could call 'official crime' — offences to which the police, prosecutors and courts pay attention and with which they deal. To talk meaningfully about crime in a social context, one must talk about 'official crime' and not 'total crime'. Offences cannot be treated as simple entities on their own, but must be considered in the context of their reciprocal relationship with the law and law enforcement. I call this 'reciprocal' because the number and sorts of offences committed will have an effect on the nature of the law and the law-enforcement agencies; but, in turn, the question of which acts and persons the law-enforcement agencies choose to treat as criminal (or more likely, on which they choose to concentrate their law-enforcement priorities) will itself affect which acts and people end up being punished by the courts; which in turn will affect the statistics of 'official crime'. This present study examines 'official crime' in the Black Country — those acts in violation of the criminal law, and their actors, *which the agencies of authority treated as criminal.* It looks at the social determinants of 'official crime' — the factors affecting persons who committed offences, and affecting the agencies of law enforcement, prosecution and conviction, which combined to give the numbers and sorts of acts and persons which came up for trial in court.

The information on the offences and offenders dealt with in court is important for a number of reasons. It was these figures of people committed to trial which influenced people's ideas at the time about what was happening to crime and law and order. These figures also influenced subsequent figures of committals to trial by stimulating changes in the apparatus of the law — e.g. the establishment of police forces, reform of the penal system. And this information can tell us something of how the police, judicial and penal systems of the time worked. These figures — of offences and offenders tried by the courts — are thus 'social facts' of some importance. Whatever may be the truth about 'total crime', it was against these people, who made up the statistics of 'official crime', that the state machinery for law enforcement and punishment was used. And studying this information may throw light not only on the offences, offenders, police, courts and prisons, but also on some wider features of their society — its degree of tolerance of political and social dissent; the level of violence deemed normal and acceptable, both from its citizens and from its police agencies; attitudes towards property rights in the society; the status which the law and its agents occupied in the minds of the mass of the population, and the degree to which they showed an acceptance of the legitimacy of the state and its laws.

This study looks at the people and offences brought up for trial in the Black Country over the period 1835-60, putting this information within the context of contemporary developments in law enforcement and prosecution. In analysing this information, I have made use of some of the ideas developed in the work of a number of sociologists whose approach has been grouped under the loose title of 'The Interactionist Perspective'.[5] A central tenet of this perspective is to treat crime as one of a number of types of social deviance and to focus attention not only on the acts of the offenders, but also on the part played by the reaction of the authorities in defining, labelling and punishing a particular set of acts as deviant. This can be summed up in the statement: 'Deviance is not a property *inherent* in any particular kind of behaviour; it is a property *conferred upon* that behaviour by the people who come into direct or indirect contact with it.'[6]

Since the laws and rules of all societies have not always and everywhere been the same, the criminality of an act is not something absolute which is inherent in that act, but can only exist as something relative to the laws of that particular society. For instance, in Puritan seventeenth-century Massachusetts, even such minor infractions as non-attendance at church, drinking too much, wearing inappropriate clothes, having hair too long, cursing, and all breaches of the code of sexual behaviour, were punishable and punished by the colony's courts of law.[7] Several studies have shown that the official policies of law enforcement and the varying ways they are carried out will affect the amount and nature of officially recognised criminal deviance in that society — that is, the amount and nature of 'official crime'. The crime rates which any society produces, which show the magnitude of 'official crime', will be produced by a process of interaction between those who make and enforce the laws and those who break the laws.[8]

The official crime rates are acknowledged by all criminologists to fall short of giving a picture of 'total crime', because they fail to record those offences which have not come to official attention; a number of criminologists have tried ways to correct or improve this.[9] But Cicourel and Kitsuse have suggested that the official crime rates, though imperfect for the purpose of trying for the unattainable goal of a picture of 'total crime', are useful precisely *because* of their imperfection, since they represent the end result of the process of interaction between the authorities and the lawbreakers, and can be used to give a picture of that process in action.[10] In this study, I analyse the information yielded by the court records as reflecting this sort of interaction.

A brief discussion is necessary of the sources which are used for this purpose. There are basically three sorts of criminal statistics, which make up the criminal statistics of England and Wales today, and have done so since 1857.[11] These are: (1) the number of indictable offences known to the police (Crimes Known to the Police); (2) the number of people committed to trial for indictable and summary offences (Committals to Trial, Indictable and Summary); (3) the number of people imprisoned on conviction (Prison Commitments). To these one can add another total, which would come before (3), and that is the number of people found guilty on trial, indictable or summary (Guilty on Trial, Indictable or Summary). Of these sets of figures, the largest total will be the Crimes Known to the Police, since it consists of all offences which are reported to the police by members of the public, or which are observed by members of the police themselves — whether or not someone is subsequently prosecuted for that offence. The other totals, in descending order of their magnitude, will be the Committals to Trial, then those Guilty on Trial, and finally, smallest of the four, the Commitments to Prison. The descending order of magnitude reflects the various stages of the working of the system: there will be some reported offences for which no suspect is committed for trial; some committals to trial which are not convicted; and some of those convicted who are not sent to prison.

Modern criminologists rely on the Crimes Known to the Police for constructing crime rates, on the principle that, although these figures will be deficient because they fail to include the 'dark figure' of offences which do not come to official notice, they are nonetheless the closest one can get to a picture of 'total crime' before the workings of the machinery of law enforcement and justice have diminished these totals.[12] But we have already indicated that this study is not concerned with searching for 'total crime', but rather with studying what was dealt with by the police and the courts. In any event, figures of Crimes Known to the Police were not collected and published in England until 1857, at the end of our period, when police forces were established all over the country. The basis of this study comes from an analysis of Indictable Committals to Trial in the Black Country, from which the two smaller sets of figures — those found guilty, and those sent to prison — are also available.

The annually published criminal statistics gave their totals on a national and county basis only; these published figures were not, and cannot now be, broken down by town or area. To get at the figures and fuller information than simply bare totals, for the Black Country committals to trial for 1835-60, the original Quarter Sessions and Assizes records were used, from which the totals were compiled and the information recorded.[13] These court records cover only the *indictable* committals and not trials for *summary* offences,[14] which means that they refer only to trials for relatively serious offences (larceny, robbery, burglary and housebreaking, fraud, forgery and coining, murder, manslaughter, rape, the more serious assaults and riots) and not the minor offences (vagrancy, drunkenness, minor assaults and breaches of the peace, breaches of licensing laws and local acts, etc.) which were tried summarily.

Examining these court records and the contemporary law-enforcement and judicial systems, one can see that the figures which are produced do indeed stem from a process of interaction. Leaving aside, for the moment, the social forces which will exert influence on trends in the figures, one can isolate five factors which interact to produce the figures themselves.

(1) The Actual Number of Acts being Committed in Breach of a Law

This is naturally the most important of the five factors which interact to produce these totals; but it cannot be considered the sole, or even the dominant, factor. It is important to try to isolate this factor, and to estimate the effect which social forces such as, for instance, the state of employment and the trade cycle, had on this factor; but it would be a mistake to see changes in the figures of committals of trial as reflecting *only* changes in the number of illegal acts being committed. They reflect *also* changes in the policies and activities of the authorities, as indicated in the other four factors below; the committal figures represent a resultant produced by the activities of those who broke the law, and those who made and enforced it.

(2) The Criminal Law

The numbers of people being committed to trial, and the numbers being convicted, would have been affected by changes in the criminal law over this period.

(a) Changes in the Penal Code

Between 1808 and 1841, the more than 200 capital offences on the statute book were reduced to eleven, and after 1841 executions were carried out only for murder.[15] As the scope of hanging was restricted, so that of transportation was correspondingly increased. But transportation to New South Wales ceased in 1840, though it continued to Van Diemen's Land throughout the 1840s and began, in small numbers, to Western Australia in 1849. In 1853 transportation to Van Diemen's Land was stopped, and transportation continued only for small numbers of very long-term sentences to Western Australia until all transportation was ended in 1867. From 1853, penal servitude, in the new prisons being built on the Pentonville model, increasingly replaced transportation as the sentence for most serious crimes; while the expansion in prison accommodation enabled more short-term custodial sentences to be used.[16]

Thus, in the space of about forty years,[17] the form of punishment prescribed for serious crimes twice changed radically in form; the idea became established of prisons as places for regular short-term confinement of less serious offenders rather than primarily as places to keep debtors and prisoners awaiting trial, execution or transportation.

It is not quite clear exactly how much effect these changes could be expected to have had on the totals of committals, though it was suggested at the time that the abolition of capital punishment would have made prosecutors more willing to prosecute.[18] These changes certainly affected the sentences, and possibly the verdicts, of the courts and had a general effect on the capacity of the courts and penal institutions to handle the number of offenders tried.

(b) Changes in the Law relating to Criminal Procedure

There were a number of instances of this; the most significant in our period were the Juvenile Offenders Acts (JOA) of 1847 and 1850, and the Criminal Justice Act (CJA) of 1855, which allowed previously indictable larcenies to be tried summarily by Justices in Petty Sessions. These Acts had the effect of greatly increasing the number of prosecutions for larceny.[19] Other changes might have affected the number of convictions — for instance, it was urged against the Prisoners' Counsel Act of 1836, which for the first time allowed counsel to address the jury on behalf of a prisoner accused of a felony, that it would lead to a great increase in the rate of acquittal of guilty persons.[20]

(c) Changes in the Substantive Definition of Offences

Such changes — the creation of new offences, extension of an existing offence, or abolition of all or part of an offence — would naturally affect the figures of prosecutions. However, no such substantive change in the definition of offences appears to have taken place during our period.

(3) The Administrative and Judicial Authorities

The most important institution affecting the Black Country in this respect was the local magistracy. Over the period 1835-60, the magistrates' judicial function remained crucial and increased in scope in some respects. There was an increase in the number of JPs for the Black Country: Walsall acquired its own Borough Quarter Sessions and Borough magistrates in 1836, and Wolverhampton its own Borough magistrates in 1848; the number of Staffordshire and Worcestershire county magistrates for the Black Country increased from less than forty in 1833 to 104 in 1859; and a stipendiary magistrate was appointed for South Staffordshire in 1846. These JPs played an important role in law enforcement and in initiating prosecutions; the fact that, over this period, their social composition changed from basically a landowning group to one dominated by the industrial entrepreneurs of the area, had an important effect on the way they carried out that role.[21]

(4) The Law-enforcement Agencies

Here there is an obvious effect to be expected on the number of persons brought to trial. In 1835, the only agents of law enforcement in the Black Country were parish constables and some bodies of town watchmen maintained under local Improvement Acts. Gradually, 'New Police' forces were introduced into the area until, by 1845, each part of the area was under one of three organised, paid, uniformed police forces (after 1848, four forces). This change, and the gradual growth in size and efficiency of the forces, could be expected to have increased the number of people arrested for offences, to have widened the scope of 'official crime' against which the agencies of the law took action, to have set a higher standard of public order to be observed, and to have improved the efficiency with which prosecutions were conducted.

(5) The Process and Personnel of Prosecution

This is dealt with in detail in chapter 4. The most important feature of the early nineteenth-century English prosecution system was that it was one of private prosecution, relying on prosecutions being brought by the victims of offences. So the figures reflect those crimes which victims chose to prosecute.

There were a number of reasons why a victim might choose not to prosecute, including unwillingness to invoke the law at all, fear of retaliation by the offender, reluctance to inflict the severe penalties prescribed by law and, by far the commonest reason, unwillingness to incur the loss of time and expense involved. By the 1830s, the courts were empowered to award the costs of a felony prosecution and most misdemeanour prosecutions to a prosecutor and the witnesses, provided the evidence was sufficient to commit the accused for trial; but if there was no committal, then no expenses were reimbursed. Even for those who felt sure that they would get a committal and thus get paid the expenses of the prosecution and something for their loss of time, the trouble and loss of working time involved in having to travel to the county town and wait for their case to come up at Quarter Sessions or Assizes, was still a strong disincentive to prosecute for many. The great increase in prosecutions for larceny which took place following the Criminal Justice Act (CJA) of 1855, by which the time, trouble and expense of prosecution were greatly reduced, is an indication of how many potential prosecutors had previously been deterred by these factors. Another change over this period is that the police forces, as they became established, took on a growing responsibility for the prosecution of many offences.

So the figures of committals to trial are not a straightforward index of 'total crime', but are the product of the interaction of a number of factors. By studying them within the context of the law-enforcement and judicial agencies of the time, we can get a picture of what offences were being committed and punished; what people were committing the offences; what people were the victims of, and were prosecuting, the offences; and what means the authorities were using to maintain social and legal control of the society.

It must be made clear, before we get on to the material itself, that this study is based only on the committals for trial *on indictment* at Quarter Sessions and Assizes; it does not cover the offences tried *summarily.* The distinction between these is basically a procedural one — an indictable offence had to be tried before a jury and a judge or full Bench of magistrates, with the jury deciding the verdict and the judge or magistrates pronouncing sentence; in a summary trial, the offence was tried by one or more (usually two) magistrates, who sat without a jury and decided both verdict and sentence. This procedural distinction coincided, on the whole, with a distinction as to the degree of seriousness of the offence — serious offences being indictable. But this borderline between indictable and summary offences was not hard and fast for every type of offence, and for some categories of offence an act could be tried summarily *or* on indictment, depending on how seriously the nature of the act was viewed.[22]

However, by and large, all the more serious offences were tried on indictment — *all* robberies, housebreaking and burglary, frauds, forgery, homicides, sexual offences against the person, aggravated assaults, and all larcenies; and *the more serious* common assaults and offences of riot. Indictable committals included all the trials for crimes considered by the community as at all serious, reaching as far down the scale as larcenies of very small amounts. They excluded the very wide and vaguely phrased minor categories of offence — such as vagrancy, drunkenness, breaches of licensing laws and of local Acts, and the lesser categories of assault and breaches of the peace.

Notes

1. E.H. Sutherland and D.R. Cressey, *Criminology*, 8th edn. (New York 1970), p.4.
2. N. Walker, *Crimes, Courts and Figures* (Harmondsworth 1971), pp.12, 15, 21, 36-7; *Select Committee on Criminal Commitments and Convictions* (2nd Report), P.P. 1828, VI, p.430; A.G.L. Shaw, *Convicts and the Colonies* (London 1971), p.163; Tobias, *Crime*, p.65.
3. Walker, *Crimes, Courts and Figures*, pp.17-18.
4. e.g. Michael Banton pointed out, in his survey of the police departments of two southern cities of the United States in 1962, that the police and the courts paid much less attention to assaults and homicides committed by blacks against blacks, than to comparable offences by blacks against whites, or by whites against whites. The latter two categories were regarded as serious and requiring action as threatening the [white] community; the former category of offences was regarded as normal and to be expected among the black community (M. Banton, *The Policeman in the Community* (London 1964), pp.172-3).
5. This is the term used as the title of a collection of articles by some of these sociologists – E. Rubington and M. Weinberg (ed.), *Deviance: The Interactionist Perspective* (New York 1968). The chief works of this perspective on which I have drawn are: A.V. Cicourel and J.I. Kitsuse, 'A Note on the Uses of Official Statistics', *Social Problems* 11 (autumn 1963) pp.131-9; A.V. Cicourel, *The Social Organisation of Juvenile Justice* (New York 1968); H. Becker, *Outsiders: Studies in the Sociology of Deviance* (New York 1963); H. Becker (ed.), *The Other Side: Perspectives on Deviance* (New York 1964); Kai T. Erikson, *Wayward Puritans. A Study in the Sociology of Deviance* (New York 1966); E.M. Lemert, *Human Deviance, Social Problems and Social Control* (Englewood Cliffs, New Jersey 1967); J.H. Skolnick, *Justice Without Trial: Law Enforcement in Democratic Society* (New York 1966). In S. Cohen (ed.), *Images of Deviance* (Harmondsworth 1971), some of the concepts of this school are applied to a series of English studies; M. Phillipson draws rather uncritically on these American works in his *Sociological Aspects of Crime and Delinquency* (London 1971). A critique of this perspective is offered in Jack P. Gibbs, 'Conceptions of Deviant Behaviour: The Old and the New', *Pacific Sociological Review* (spring 1966), pp.9-14.
6. Erikson, *Wayward Puritans*, p.6 (italics in the original); see also Becker, *Outsiders*, p.14.
7. Erikson, *Wayward Puritans*, ch.4.
8. Ibid., chs.1, 4; Cicourel, *Social Organisation;* E.M. Lemert, 'Social Structure, Social Control and Deviation' in Lemert, *Human Deviance*, pp.3-30; Skolnick, *Justice Without Trial;* Becker, *Outsiders*, p.163.
9. See T. Sellin, 'The Significance of the Records of Crime', *Law Quarterly Review*, 67 (1951), pp.489-504; T. Sellin and M. Wolfgang, *The Measurement of Delinquency* (New York 1964), chs.1-4, 8-20; Walker, *Crimes, Courts and Figures*, pp.22-8, 69-75; *Report of the Departmental Committee on Criminal Statistics* (W. Perks, chmn.), (HMSO 1967).
10. Cicourel and Kitsuse, 'A Note on the Uses of Official Statistics', p.136.
11. The best discussion of these statistics and their uses is in Gatrell and Hadden, 'Criminal Statistics', pp.336-62.
12. See Walker, *Crimes, Courts and Figures*, pp.22-8; Sellin, 'The Significance of the Records', pp.497-8.
13. For details of these sources and their compilation, see Appendix I.
14. The distinction between indictable and summary offences is discussed in Appendix II.

15. For a full account of these reforms, see L. Radzinowicz, *A History of English Criminal Law and its Administration from 1750*, 4 vols. (London 1948-68), vols.1 and 4.
16. Shaw, *Convicts and the Colonies;* U. Henriques, 'The Rise and Decline of the Separate System of Prison Discipline', *Past and Present*, 54 (1972), pp.61-93.
17. Only one important capital offence was abolished before 1820; most of the abolitions came in the 1820s and 1830s – though it is true that by 1801 only about 10 per cent of capital sentences were being executed, the rest being commuted to transportation (Radzinowicz, *History*, vol.1, pp.151-60).
18. See *Select Committee on Criminal Laws*, P.P. 1819, VIII, pp.3-270.
19. For details of these Acts, see appendix I; for details on the increase in prosecutions, see chs.4, 5 and 6.
20. See ch.4.
21. See section on Industrial Thefts, ch.6; D. Philips, 'The Black Country Magistracy 1835-60; a changing local élite and the exercise of its power', *Midland History* (spring 1976).
22. For a full discussion of this, See Appendix II.

3 THE OLD AND NEW POLICE

It appears desirable for the sake of order and better security of property that an efficient system of police should be adopted and placed in respectable hands. For the last twenty years and upwards, the only persons who would undertake the office of constable have been men of idle habits and no character.
(Return from a Hampshire Poor Law Union, quoted in *RC on Constabulary Force* (1839), p.103.)

At this time [1830s] Darlaston, although a big and important town, had neither magistrate nor courthouse. An infirm old man acted as the constable, watchman and beadle. If he wanted to take anyone up, he had merely to go to the culprit and say 'Come'. Strangely enough, the men thus apprehended nearly always did as bidden, and were then walked off to Bilston, one mile distant, where there was a magistrate.
(William Derrincourt, *Old Convict Days* (London 1899; Penguin 1975), p.10.)

That in consequence of the present inefficiency of the Constabulary Force, arising from the great increase of Population, and the extension of Trade and Commerce of the country, it is the opinion of this Court, that a Body of Constables appointed by the Magistrates, paid out of the County Rate, and disposable at any point of the Shire, where their Services might be required, would be highly desirable, as providing in the most efficient manner for the prevention, as well as detection of offences, for the security of person and property, and for the constant preservation of the public Peace.
(Resolution passed by Shropshire QS in January 1839, sent by Home Secretary to all county QS for discussion.)

I

In 1835, there was no police force in the Black Country; in 1860, it possessed four police forces with a total strength of 262. It had changed from being an 'unpoliced society' — where police functions were carried out (if at all) by citizens or their appointed constables, to a 'policed society' in which a paid police force operated, relying not only on coercion, but also on the moral assent of most of the population to the role of a police force as enforcer of law and order.[1]

The chief national landmarks in the introduction of police forces were: the *Metropolitan Police Act* (1829), establishing the first paid, uniformed force for the London metropolitan area; the *Municipal Corporations Act* (1835), which made it obligatory for all incorporated boroughs to set up police forces under the control of a Watch Committee appointed by the Borough Council; the *County Police Acts* (1839 and 1840), which were permissive Acts, allowing, but not compelling, county Quarter Sessions to set up professional county police forces; the *County and Borough Police Act* (1856),[2] which made it compulsory for all counties and boroughs to establish police forces; three Inspectors of Constabulary were appointed, under this Act, to assess the efficiency of all the forces and make annual reports to Parliament; forces certified efficient would qualify for a Treasury grant of one-quarter of the cost of the pay and clothing of the force.[3] These Acts took some time to become effective at the local level. This chapter is concerned with how and when the Black Country policing arrangements changed from the traditional agencies to police forces, how the traditional and new police agencies operated in practice, and how this affected the process of law enforcement in the Black Country.

II

In 1835, the authorities for apprehending and detaining offenders, and for repressing disorders, were basically the traditional parish constables, supplemented in the larger towns by a locally raised and paid watch force.[4]

Parish constable is an office dating back to Anglo-Saxon and Norman times. It was an unpaid, elective office, rotating annually; every inhabitant had to serve as constable if chosen by the parish vestry. By the nineteenth century, it was normal for citizens to pay deputies to perform their duties as constable. By the 1830s, the average constable of a Black Country town held the post for a number of years; but many of them still practised a trade as well. Their deputy's wage was not very large; most of their police remuneration came from fees for executing warrants, serving summonses and appearing in court.

As well as having parish constables, the larger Black Country towns had raised their own forces of paid watchmen (sometimes called a 'Watch', sometimes a 'police force')[5] to patrol the streets, especially at night. Walsall had a night watch from 1811, and in 1832 established a 'police force' of three men; Wolverhampton had a night watch from

1814 till 1837, when it established a 'police force'; Dudley had a night watch from 1816, and acquired a 'police force' of nine men in 1840.[6] Bilston had a night watch, though it was probably not very large or effective.[7]

These were the two chief sources of normal law enforcement in the Black Country in 1835; but there were auxiliary forces for use in times of disorder. If the magistrates feared that 'any tumult, riot or felony. . . might be reasonably apprehended', they could nominate and swear in ordinary citizens as special constables.[8] Being without any special training, and being armed only with truncheons, special constables were not effective forces to use against disorders,[9] but they were always sworn in for such emergencies. As a rule, this was only when riots were anticipated, but they were also used to protect property and prevent disturbances when railway labourers were laying track across remote and poorly policed areas.[10] Should the Specials prove insufficient to cope with a disorder, the magistrates could (with Home Office consent) call in the military — the local Yeomanry, the Enrolled Pensioners, or the Regular Army, cavalry or infantry.[11] Resort to these military forces when disorder threatened remained common until the end of the 1850s. At this stage, the normal police authorities were inadequate to cope with any but the very smallest disorders.

III

The first 'New Police' force in the Black Country was a borough force in 1835 for Walsall, the only incorporated town in the Black Country. Under the Municipal Corporations Act, Walsall's Corporation was remodelled; the new Corporation appointed a Watch Committee which established a borough police force. Its total strength was four — one superintendent and three constables — from 1836 to 1838, and was reduced to three for the period 1839-41.[12]

As none of the other Black Country towns was incorporated, no other Black Country forces could be established until 1839, when Parliament passed the permissive County Police Act, allowing the magistrates in Quarter Sessions for any county to establish a paid, uniformed police for all or part of the county.[13] Of the two counties into which the Black Country fell, Worcestershire decided in 1839 to adopt the Act for the whole county;[14] Staffordshire Quarter Sessions voted in 1839 against adopting the Act for the whole county, but decided to adopt it for the area of the Southern Division of the Hundred of Offlow South.[15] This Offlow Force had a strength of twenty-one — one superintendent, two sergeants, and eighteen constables.[16] Only in November 1842 did the Staffordshire Quarter

Sessions decide to adopt the Act for the whole county and set up a Staffordshire county force under a Chief Constable.[17] Following the 1840 County Police Act, the county was divided into three districts for administrative and rating purposes: the *Mining District,* which comprised the Black Country;[18] the *Pottery District,* taking in the Potteries of north Staffordshire; and the *Rural District,* comprising the predominantly agricultural remainder of Staffordshire between these two industrial belts.[19] County forces were paid for by Quarter Sessions levying a Police Rate on the whole county; borough forces by borough ratepayers. This question of who paid for the force, and who controlled its finances and administration, was to be important in the future relations of county and borough forces.

So, from 1843 to 1860 there were 'New Police' operating throughout the Black Country.[20] In 1848, Wolverhampton became incorporated as a municipal borough and immediately established its own borough force, which continued a separate existence thereafter. All these forces gradually increased their strengths, particularly under Home Office prodding, following the 1856 County and Borough Police Act.[21] The changes in strength of these forces over the period are set out in table 1.

Table 1   Strengths of Black Country New Police Forces 1835-60

Year	Staffs. (Offlow Force, then Mining District)	Worcs. (Black Country section)	Walsall	Wolver- hampton	Total
1835	—	—	4	—	4
1840	21	6	3	—	30
1843	92	7	8	—	107
1847	100	NA	10	—	110+
1849	82	NA	10	27	119+
1853	90	NA	13	35	138+
1858	130	40	25	62	257
1860	134	40	26	62	262

NA = Not available

Sources: Reports of Supt. of Offlow Force 1840-2 (SRO Q/APr2), Staffs. C.C. Reports 1842-60 (SRO Q/SB till M. 1858; from Mich. 1858 C/PC/VIII/2/2), Worcs. C.C. Reports (WRO Q/SB); MWWC 1853-60; PRO HO 63/2 1858-60; *Return of the Number of Rural Police in each County in England and Wales. . .* P.P. 1856, p.665; *Return of Several Cities and Boroughs. . .* (1854).

IV

The expense of running a police force was a key factor in these changes in the early forces. The Walsall force took over its personnel unchanged from its local 'police force' with the addition of a superintendent, and kept its strength at only 3-4 men for the period 1835-40 — for a population which grew from 14,420 in 1831 to 19,587 in 1841.[22] The Worcestershire force set up in 1839 was kept small as a result of the persistent opposition of some of the magistrates to any greater expenditure — some had opposed the setting up of a county force at all.[23] In Staffordshire the prospective cost of a county force led to the defeat of the resolution for a force for the whole county, in 1839. The Offlow force was established as a force for part of the county only, because the magistrates of the Southern Division of the Hundred of Offlow South were prepared to accept the burden of a Police Rate as a lesser evil; they argued that their area was vulnerable because of its proximity to Birmingham, to 'gangs of depredators' from the city. A police force could supply 'an efficient night watch, and a body of men that could be called together quickly in case of any disturbance of the public peace'. Opposition still came from some magistrates on the grounds of the burden it would impose on the rates, but the motion for the force for part of the county only was carried.[24]

The opposition to a force for the *whole county*, on grounds of expense, was only overcome by a serious threat of disorder. By March 1842, twenty counties had adopted the 1839-40 County Police Acts for the whole county,[25] yet Staffordshire showed no signs of doing so and was showing signs of discontent even with the Offlow force.

At the Midsummer Sessions in June 1842, a petition was received from the ratepayers of Darlaston, asking that they be excluded from the jurisdiction of the Offlow force on the grounds that, after a trial of two years, 'they were convinced that the maintenance of two policemen parading the streets of Darlaston was a vexatious and useless burden on the rates'. A motion to this effect was put to Quarter Sessions for their next meeting, in October.[26] However, before this next meeting came the miners' strike of August-September 1842 in north and south Staffordshire. This strike, like the contemporaneous 'Plug Plot' strike in Lancashire, involved Chartist leadership and meetings, and riots leading to clashes with troops and destruction of houses and mine machinery; the riots were especially severe in the Potteries but also occurred in the Black Country.

At the next meeting of Quarter Sessions there were, in addition to the Darlaston motion, petitions from groups of ratepayers in Tipton, Wednesbury and West Bromwich (all drawn up before the riots), asking that they be exempted from the Police Rate and the sphere of operations of the Offlow force. But the Darlaston motion was now withdrawn by its proposer on the grounds that 'circumstances had since taken place which rendered it inexpedient to reduce the police force', and was replaced by a motion to extend the police force throughout the whole county.[27]

Debate on this motion took place at this Sessions and at the Adjourned Sessions in November 1842. Those magistrates favouring the introduction of a full county force generally stressed the shock which the recent riots had caused, and the need for an efficient police force to prevent similar outbreaks; those opposing it stressed the increase this would occasion in the rates.[28] Relatively little was said about the need for a force to repress more mundane and everyday crime, such as property offences; everyone seemed agreed that that was a desirable thing in the abstract, but the real debate was about whether the inconvenience of adding to the burden of the rates outweighed the fear of potential riot and destruction.[29]

As soon as Wolverhampton became incorporated in 1848 and entitled to set up its own borough force, it did so; this followed complaints from ratepayers about the corruption and inadequacy of the county force.

Before 1857, all the forces kept increases in strength to a minimum in order to keep down the expense; increases tended to be made only when the Home Office brought pressure to bear. For instance, following the Black Country riots of March 1855, for which troops had had to be called in, the Mayor of Wolverhampton received a letter from the Home Secretary, stating that the Wolverhampton force was inadequate for such a large and populous town; this meant that

> while inefficient provision is made to check the commission of ordinary crime, the civil force alone is nearly powerless in the event of any disturbance of the Public Peace. It is of great importance that there should be a sufficient Police Force in all large towns, not only for the protection of life and property under ordinary circumstances but also with the assistance of Special Constables, for the repression of any sudden disturbance of the peace without requiring, as has been too often the case, the aid of a military force.

And the Council should place Wolverhampton's force on a 'more satisfactory footing'. The letter contained a strong hint that troops would no longer be made available for the sort of riot suppression for which they had been used in the past. The Council responded immediately to this pressure and increased the force from thirty-nine to fifty-four.[30] Similarly, the offer of the Treasury grant to all forces certified 'efficient' by the Inspectors induced all the Black Country forces to make increases in 1857.

V

An examination of the normal working of the parish constables in the early part of the period and of the 'New Police' after their establishment, shows the degree of change involved in the introduction of the new forces.

The parish constables were, in 1835, the most important law-enforcement officers of the Black Country; and even after the establishment of the 'New Police' forces, they continued to play an important role. There can be no doubt about their importance:[31] in 1836, the overwhelming majority of people committed to trial in the Black Country were apprehended by parish constables; in 1839, the same is true of those committed to trial from the Worcestershire Black Country. In 1842, as might be expected, a considerably larger part was played by 'New Police' forces: all arrests from Stourbridge, Halesowen and Oldbury were by the Worcestershire county force, and all those from Walsall by the Walsall force. In the parishes under the Offlow force, arrests were divided about 40-60 per cent between the Offlow force and the parish constables respectively; and in Wolverhampton and Dudley, with their local watch forces, even though the local policemen accounted for the majority of arrests, the parish constables still handled a substantial proportion in each town. And of course, those parishes without a 'New Police' or watch force still relied totally on the parish constables for their arrests. Even in 1847 in Staffordshire, and in 1851 in Worcestershire, by which stage the county forces had been established for four and eleven years respectively, the parish constables still played a part in the arrest of those committed to trial, though their share had shrunk considerably from that in 1842. Parish constables continued to be appointed in Staffordshire until at least 1865;[32] it was not until 1872 that an Act was passed removing the obligation on parishes to appoint constables. It is probable that, well before this Act, the office of constable had already become obsolete and a mere formality, but exactly when this took place is not clear; certainly it was still functioning throughout the 1840s and was still in action in 1851.

Most accounts stress the unfitness of the parish constables, as part-time police officers, for the job of coping with the problems of law enforcement in industrial and urban environments.[33] However, in the 1830s and 1840s each Black Country town and parish had from two to six constables who kept the office for many years, and who carried out the normal police functions (searches, arrests, prosecutions, serving warrants). This long service as constable gave them considerable experience in law enforcement and many seem to have regarded themselves as full-time policemen; a number of them went on to join the new county and borough police forces of the Black Country.[34]

This stress on long service and police experience might seem to conflict with the usual accounts in police histories, which stress the corruption and inadequacy of the parish constable system; but perhaps they could exist together. The allegations of inefficiency seem to have some basis of truth; the parish constables did not form an organised patrolling group, which meant that they could not fulfil much of a preventive police function; and the fact that they relied largely for remuneration on fees paid or expenses claimed for each case brought or each warrant served, was said to tend to encourage parish constables to bring needless prosecutions and perhaps even give false testimony in order to get convictions.[35] But it is possible for them to have been seen as inefficient in certain respects (notably in the repression of large-scale public disorders, in finding the perpetrators of crimes of which the victims could not name the offenders, and in preventing the commission of offences) and relatively efficient in others (such as breaking up small disorders, and dealing with thefts, assaults or robberies where the victim either knew, or had a fairly strong suspicion, who the offender was).

Larcenies of this latter type form the bulk of the cases in the Quarter Sessions Calendars; typically, in such a case, the victim would go to the constable, report the offence and state whom he suspected; the constable would then obtain a search warrant and/or warrant of arrest, and search the suspected offender's lodgings or property and/or arrest him.[36] This procedure seems to have worked more efficiently than one might think it would; particularly in the small Black Country mining villages and industrial towns, the community seems to have been a tight one in which everyone knew everyone else; fights and brawls were easily dispersed; in cases of thefts and assaults, the victims seem usually to have been able to name or make a plausible suggestion as to the offender; even in robberies and burglaries the victims seem surprisingly often to be able to identify the offenders or give a description which results in their being easily found.[37] (At least, this is true of most of this sort of case *which got to the courts:* those in which such identification was not possible did not often get to the courts, presumably because there was no efficient means, in such a case, of finding and prosecuting the offender.) Even in the larger towns, like Wolverhampton and Dudley, evidence given by witnesses, especially by constables, indicates that it was surprisingly easy to find a particular person being sought as a suspected offender. And since many offenders were caught in the act (for example, by a watchman or an employee while stealing coal) or were strongly suspected by the victim, all the constable had to do in such cases was take into custody the offender caught red-handed, or search the belongings of the suspected offender and, if the stolen property was found, arrest him.

The constables could be seen as basically adequate for dealing with such 'normal' crime, but their great defect was particularly felt in cases where they had to deal with serious violence, robberies or burglaries committed by organised gangs on a large scale, or large-scale public disorder;[38] also in their lack of a preventive role. Hence, the early watch forces established in the larger towns, Wolverhampton, Dudley and Walsall, were night watches, sometimes for the winter months only, the intention being by patrols to prevent the commission of crime during those hours of darkness. An important element in the establishment of the Walsall, Wolverhampton and Dudley local forces, and of the Staffordshire county force, was exposure of the inadequacy of the parish constables in coping with large-scale disorders.[39]

The parish constables tended to operate on a small, domestic scale; in a large town like Wolverhampton there was a local goal where prisoners could be kept before being brought before a magistrate, but in most of the other towns there was only a very small lockup or no lockup at all. The constables tended to operate from their own houses as a base; it was here that complainants came to find them to ask them to get a warrant or arrest someone (in many depositions, the witness records: 'I went to the constable's house and he then came with me. . .' or '. . .but he was out and I had to return later. . .'). Often a constable would detain a prisoner in his own house, chaining him to prevent escape. Naturally, this system was open to abuse, especially in the smaller towns and villages, where there was relatively little supervision of the constables.[40]

The system could cope adequately after a fashion with prisoners brought in for small thefts or assaults, who could either be bailed, or

kept one night and then committed or tried by a magistrate, after which
those committed to trial could be sent off to the county prison; but it
could not cope with a sudden large influx of prisoners, such as occurred
after a riot was suppressed, or any other sudden spate of arrests. The
constables were subject to the control of, and answerable only to, the
magistrates; and the evidence suggests that the magistrates did not
exert themselves greatly to check abuses, unless they became flagrant —
for instance, in the two cases of constables who chained prisoners cited
in note 40, the magistrates had done nothing to prevent these practices,
and made statements in defence of the constables concerned.

Though this system *could* work reasonably efficiently in dealing
with routine offences, this did not mean that it always *did* work
efficiently. It placed a large amount of power in the hands of the few
semi-permanent constables who could decide whether or not to respond
to a victim's request and apply for a warrant. It tended to work in
favour of those with money and property. A constable was more likely
to take up an investigation if the prosecutor had sufficient money to be
able to repay his expenses and loss of time if no prosecution followed
the investigation through failure to gather sufficient evidence.[41]
Conversely, it was easier for a man with money to persuade a constable
to 'compound a felony' by abandoning a prosecution against him.[42]

Most police histories have followed the Royal Commissions on
County Rates (1836) and on the establishment of a Constabulary Force
(1839) in the view that the constable was usually illiterate and 'most
commonly an uneducated person from the class of petty tradesmen or
mechanics', who held office for one year only.[43] This was not true of
the Black Country constables of the 1830s: as has been mentioned,
they tended to be long-serving; and examination of the depositions of
constables in the Staffordshire and Worcestershire Quarter Sessions
shows that the overwhelming majority of them could sign their names.
Most of them signed with an easy and flowing handwriting which
suggests that they used their writing skills fairly regularly — and this in
an area in which over 50 per cent of adult males were unable to sign
their names.[44] The image of the illiterate, ignorant, annually rotating
parish constable, quite inadequate for the task he had to perform, is
so firmly fixed in most historical accounts that they never seem to ask
why, if that was the case, the system continued to work until the 1840s
without any serious breakdown of law and order in those communities
which relied on parish constables. The system had many flaws, but it
coped with much of 'normal' crime and small-scale disturbances.

It is difficult to discover much about the occupations of the active

Black Country constables in the 1830s and 1840s: systematic lists of
parish constables are only available from 1843 onwards, and the
occupations are only given of those appointed for the Southern Division
of Offlow South; only in the 1850s is information given on the
occupations of all the parish constables. But some deductions can be
made from these data (table 2). Table 2 confirms that some of the
long-serving constables had no other occupation — the two listed simply
as 'constable' were both long-serving and active constables of West
Bromwich. It shows that the constables were drawn primarily from
farmers, artisans and tradesmen; there were very few manual workers
or labourers. It is not clear, however, how far some of these may have
been occupations in name only, in which the man in fact spent most
of his time on police work. It is clear from other evidence (directories,
depositions) that some of the constables did carry on regular trades, but
this is not necessarily true for all of those for whom an occupation is
listed; nor does this sample cover the constables of Wolverhampton and
Dudley, who were among the longest-serving and most experienced
constables. But it does seem to be the case that the social background
of the constables was that of farmers (in the more rural parishes) and
small tradesmen and artisans (in the towns).

Table 2   Occupations of Parish Constables appointed for the Southern
Division of the Hundred of Offlow South, Staffs. 1843-8

Occupation	No.	Occupation	No.	Occupation	No.
Farmer	23	'Constable'	2	Ferrule maker	1
Butcher	11	Watchman	1	Pumpmaker	1
Blacksmith	7			Engraver	1
Shoemaker	6	Baker	1	Gunlock forger	1
Carpenter	4	Miller	1	File maker	1
Grocer	3	Dealer	1	Glass cutter	1
Maltster	3	Huckster	1	Moulder	1
Agent	3	Pawnbroker	1	Engineer	1
Cooper	2	Mercer	1	Mechanic	1
Builder	2	Cattle dealer	1	Road surveyor	1
Bricklayer	2	Nurseryman	1	Stone mason	1
Brickmaker	2				
Ironfounder	2	Tailor	1	Labourer	1
Miner	2	Coachsmith	1		
	72		13		12

TOTAL: 97

Source: Lists of Parish Constables 1842-63 (SRO Q/APr 3).

VI

The evidence suggests that the change from parish constables to New Police forces in the Black Country was not a sharp break from inefficient confusion to efficient organisation, but a much more gradual change. The Walsall force was a virtual continuation of the town's old watch force, under another name, and had a strength of only three to four men for its first six years (table 1). The Offlow force operated at night only.[45] The Worcestershire force began with only six men for its Black Country areas.[46] The Mining District section of the Staffordshire county force, which replaced the Offlow force, was better organised, operated by day and night, and maintained a higher ratio of police to population;[47] but its efficiency was impaired in its early years.

To gain a picture of the early police forces, the personnel and functioning of the Offlow force and of the Staffordshire county force will be examined; the Offlow force because it was a small force which lasted for only three years, on which a fair amount of material is available; the Staffordshire force because it covered 70 per cent of the Black Country population, and there is a large amount of material available on its composition and functioning. Reference will also be made, where relevant, to the Wolverhampton borough force.[48]

Both the Offlow and Staffordshire forces were set up by the Staffordshire Quarter Sessions, which appointed their commanding officers — a Superintendent for the Offlow force and a Chief Constable for the county force. The Chief Constable of a county force had considerable independence and powers of his own; he appointed and removed members of the force; he was appointed by Quarter Sessions but thereafter their control over his actions was relatively slight; Quarter Sessions decided on increases or reductions in the size of the force, but even here the Chief Constable's recommendations would carry great weight.[49] This meant that Quarter Sessions preferred to appoint as Chief Constables men of good social standing, with local county family connections, and especially with distinguished military records.[50] A Chief Constable could have considerable individual impact on the personnel and operations of his force.

The Superintendent of the Offlow Force, Wray, was quickly appointed, without any competition for the post; he had been an army officer for four years and then an inspector in the Metropolitan Police for eight years.[51] But for the post of Chief Constable of Staffordshire in 1842 there were forty-seven applicants, nineteen of them former army or naval officers, and nineteen (with considerable overlap here) with previous police experience; of the short list of seven, all had previous military and/or police experience.[52] The man chosen was John Hayes Hatton, who had been Chief Constable of the East Suffolk County Force from March 1840, and before that had been for seventeen years in the Irish Constabulary, ending as a Chief Constable, chiefly in County Wicklow of which he was a native.[53] Another of the applicants, Colonel Gilbert Hogg, was appointed Deputy Chief Constable of the force and Superintendent of the Mining District; he succeeded Hatton as Chief Constable in 1857. Hogg, who also came from Ireland, had a distinguished military career, serving in the British Legion in Spain in the 1830s; he had been in the Manchester Police Force from 1839 to 1842.[54]

There was a fair degree of turnover among the officers in the early years of the force. Seven superintendents and twelve inspectors were appointed. Three of the superintendents resigned and were replaced within the first year, and another resigned in 1845. Of the inspectors, one was discharged immediately, two each were dismissed during 1844 and 1845 while resignation removed another three in 1844, three in 1845 and one in 1846.[55]

This high turnover is even more marked in the case of the men (constables and sergeants) of the Staffordshire and Offlow forces. Police historians have stressed the difficulties which all the early police forces experienced in getting suitable recruits who would accept both the discipline of a police force and the need to commit themselves to a full-time police career; drunkenness was a particular problem among the early recruits.[56] The result was a high rate of dismissals and resignations, as the Offlow, Staffordshire and Wolverhampton forces show.

Twenty months after its establishment, the Offlow force contained only five of its original twenty constables; there had been a turnover of over 300 per cent in the other fifteen constables.[57] Table 3 shows how soon they left, and whether they resigned or were dismissed. 'Resigned' may mean that the recruit genuinely wanted to leave the police, but some names are endorsed 'allowed to resign', meaning that he was allowed to resign to avoid the stigma of dismissal.[58] Of the first twenty constables appointed, two were dismissed or resigned and were then reappointed and dismissed again within a short period.

The Staffordshire force had a similar high turnover among its initial recruits; of the 210 constables appointed between December 1842 and April 1843, 104 left during the course of 1843, and another twenty-nine during 1844; by 1 January 1848, only forty-six of the original 210 were still in the Force (table 4). Furthermore, a number of those who were dismissed or who resigned were reappointed to the force – table 4 lists numbers of those who were officially recorded as having been reappointed; probably the number was greater than this. Many of these were reappointed within a few months of their original dismissal or resignation, and most of them were dismissed or resigned again. Hatton, the Chief Constable, gained a bad reputation for reappointing dismissed men, as will be seen below; and a number of examples lend weight to this charge. For instance, Sergeant Michael Stewart was dismissed for misconduct in November 1847, following a Police Committee investigation into mismanagement and corruption in the Mining District headquarters at Wolverhampton; but he was reappointed on 1 January 1848, at his former rank; he remained in the force, and became a Superintendent in 1865.[59]

Table 3   Constables in the Offlow Force February 1840 – September 1841: Length of Service and Manner of Leaving*

Period of Service in the Force	No. of Constables Leaving the Force				No. of Constables Still Serving+
	Total	Dismissed	'Resigned'	'Allowed to Resign'	
Less than 1 month	8	6	1	1	
1 month	2	0	1	1	3
1-2 months	2	0	0	2	1
2-3 months	7	3	2	2	3
3-4 months	4	1	1	2	0
4-5 months	4	2	0	2	0
5-6 months	4	2	1	1	0
6-12 months	11	2	5	4	7
12-20 months	4	2	1	1	2
20 months					5

* Manner of leaving as recorded in the Superintendents' Reports (SRO Q/APr 2).

+ This column of constables still serving adds up to twenty-one, though the officially recorded strength of the force never changed from twenty constables. These are the constables assumed to be still serving in the force at the end of September 1841, as there is no record of their leaving.

Table 4 Constables in the Staffordshire Force December 1842 —
        January 1848: Length of Service and Manner of Leaving*

| Number of Constables | Date of Appointment to Force | | | | | Total |
	Dec 1842	Jan. 1843	Feb. 1843	March 1843	April 1843	
TOTAL	120	55	15	14	6	210
1843						
Dismissed	48	10	4	5	2	69
Resigned	22	7	1	3	0	33
Died	1	0	1	0	0	2
1844						
Dismissed	6	3	1	2	0	12
Resigned	11	4	1	0	1	17
Died	0	0	0	0	0	0
1845-48						
Dismissed	6	2	0	0	0	8
Resigned	10	7	3	1	1	22
Died	0	1	0	0	0	1
Still serving 1 January 1848	16	21	4	3	2	46
Listed as Reappointed:+						
After dismissal	15	5	1	2	0	23
After resignation	17	9	2	1	3	32

* Taken from Register of Members of the County Force 1842-63 (SRO C/PC/VIII/
  4/1/1). The category 'Allowed to Resign' is not distinguished from 'Resigned'
  in this Register.

+ In the totals of dismissals and resignations, each constable is only counted once.
  Most of those reappointed again resigned or were dismissed subsequently
  (some were reappointed twice and dismissed three times in all); second
  dismissals or resignations for any man have not been counted in the main
  part of the table.

The Wolverhampton force had similar problems with turnover of men;
no figures are available on its first few years but the figures for 1859,
the twelfth year of its existence (table 5(a)), show that even by then,
about half of the men had less than three years' service in the force,
and over one-quarter had less than one year. Table 5(b) shows the large

numbers who resigned or were dismissed in the years 1853-60 — in a force whose strength was thirty-five in 1853 and sixty-two in 1860. The reasons for dismissal are listed for many. By far the commonest reason is drunkenness while on duty, or persistent drunkenness; other fairly common reasons are commission of an assault (on a civilian or a fellow policeman) and neglect of duty, breach of regulations, insubordination, etc. Rarer instances involve conviction for an offence, being absent without leave, and dismissal following a civilian complaint.

This high turnover (and the reappointment of men who had been dismissed or had resigned) must have affected the operating efficiency of these forces, particularly in their early years: the Offlow force was probably never a very efficient force for the three years of its existence — at any given moment the core of experienced, trained men in the force was very small; the Staffordshire and Wolverhampton forces were hampered by this problem in their early years.

The recruitment of policemen was related to their wages. A policeman starting in the Staffordshire force would start as a constable, 4th class, at 15s a week in the 1840s (17s from 1853) (table 6(b)). These wages could not compete with the wages of skilled industrial

Table 5   Turnover in the Wolverhampton Force 1853-60.

(a) Length of Service in the Force of Members (Officers and Other Ranks) of Wolverhampton Force at September 1859

			Years of Service					
Less than 1	1-2	2-3	3-4	4-5	5-7	7-10	10-12	Total
16	1	14	6	5	6	7	6	61

(b) Dismissals, Resignations, etc. 1853-60

Manner of leaving	Number							
	1853	1854	1855	1856	1857	1858	1859	1860
Dismissed	3	2	5	5	9	9	2	5
Resigned*	1	8	14	19	20	12	7	14
Deserted		1			1			
Reappointed							1	1

* Resigned includes those 'allowed to resign'.

Source: MWWC 1853-60.

Table 6 Rates of Pay in the Staffordshire, Offlow and Wolverhampton
        Police Forces

(a) Officers (per annum)

Year	CC	DCC	Staffs. County Supts.	Inspectors	Wolverhampton CC	Inspectors
1840	(Offlow Force) £150					
1843	£150	£120	£80-£100	£65-£80		
1846	£400	£140	£90-£120	£70		
1851	£350	£140	£90-£120	£70		
1853	£350	£140	£94 10s-£126	£68 5s-£78 15s		
1854					£250	£65-£70 4s
1855					£280	£65-£70 4s
1857	£400		£109 4s-£126	£70-£80	£200	£62 8s-£78
1858					£300	£72 16s-£78

(b) Other Ranks (per week)

Year	Staffs. County Sgts.	Constables	Wolverhampton Sgts.	Constables
1840 (Offlow)	20s	17-18s		
1843	19-21s	15-18s		
1846	21-23s	15-20s		
1851	21-23s	15-20s		
1853	22-24s	17-21s		
1854			22s	16-21s
1855			22s	17-21s
1857	22-23s	19-21s	21-23s	17-22s
1858			23s	17-22s

CC = Chief Constable   DCC = Deputy Chief Constable

Sources: SRO Q/SB Staffs. C.C. Reports; SRO Q/SOp 1833-60; SRO Q/ACp 3,
    Police Return to Home Office, February 1840; MWWC.

and building workers in the Black Country; when in employment, the
miners could always earn better wages than the police; only labourers,
nailers, chainmakers and workshop metal workers might find themselves
attracted by these wages into the police, especially in times of

depression and low wages.[60]

Continual concern was shown in Quarter Sessions over the problem of finding sufficient suitable men at these wages. Fierce debates took place over attempts to cut or to increase the policemen's wages, in which comparison was continually made with the wages of other manual workers. In a debate in 1851 on a motion to cut the wages of the policemen by one shilling a week, Lord Wrottesley argued that their wages should rather be increased:

> Fifteen shillings a week was too little to give to men who had to fill the duties of a police officer. A mere labourer taken from the plough would not be sufficient for the office. . .Fifteen shillings was a sum little more than he gave his own waggoners, and was not sufficient for police officers.

He was supported by other magistrates, who pointed out that some skilled workers received twenty-five and thirty shillings a week. The Hon. F. Gough, pursuing this line, argued:

> Considering that the greater part of the men who were employed in this force were exposed to great temptations, he thought they ought to select them from a higher grade than labourers receiving fourteen or fifteen shillings a week.

But against this, a number of magistrates supported the line of Mr. Barker that, while it was true that skilled workers' wages were higher,

> they did not, however, want a skilled labourer in a police station. It was from the working population that the individuals constituting the police force were generally raised.[61]

There was agreement that the basic constable's wage excluded skilled workers as potential recruits; the debate was over the desirability of this result. The motion for a wage cut was defeated on that occasion but the constable's basic wage was not substantially raised and the catchment area for recruitment remained basically labourers.

This is borne out by the previous occupations listed for constables and sergeants in the Staffordshire force. Of the 210 constables appointed to the force between December 1842 and April 1843 (whose turnover has already been discussed), the previous occupation before joining the force is listed for only thirty-six; within these thirty-six the commonest occupations are 'labourer', 'farmer', and artisan (carpenter, joiner, shoemaker, chairmaker), and there are four each listed as 'soldier' and 'police'.[62]

A more reliable idea of previous occupations of constables can be had from the 1842-94 Register,[63] which lists the previous occupation for all constables and sergeants *except* the initial 210, for 1843-60 (Table 7). By far the commonest previous occupation given is 'labourer'; this may mean industrial, building or agricultural labourer, and is probably a mixture of industrial and agricultural labourers. Within the Black Country itself, 'labourer' would probably mean industrial labourer; but taking into account the thirteen entries of 'farmer', and the fact that other industrial areas made use of farm labourers from surrounding agricultural areas to man their early police forces,[64] a high proportion of those 'labourer' entries probably refer to farm labourers, brought in from the agricultural areas of Staffordshire, Worcestershire and Shropshire. Agricultural labourers were one group who would see 15s as an improvement on a basic wage of about 10s a week.[65] Some in the category 'labourer' are probably industrial labourers; but very few other industrial and mining workers were induced to join the force. It is noticeable that farmers, artisans and small tradesmen, the men who made up the bulk of the parish constables (Table 2), are prominent in the Staffordshire force.

What previous experience, of police or related work, did the officers and men of the initial Staffordshire force bring with them? Of the ten superintendents appointed between December 1842 and April 1843, all listed previous public service: one came from the Irish Constabulary (specifically recommended by Hatton) and one from the Army; the bulk were from the Metropolitan force, the Manchester and Birmingham forces (set up on the Metropolitan model under government supervision),[66] and the Stafford borough force. Of the eighteen inspectors, fourteen listed previous public service – nine in borough forces, and two each in the Army, Irish Constabulary, other English county forces, or Metropolitan force (with some overlap, some having served in more than one force). Available information on the native counties of these officers shows that only one came from Staffordshire, seven from other English counties and five from Ireland.[67]

Of the 210 new constables recruited between December 1842 and April 1843, 156 had some previous police or military service – in some cases, service in more than one force or in the Army and a police force (Table 8). Very few came from the Metropolitan force, but the

Table 7   Previous Occupations of Constables and Sergeants
Appointed to the Staffordshire County Force 1843-60

Previous Occupation	No.	Previous Occupation	No.
'Labourer'	75	Publican	2
'Farmer'	13	Porter	2
Shoemaker	13	Engineer	2
Servant	13	Wheelwright	1
Baker	8	Wheel fitter	1
Butcher	8	Carpenter	1
Blacksmith	7	Whitesmith	1
Weaver	6	Clock case maker	1
Gamekeeper	4	Locksmith	1
Groom, Coachman	4	Keysmith	1
Sawyer, Wood cutter, Lath cleaver	4	Currier	1
Miner	4	Tanner	1
Potter	3	Japanner	1
Tailor	3	Hatter	1
Grocer	3	Printer	1
Clerk	3	Stone Mason	1
Gardener	3	Maltster	1
Miller	2	Warehouseman	1
Jeweller	2	Sailor	1
Soldier	2	TOTAL:	202

Source: 1843-60 entries in Register of Staffs. Force 1842-94 (SRO C/PC/VIII/
4/2/1).

Government-controlled Manchester, Birmingham and Bolton forces
supplied more than a quarter of all the men with previous experience;
while existing local forces — Offlow force and local town forces —
contributed one-fifth.

But there is no way of telling how much this 'previous public service'
really meant — it could mean a man who had learned police skills
through experience in a force, or it could mean a man who had been
dismissed or had resigned from his previous force within a few months.
The subsequent record of dismissals and resignations of these 210
constables suggests that previous police experience did not mean much
in terms of reliability and efficiency.

The counties of origin of these same 210 (Table 9) show that only

Table 8 Previous Public Service of the Constables Appointed to the Staffordshire County Force, December 1842 - April 1843*

Service	No.+	Service	No.
Metropolitan Police	9	Irish Constabulary	13
Manchester, Birmingham or Bolton Police	55	Dublin Metropolitan Police	13
Borough Police Force	25	Offlow Force	14
English County Force (excluding Offlow Force)	4	A Staffordshire or Black Country Local Police Force (Wolverhampton, Dudley, Potteries, Stoke)	22
Army	13	Listed simply as 'Police'	8
		NONE, or Not Listed	54

* SRO C/PC/VIII/4/1/1.

+ Of 210 constables listed, 156 have some previous public service; the numbers listed here add up to 176 because a number have service in more than one police force, or in the Army and police force(s) behind them.

Table 9 County of Origin of Constables Appointed to the Staffordshire County Force, December 1842 - April 1843

County or Area	No.
Staffordshire	82
Neighbouring County (Worcestershire, Warwickshire, Shropshire, Cheshire, Derbyshire)	20
Other English County	41
Ireland	56
Scotland	10
Not Listed	1
TOTAL	210

Source: SRO C/PC/VIII/4/1/1.

half were of local origin — from Staffordshire or a neighbouring county; more than one-quarter were of Irish origin.

The ages of new constables tended to be in their twenties and thirties (Table 10). Most of the younger men joined in the first month,

December; January shows a higher proportion of older men. The January recruits show a much better record on resignations and dismissals than the December group (Table 4), which suggests that the younger men initially joined eagerly but soon wanted to leave or were thrown out, while the older men (with somewhat more police experience behind them) were found to make the steadier policemen.

To sum up the Staffordshire force in its early years. It was commanded by a Chief Constable from an Irish Constabulary background, under the loose control of a Quarter Sessions concerned to keep down the county police rate. Below the Chief Constable came the superintendents, in charge of the county's three districts and of divisions within those districts; after the initial resignations in the first year they were a stable and long-serving group. Beneath them came the inspectors, with a much higher turnover of dismissals and resignations. Finally, the bulk of the force — sergeants and constables — had a very high rate of turnover and of reappointment, which must have impaired the efficiency of the force in these years.

Table 10   Ages of the 204 Constables Appointed to the Staffordshire County Force, December 1842 - March 1843

Age of Constables	Date of Appointment to Force			
	Dec. 1842	Jan. 1843	Feb. 1843	March 1843
Less than 20	2	0	0	0
20-29	83	19	6	10
30-39	33	26	9	4
40 and over	2	6	0	0
Not given	0	4	0	0
Total Number of Constables	120	55	15	14

Source: SRO C/PC/VIII/4/1/1.

VII

Now to look at the Mining District section of the Staffordshire force as it operated in the Black Country.[68] Until 1848, Wolverhampton was included within the Mining District and the Deputy Chief Constable had his headquarters there.

Most of the Mining District force was concentrated in the larger towns — Wolverhampton, West Bromwich, Bilston. The non-urban parishes (such as Sedgley, Tipton, Kingswinford) in which large populations were scattered in mining and ironworking villages, were more scantily policed. The impact of the new force was largely felt in the towns.[69] The main experience which most of the non-urban areas would have had of the early police force was of one constable patrolling on foot. These areas were also short of lockups and police facilities.[70] Smethwick, a fast-growing town (population 2,676 in 1831, 13,379 in 1861), was held by its inhabitants to be especially vulnerable to criminals because of its proximity to Birmingham; yet the town had only one police constable, with another two stationed in the neighbouring rural parish of Harborne; as late as 1857, Smethwick inhabitants petitioned Quarter Sessions to increase this number.[71]

With such small numbers of policemen available for the non-urban areas, their role remained essentially the old reactive 'parish constable' one, rather than a new, more active preventive police role; it is not surprising that parish constables continued to be appointed and made use of, in these areas. In any emergency, such as a strike or threatened riot, men could be drafted into the area from the urban centres, but in normal times such areas would not see many policemen.

In 1848, Wolverhampton got its own borough force. The Mining District headquarters moved to West Bromwich and the non-urban areas were gradually given a larger number of policemen. But even this increase came in the form of police stations housing only a single constable, so these areas were still a long way from experiencing the effects of a numerous patrolling police force.

The Inspector of Constabulary, in his first report in 1857, recommended an increase in the force in view of the population and industry of the area. Staffordshire Quarter Sessions set up a committee to look into the strength of the force, which endorsed the need for an increase; the material they gathered provides much information about the operations of the force. The Mining District was increased by nineteen men.[72] Thereafter, the Staffordshire force was always rated 'efficient' by HM's Inspector; the non-urban areas were probably seeing more of a permanent police presence by then. The cities were also being more heavily policed: the Inspector prodded Wolverhampton into raising its borough force from thirty-six to sixty-two for its population of nearly 60,000; Walsall, with a population of 35,000, increased its force to twenty-six; and Dudley had a detachment of the Worcestershire county force.[73] By 1860, the Black Country forces could be said to be approaching the idea of a modern police force in terms of strength and operating efficiency; but in the 1840s and 1850s they fell short of this role, especially outside the large towns.

The operation of the force would have been affected by the 'police ideology' which it developed — the ideas which the Quarter Sessions, Chief Constable, superintendents and ultimately the constables themselves, held about the functions and primary goals of their police force.[74]

The early Staffordshire force seems to have been based, at least partially, on a paramilitary model, with emphasis placed on the repression of riots and disorders. It has already been noted that the *raison d'être* of the Staffordshire force, and the argument which overcame the claims of financial stringency, was the need for a force which could prevent a repetition of the riots of August 1842. The new Chief Constable, Hatton, had made his name and gained most of his experience in the paramilitary Irish Constabulary, much of whose task had been the repression of agrarian disorders. His testimonials from Irish landowners and magistrates, and the newspaper account of his appointment, stressed the part he had played in suppressing the activities of the Ribbonmen in County Louth and the anti-tithe agitation in County Wicklow; the latter involved his constabulary in co-operating with dragoons and Yeomanry in dispersing and quelling riotous crowds. There is no mention in any of his testimonials of commendation for more 'normal' police duties — the stress is on riot control and repression of disorders.[75] Hogg (the candidate for Chief Constable in 1842 who was appointed Deputy Chief Constable, and who succeeded Hatton as Chief Constable in 1857) likewise stressed his military service and the prominent role he had played, while in the Manchester police force, in repressing the August 1842 disturbances in Lancashire.[76]

County forces were still new institutions, with no models provided by precedent or by the Home Office as to how they should be run; it was largely left to Quarter Sessions and the Chief Constable to determine their own organisation and priorities.[77] Commanding officers were likely to turn to the type of organisation of which they had had experience in commanding men.

Hatton was clearly influenced by his paramilitary model. The easiest way for him and his officers to train inexperienced recruits was to drill them in military discipline and send them out to patrol the streets. Developing skills of preventive and detective police work in them took much longer. Much of the energy of the force and its organisation, especially in the early years, was directed towards the repression of disorder. One of the first steps which Hatton took with his new recruits was to give them military drill, including sword drill with cutlasses.[78] This same military emphasis can be seen in the Wolverhampton Force, under Colonel Hogg and his successor Captain Segrave – the men had to go through regular drilling under an instructor, and were marched on and off their beats; following the riot in the Wolverhampton area in March 1855 and a reprimand from the Home Secretary for their ineffectiveness in checking public disorders, the force issued cutlasses to each member.[79]

In the Staffordshire force, from the start, considerable attention was paid to the role of the force in preserving public order; this applied primarily to political and industrial agitation – the shock of Chartism and the disturbances of the early 1840s had determined the authorities to strengthen the machinery for repressing such disorders[80] – but it applied also to minor disorders, disorderly gatherings, etc.[81] By the mid-1850s, the Staffordshire force had become skilled at handling riot situations, strikes and public meetings, while it is not evident that they had reached the same degree of skill in preventive and detective work involving more routine crimes.

However, the paramilitary aspect of the force and the parallel with the Irish Constabulary must not be overstressed; the Staffordshire force never became a gendarmerie armed with firearms – their normal weapon was the truncheon, and even cutlasses were only issued in special circumstances of danger or unrest; nor were they stationed in groups in strategically positioned barracks around the country, as was the case with the Irish Constabulary – the Staffordshire force operated from police stations in the centres of the towns and lived at home. The similarities lie in their officers and command structure, and their emphasis on drill and the need to combat disorder; but they go no further than that.

The methods and freedom of operation of the force were also much affected by tight control of their budget; the Staffordshire Quarter Sessions wished from the start to keep the police rate as low as possible. The expense of a police force was the chief ground on which the establishment of the force had been initially opposed; even after its establishment, motions for its abolition or reduction in size, or for cuts in police pay, continued to come up at Quarter Sessions.[82] These motions did not succeed but they had an effect in making Quarter Sessions and their Police Committee, and the Chief Constable very cost-conscious in relation to the force. Expenditure on the force was kept to a minimum, constables' wages were kept low and ways were continually sought to justify the existence of the force as a source of monetary saving to the country. Throughout the 1840s, the force experienced financial stringency and the Chief Constable continued to stress the savings to the county effected by the force, to protect it against cuts in size and expenditure.[83]

In 1846, Hatton managed to get an increase in the size of the force and a general pay rise; but in 1851 Quarter Sessions economised by cutting Hatton's pay. There was another general pay rise in 1853, and a rise for some ranks in 1857. By this time, the extra duties which the police force were performing in order to save the county money included: conveying and maintaining prisoners; building and repairing lockups; inspecting weights and measures; attending inquests; inspecting vagrants, Union workhouses and lodging-houses; paying parish constables and special constables; acting as Inspectors of Nuisances.[84]

VIII

The impact which the new Staffordshire force had on the situation in the Black Country in the period 1842-60 can be analysed, falling into three rough stages: (1) From its establishment to about 1848; (2) 1848-57; (3) 1857-60.

(1) From establishment to 1848

In this period the force could not have been functioning with great efficiency nor providing a marked contrast to the old system of parish constables and local watch forces. Indications of this are: the high turnover of men and officers in the first five years; the methods of operation of the force in these years, which left the non-urban areas with few policemen; and the emphasis on keeping down the police rates. In its early years, the force was not getting much co-operation from the public. It met hostility from Chartists and Radicals, and some violence from individual members of the public. Throughout these early years, Quarter Sessions were petitioned by parishes wanting to opt out of the jurisdiction of the force and the payment of the police rate.[85] Organised political hostility to the force seems to have died away in Staffordshire within a few years, as did the attempts to be exempted from the force, after a few more years; even violence towards the force by individuals seems to have greatly diminished by the 1850s.

But the 'New Police' had not totally extinguished the parish constables as law officers; recognisances and depositions show that people were still making use of parish constables as law-enforcement officers as late as 1847. This is especially true of the non-urban parishes such as Kingswinford, Rowley Regis and Sedgley but is found even in Wolverhampton. This might indicate a preference for the old parish constables over the new policemen; more likely, in most cases, it reflects the fact that the new police were not able, in their early years, to cope fully with all the necessary police functions.

There was considerable rivalry and ill-feeling between parish constables and the new police. The 1839-40 County Police Acts gave the county police constabulary powers, but they did not remove those powers from the parish constables; this left, legally, two parallel systems of policing with no common control or connection. In the early years of the police forces, there were conflicts with the parish constables over the right to use existing lockups and police facilities.[86]

The pettiness and bitterness of the rivalry is brought out in a case, previously cited, of ill-treatment by a parish constable in 1845.[87] Mary Heseltine's father complained to the Sub-Inspector of Police at Wolverhampton that she had been ill-treated by Fellows, the Bilston parish constable. In his defence, Fellows alleged that the whole charge had been trumped up against him; why, he asked, had the complaint been made to the police and not to the Bilston magistrates? He continued:

> . . .but that would not suit the man who thus basely trumps up a
> charge of cruelty towards the prisoner – no – he prefers going in a
> wily manner to one placed in authority in the Police Force at
> Wolverhampton to make his false charge, to one, who he well
> knows, would use his utmost powers to injure the reputation and
> if possible, annihilate every Parish Constable in the county.[88]

This suggests that Fellows saw the power struggle between the rising new police and the dying parish constables as dwarfing all other issues in importance. His shrill tone shows almost paranoid hostility towards the police.

This sort of conflict between rival enforcers of the law was made easier by the loose structure of the normal administrative and judicial channels. The other documented case of ill-treatment of a prisoner by a Black Country parish constable in 1845 showed rivalry and lack of co-ordination between the separate Petty Sessions in the area: the complainant Eliza Price was able to get Joseph Newey convicted of an assault on her (committed on 3 April) at the Wordsley Petty Sessions on 7 April; yet Newey was able at the Kingswinford Petty Sessions on

7 April to get a warrant against Eliza Price for assault on him, arising out of the same act. This came about because, as the Commissioner reported in this case, two separate Petty Sessions had been established for the same district, without any division of jurisdiction being agreed between them; as a result

> unseemly jealousies amongst the magistrates and conflicts of authority, as must naturally have been expected, have frequently occurred, tending to bring into disrepute the administration of justice. . .Each bench of justices has its admirers, and the constables and even some of the police force seemed to me to be infected with partizan spirit.[89]

In each area, the magistrates for that Petty Sessions division could decide for themselves what attitude to take to the parish constables; if they chose to favour them by letting them, rather than the police, serve warrants and execute summonses, this could keep alive and exacerbate the rivalry. It made it impossible for the police to check or control the number of arrests made and prosecutions brought in that area.

The Staffordshire force itself shows evidence in these early years of dissensions among its officers, and of financial irregularities. The Chief Constable controlled the appointment of men and the spending of money. Hatton gained a reputation for reappointing men who had been dismissed or had resigned — a practice banned by a regulation of the Home Secretary as early as 1840.[90]

In July 1847 an anonymous letter to Quarter Sessions — possibly written by a member of the force — accused Hatton of tolerating drunkenness and inefficiency, reappointing dismissed men and lining his own pockets. The Police Committee investigated this and exonerated Hatton of the main charges, but found that there had been some financial irregularity in his favour.[91]

In October 1847, an enquiry into the running of the Mining District headquarters at Wolverhampton showed irregularities in the accounts. Deputy Chief Constable Hogg was demoted to superintendent and removed from Wolverhampton; Inspector Casey was fined five pounds and also moved away from Wolverhampton; and Sergeant Stewart was dismissed. In his defence, Casey attacked his superior, Hogg, claiming that he was trying to pin the charges on to Casey.[92] There was also personal animosity between Hatton and Hogg, the two most senior officers of the force.[93]

All this suggests that the Staffordshire force could not have been functioning very efficiently between the time of its establishment and 1848. However, it was successful in ensuring that there was no large-scale outbreak of disorder in this period; and the force vigorously enforced the law against minor disorders. This was probably due to the emphasis given to the public order role of the force; they were trained for the dispersal of riots and the prosecution of disorders in the streets, but in dealing with the 'normal' offences of larceny and robbery their methods do not seem to have been a significant advance on those of the parish constables.

(2) 1848 to 1857

The administration and effectiveness of the force seem to have improved after 1848. For one thing, as has been mentioned, after 1848 more police stations began to be established in the non-urban areas, ensuring more of a real and permanent police presence in those areas. Secondly, Quarter Sessions set up police committees in 1848 to exercise supervision of the finances of the force, though it was not until 1855 that the handling of the receipts and expenditure of the money of the county force was transferred from the Chief Constable to the County Treasurer.[94] The active role of the parish constables declined markedly in the 1850s, and clashes between them and the police seem to have died out. In the force, the turnover in men and officers was diminishing; dismissals and resignations for drunkenness and insubordination continued to be a problem well into the 1850s, but not on the same scale as the turnover of the early years. Serious public opposition to the force had virtually ceased by the 1850s;[95] and the police were gradually developing a confidence in themselves and their police role.

But this change should not be seen as very large or sudden — a number of the earlier problems and weaknesses of the force continued after 1848. A considerable turnover of men continued: for the year May 1855 to May 1856, fifty-six men were dismissed and thirty-six resigned — from a total force of 279. A return sent to the Home Office stated that during the year of 1856, seventy-one constables had been dismissed and sixty-eight had resigned from the county force, out of a total force of 280. (The respective figures for the Mining District were twenty-three dismissed and twenty-one resigned out of a total of ninety-three). Turnover, even at that stage, was between 33 and 50 per cent.[96]

Signs of dissatisfaction with Hatton's running of the force appeared in Quarter Sessions in 1849; in 1851, they reduced his salary by £50.[97] In 1852 there was another enquiry into the Mining District force, which showed that internal discipline was lax and the journals and reports of the senior officers had been inadequately kept. The Police Committee warned Hatton that if no improvement was made in the Mining District, they would recommend his dismissal.[98]

The question of reappointment of men who had been dismissed or had resigned for some misconduct came up a number of times. Quarter Sessions reprimanded Hatton for this practice on a number of occasions, and pressed him for regular returns to Quarter Sessions of the number and past records of men reappointed — but the practice continued.[99] Hatton resigned as Chief Constable in December 1856 under strong pressure from Quarter Sessions over another enquiry into corruption in the force.[100] And overall, the constraints of financial stringency on the strength and facilities of the force remained.

So the force was still encountering a number of problems in settling into a smooth routine. But it did show itself to be operating efficiently in at least one area — control of public order. In March 1855 a large miners' strike was handled by the police without any serious rioting ensuing; this included an incident in which a force of thirty Mining District police dispersed a crowd of 3,000 miners armed with sticks and stones, without any serious violence or injury. Similarly, they coped without disorder or clashes with the 'Dear Bread' agitation of November-December 1855, and with the miners' strikes of November 1857 and August-November 1858.[101] The efficiency and confidence with which the police handled these situations form a striking contrast to the alarm and lack of co-ordination which marked the authorities' handling of the 1842 disorders. The police dealt with the four episodes of the 1850s with a minimum of confrontation and violence, and the authorities commended their handling of the situations.[102] The contrast between the confident and commendatory tone used by the authorities in these episodes and their tone in 1842 (especially that of the magistrates who tended to be the most alarmist)[103] shows the extent to which the development of the police force over those 13-16 years had given the local authorities a feeling of confidence in their ability to handle public disorder.

(3) 1857 to 1860

As with the other two stages, this is only a roughly defined period, but it chiefly covers the changes in the force following the 1856 County and Borough Police Act and the beginning of government inspection of police forces. It also coincides with the resignation of Hatton as Chief Constable, and his replacement by Colonel Hogg. Selection of Hogg involved no change in Quarter Sessions policy. Hogg had a distinguished military record and the other four candidates shortlisted with Hogg for the post were all ex-army officers.[104] Hogg had police experience in the Staffordshire force as its second-in-command and in command of the Wolverhampton force; he made no administrative changes on becoming Chief Constable.

The chief impact of the County and Borough Police Act lay in its provision that the Treasury would pay a grant of one-quarter of the cost of the pay and clothing of all forces certified efficient by the inspectors. This meant that for the first time local forces would receive income from sources other than county or borough rates. With this incentive, all the Black Country forces increased their strengths to totals rated 'efficient' by the inspectors. The Treasury grant meant that the tight financial stringency imposed on the forces began to be relaxed slightly. In the Staffordshire force, the increased strength of the Mining District section meant a higher ratio of police to population and to area covered, in the non-urban areas.[105] Following increases in their strength, the Staffordshire force and the other Black Country forces were certified 'efficient' by the Inspector of Constabulary; the test of efficiency was the ratio of size of force to population being policed.[106]

Whereas in the two earlier stages the force seems to have been more active and efficient in repression of disorder than in its concern with 'normal' crime, it seems to have extended and improved its handling of 'normal' crime after 1857. This is partly due simply to the increased strength of the force after 1857, which facilitated more thorough patrols and detection throughout the area. More important, fear of public disorder was becoming less pressing as the threat and memory of the 'Hungry Forties' receded; it was being replaced by a growing concern with 'normal' crime (chiefly property offences and individual violence), especially juvenile crime. These had been matters of concern before but up to the 1840s 'normal' crime was often seen as being linked to disorder as part of a general 'social threat'; from the 1850s, it came to be seen much more as a 'social problem' — requiring attention but lacking the urgency imparted to the earlier views by the fear that 'normal' crime might be part of a general social breakdown.[107]

What effect did all these police developments have on the numbers of people arrested, the numbers committed to trial, the general standard of public order? Obviously, by 1860, the position in the Black Country was considerably changed from what it had been in 1835, with four reasonably large police forces taking the place of the parish constables and local town forces. The change in personnel and operating efficiency, as has been shown, was not a sudden one, yet between 1835 and 1860 a marked change can be seen.

Studies of the introduction of new police forces into communities suggest that one immediate effect which they produce is a marked increase in prosecutions for minor public order offences — brawls, drunkenness, disorderly conduct in public, etc. The new police bring with them a heightened sensitivity to disorder which has previously been tolerated or at least not punished by legal sanctions; the imposition of this new order is initially resisted by the people who feel its effects, resulting in a sharp initial rise in prosecutions for such offences.[108] A similar effect followed the establishment of the Staffordshire force; there was an immediate attempt by the police to curb rowdy public behaviour and break up public recreations of doubtful legality.

The Black Country was well known for its boisterous wakes and fairs and its rough sports — bullbaiting, prizefighting, cockfighting, dogfighting. These were the traditional recreations of the Black Country working class.[109] From the early nineteenth century, opposition to these occasions and sports had been gathering force from the 'respectable' classes, especially from the clergy, manufacturers, some magistrates, and large numbers of the middle class; societies were founded to put an end to these blood sports; wakes and fairs were attacked as occasions which encouraged drunkenness, crime and immorality; the blood sports were attacked as cruel and barbarous and often leading to public disorders.[110]

The legal position of the blood sports was uncertain until the 1830s because there was no statute on the subject — people and societies prosecuting for these sports did so under the common law offence of common nuisance or breach of the peace. In 1835, a Cruelty to Animals Act was passed, explicitly making illegal all blood sports which involved the baiting of animals; cockfighting was explicitly prohibited by an 1849 Act.[111] Magistrates had taken action against prizefights since the late eighteenth century (for the common law offences of breach of the peace or unlawful assembly), and continued to do so in the nineteenth century. But prizefights continued to be held in out-of-the-way places, and to be supported by a number of members of the gentry. The Chairman of Staffordshire Quarter Sessions remarked, in a charge to the Grand Jury in 1836:

He had to observe that since the last Sessions, there had been in this county one of those disgraceful exhibitions called 'prize fights', and an attempt at another which, however, had failed. A great number of that description of persons who attended exhibitions of this nature were with difficulty persuaded that there was anything wrong or unlawful in them. He (the Chairman) considered that there was a great deal of harm in them; they were always attended by a description of persons who were dangerous to the peace of any country — reputed thieves — pick-pockets — and those classes of persons who were a disgrace to any society.

He went on to say that such fights were clearly illegal, and that all who attended a fight were, in law, equally guilty of the injuries inflicted, and appealed to 'respectable persons' to help put a stop to such fights.[112] Like prizefights, bullbaiting ceased to be held in public after the 1835 Act, but continued to be held in secret places in a number of Black Country towns until well into the 1840s; the same was true of cockfighting and dogfighting.

This was known to the magistrates and the parish constables, but they exercised a fair degree of informal toleration; some prizefights were broken up, but in other cases the crowd would be too large, or the local support for the fight too strong, for the constable to be able to disperse the crowd, and he would turn a blind eye. Similarly, bullbaitings were broken up, cockfights and dogfights were raided — when they were blatant and attracted large crowds; when they were kept unobtrusive and small they were often left alone or simply warned to move elsewhere by the constables.[113] Similarly, brawls and public drunkenness among the working class did not often result in the parish constables taking action against those involved, unless someone specifically made a complaint or brought a prosecution.

The coming of the new police changed this. The police constables (especially in the larger towns) were sent out on to their beats with the idea that their function was to maintain public order and prevent crimes — one might say they were being sent out looking for trouble.[114] This is made explicit in the report of the Chief Constable to Quarter Sessions after the first nine months of the force. He emphasised that the force had prevented 'all attempts at Outrage and disorder' which might have been expected from the continuance of unemployment, distress and Chartist agitation in the Black Country and Potteries; and then stressed that the force had been used to crack down on 'Races, Fairs and Wakes by which riot and drunkenness have not only been checked but many thieves and abandoned characters who resort to such places to the terror and annoyance of the well disposed have been greatly foiled'.[115] There was also a general police campaign against drunkenness, disorderly behaviour and fighting in the streets, and against the hitherto tolerated blood sports. Middle-class opinion had moved decisively against such 'barbarous' sports, and the activities of the animal protection societies ensured a regular stream of prosecutions for these sports; a sport like bullbaiting was impossible to keep secret against any determined opposition. The new police played an important role in stamping out these sports, especially cockfighting and dogfighting, which were much easier activities to hide; the police sought them out, broke them up, arrested and prosecuted the participants.[116]

The result of this general police crackdown was, as might be expected, a great increase in the number of minor offences of public order tried summarily; evidence for this is fragmentary, since there is no regular recording of the number and sorts of offences tried summarily before 1857, but it can be pieced together. The reports of the Offlow Force Superintendent for 1840-2 show that most of the arrests made were for summarily-tried minor public order offences.[117] Staffordshire force reports for 1845-7 show a decrease in reports of serious crimes but a continuing increase in arrests for minor public order offences ('Intoxication, Breaches of the Peace and Disorderly Conduct'). They also show an increase in the number of people charged with assaulting or resisting police in the course of their duty; the 1846 report pointed out that there were 'repeated assaults made on the Police whilst employed to keep order at places of public resort'.[118] Similarly, the Stourbridge Town Commissioners tried to stamp out the rowdy celebration of Guy Fawkes night in 1842; when the people gathered and let off fireworks 'the police felt called on to interfere and the consequence was that a collision took place'.[119] The increase in assaults on policemen is presumably due to their increase in numbers and general obtrusiveness; this policy of enforcing the law against illegal sports, disorderly gatherings, drunkenness, etc. must have made them unpopular at a time when they had not yet become accepted as a permanent and traditional institution.

The new police thus inflated the number of trials of summary offences with this increase in public order cases; what effect, if any, did they have on the figures for indictable committals to trial during the period covered by this study? One might expect an initial inflation of the figures, as the coming of the police forces should mean that more offences are successfully detected and their perpetrators arrested; later on, the police might be expected to cause a decline in the figures as their preventive and deterrent effect takes hold. But this seems too simple a way of looking at the issues. It has been shown that there was a difference in the methods and efficiency with which the police operated with respect to the maintenance of public order, and against more routine crime, so we can consider separately the effect on the figures for these sorts of offences. For public order offences the coming of the police seems to have resulted in a small increase in indictable committals for 1843-5; and thereafter a decrease in indictable committals over the next sixteen years.[120] The great increase in prosecuted public order offences which followed the establishment of the police came in summarily-tried offences, not indictable offences.

In the case of the offences other than public order ones (property offences, housebreaking, forgery and fraud, offences against the person) the position is more complex. In the system of private prosecution prevailing at that time, most prosecutions for these offences were brought by the victims,[121] who often knew or suspected who the offender was; this chapter has argued that, for handling cases of this sort, the parish constables were reasonably competent and that the change to the New Police did not amount, in the first few years, to a sudden change to greater efficiency and total supersession of the parish constables, especially in the non-urban areas. On the other hand, by 1860, it seems certain that the police forces were having more effect on the detection, and possibly the prevention, of crimes than the old parish constables and watch forces had done; and the police were certainly, by 1860, assuming an important role in the process of prosecution.[122] But was this a sudden or gradual change? It seems unlikely on the evidence that there was a sudden change in the 1840s; even in the large towns, the figures for prosecution of these offences do not show any marked increase for the years following the introduction of the police forces. It seems likely, then, that the effect of the police forces on the figures of these non-public order offences was a gradual one which it is impossible to isolate, probably stronger in the 1850s, when the police began to improve in efficiency, than in the 1840s.

Notes

1. For a discussion of the change embodied in these concepts, see Allan Silver, 'The Demand for Order in Civil Society; a Review of Some Themes in the History of Urban Crime, Police and Riot' in D.J. Bordua (ed.), *The Police: Six Sociological Essays* (New York 1967), pp.6-15.

2. 10 Geo. IV c.44; 5 and 6 Will. IV c.76; 2 and 3 Vict. c.93, and 3 and 4 Vict. c.88; 19 and 20 Vict. c.69.

3. Accounts of the establishment and growth of the police forces of England and Wales are found in: T.A. Critchley, *A History of Police in England and Wales 900-1966* (London 1967), and in the series of books by Charles Reith – *A New Study of Police History* (Edinburgh 1956), *The Police Idea* (London 1938), *Police Principles and the Problem of War* (London 1940), *British Police and the Democratic Ideal* (London 1943), and *The Blind Eye of History* (London 1952). Reith's books are written from a highly conservative standpoint which makes police history a form of teleology. Critical assessment of the working of the respective Acts on a local level and of the administrative efficiency of the new forces can be found in articles by J. Hart, 'Reform of the Borough Police 1835-1856', *English Historical Review,* 70 (1955), pp.411-27, and 'The County and Borough Police Act 1856', *Public Administration,* XXXIV (winter 1956), pp.405-17, and by H. Parris, 'The Home Office and the Provincial Police in England and Wales 1856-70', *Public Law* (1961), pp.230-55. Radzinowicz, *History,* has a large amount on the development and acceptance of police ideas and on the establishment and growth of the police forces, especially vol.4 on the establishment of the Metropolitan force and of borough and county forces in the provinces. F.C. Mather, *Public Order in the Age of the Chartists* (Manchester 1959), thoroughly examines the Old (parish constables) and the New Police in their role as repressors of public disorders in the late 1830s and 1840s.

4. A High Constable also existed for each Hundred of the county – a salaried officer paid by county Quarter Sessions; in theory he had powers of control over the parish constables in his Hundred, but by the 1830s this control was purely nominal (see *Report of Commissioners for Inquiring into County Rates,* P.P. 1836, XXVII, p.36; Mather, *Public Order,* p.75). There were three High Constables in the Black Country area but they had little role in normal law enforcement, except in rare instances involving public disorders (e.g. SRO Q/SB E. 1836).

5. These 'police forces' are not to be confused with the 'New Police' forces which were established under the Municipal Corporations Act 1835 or the County Police Acts of 1839 and 1840 – the basic English county or borough police forces which still form the police of England today. The local 'police forces' were raised by Town Commissioners or councils under powers granted by local Improvement Acts, or under the Lighting and Watching Act 1833 (3 and 4 Will. IV c.90) which enabled a parish rate to be levied to pay a force of watchmen. These forces were under the control of the Town Commissioners and the local parish constables usually acted as superintendents for the forces. As 'New Police' forces were introduced, they superseded these local 'police forces'.

6. J.H.A. Collins, *History of the Former Walsall Borough Police Force* (Brierley Hill 1967), p.1; A. Thorley, *The History of the Former Wolverhampton Borough Police Force* (Brierley Hill 1967), pp.2-3; W.A. Smith, 'The Town Commissioners in Wolverhampton', *Journal of West Midland Studies,* 1 (December 1967), pp.39-40; G. Chandler and I.C. Hannah, *Dudley as It Was and As It Is Today* (London 1949), pp.148-59; MDTC, 31 January 1840.

7. TLB, Talbot to Home Secretary, 2 January 1842.

8. 1 and 2 Will. IV c.41; this Act required that this reasonable fear be sworn to by a creditable witness in front of two magistrates, and that the magistrates be of the opinion that the ordinary peace officers were inadequate.

9. See Mather, *Public Order,* pp.81-7, and the lack of confidence in the usefulness of special constables expressed by magistrates throughout this period (PRO

HO 40 and 45 *passim).*

10. SRO Q/SBm 24, Leics. Clerk of Peace to Staffs. Clerk of Peace, 15 March 1838; Q/SOp HO Circular to Clerks of Peace, 23 October 1838.

11. See Mather, *Public Order,* ch.5. The Enrolled Pensioners were a force intermediate between special constables and troops – they were soldiers or sailors receiving a government pension who were called up and forced to enrol as special constables (on pain of losing their pensions); they were drilled, armed and placed under military discipline.

12. Collins, History, pp.1-2; *Return of the Several Cities and Boroughs of Great Britain, their Population respectively, the Number of Police, and the Cost of the same in each, in each year from their Establishment. . .* P.P. 1854 LIII (345), p.509.

13. 2 and 3 Vict. c.93. This is generally referred to, together with the amending 1840 County Police Act (3 and 4 Vict. c.88), as the County (or Rural) Police Acts 1839-40, which formed the legal basis of all county forces before 1856. The 1840 Act laid down that any area which now came under a county force and which had previously established its own 'police force' under the Lighting and Watching Act, had to disband that force; and it allowed the magistrates in Quarter Sessions to divide the county into separate divisions for purposes of rating the divisions at different rates.

14. (Anon.) *Worcestershire Constabulary: History of the Force* (Hindlip 1951), p.1. The Stourbridge and Halesowen divisions of this force covered the Black Country areas of Stourbridge, Halesowen and Oldbury, Cradley and the Lye, and Oldswinford. Dudley was excluded, since, as a detached part of the county, it could not, in terms of 2 and 3 Vict. c.93, be included in the county force (WRO Q/SB Ea.1840). Dudley was not included in the county force until 1845.

15. *SA* 23 November 1839. The Southern Division of the Hundred of Offlow South comprised just under half of the area of the Black Country – the eastern part – and about one-third of its population. Walsall, though falling within this division of the Hundred, was not included in the area of jurisdiction of the force, since it had its own force. This force is referred to, for convenience, as the 'Offlow force'. It came into existence as a police force in February 1840.

16. The proposer of the resolution, Lord Dartmouth, claimed that this would give a ratio of about one policeman per 2,000 inhabitants – but this was using the 1831 census figures. Using the 1841 census figures (the strength of the force did not alter between 1840 and 1842) gives a population for this division (excluding the Walsall Borough area) of 78,275 – a ratio of one to over 3,700 inhabitants.

17. *SA* 8 November 1842.

18. The Offlow force was merged into the Mining District of the county force. Wolverhampton had to disband its local 'police' and come under the Mining District force. All other Staffs. Black Country towns (except Walsall, with its own borough force) came into the Mining District of the county force.

19. Until May 1844, the Rural District did not have a full county force establishment but only a number of paid superintendents, supervising paid parish constables. This was done under the Parish Constables Act 1842 (5 and 6 Vict. c.109) which was an attempt to improve the efficiency of parish constables without resorting to the organisation and expense of a full force. It was not a success in any county, and in Staffordshire in May 1844 the Rural District became a full section of the county force, like the Mining and Pottery Districts.

20. With the initial exception of Dudley, which only came under the

Worcestershire force in 1845 — see note 14 above.

21. This held out an inducement to small forces to increase their size or amalgamate with other forces, by the offer of an Exchequer grant of one-quarter of the cost of the pay and clothing of the force, to all forces certified 'efficient' by the Inspectors. 'Efficiency' was assessed primarily in terms of the ratio of police to population.

22. This gives a ratio of one policeman to over 4,000 inhabitants; the efficient ratio for large cities was reckoned by the Home Office to be one to 400-800 inhabitants; for non-urban areas one to 1,000-2,000.

23. *Worcs. Constabulary Hist.,* p.1; *Berrows Worcester Journal,* 9 April 1840, report of QS.

24. *SA* 23 November 1839, report of Mich. Adj. QS.

25. Critchley, *History,* p.89.

26. *SA* 2 July 1842, report of QS.

27. *SA* 22 October 1842, report of QS.

28. Ibid., and *SA,* 12 November 1842, report of Mich. Adj. QS.

29. On this point, see also *Midland Mining Commission* (1843) and *SA* 5 November 1842, report of Wolverhampton meeting protesting against the motion to establish a county force.

30. MWWC 3 April 1855.

31. The following statements are based on the recognisances and depositions for Black Country cases in the Staffs. and Worcs. Quarter Sessions for 1836 and 1842, for Worcs. alone for 1839 and 1851, and for Staffs. alone for 1847. An estimate has been made of the relative frequency with which parish constables and other police officers appeared as prosecutors or arresting officers and witnesses.

32. SRO Q/APr3, 'Lists of Parish Constables appointed under 5 and 6 Vict. c.109, 1843-1865'.

33. This view was strongly put in the Report and evidence of *RC on County Rates* (1836), pp.9, 167-9; and in *RC on Constabulary Force* (1839), pp.89-108.

34. Sources cited in notes 31 and 32 above; MDTC, January 1852; SRO C/PC/VIII/4/1/1, Register of Members of Staffs. County Force 1842-63; MWWC.

35. See *SC on Criminal Commitments* (1828), p.484; *RC on County Rates* (1836), pp.11, 14, 41.

36. Derived from a study of cases in 1836 and 1842 — depositions and newspaper reports.

37. See Freeman, *Stories and Sketches,* on the two Bilston constables in the 1830s. William Derrincourt, *Old Convict Days* (London 1899), describes the constable in Darlaston in the 1830s as working this way; Derrincourt was transported in 1839, having been caught by the constable of a Black Country town (pp.10-11, 24-6). [Charles Shaw], *When I was a Child, by an Old Potter* (London 1903), describes the constables at work in this period in Tunstall, a Potteries town very similar to the Black Country mining towns.

38. On the inadequacies of parish constables for dealing with public disorders, see evidence of High Constable of Birmingham to *SC on Criminal Commitments* (1828), p.461, and Mather, *Public Order,* pp.76-80. 'An Old Potter' states that the one occasion when a rioting crowd refused to disperse at the constable's approach was during the 1842 strike, when a crowd of colliers gathered to smash the machinery at a colliery; when the constable tried to intervene, they threw him into a pit of water and nearly drowned him, and then carried on destroying the machinery (*When I was a Child,* pp.32-3).

39. Above, p.57 for Staffs. county force. The Walsall force was set up in 1832

following large Reform Bill disturbances; the Dudley force following Chartist demonstrations in 1839.

40. See *Report of the Commissioner relating to the alleged Ill-treatment of Eliza Price by Members of the Staffordshire Constabulary*, P.P. 1845, XXVII, pp.249-56; and 'Case of Ill-Treatment of a Prisoner, Mary Ann Heseltine, by John Fellows, Constable of Bilston' (SRO Q/ACp, 3 August 1845). In both these cases, the constables chained up their prisoners overnight; and the evidence makes it clear that this was normal practice for constables. Scandal only arose in these particular cases because of the prisoners involved – in the Eliza Price case, a pregnant woman, and in the Bilston case, a thirteen-year old girl. The one constable of Kingswinford had advised the other to chain up Eliza Price 'as he had been in the habit of doing for years, there being no lockup house in that neighbourhood, or other means of securing prisoners' (*Case of Eliza Price*, p.251).

41. *RC on County Rates* (1836), pp.12-13, 45, 61, 165, 167, 170, 177, 188, 206-8, 211; and see ch.4.

42. See *SA*, 22 October and 29 October 1842 – report of trial of constables Onions and Price of Kingswinford for compounding a felony. The evidence in this case suggests that it was a fairly frequent practice. The two constables were fined lightly, which was unlikely to deter them seriously from continuing the practice. On the general problem of parish constables compounding felonies, see *RC on County Rates* (1836), pp.33, 177; *Report from the Select Committee on the Police of the Metropolis*, P.P. 1828 (533), VI, pp.9-14.

43. *RC on County Rates* (1836), p.8.

44. On the Black Country literacy rate, see Table 19.

45. The number of men is 'too small to be as efficient as I should wish' because of the large area of ground over which they have to patrol, so 'I have placed the whole of them on duty at night, finding it impossible to cover the ground, if any of them were taken for day duty' (1st Report of Supt. of Offlow force, April 1840). This remained true of the force (5th and 6th Reports, April and June 1841) (All reports SRO Q/APr 2). The low ratio of police to population of this force has been noted – note 16 above.

46. Police Committee Reports WRO Q/SB 1840. Two of these six men were superintendents; there were only four constables to patrol a district with an area of 11,565 acres and a population, in 1841, of 31,678 – a ratio of one policeman to more than 5,000 inhabitants and to nearly 2,000 acres.

47. Mining District initial strength 96; 1841 population of the area 210,534 – one policeman to about 2,200 inhabitants.

48. The following section draws largely on these sources: *Offlow Force:* Supt.'s quarterly reports to QS, April 1840 - December 1842 (SRO Q/APr 2); *Staffs. County Force*, especially *Mining District:* Registers of members of County Force 1842-63 (SRO C/PC/VIII/4/1/1) and 1842-94 (4/2/1); newspaper reports of the establishment of the force and appointment of the Chief Constable; letters of application for the post of Chief Constable and incidental information on the early years of the force (SRO Q/ACp 3); information on the running of the force (SRO Q/ACp 5); Chief Constable's quarterly reports to QS 1843-58 (SRO Q/SB) and October 1858 to April 1861 (printed in SRO C/PC/VIII/2/2); Quarter Sessions Order Books (Q/SOp); *Wolverhampton Force:* MWWC 1853-60.

49. Critchley, *History*, pp.124-5, 141-4.

50. Ibid., p.141; W.L. Burn, *The Age of Equipoise* (London 1968), p.172, for examples of this in other counties. There is an indication of this in the letters which Chief Constable Hatton sent to the Lord Lieutenant; the tone is that of

a brother magistrate writing to the Lord Lieutenant (HC 5/6/1).

51. *SA* 4 January 1840, report of QS.

52. SRO Q/ACp 3.

53. SRO Q/ACp 3, applications and testimonials for post of Chief Constable, November 1842; *SA* 26 November, 3 December, and 31 December 1842; C. Prescott, *The Suffolk Constabulary in the Nineteenth Century* (1967), pp.11-16.

54. *SA* 3 December 1842; SRO Q/ACp 3. Wolverhampton also chose military men to lead their borough force: their first Chief Constable was this same Col. Hogg (1848-57); when he left in 1857 to take over the Staffs. county force, he was succeeded by Captain Segrave, of the 12th Regiment (MWWC 6 and 14 April 1857).

55. SRO C/PC/VIII/4/1/1. The reason for removal is listed for three of the inspectors. One was dismissed in 1844 for 'Insubordinate Conduct'; one in 1845 for writing an anonymous letter to the newspaper about his superintendent; and one who 'resigned' in 1844 did so because of 'Drunkenness'.

56. Reith, *A New Study,* pp.145-8; Critchley, *History,* pp.145-7; Burn, *Age of Equipoise,* pp.172-3.

57. SRO Q/APr 2, Supt.'s Report October 1841.

58. e.g. one Staffs. constable's entry is endorsed 'Dismissed 18th Feb. 1856. Allowed to Resign 18th Feb. 1856' (SRO C/PC/VIII/4/1/1). The Wolverhampton entries are more explicit: one constable was convicted of an unprovoked assault on a civilian and was to be dismissed 'but in consequence of his previous good character, the Chief Constable allowed him to resign his appointment forthwith'. Another was allowed to resign 'his general conduct not being satisfactory'; two were 'ordered to resign'. (MWWC 15 December 1856, 7 September 1857, 3 September 1860, 29 October 1860). One Wolverhampton constable was allowed to resign during his first month in the force, the Chief Constable 'believing him to be too timid for Police duty' (MWWC 3 December 1860).

59. SRO C/PC/VIII/4/2/1. There are a number of other examples here of men dismissed and reappointed within a few months at their old rank.

60. Black Country wage rates are hard to obtain because of the existence of piecework in mining and ironworking, and the fluctuations in earnings due to short-time working. The wage rates cited here are based on G.J. Barnsby, 'The Standard of Living in the Black Country during the Nineteenth Century', *Ec. Hist. Rev.,* XXIV (1971), pp.220-39. Of necessity, some are rough estimates, made by Barnsby or by myself from Barnsby's figures. These are wage rates for the 1840s and 1850s per week:

Skilled Workers

Skilled Ironworkers (Puddlers, Rollers, Furnacemen)	40s to 80s
Engineers	30s
Bricklayers and Carpenters	21s to 24s

Semi-skilled and Unskilled

Miners	16s to 30s	Chainmakers, nailers	8s to 16s
Labourers	14s to 15s	Lock and key-makers	7s to 15s

61. *SA* 4 January 1851, report of QS.

62. SRO C/PC/VIII/4/1/1.

63. SRO C/PC/VIII/4/2/1.

64. The head of the Manchester borough police told a Select Committee in 1852 that his constables were agricultural labourers from Derbyshire, Yorkshire and Cheshire *(Second Report from the Select Committee on Police,* P.P. 1852-3, XXXVI, p.195).

65. *SC on Police (1st Report)*, P.P. 1852-3, XXXVI, p.28.
66. For the establishment of these two forces and the Bolton force by Act of Parliament in 1839, see Mather, *Public Order*, pp.119-22; Critchley, *History*, pp.80-4; Radzinowicz, *History*, vol.4, pp.255-9.
67. SRO C/PC/VIII/4/1/1.
68. This section is based on information in C.C. Reports, in SRO Q/SB 1842-60 and in Q/ACp 5.
69.

	Sedgley	Tipton	Kingswinford	Wolverhampton
Population 1841	24,819	18,891	22,221	36,382
Police strength 1845	7	6	8	26

70. *Case of Eliza Price*, p.254.
71. SRO Q/SB E. and Ea. 1857. A similar petition in this same bundle, from the ratepayers of Brockmoor in Kingswinford parish, states that the town has 3,500 inhabitants but no policeman, and asks for one to be stationed there.
72. Ibid.
73. PRO HO 63/2 1858-60.
74. See Banton, *Policeman in the Community;* Skolnick, *Justice Without Trial.*
75. *SA* 31 December 1842; testimonials in SRO Q/ACp 3.
76. *SA* December 1842; SRO Q/ACp 3.
77. Evidence given to the 1853 Select Committee on the Police makes it clear that the organisation and activities of county forces varied widely, and depended heavily on the ideas and policies of each Chief Constable *(SC on Police, 1st and 2nd Reports;* Radzinowicz, *History*, vol.4, pp.283-91).
78. *SA* 17, 24 and 31 December 1842. The drilling continued to be a feature of the force; all recruits had to undergo a period of probationary training and regular periodical drill, including drill in the use of cutlasses, with much marching. They were given careful training in how to act as a body in dispersing potentially riotous crowds (SRO Q/ACp 1/1 Police Cttee Mins. 29 October 1853; Q/SB Ea 1857).
79. WCL L3522/1408, 'Outline of Duties and General Instructions of Wolverhampton Police...', pp.8-9, 11; MWWC 3 April 1855.
80. Mather, *Public Order*, pp.112-40; PRO HO 41/16 to 20.
81. C.C. Reports (SRO Q/SB E. and M. 1846, E. 1848; Q/ACp 3, Mich. 1843).
82. SRO Q/SOp.
83. C.C. Reports (SRO Q/SB Ea., M., and Mich., 1843; Ea. 1845; E. 1851). To save the county money, police were used to perform duties outside strict police work.
84. C.C. Reports (SRO Q/SB Ea. 1846, E. 1851); Report of Special Committee (SRO Q/SB M. 1846); SRO Q/SOp 1853 and 1857; Q/SB E. and Ea. 1857. Similarly, in the Wolverhampton force, the Chief Constable was also the Inspector of Lodging Houses, and in Dudley a police inspector did this job (MWWC; MDTC 9 January 1852).
85. *Northern Star,* 1840 and 1842; *Staffordshire Examiner,* an Anti-Corn Law paper, 1840, especially August 1840; SRO Q/APr 2, 1st Reports of Supt. of Offlow Force; C.C. Report July 1848, in *SA* 1 July 1848; SRO Q/SOp 1844 and Q/ACp 3.
86. e.g. in Worcs. — *WH* 8 January 1842.
87. 'Case of Ill-Treatment of Mary Heseltine', SRO Q/ACp 3, August 1845.
88. Ibid.
89. *Case of Eliza Price,* p.253.
90. SRO Q/ACp 3, Circular from HO to Clerk of Peace, 5 October 1840.
91. SRO Q/ACp 5, July 1847.
92. Ibid., October - December 1847.
93. See entry on Hogg in Register SRO C/PC/VIII/4/1/1; statement by Hon. and

Rev. A. Talbot in *SC on Police, 2nd Report* (1853), p.179.

94. SRO Q/ACp 1/1 and 1/3; Q/SOp Mich. 1855.

95. See Talbot's evidence to SC – 'the opposition to the force has completely died away' *(SC on Police, 2nd Report,* 1853, p.182). Parish petitions were no longer asking for permission to opt out of the police force sphere but instead asking for an increase in the number of policemen stationed there – e.g. Rowley Regis parish vestry had fiercely opposed the establishment of the force in 1842; in 1855 they petitioned asking that the force stationed in the parish be increased.

96. SRO Q/SB Ea. 1857. Strengths from: *Return of the Number of Rural Police* (1856); and Chief Constable's Returns of Strength for August-December 1856 (SRO Q/SB E. 1857).

97. SRO Q/SOp Ea. 1849; *SA* 4 January 1851, report of QS.

98. SRO Q/ACp 1/1 General Police Cttee Mins. 10 April, 24 April and 1 May 1852.

99. Return of all constables in the Staffs. force who have been discharged or dismissed and reinstated, with the remarks by the Chief Constable (SRO Q/ACp 5, December 1855); Q/SOp M. and Mich. 1856; Q/ACp 5, M. Adj. 1856.

100. In January 1856, the Police Committee dismissed a superintendent in the Potteries District after an enquiry had shown that he was using police constables to deliver the letters of a Loan Society to which he belonged. Hatton strongly supported the superintendent and his right to use his men in this way. The Police Committee expressed dissatisfaction with Hatton's behaviour on this issue; they also investigated the number of dismissals and reappointments in the Potteries District and reported that he had reappointed too many men dismissed for misconduct (SRO Q/ACp 1/1 General Police Cttee Mins.; Q/SB M. 1856, C.C. Report).

101. HC 5/6/1 and 2; PRO HO 45/O.S. 6378 November-December 1857, August-October 1858. These four episodes are discussed in greater detail in D. Philips, 'Riots and Public Order in the Black Country 1835-60', in J. Stevenson and R. Quinault (ed.), *Popular Protest and Public Order* (London 1974).

102. Commendation by Lord Lieutenant, magistrates and Chief Constable in: *SA* 7 April 1855, report of QS; HC 5/6/1 March-April 1855; PRO HO 45/O.S. 6378 Hatherton to HO 13 and 14 August 1858.

103. PRO HO 41/16 and 17, HO 45/260; Mather, *Public Order, passim.* These show local authorities' fears and lack of confidence in their local forces for dealing with the 1842 disorders.

104. SRO Q/SOp E. 1857.

105. SRO Q/SB E. and Ea. 1857, Supt. McKnight's report and tables on the Mining District.

106. The discipline of the force and the area covered by it were also taken into account, but discipline was usually also measured arithmetically by whether the force had enough officers to supervise the constables on duty continuously and regularly. The 'efficient' ratio of police to people was set by the Home Office, and varied according to circumstances; a higher ratio was felt necessary for boroughs than for counties (Parris, 'Home Office and Provincial Police', pp.231-3).

107. See Silver, 'Demand for Order', pp.1-5; Gatrell and Hadden, 'Criminal Statistics', p.338. Apocalyptic statements about the dangers of crime, such as those quoted at the beginning of ch.1, were not encountered after the 1840s.

108. R. Lane, 'Urbanization and Criminal Violence in the 19th Century; Massachusetts as a Test Case' in H.D. Graham and T.R. Gurr (eds.), *The History of Violence in America* (London 1969), pp.468-84; Macnab, 'Aspects',

      pp.226-9, 243, 264-5.
109. See R.W. Malcolmson, *Popular Recreations in English Society 1700-1850*
      (Cambridge 1973); M. and J. Raven, *Folklore and Songs of the Black Country*
      (Wolverhampton 1965-6), 2 vols.; R. Palmer and J. Raven (eds.), *The Rigs of
      the Fair* (Cambridge 1976); Freeman, *Stories and Sketches*, pp.46-7, 62-71.
110. Malcolmson, *Popular Recreations*, pp.118-57; Raven, *Folklore*; [Anon.],
      'The Towns of the Black Country' (WCL, articles from the *Daily Post* 1865),
      articles on Wednesbury, Willenhall, Darlaston; A.C. Pratt, *Black Country
      Methodism* (London 1891), pp.93, 141.
111. Malcolmson, *Popular Recreations*, pp.123-4.
112. *SA* 9 January 1836, report of QS.
113. Malcolmson, *Popular Recreations*, pp.134-5, 145-6; Freeman, *Stories and
      Sketches*, pp.34, 65-8, 87-8, 182, 222.
114. Freeman gives an example of this. When the new police came to Bilston
      in 1843, 'drunkenness and street fighting were then very rife and the new
      constables were eager to show their qualities in dealing with the trouble' and
      immediately provoked clashes with some of the local inhabitants with whom
      the parish constables had kept a relationship of mutual tolerance and
      non-interference provided they did nothing seriously wrong (*Stories and
      Sketches*, pp.29-30).
115. SRO Q/SB Mich. 1843, C.C. Report.
116. *SC on Police (2nd Report)* (1853), p.182; Malcolmson, *Popular Recreations*,
      pp.125-6; Pratt, *Methodism*, p.93.
117. SRO Q/APr 2, Supt.'s Reports 1840-2.
118. SRO Q/SB E. and M. 1846, E. 1848 − C.C. Reports.
119. WRO Q/SB E. 1842, C.C. Report.
120. See Philips, 'Public Order', pp.165-9.
121. See Chapter 4.
122. Ibid.

4 THE SYSTEM OF PROSECUTION AND THE PROSECUTORS

No measure of improvement, it is believed, would be more generally acceptable than that of committing the duty of prosecution to public officers. . .It is a strange and discreditable defect in our system of criminal law, that it makes no provision on this subject, and, consequently, throws the burthen of proceeding on the party injured. (*Report of RC on County Rates* (1836), p.33.)

I

In nineteenth-century England, prosecution of crimes was essentially the responsibility of the private citizen. Theoretically, this remains the position in England even today, though in practice the police now handle most prosecutions. But in the nineteenth century the burden of prosecution really did rest on private individuals; there was no public prosecutor — even the position of Director of Public Prosecutions was not created until 1879. It was up to the individual who had been harmed by an offence to ensure that the offender was prosecuted; the state would control and to some extent assist the process, but the essential responsibility for carrying through the prosecution rested with the aggrieved citizen. The great English legal historian, Maitland, writing in 1885, saw this as a point of national pride:

> To speak of the English system as one of *private* prosecutions is misleading. It is we who have *public* prosecutions, for any one of the public may prosecute; abroad they have *state* prosecutions or *official* prosecutions.[1]

To illustrate the workings of the prosecution system at the time, a sample case has been selected, to be followed through from the commission of the offence to the passing of sentence. This particular case was selected because it typifies many of the features of the common offence and prosecution, and because information is available on all stages of the process for this case.[2]

George Rose, a labourer from Perry Barr, heard footsteps under the window of his house and a noise of coal being taken, at about 10.30 on the night of 8 November 1841. He woke up Edward Bayley who lodged with him, and the two of them saw two men leave the house. They then went in search of the men, found them eventually in a lane, each with a lump of coal on his back, and took them in custody. They took the two men, John and Henry Medcalfe, back to Rose's house, and then gave them in charge to the Handsworth constable, Richard Aston.

This incident took place in 1841, before the establishment of the Staffordshire county force. In this period, detection and apprehension of the offender were often carried out by the victim and people assisting him. The police would only enter the picture when the accused was handed over to them for safe-keeping, or if the victim wanted the constable to get a warrant to search the lodgings of the man he suspected. The coming of the 'New Police' forces changed this situation to some extent, with the police taking a more active detective role; but, as we have seen, this change came only gradually and in the larger towns. In the smaller towns and villages, even the 'New Police' continued to play an essentially parish constable-type reactive role.

The Medcalfes were handed over to the constable Aston late at night, and Aston locked them up in his house for the night —a normal procedure for parish constables. Next morning, they were taken before a magistrate for preliminary examination. This took place before a local magistrate — in this case John Edward Piercy, a large West Bromwich coalmaster. Rose, Bayley and Aston made sworn statements before Piercy, which were set down in depositions and signed by them. Rose's and Aston's depositions said that John Medcalfe had admitted taking the coal, had claimed that it was his first offence, and had said to Rose: 'George, forgive me. I'll pay you twice the value of the coal if you'll forgive me.' The coal was valued at one shilling. The two prisoners made no statement at this stage.

The magistrate now had to decide whether to discharge the prisoners, try them summarily, or commit them for trial on indictment at Quarter Sessions or Assizes. Minor offences would be tried summarily; some offences, such as assault and riot, could be tried either summarily or on indictment depending on the seriousness of the case; serious offences had to be tried on indictment.[3] The Juvenile Offenders Acts (JOA) of 1847 and 1850 later allowed summary trial for larcenies such as the one of which the Medcalfes were accused, if committed by juveniles under the age of sixteen; and the Criminal Justice Act (CJA) of 1855 allowed summary trial, for accused of all ages, for larcenies of under the value of five shillings if the accused agreed to a summary trial, and for larcenies of five shillings and over, if the accused pleaded guilty. The Medcalfes were not juveniles, being aged twenty-one and nineteen; but

after 1855 the CJA would have enabled them to elect summary trial
for this offence. They would probably have done so if given the choice –
98 per cent of people charged with such offences elected summary trial
in the period 1856-60. But in 1841 the magistrate did not have this
option, and Piercy committed the Medcalfes for trial at Quarter Sessions

The magistrate made this decision – to discharge the prisoners or
commit them for trial – on the basis of whether the evidence presented
by the prosecutor warranted the case going forward for trial. We can
estimate, from Black Country material, what proportion of persons
brought up for preliminary examination were discharged, summarily
tried, and committed for trial. For the years 1845-7, of the persons
examined by Black Country magistrates for possibly indictable offences,
14-18 per cent were committed for trial, 41-47 per cent were tried
summarily and 38-43 per cent were discharged.[4]

So, well over one-third of cases were normally discharged at the
preliminary examination, on the grounds either that the evidence was
insufficient to support a prosecution or that the facts disclosed too
trivial a situation to warrant prosecution – a discharge was often
coupled with an admonition or a reprimand. The offences which were
committed for trial were homicides, the more serious assaults, sexual
offences, robbery, housebreaking, larcenies and other property offences.
Larcenies always made up about 75 per cent of all offences committed
for trial, and before 1847 could only be tried on indictment, if they
were tried at all.[5]

The Medcalfes were committed for trial at the next Quarter Sessions.
They were not given bail – presumably they would not have been able
to afford it themselves nor to find people who could put up bail for
them – so they were committed to the county gaol in Stafford on 9
November 1841, to await trial at the Staffordshire Epiphany Quarter
Sessions of 1842, which began on 4 January 1842.

Defendants could find themselves in gaol awaiting trial for up to
three months, depending on when they were arrested and when the
nearest Sessions or Assizes was. The commonest arrangement of
Sessions and Assizes in the period 1835-60 was to have five Sessions
and two Assizes during the year; these were as follows:

Epiphany Quarter Sessions held between 29 December and 7 January,
   trying people who had been committed for trial between the end
   of October and the end of December.
Epiphany Adjourned Sessions held between 27 February and 6
   March, trying those who had not been dealt with by the Epiphany

Sessions, and those committed in January and February.

Spring (or Lent) Assizes held in mid-March, to try the more serious
offences, which Quarter Sessions did not deal with, but also
trying some of the less serious offences if the gaol was crowded.

Easter Quarter Sessions held between 4 and 8 April, trying the less
serious offenders committed for trial in March.

Midsummer (sometimes Translation) Quarter Sessions held between
29 June and 6 July, trying those committed during April, May
and June.

Summer Assizes held in the last week of July, and covering the same
field as the Spring Assizes.

Michaelmas Quarter Sessions held in the third week of October,
trying those committed during July, August, September and
early October.

This was the minimum number of Sessions and Assizes held in any of
the years under discussion; often, pressure of the number of cases to be
dealt with meant the addition of extra Sessions and even an extra
Assize. In Staffordshire, in many years, an Adjourned Midsummer
Sessions was held some time between mid-July and early August, to
cope with the large numbers awaiting trial at the Midsummer Sessions,
and lessen the burden of the Michaelmas Sessions. In the 1850s
Adjourned Easter Sessions, held in the middle of May, and Adjourned
Michaelmas Sessions, held in late November, were brought in to help
cope with the large numbers for trial, so that 1854 and 1855 have eight
Quarter Sessions as well as Assizes. After 1855, the effect of the CJA
was to relieve the pressure on the Quarter Sessions, by transferring large
numbers of cases to summary trial, and the annual number of Sessions
fell again to six or five. The number of Assizes was also increased to
cope with extra work: in 1842, a Special Commission of Assize was sent
to Staffordshire in October, to try people charged with the riots of that
summer; in 1843 and 1844 a Winter Assizes, held in December, was
added to the two regular Assizes; this ceased in 1845, but returned in
1855 and was held each year thereafter up to 1860.

With his decision to commit the Medcalfes for trial, the magistrate
also took steps to ensure formally that George Rose would carry
through the prosecution he had begun. Rose was formally bound over
to prosecute the Medcalfes, signing a recognisance binding himself to
pay £40 unless he 'did then and there prefer or cause to be preferred a
Bill of Indictment to the Grand Jury against John Medcalfe and Henry
Medcalfe for stealing a quantity of coal' etc. Rose was now bound to

bring his Bill of Indictment before the Grand Jury at the next Sessions, and if it was found to be a True Bill, to bring it before the court and. give evidence on it. If he did this, regardless of the verdict in the case, he would have discharged his recognisance, and would not have to forfeit any money. If he failed to turn up to present the Bill of Indictment and give evidence, the accused would go free, and Rose's recognisance of £40 would be estreated — the court would take action to recover the money from him. Similarly, the witnesses were bound over on recognisances to give evidence in the case — in this instance, Rose's witnesses were his lodger Bayley and the constable Aston; each of them bound himself in £20 to give evidence.

This was the standard procedure of binding over prosecutors and witnesses; on occasion the money varied — usually it was £40 for the prosecutor and £20 for the witnesses, as here, but sometimes it was £20 for the prosecutor and £10 for the witnesses. Where the accused was given bail, it was done on a similar system, the accused himself and one or two sureties binding themselves in sums of money for the accused's appearance in court, which they would have to pay if he failed to turn up.

In the Medcalfes' case, the victim of the offence, George Rose, was himself the prosecutor. This was the pattern of the majority of cases in the 1830s and 1840s, but not of all. In most cases of coal-stealing, for instance, the prosecutors were not mere labourers like Rose, but large coal and iron firms.[6] In these cases, the proprietors did not have the time to attend in court and conduct the prosecutions in person, so the man bound over to prosecute would be the coal and iron master's agent or an employee. When a woman was the victim of an offence, the actual prosecution would sometimes be done by her husband (if married) or father (if single); more commonly, she would prosecute but her father or husband — occasionally even the constable — would bind himself for the money in the recognisance; widows, however, generally entered into their own recognisances. Sometimes a wife would prosecute her husband's case, or a son his father's case. Even before the establishment of the 'New Police' forces, the parish constables and watchmen were bound over to do some of the prosecution — though in a distinct minority of the cases; as the new police forces developed, so they took over more of this prosecuting role.

Using those recognisances which survive for Staffordshire and Worcestershire Quarter Sessions (none survive for Assizes) for 1836 and 1842, we can set out who the prosecutors were (Table 11).

Table 11 shows that the responsibility for most prosecutions in the

Table 11   Black Country Prosecutors in Staffordshire and Worcestershire
Quarter Sessions 1836 and 1842

Person Prosecuting	Percentage	
	1836	1842
Victim	79.6	63.9
Victim's employee	5.1	14.8
Constable/policeman	7.1	10.1
Victim's husband/father/son/wife	5.1	2.4
Other person bound for victim*	0.0	2.4
Other person	3.1	6.4
TOTAL	100.0	100.0
	n = 98	n = 377

* Victim prosecuted, but someone from outside victim's family bound himself in the recognisance.

Sources: SRO Q/SB E., E.Adj., and Ea. 1836; E., E.Adj., Ea., M., M.Adj. and Mich. 1842 (Staffs. Recognisances). WRO Q/SB E., E.Adj., and Ea. 1836; E.Adj. 1842 (Worcs. Recognisances).

pre-police period rested with the victims of the crimes themselves. Virtually all the prosecutions by the victim's employee were prosecutions for industrial thefts; their large increase from 1836 to 1842 is due to the large increase in industrial theft prosecutions.[7] These are equivalent to prosecution by the victim himself, since it was the coal and iron masters whose property had been stolen, who decided on these prosecutions and instructed their employees to prosecute. Taking these two categories of prosecution — by the victim and by his employee — together, we see that over 80 per cent in 1836 and almost 80 per cent in 1842 of all prosecutions were brought by victims themselves. There was a small increase, from 1836 to 1842, in the proportion brought by the police, since in 1836 there was no 'New Police' force for the area, whereas by 1842 the Worcestershire and Offlow forces were in operation for part of the area and were taking responsibility for a slowly increasing proportion of prosecutions. But predominantly, this was still very much a private prosecution system.

Once he had been bound over, it was the responsibility of the prosecutor to ensure that the Bill of Indictment against the accused was presented and fully supported at the trial. Once the Medcalfes had been committed to Stafford goal, the magistrate forwarded the depositions, setting out the prosecution case, to the Staffordshire Clerk of the Peace, who was a solicitor in Stafford (if it had been a case for the Assizes, it would have gone to the Clerk of Assize). The clerk then framed a Bill of Indictment from the depositions — he would always do this unless the prosecutor chose to retain and use his own solicitor for this purpose.

There is another way in which an accused might reach the court; in cases of homicide, a coroner's jury would hold an inquest on the dead body, and return a verdict of what they thought had caused death. Their verdict was to establish what had happened, not who was guilty, but if they returned a verdict of murder, manslaughter or infanticide against a particular person, that person could be directly committed for trial at Assizes by the coroner.

The next important stage came when the Sessions (or Assizes) opened. The county magistrates (at Quarter Sessions) or judges (at Assizes) took their seats on the Bench. But all cases had first to go before a Grand Jury before they could be heard by the court.

A Grand Jury is not to be confused with an ordinary or petty jury, which renders its verdict on the facts in a trial; a Grand Jury was a jury of presentment, whose function was to determine whether the prosecution had made out a *prima facie* case in each indictment. At the beginning of each Sessions, the Chairman of Quarter Sessions (at Assizes, the senior judge) would deliver his Charge to the Grand Jury. Theoretically, this was meant to set out the current state of the law and advise the jurors on any difficult points of law arising from cases in that particular calendar. But the chairmen and judges also used this opportunity to hold forth, to the county gentlemen on the Grand Jury and to the wider audience gathered for the Sessions or Assizes, on issues such as the state of crime in the county, the state of the law, the efficacy of penal measures, the need for increased education and religious teaching, and for greater obedience to the law.[8]

The Grand Jury then retired to a private room, and there considered the merits of each case, relying only on the Bills of Indictment and the depositions. They could also call in the prosecution witnesses individually and examine them, but no one else was allowed to be present during the examination of each witness; all these proceedings were held in secret, and nothing of the proceedings was allowed to be divulged. The idea was that the Grand Jury should act as a sort of sieve, filtering out those prosecutions brought frivolously or on insufficient evidence. For each case, they endorsed the Bill of Indictment 'True

Bill', or 'No True Bill' (this latter was also known as 'ignoring' the Bill, since it had formerly been marked 'Ignoramus' — 'we do not know'). If they found it to be a 'True Bill', the accused went for trial; if 'No True Bill', he was discharged immediately. A discharge was not the same as an acquittal, and it was possible — though unusual — for a man against whom an indictment had been thrown out by a Grand Jury to be indicted again for the same offence.[9]

The Grand Jury was thus performing a similar function to the magistrate at the preliminary examination, its purpose being to throw out unnecessary or unsupported prosecutions. In course of time, the preliminary examination became more important, and the Grand Jury hearing more of a formality; Maitland, writing in 1885, stated that 'nowadays' preliminary examinations had become so usual 'that for a grand jury to ignore a bill has become a rather rare event'; and in 1933 Grand Juries were finally abolished in England and Wales.[10] But in our period, Grand Juries were still a very important feature of court procedure. Even though preliminary examinations were held first, many Black Country Bills of Indictment were 'ignored' — of the 16,261 cases which came to Quarter Sessions or Assizes over the period 1835-60, 1,202 (7.4 per cent) were discharged as 'No True Bill'.

A Grand Jury had to consist of at least twelve, and not more than twenty-three, men; there could be no indictment carried forward to the court unless at least twelve of them concurred in finding it a True Bill. Property qualifications for Grand Jurors were the same as for petty juries (see below), but Quarter Sessions Grand Juries tended to be selected from a slightly higher social and economic stratum than petty juries, while Assize Grand Juries were drawn from a distinctly higher class, being made up of county magistrates, mayors of boroughs and coroners.[11]

The case against the Medcalfes was found to be a True Bill, and their case came up for trial in the Quarter Sessions before a Bench of county JPs, presided over by the Chairman of Quarter Sessions, and a petty jury. The accused were asked how they pleaded; John Medcalfe, the elder brother, pleaded guilty, and Henry Medcalfe not guilty. In all, at least one-third of persons coming up for indictable trial from the Black Country in 1842 pleaded guilty.[12]

Against John Medcalfe, the depositions from the preliminary examination, plus his plea of 'Guilty', were enough to convict him; but the prosecutor now had to present a case against Henry. The prosecutor might do this in person, but by the 1830s it was becoming more usual for the services of counsel to be used for this purpose, to ensure that the prosecution was carried through successfully. Similarly, it was possible for the accused to be represented by counsel. Until 1836, this latter right was limited — persons accused of a *felony* could engage counsel only to cross-examine witnesses and argue points of law, but counsel were not allowed to address the jury on behalf of the accused. This was changed by the Prisoners' Counsel Act of 1836 (6 and 7 Will. IV, c.114), which allowed counsel retained for prisoners accused of felony to address the jury on their behalf. This Act was strongly opposed, at the time of its passage, by lawyers, judges and magistrates, who claimed it would make proceedings longer and more expensive, and would enable more guilty felons to escape conviction; but it soon became part of the normal criminal procedure.[13]

Counsel for both prosecution and defence could be briefed from among the barristers who 'travelled the Circuit', attending all the Quarter Sessions and Assizes held on one particular circuit; for the Black Country it was the Oxford Circuit, which took in the counties of Staffordshire, Worcestershire and Shropshire.[14] The newspaper reports of trials at the Staffordshire and Worcestershire Sessions and Assizes show that there was a pool of between thirty and forty barristers who interchangeably took the prosecuting and defending roles in these trials. These would have to be paid for, by both prosecutor and defendant. There was no form of legal aid for defendants. Fees for criminal cases on the circuits were low by barristers' standards, usually only one guinea — two guineas at the outside; and often in criminal prosecutions the brief was handed to the prosecution counsel directly by the Clerk of the Peace or county solicitor, so there would be no separate solicitor's fee for the prosecutor to pay; if a solicitor was employed, that would be another guinea. For defendants, it was a commonly accepted convention that in murder cases a judge should ask counsel to defend a poor defendant, and that counsel should do so without asking any fee. But for all criminal charges other than murder there was no provision of free legal services for defendants, and even the guinea for counsel's services was well beyond the reach of many defendants.[15]

Analysing the available cases for 1843,[16] we find that, for all types of offence taken together, counsel were retained for the prosecution in 52 per cent of cases, and for the defence in 25 per cent; 46 per cent had no counsel employed by either side. If we divide up the types of offence we find, not surprisingly, that the more serious the offence was, the more likely it was that both prosecutor and defendant (or at least one of the defendants) would employ a barrister. Taking all the non-larceny offences together (a category including fraud and currency offences, robbery, breaking and entering, assaults with wounding, sexual offences, homicides and riots), we find that 63 per cent of these had counsel for the prosecution and 49 per cent for the defence; only 30 per cent had no counsel engaged at all. For the more serious of these offences (homicides, assaults causing grievous bodily harm, burglary, robbery), tried at Assizes, almost all cases had a barrister for the prosecution and most of these also had defence counsel.

But in the larceny cases (which were by far the most common, and also the less serious, cases),[17] only 48 per cent employed a barrister for the prosecution, and only 16 per cent briefed counsel for the defence; in 52 per cent of the cases, no barrister was employed by either side. This sample probably *overstates* the proportion in which counsel was employed, since it relies on those cases for which the newspapers reported details; and the cases for which the newspapers left out the details were usually the small ones for which counsel were unlikely to be employed.

Of those larceny cases in which there was no counsel for either prosecution or defence, 65 per cent were cases in which the accused pleaded guilty. But it seems clear that, even where the accused pleaded not guilty to a larceny charge, the prosecutor often felt the case to be simple enough not to require the service of a lawyer;[18] while the bulk of those accused of larceny and pleading not guilty were not legally represented — presumably because the gravity of the charge and the possible penalty were not sufficient to justify the necessary expenditure.

Defence counsel were very seldom employed in cases in which the prosecution did not also retain counsel; in the 350 cases analysed here, there were only six such instances, whereas there were 102 cases in which the prosecutor had a barrister but the defence did not. Tobias claims that the Prisoner's Counsel Act of 1836 placed the prosecutor at a disadvantage in situations where the defence employed counsel and the prosecution did not;[19] but, as our analysis shows, such a situation was only encountered in the exceptional case. The two Medcalfe brothers had no legal representation, but the prosecutor, Rose, briefed counsel to conduct the prosecution.

The trial proceeded before the Bench of county magistrates at Quarter Sessions (or a High Court judge at Assizes) and the petty jury, the jury deciding the questions of fact in the case and the verdict — guilty or not guilty — while the Bench ruled on points of law and pronounced sentence. At the Assizes, it was the judge who controlled the conduct of the trial — he gave the charge to the Grand Jury, ruled on points of law, summed up the evidence of the jury, and formulated and pronounced sentence. At Quarter Sessions, each Bench of JPs elected a Chairman, who performed many of the functions of the judge at Assizes — charging the Grand Jury, ruling on the law, summing up, and *pronouncing* sentence — but the sentence itself was *formulated* by all the JPs on the Bench.[20]

The social composition of petty juries had been fixed by the Juries Act of 1825 (6 Geo. IV, c.50), which laid down that the people liable for jury service were men who: owned freehold land worth at least £10 a year, occupied a dwelling of at least £20 annual rateable value, or occupied a house with at least fifteen windows. This ruled out the bulk of the working class.[21] Jury lists were made out by the High Sheriff of the county. The Overseers of each parish drew up lists of eligible men, from which the Sheriff made out the jury lists; the county JPs then had the final right to amend these lists.[22]

Analysis of a jury list for Staffordshire for this period shows a predominance of farmers, with the rest made up of small tradesmen, artisans and skilled manual workers.[23] Comparison of this with lists of Grand Jurors for Quarter Sessions shows a slightly higher social status for the members of the Grand Juries: over half of each Grand Jury is made up of tradesmen and farmers, but each Grand Jury also includes a significant proportion made up of gentlemen, ironmasters, manufacturers, bankers, and members of professions (other than the law) — groups which are not found in the petty juries — and Grand Juries include very few artisans or skilled manual workers.[24] The Assize Grand Juries were recruited from a much higher social stratum — the county and borough magistrates.

The trial proceeded, with the prosecutor calling his witnesses and examining them; the accused, or his counsel if he had legal representation, could cross-examine them. The accused could then call witnesses for the defence. Throughout this period, however, the accused was not allowed himself to give evidence on oath in his defence — this right was only allowed to accused persons in 1898; before this, the only direct statement he was allowed to make during the trial was an unsworn statement, made right at the end of the trial; such a statement naturally did not carry much weight, since it was not made on oath, and could not be tested by cross-examination or the bringing of evidence to refute it.[25] He could call witnesses in his defence but, unlike the prosecution, the expenses of defence witnesses attending the trial were not reimbursed.[26] If the accused called no witnesses, then the prosecuting counsel could sum up the evidence for the prosecution to the jury; if the accused called witnesses, the prosecutor had the right to reply after they had been heard. The Chairman (at Quarter Sessions) or judge (at Assizes) then summed up the evidence for the jury, who decided on their verdict.[27]

Observers had long stressed the liberal nature of English criminal procedure, the way in which it held the accused innocent until proved guilty beyond reasonable doubt. Study of a large number of the ordinary Quarter Sessions and Assizes cases shows that this claim was more than just a rhetorical flourish — in terms of criminal procedure during the progress of a case, the accused really did receive the benefit of any doubt. In addition, English legal procedure was technically very strict, offering numerous technical points on which a prosecution might be thrown out. In the eighteenth century, this strictness had been one of the safeguards used to save defendants from the capital provisions of the 'bloody code'; and the strictness continued even after the repeal of most of the capital statutes.

Courts insisted on strict tests of identifying alleged offenders and alleged stolen property, in which the benefit of any doubt went to the accused.[28] And the indictment had to be absolutely correct; an error in the indictment — in the prosecutor's name, in the description of the stolen goods or their ownership — no matter how trivial, was enough to wreck the prosecution. The indictment was a long document couched in elaborate legal language, and offered a fair amount of scope for error in some detail. A perfect example of such acquittal due to error is given in the following report of a case in the *Staffordshire Advertiser:*

Mary Ann Boam. . .[took] her trial on an indictment charging her with stealing one shilling in silver, twopence in copper, and three caps, the property of George Plunket Tunney. Mr Welch appeared for the prosecution, and Mr Woolrych for the defence.

The prosecutor, a draper,. . .was called into the witness-box and stated that his name was Gerald Plunket Tunney.

Mr Woolrych upon this said he would save the Court any further trouble in reference to this case, as the indictment laid the articles as the property of *George* Plunket Tunney.

The objection was fatal, and the prisoner was discharged.[29]

Similarly, Ann Thompson, in 1837, and John and Samuel Smith, in 1842, were respectively acquitted at the direction of the Chairman of Quarter Sessions because in each case the property they had taken belonged to *two* people and not to the *one* named in the indictment.

Joseph Palmer, charged with obtaining eighteen shillings by false pretences, was acquitted at the Chairman's direction because he had, in fact, obtained £1. John Harris was charged with the manslaughter of Maria Griffiths, a girl aged seven, by knocking her down with his waggon. The killing of the girl by the waggon was proved, but

> no evidence having been given that the name of the child who had been so unfortunately killed was Maria Griffiths, as stated in the indictment, it was objected on behalf of the prisoner that the indictment was not sustained by the evidence, and his Lordship directed a verdict of not guilty.[30]

Similarly, if the prosecutor or one of his witnesses failed to turn up at the trial, the trial was not postponed, but the accused was immediately set free.[31] The problem of trivial errors in the indictment wrecking the prosecution was to some extent remedied by the Criminal Procedure Act 1851 (14 and 15 Vict., c.100), which enabled the courts to amend mistakes in the indictment in names, places, descriptions of property and ownership, in all cases where these were not considered material to the merits of the case.[32] Thus, although the system of legal procedure made adequate legal counsel and a full defence difficult for many accused, it did also impose the requirements of strict technical correctness on the prosecution, left a number of loopholes open to the defence and ensured, on the whole, that the onus of proof really did have to be discharged by the prosecution. The Chairman or judge would try to ensure a fair hearing for those prisoners without counsel; and even the prohibition on defendants giving evidence in their own defence was meant in theory to protect them against self-incrimination. These points do not negate the considerable bias which the system contained, particularly against lower-class accused, but they must be borne in mind in any full picture of the working of the prosecution system.

In the Medcalfes' case, the prosecuting counsel called as witnesses Rose himself and the two others who had given evidence at the preliminary examination. John Medcalfe had pleaded guilty; Henry Medcalfe did not bring any evidence in his own defence, and, after the Chairman had summed up, the jury found him guilty. The magistrates on the Bench then conferred together, and the Chairman pronounced their sentences — two months in the House of Correction at Stafford with hard labour for John Medcalfe, and four months with hard labour for Henry. The Medcalfes were then led away to serve their sentences.

Quarter Sessions was competent to impose any penalty, except death, or transportation for life for a first offence — these could only be imposed by Assizes.[33] It is unlikely that the Medcalfes would have wanted to appeal against their verdicts or sentences, but even if they had wanted to they would have been unable to do so. There was no machinery of appeal in criminal cases at all.[34]

However, the power of the Crown to grant absolute or conditional pardons was much used, usually to commute sentences of death. The reforms of the 1830s, in particular those of 1837 and 1841, left eleven capital offences on the statute book; but in practice, after 1836 executions were only carried out for murde. and attempted murder, and after 1841, only for murder. In the case of persons found guilty of any of the other capital offences, the judge would be bound by law to pronounce the sentence of death, but would then recommend to the Home Secretary that the sentence be commuted to a term of transportation. This recommendation was always accepted, and it became a routine procedure — the judge would *record* the sentence of death in court and announce that he would make a recommendation to mercy, if he intended that the execution should not go through.[35] This became so standardised that the Calendars of trials of prisoners would list the sentence as 'Sentence of death recorded' if it was clear that it was going to be commuted, and 'Sentence of death confirmed' if the judge intended the sentence to be carried out. In all, in the Black Country for the twenty-six years 1835-60, eighty-one sentences of death were pronounced, of which sixty-eight were 'recorded' and only thirteen 'confirmed' (three of those thirteen came in 1835 before the last batch of statutes abolishing capital offences). Even when the sentence was 'confirmed' by the judge, it was still possible for the Home Secretary to commute it, and only four of these thirteen Black Country death sentences were executed.

One can take an example of the way this procedure worked from the case of John Yates: Yates, together with two other men, was found guilty of highway robbery, committed with violence and severe infliction of injuries. Yates's defence counsel called a number of witnesses who testified to Yates's good character. The jury found Yates guilty, but recommend that he be transported for seven years.' character he had received'. Yates's sentence is reported as follows: 'Sentence of death was recorded against John Yates, but the learned Judge said he would recommend that he be transported for seven years.' In other words, the death sentence was a formality, imposed on the judge by the state of the law; the reality was that it would be automatically commuted to transportation.[36]

II

As this discussion has shown, this was a system of private prosecution; and the decision whether or not to prosecute someone lay predominantly in the hands of private citizens. This reliance on private prosecutors entailed defects in the system which some observers had criticised from the mid-eighteenth century onwards; two particular problems stood out. The first was the expense of prosecuting and the effect this might have in deterring potential prosecutors; the second was the absence of effective state control over the process of prosecution.

On the first problem, Alexis de Tocqueville noted in 1833:

> Officers of the police are paid so little by the State that the interested parties are allowed to pay them themselves, so that justice is only within the means of the rich, which, in criminal cases, is a great social evil. . .There is no official charged with a duty to prosecute, which both makes worse the defect mentioned above, that of placing justice out of reach of the poor, and means that the criminal law is never enforced continuously or firmly.[37]

By 'officers of the police', Tocqueville meant the parish constables; similar criticisms of the parish constables and the prosecution system form the subject matter of the *Second Report of the Commissioners for Inquiring into County Rates* (1836).

This report, and most of the other evidence on prosecution at this time,[38] make it clear that the chief factor deterring potential prosecutors from prosecuting and constables from investigating reported offences, was the time and expense which these would involve. Other factors mentioned include: reluctance of prosecutors to inflict capital punishment for small property offences;[39] fear of possible retaliation by the offender or his associates; and unwillingness to invoke the law at all. By 1835, the death penalty had been repealed for all offences against property except burglary (for which it was repealed in 1837), so the first factor no longer had any importance and the other two will be discussed below; but it is clear that expense was the chief deterrent to prosecution.

One can show this by outlining the trouble and expense involved for the individual bringing and seeing through a prosecution such as the example of the Medcalfes set out above, assuming for the moment that the individual received no financial help at all for this purpose. It would *people not turn in crime problem cont...*

begin with the citizen discovering that some offence had been
committed against him – theft, housebreaking, fraud, assault, etc. If
he was quite clear who the offender was, he might institute the
prosecution entirely by himself, but more probably he would call in
the constable or (after their establishment) the police force. Here he
would probably find that, unless he had a clear idea of who the
offender might have been, where the offender and the stolen property
might be found, etc., the police would not take up the case any further,
unless he could guarantee the payment of their expenses – the reasons
for this are discussed below.

If the prosecutor could ensure that he or some police officer found
and apprehended a suspect, he would then have to gather witnesses
who could testify to the offence. He and the witnesses would have to
appear before the magistrate at the preliminary examination, for which
they might have to travel some distance; the examination itself, plus the
travelling and the waiting for other cases to be taken first, would mean
that most of a working day would be taken up this way. If the
magistrate committed the accused for trial, the prosecutor and his
witnesses would have to be bound over for sums of money – £40, £20,
£10 – which they would forfeit if they failed to prosecute or give
evidence. There would also be fees to be paid to the magistrate's clerk
for issuing the warrant of arrest, taking the recognisances, and often for
furnishing copies of the depositions.

The prosecutor and his witnesses would then have to travel to the
county town at the time of the Quarter Sessions or Assizes. The relevant
county towns for the Black Country were Stafford and Worcester;
Stafford was between fifteen and twenty-five miles, and Worcester over
thirty miles, from any Black Country town. They would have to find
accommodation in the town, and stay there several days so as to be
present at both the Grand Jury hearing (which took place at the
beginning of the Assizes or Sessions) and the trial itself (which might
be heard at any point in the Calendar – a crowded Sessions or Assizes
could last ten days). If the prosecutor made use of legal assistance for
the case, he would have to pay for the services of a solicitor and/or a
barrister. And there would be more fees – to the Clerk of the Peace
(at Sessions) or Clerk of Indictments (at Assizes) for drawing up the
indictment, to the clerks and bailiffs for attending witnesses, swearing
them in, etc. Even after sentence, if the prisoner was found guilty, the
prosecutor had to pay a fee to the Clerk of the Peace or of Assize for
the order committing the prisoner to imprisonment or transportation;
if he was acquitted or discharged, the prisoner had to pay a similar fee

himself.[40]

These were the expenses and inconveniences facing the prosecutor; but the state did give him some help. Before 1750, there had been no machinery for reimbursing prosecutors, though there had been a system of Parliamentary rewards for convictions for certain felonies such as highway robbery, coining, burglary and sheep-stealing.[41] An Act of 1752 (25 Geo. II, c. 36) gave the court power, *if the prosecutor was poor,* and if he secured a *conviction* for *felony*, to award him 'such sum as the court should think reasonable as a compensation for the expense, loss of time, and trouble incurred in carrying on the prosecution'. This allowance was payable by the county out of its county rate; the reason for this reimbursement was made clear in the Act's preamble which stated that the expense of prosecuting had deterred many persons from prosecuting for felonies, which had had the effect of encouraging theft. A 1754 Act (27 Geo. II, c. 3) made a similar provision for poor persons appearing on their own recognisances as *witnesses* in felony cases in which a conviction was returned.

A 1778 Act (18 Geo. III, c. 19) extended this in a number of ways: all witnesses, whether poor or not, and whether appearing on their own recognisances or on subpoena, and all prosecutors, without regard to their financial circumstances, would get the allowance. Prosecutors would now get it as long as a Bill of Indictment was preferred, even if the prisoner was acquitted, while witnesses would get it even if no Bill of Indictment was preferred. By this Act, and an 1801 Act, the county would also pay the reasonable expenses incurred by constables in conveying offenders to prison. A 1779 Act (19 Geo. III, c. 74) and an 1815 Act (55 Geo. III, c. 50) respectively placed on the county the burden of paying the fees to the Clerks of Assize and of the Peace, on conviction and on acquittal, in felony cases (though not for misdemeanours). Bennet's Act in 1818 (58 Geo. III, c. 70) abolished the fixed Parliamentary rewards for conviction on capital property offence charges, and empowered the courts to award an allowance for loss of time and trouble to all prosecutors and witnesses in all felony cases (including those for which the rewards had up to then performed the function of reimbursement). Furthermore, the allowance would now include the expenses incurred, not only in carrying on the prosecution, but also in preferring the indictment and in appearing before the Grand Jury; and it was, of course, awarded regardless of whether or not there was a conviction. The courts could also grant a reward to those who had been active in *apprehending* a person accused of a felony — whether or not he was convicted. This Act arose out of the Second Report of the Select Committee on the State of the Police of the Metropolis, which reported:

> The only impediments that are met with upon the general subject of legal prosecutions are of two kinds, First, The Expenses of the prosecution: — Secondly, The severity of the laws, which often deter men from pursuing the offender to conviction; so that if the parties prosecuting were assisted in their expenses by an allowance, and the witnesses remunerated for loss of time, the public justice of the country would be no more interrupted than under the present practice [the 'blood-money' system of rewards].[42]

At this stage, then, prosecutors and witnesses in *felony* cases were reasonably well provided for, in terms of recovering their expenses incurred: during the trial, in preferring the indictment, and in appearing before the Grand Jury. However, there was no provision at all for prosecutors and witnesses in *misdemeanour* cases — even though these included offences such as: uttering base coin, obtaining property under false pretences, assaults, perjury, and most forms of riot; while even for *felonies* there was no allowance for expenses incurred *before* the actual drawing up of the indictment. This was largely remedied by Peel's Criminal Justice Act of 1826 (7 Geo. IV, c.64) which extended the area of recoverable expenses to include the cost of attending the committing magistrate's preliminary examination, and also allowed these expenses to be awarded for *certain misdemeanours:* assault with intent to commit a felony; assault on a peace officer in the execution of his duty; assault in pursuance of a conspiracy to raise wages; obtaining property by false pretences; perjury; misdemeanour for receiving stolen property; riot; and several others.[43]

This was the last of the statutes passed which dealt with the reimbursement of prosecutors and witnesses, and this remained basically the position for the rest of the period under consideration. If a suspect was apprehended, examined by a magistrate, and committed to trial for any felony or one of the misdemeanours listed above, then the prosecutor and witnesses would be reimbursed for their trouble, loss of time and expense, even if the Bill was thrown out by the Grand Jury or the accused acquitted on trial. If a parish constable was involved in the case, he could recover the cost of detaining the suspect in custody, the cost of conveying him to gaol and to court, fees for serving warrants, etc., and an allowance for time and trouble involved in attending to give evidence at the preliminary examination and the trial.

However, if it was one of the misdemeanours *not* covered by the 1826 Act, the prosecutors and witnesses could not recover any expenses; these were not frequent or serious and hence this was not a serious gap. More important, if the suspect was *not* committed for trial, then prosecutor and witnesses could not recover any costs they might have incurred in finding and apprehending the suspect and bringing him before the examining magistrate; and in such a case the constable could not recover the costs of the investigation nor the expenses of appearing before the magistrate. The result was to make parish constables reluctant to enter on investigations unless there was a strong probability of finding a suspect against whom the evidence would be strong enough to ensure a committal, or alternatively the prosecutor could afford to guarantee personally the expenses incurred by the constable in his investigation. This led to a situation in which a constable was unlikely to take up a difficult investigation unless the prosecutor could personally pay him his expenses.

A number of cases were cited in evidence to the Commissioners on County Rates, of constables who pursued investigations at their own expense, for which they failed to be reimbursed, and of poor prosecutors unable to have their cases followed up because of inability to pay the constable's expenses; and this remained the case through the 1850s.[44] This was one of the grounds on which reformers urged the replacement of the constables remunerated by fees, by a regularly-paid police force; in the 'New Police' forces, each police officer was paid regular wages and was prohibited from taking individual rewards, fees, or gratuities from the public or the magistrate. Yet, even in the New Police, the cost of undertaking investigations — especially outside the immediate vicinity — remained a problem, and still made it considerably easier for the processes of justice to be set in motion for the richer than for the poorer prosecutor. For instance, the Chief Constable of the Wolverhampton Borough Force reported that in the months July-December 1856 and 1857, there had been fifty-nine reported cases of thefts from dwelling-houses by lodgers, and only one of these cases had been brought to justice. He explained this discrepancy:

Nearly in all instances the parties leave the Town, *the persons complaining being of the working classes,* have *no means to pay* the officers' expenses to go in pursuit.[45]

Clearly there remained considerable holes in this makeshift system which prevented it from being able to enforce a uniform and effective prosecution of offences. The reimbursement of expenses, and allowances for travel, loss of time and trouble, might compensate for the expense involved in a prosecution once properly set in motion. But there remained these gaps in the early stages of the process, which meant that if the victim failed to bring his case to the point where a *prima facie* case could be made out against someone, he would never recover his initial outlay spent on searching for the offender. Trying to find the person who had committed an offence against oneself was a distinct gamble, which might result in one just losing more money without having anything to show for it.

It was this failure of any official body to guarantee the expenses incurred before committal, or to take over the investigation of a case at this stage from the prosecutor himself, that reveals the largest flaws in the system, and which came in for the most criticism. A number of cases were cited to the County Rates Commissioners of poor people who wished to follow up crimes committed against them, but: were unable to afford to pay out of their own pockets the initial expenses of the investigation and prosecution; declined to initiate such investigations on the grounds that the procedure would cost them much more than the value of the initial loss suffered; or compounded with the offender and dropped the prosecution in return for a sum of money. For instance, a poor man who kept bees for a living had a hive stolen; two men saw who had taken the hive and told him; he went to the house of that man and found the hive, but with the honey gone. He asked the two men to come with him and give evidence before a magistrate, but they were at work, and demanded that he pay them five shillings each for their loss of time. He could not afford this, so went looking for a magistrate on his own; but none of the magistrates in his own or nearby parishes could be found at home, though he tried for several days to find one. Then the offender, hearing he had been to a magistrate, went to him and paid him £5 to drop the prosecution, which he did. In this particular case, he was able to recover some money, but in many cases inability to pay the initial expenses meant inability to find out anything more about the case. As the Commissioners commented:

The expense and difficulty attending every case in first bringing it before a magistrate, are said to operate as a check to the punishment of criminals. The uncertainty of finding magistrates at home, when they reside at a distance, materially aggravates the inconvenience.

These impediments to justice greatly increase the offender's chances of escape, and offer strong inducements to accept of composition [i.e. accepting money in return for dropping the case].[46]

Even where the case did go far enough to justify full reimbursement of expenses, it was always *repayment* of expenses already incurred by the prosecutor; if he did not have the money to lay out in the first place he could not proceed with the prosecution. And the award of expenses was a discretionary one by the court. It always lay in the power of the judge or magistrates to decide that the prosecution had been maliciously or unnecessarily brought, and disallow all or part of the expenses claimed;[47] for instance, the judge might hold that the prosecution had not needed the services of a lawyer, and disallow the claim for legal fees. And even if the full expenses were awarded, they did not always cover the legal costs of the case; nor did all prosecutors find them adequate recompense for all the trouble and time involved. On the other hand, the system was so loose that it was alleged that opportunities for exploiting it were legion, and that prosecutors and constables brought prosecutions unnecessarily, called too many witnesses, and falsified their mileage and subsistence claims in order to profit from the reimbursement. The Recorder of Birmingham, in a Grand Jury Charge in 1839, summed up the weaknesses of the system:

> . . .it is quite evident that, unless prosecutors and witnesses were remunerated to an amount which might furnish a motive to fabricate charges against the innocent (to say nothing of the burthens which would be accumulated on the ratepayer), much loss and inconvenience must still fall on individuals taken from their occupations and detained at a place remote from their dwellings. Nor would money, however lavishly expended, be in all cases a compensation for this enforced absence.[48]

The second major problem was that of control over the system and over the discretion of prosecutors to prosecute. For the Crown, the Attorney-General controlled state prosecutions — prosecutions for treason and political offences, serious murders (chiefly in London), and prosecutions brought by government departments — and the Treasury Solicitor conducted these on behalf of the government. But state prosecutions were only a tiny handful of all the prosecutions brought in the courts of England and Wales. In the vast majority of cases it was the private prosecutor who conducted the case. And with

Table 12   Average Expense of Prosecutions

Year	Staffs. QS £ s. d.	Staffs. Ass. £ s. d.	Worcs. QS £ s. d.	Worcs. Ass. £ s. d.	Walsall QS £ s. d.	England QS £	England Ass. £
1829-31	7 3 10	19 1 6	6 19 11	19 0 7	NA	8	20
1832-4	6 15 10	18 3 6	8 11 3	19 9 3	NA	8	20
1833	6 13 11½	NA	10 5 7½	NA	NA	NA	
1835	6 17 2	20 11 9	NA	NA	3 2 0	NA	
1836(1st quarter)	5 11 9	21 1 2	NA	NA	3 17 3	NA	
1852	7 0 0	19 0 0	NA	NA	NA	NA	
1853	9 12 4	22 7 10	9 9 6	21 7 7	7 0 0	NA	
1854	7 0 0	16 0 0	NA	NA	NA	NA	

NA = Not available;   QS = Quarter Sessions;   Ass. = Assizes

Sources: *RC on County Rates* (1836), Appendix C; Staffs. Quarter Sessions Treasurers' Accounts 1835 and 1836 (SRO Q/SB E. and M. 1836); *SC on Public Prosecutors* (1st Report 1855), Mins. of Evidence and Appendix 3.

him lay the power to decide whether or not he prosecuted at all in that case; whether he pressed his case vigorously, allowed it to fail, withdrew his charge, or compounded it for money; whether he gathered sufficient evidence to sustain a prosecution. There was no easy way the government could control this. A magistrate could bind a man over to prosecute, but if this was done and he then failed to prosecute, all that happened to him was that he estreated his recognisance of £40 or £20. If the aggrieved party was unwilling to prosecute, the authorities could not force him to do so; and they could not easily ensure that that offence was prosecuted. As the Royal Commission of 1839 put it:

> To give to private individuals the power of determining whether the law shall be enforced or not, is in effect to give them a *veto* on the acts of the legislature — to give them more than the power of pardoning, and abandoning to them the prerogative of mercy.[49]

Criticism of the system chiefly centred on the absence of any official person or body responsible for seeing that prosecutions were instituted, properly prepared, and fully carried through whenever and wherever they should be felt to be necessary. The chief remedy suggested was the establishment of some form of public prosecutor to fill this role, such as was found in Scotland, Ireland, the United States and France. In 1855, a Bill to establish a form of public prosecution was introduced into the House of Commons, and the Select Committee set up to consider the Bill reported in favour of such a system. The Bill was subsequently dropped, but the Select Committee report contains much testimony from lawyers, magistrates, policemen, clerks of courts, and law officers of the Crown, expressing dissatisfaction with the current system and exposing its deficiencies.[50] Basically, the Committee's criticisms could be summed up in the paragraph which it quoted from an earlier investigation into the Criminal Law:

> The existing law is by no means as effectual as it ought to be; the duty of prosecution is usually irksome, inconvenient, and burthensome; the injured party would often rather forego the prosecution than incur the expense of time, labour, and money. The entrusting the conduct of the prosecution to a private individual opens a wide door to bribery, collusion, and illegal compromise. . . The injured party may be helpless, ignorant, interested, corrupt; he is altogether irresponsible, yet his dealing with the criminal may effectually defeat justice. On general principles it would evidently be desirable to appoint a public prosecutor.[51]

In the absence of state control, the crucially important decision whether or not to prosecute a particular offence lay in the hands of the private individual — and, effectively, of the private individual with money, because of the costs of the system. The system best served those who had the money, time and inclination to prosecute particular offences against themselves.

The state exercised virtually no control over the vital area of the discretion to initiate a prosecution; it was also unable to ensure that a prosecution, once begun, would be adequately carried through. And it offered little assistance in this area to the private prosecutor. All the prosecutor had when he left the preliminary examination was a copy of the depositions relating to that prosecution; from this he had to prepare a full case for presentation in court. As that veteran law reformer Lord Brougham said:

> The prosecutor, who is not a man cognizant of the law, comes to the assizes or the sessions, goes before the grand jury, and prefers a bill upon the depositions; but there is no one whose office it is to

look, prior to that time, to see that the evidence upon which the magistrate committed is all the evidence which can be procured, or is at all events sufficient evidence to prove the case.[52]

The obvious answer was for the prosecutor to employ an attorney or solicitor for this purpose, to prepare the brief of the case. The problem here was that a poor man would only be able to afford to pay his attorney the guinea which the court would award as his expenses — which was the minimum fee which an attorney would accept. This meant that well-established attorneys, being able to demand higher fees, would not take such cases. Attorneys without good practices, to whom even the guinea was attractive, would take such cases and would get their guinea fee regardless of how the case turned out; such 'low attorneys' were said to take very little trouble in preparing such cases, which often failed in court as a result. Staffordshire was said to be one of the worst counties for this; as C.S. Greaves QC (who had practised for many years in Staffordshire) said:

> It is very well known there [Staffordshire] that though the costs are at a very low rate, there is a perfect hunt for the prosecutions by low attorneys. . .the consequence is that they get hold of the prosecutors who are poor, and incompetent to carry on the prosecution; it gets into their hands, and they never take the least trouble about it, any more than giving counsel a copy of the depositions with the fee on the back of the brief, and they let the case take its chance at the assizes.[53]

If one wanted to be sure of success in one's prosecution, one had to be able to pay for good, competent legal assistance; this cost considerably more than the reimbursement allowance for a lawyer, and hence was out of reach of the poor prosecutor.

There is a good illustration of the importance of money, both in the initial investigations to begin the prosecution and in the legal preparation of a case for the Sessions, in the Associations for the Prosecution of Felons which were established and operated throughout England in this period. These began as associations of property owners in areas in which the police protection of property and the means provided for prosecution were felt to be inadequate. These were found throughout England and Wales, predominantly in rural areas though also in some urban and industrial areas; they flourished mostly before the coming of the 'New Police', though they continued in some areas well after the initial establishment of a 'New Police' force. There were estimated to be over 500 of them in existence in 1839.[54] Probably the best-known such example is the High Barnet Association, serving the area of Hertfordshire on the edge of London, about which evidence was given to the Royal Commissions of 1836 and 1839.

The Black Country had a number of these associations; they certainly existed in Wednesbury, Halesowen, Bloxwich, Tipton, Dudley, Bilston and Stourbridge, and probably in a number of the other towns and parishes.[55] No records for the Black Country associations survive; but the Minute Book is available of the Chillington Association for the Prosecution of Felons. Chillington is an area on the edge of the Black Country, about six miles north-west of Wolverhampton; the Association covered the liberty of Chillington and the town and parish of Brewood, both predominantly agricultural areas; its records are available from the time of its establishment in 1828 until its dissolution in 1859.[56]

Basically the associations came into existence to remedy defects in the existing state of the police and reimbursement for prosecution. Associations consisted of local property owners, who came together, usually in fairly small numbers (the Chillington Association never had more than thirty members, elected by invitation only) to facilitate the process of search for, and prosecution of, offenders against themselves. The Chillington Association was led by the local lord of the manor, included the local clergyman, and consisted mainly of farmers, with a few innkeepers and tradesmen from the town. Each paid an annual subscription to the Association, and they met once a year to elect a committee which ran the affairs of the Association for that year.

Whenever a member of the Association had some offence committed against him (usually something stolen from him), he would come to the committee and ask for assistance in searching for, and prosecuting, the offender. If the committee agreed that this was a case deserving to be taken up by the Association (which they usually did), they would relieve the member of the responsibility and expense of the investigation and prosecution by conducting it on behalf of the Association, and paying for it from Association funds.

The committee had a number of ways of trying to find the offender. They had a regular list of rewards payable on conviction, ranging from £21 for serious crimes such as highway robbery, horse stealing or arson, to two guineas for damaging farm property; a list of these rewards was regularly published in the local press, and after a crime had been reported to them the committee would put advertisements in the local press and issue handbills for local circulation. If it was a theft of animals such as horses or cattle, the Association would send out its patrols. Each member was assigned a particular route along which he or a paid substitute had to ride, when called upon to do so by the Association, looking for traces of the missing animals; if any information was obtained of the missing animals, he had to carry on the search until he either found the animal or the thief or lost all traces of the trail. Finally, and most importantly, the Association would pay the expenses incurred by the local constable or his assistants, by the patrol riders going beyond their assigned routes in pursuit of the missing property and the offender, or by private individuals who helped to arrest the offender. The result was that the expenses of search and apprehension before committal — those that were least certain to be repaid by the county, and whose absence deterred so many prosecutors from proceeding — were guaranteed, and men were supplied for the function of search and apprehension.

The Association took care of the second problem as well — the cost of preparing a well-constructed case against the offender. Every association retained a regular solicitor, to whom the conduct of prosecutions was entrusted, who was paid far more than the normal guinea allowed by the county; the Chillington accounts show that he was paid between £4 10s and £6 for each prosecution. The Chillington Association also regularly paid a fee, and often a reward as well, to the local constable for every case which he investigated on their behalf. Their minutes make it clear that the local constable worked very closely with the Association — whenever they reported an offence, he would set off in search, confident of his expenses being paid, plus a fee, and if a conviction was secured, a reward. Whenever he detained suspicious characters with property in their possession, he would immediately consult the Association as to whether any of them had experienced a theft.[57] One can see clearly how important money was for the success of the Association's investigations and prosecutions, from the large part of their expenses which was *not* covered by the county allowance. For instance, the Association paid £15 3s 10d for the apprehension and prosecution of a man for stealing wheat, made up of the constable's charges, the expenses of the committal proceedings at Wolverhampton, the solicitor's bill, the expenses of four witnesses and their transport and accommodation costs for the Quarter Sessions. The county made an allowance of only £7 19s 6d for this prosecution — so the Association had to pay just under half the cost themselves. By contrast, in two cases in March and April 1849, the cases were felt to be so clear and straightforward that it was decided that it was not

necessary to employ a solicitor or barrister for their prosecution, so
that no expense would be incurred, *'except what the County paid'* —
in other words, the county allowance was seen as adequate to cover
only the very simplest and clearest cases; as soon as there was any
complexity and need to employ legal counsel, then private expenditure
was needed.[58] Similarly, the table in the County Rates Report shows
that well over half the cost of the prosecutions brought by the
associations listed there was borne by the associations themselves.[59]
The Commissioners commented:

> The extra expenses defrayed by associations are said to consist
> chiefly of expenses prior to commitment, a larger sum paid to the
> attorney for preparing the brief, and a higher fee paid to the counsel,
> than are sanctioned respectively by the county allowance.[60]

Most of the associations were not major forces in law enforcement. The
Barnet Association maintained a full-time paid patrol force of six men
and one superintendent which patrolled the local roads, as well as
prosecuting offences against its members; but they seem to have been
exceptional in the thoroughness of the private preventive police force
which they established. The Chillington Association only sent out its
patrols (made up of members or their servants) *after* an offence had
been committed, and for a short time only; they did no permanent
patrolling. They, and most other associations, were essentially organs
for apprehending and prosecuting offences against their members, not
for preventing crime; and most of them did not deal with a large
number of offences — presumably, if they had had to, they would
have been unable to function so easily. The Chillington Association
dealt with only one or two offences a year — these were mostly thefts
of farm produce or animals, with an occasional burglary or theft from
a shop; the Wednesbury Association handled only six prosecutions in
four years, the Halesowen Association five in the same period.[61]

The real importance of the associations lies in the clear illustration
they provide of the inadequacy of the official prosecution system when
not supplemented by private resources. The Royal Commission on the
police saw the existence of the associations as 'proof of the prostrate
condition of the penal administration of the country' and the County
Rates Commissioners held that 'it may safely be inferred from this,
that the expenses allowed for prosecutions are still inadequate'.[62]
They provide an institutional representation of the point that
enforcement of the law and prosecution were easier for the propertied

than for the propertyless. The principle underlying the whole system
of prosecution was that of state assistance for private entrepreneurs
with a cause to prosecute. The Associations carried this to its logical
conclusion by establishing corporate enterprises for the more efficient
execution of this principle; and, as in any capitalist enterprise, the
corporation with capital had a clear advantage over the individual with
none.

We noted in the last chapter that large property owners were often
opposed to the establishment of police forces, requiring as they did the
levying of a police rate, which would fall most heavily on their
property, to pay for police for the whole county. Where property
owners had active Associations for the Prosecution of Felons in
existence, this attitude is easy to understand. They paid their
subscriptions to their Association, which protected their property alone.
Why, then, choose to pay rates to a police force to serve the whole
county, which would spend much of its time protecting other people's
property? The ratepayers of Kesteven, in Lincolnshire, resisted a police
force on these grounds as late as 1853. Their Chief Constable
maintained that his parish constables plus the local associations were
quite sufficient for the prevention and detection of local offences. But,
under close questioning, he admitted that the associations only took
action on offences against their own members; and that the example
he had cited to show the efficiency of the combination of constables
and associations — that of the breaking-up of a large sheep-stealing
gang — had only been made possible by the private exertions of a
wealthy landowner and his servants. 'In all probability,' he admitted,
'if he had been a poor man, he would not have had the means or the
ability to have exerted himself.'[63]

III

We can now look at who the actual prosecutors of offences were in the
Black Country courts. Table 13(a), (b) and (c) sets out, on the basis of
recognisances for five sample years, the occupational groups from which
the victims of offences came, the extent to which the victims themselves
prosecuted, and who prosecuted in cases where the victim did not do so
himself.

Table 13(b) shows clearly that most prosecutions were brought by
the victims themselves. The majority of the coal and iron masters'
prosecutions were handled by someone other than the victim, but these
were all the work of an agent or employee of the coal and iron master
acting under his instructions. Table 13(c) shows that the police were

Table 13 (a)   Victims of Offences Dealt with at Black Country
Quarter Sessions 1836, 1839, 1842, 1847, 1851

Occupation of Victim	Percentage				
	1836	1839	1842	1847	1851
	S & W	W	S & W	S	W
Unskilled Manual	30	17	20	15	14
Skilled Manual	24	30	16	14	15
Retail Trade	29	22	25	26	32
Coal and Iron Master, Manufacturer	8	11	21	26	20
Farmer	0	7	6	6	3
Gentry, Clergy	0	0	1	4	1
Other Commercial	0	0	1	0	0
Profession, Agent	1	0	1	2	0
Clerical Staff	1	0	1	4	0
Spinster, Widow, Child	6	13	4	3	13
Police, Constable	1	0	2	0	0
Govt., County*	0	0	2	0	2
TOTAL	100	100	100	100	100
Number	89	54	359	66	98
Occupation not available	10	14	29	7	13

S = Staffordshire;   W = Worcestershire

* Offences with no individual victim, whose prosecution would be felt to be a matter of public interest by the government or county authorities; the offences in these particular instances are riot and coining.

Table 13 (b)   Prosecutors of Those Offences

Occupation of Victim	Percentage									
	1836		1839		1842		1847		1851	
	V	O	V	O	V	O	V	O	V	O
Unskilled Manual	96	4	56	44	91	9	50	50	86	14
Skilled Manual	90	10	81	19	98	2	67	33	87	13
Retail Trade	88	12	100	0	87	13	71	29	77	23
Coal and Iron Master, Manufacturer	43	57	33	67	27	73	29	71	5	95
Farmer	—	—	75	25	86	14	100	0	67	33
Spinster, Widow, Child	40	60	29	71	56	44	100	0	92	8
ALL CASES	83	17	57	43	68	32	53	47	61	39

V = Prosecuted by victims themselves;   O = Prosecuted by others.
V and O figures for each year add up to 100 per cent.

Table 13 (c)   Prosecutors in Those Cases Where the Victim Did Not
               Prosecute

Prosecutor	Percentage				
	1836	1839	1842	1847	1851
	S & W	W	S & W	S	W
Police	35	69	27	62	28
Victim's Agent, Employee	29	14	41	32	26
Victim's Spouse, Parent, Child	18	3	6	3	21
Other*	18	14	26	3	25
TOTAL	100	100	100	100	100
Number	17	29	124	34	43

S = Staffordshire;   W = Worcestershire

* Includes victim's workmate or friend, and those whose relationship and
  occupation are not indicated.

Sources: Recognisances to prosecute available for these QS:
   Staffs: E., E.Adj., Ea. 1836; E., E.Adj., Ea., M., M.Adj., Mich. 1842;
             E. 1847.
   Worcs: E., E.Adj., M. 1836; E., E.Adj., Ea., M. 1839; E.Adj. 1842; E.,
             E.Adj., Ea., M., Mich., 1851.
Only Staffs. 1842 and Worcs. 1851 have full runs of the recognisances for a
whole year. Staffs. recognisances are not available for any year after 1847.
The analysis is limited to Staffs. and Worcs. QS; no recognisances at all are
available for any Assizes, nor for the Walsall Borough Sessions. This analysis
perforce under-represents the prosecution of more serious crimes because of
the non-availability of the Assize recognisances.

increasing in importance as a prosecuting agency, particularly in the
Staffordshire part of the Black Country. (The Worcestershire figures
appear to show a decline in the prosecuting activity of the police, but
this is because the Worcestershire parish constables had been very active
in taking on prosecutions, and show an abnormally high number of
prosecutions to their credit in 1839.) By 1847, the Staffordshire county
force was handling nearly 30 per cent of all Staffordshire Black Country
prosecutions.

One can note from Table 13(a) and (b) the proportion of
occupational groups among victims and prosecutors. The two largest
groups for prosecuting offences, over the period as a whole, are retail
traders and the large industrial entrepreneurs. These people were
naturally those with the largest amount of property at risk to potential
theft. But it is notable also that the unskilled and skilled working class

together make up a large proportion of the prosecutors — never below 28 per cent, and as high as 50 per cent in 1836. This is lower than their proportion in the population of the area as a whole. But it is still surprising that this proportion is as high as it is, particularly in the case of the unskilled working class. These unskilled working-class prosecutors are made up mostly of miners, labourers and nailers.

There would seem to be good grounds for assuming *a priori* that in this prosecution system one would find very few prosecutors from the ranks of the unskilled working class. These people had relatively little property to be stolen. There were good reasons why they might have been suspicious of — perhaps even hostile to — the law and its agents. The system of prosecution did not make it compulsory for them to prosecute, and, as we have seen, gave relatively little help to the poorer prosecutors; yet, as Table 13(b) shows, most of these unskilled working-class prosecutors handled their own prosecutions.

As against these points, the detailed evidence on the Black Country offences which came to court makes it clear that these very often involved members of the unskilled working class as victims. The vast majority of assaults were committed by working-class people against other working-class people. Many of the robberies and housebreakings were committed against working-class victims. And the simple larcenies, overwhelmingly the largest category of offence, often involved: clothes taken from the washing-line, home or workplace; sheets, blankets and utensils taken from lodgings; coal taken from the domestic coalpile; poultry taken from a hutch in the yard; money or a watch stolen from the person.[64] The working class suffered these losses, and they seem to have been prepared, where possible, to prosecute for these offences.

There were certainly many offences committed against working-class victims which were not prosecuted. The most obvious instance is that of assaults — only a small fraction of the incidents which technically constituted assaults ever found their way to the courts. It is also probable that many of the thefts committed against working-class people were never formally prosecuted.[65]

Some contemporaries suggested that victims might have been deterred from prosecuting by fear of reprisals against themselves or their families by the criminals and their associates.[66] This may have had some validity for the rookeries of London, where a large, organised criminal underworld could presumably enforce its own rules. But it does not seem likely to have had more than a marginal effect in the Black Country, where there was not the same degree of criminal organisation. Most offences (at any rate, those which came to light) in

the Black Country were *not* the work of organised, professional gangs
(see chapters 6, 7 and 8), and the vast majority of offences committed
were not offences of violence. There may have been a few robberies or
burglaries which were not prosecuted because of fear of retaliation, but
overall this would have had little effect on the prosecution of most
offences.

E.P. Thompson has argued that the poorer classes would have been
unwilling to invoke the law at all. He stresses the persistence of 'popular
attitudes to crime, amounting at times to an unwritten code, quite
distinct from the laws of the land', and he states:

> The law was hated, but it was also despised. Only the most hardened
> criminal was held in as much popular odium as the informer who
> brought men to the gallows.

In support of this view, he cites examples such as poaching and
smuggling, which were condemned by law but approved and supported
by most of the community of the villages in which such activities were
carried on. But he also suggests that this was a complex phenomenon,
in which certain types of offence — wife- or child-murder, crimes which
struck at the livelihood of a community — were condemned by popular
feeling as well as by law.[67]

But if it is true that the law was despised, then one would not expect
to find any working-class prosecutors, especially for property offences.
After all, the system relied on private prosecution and there was no
official obligation on the victim to prosecute. Prosecution was a slow,
inconvenient and costly business. If one wished to recover the stolen
property and suspected who the person responsible was, it should have
been possible to inflict informal punishment on him — gather a number
of friends and get the property back by threatening to beat up the
offender, or by beating him up in addition to recovering the property.
But this does not seem to have happened in the Black Country — or, if
it did happen, it was certainly not the only way in which such events
were handled. The evidence shows unmistakably that large numbers of
workingmen prosecuted other workingmen for thefts of clothes, sheets,
coal, food, poultry, money and personal valuables from themselves;
they did not simply exact informal retribution from them, but invoked
the whole formal and cumbersome process of the law, from
preliminary examination to final sentence. This suggests two things.
First, they must have believed that the system of law had at least some
element of justice and fairness about it, and would probably uphold

their case — otherwise why bother to prosecute at all? Secondly, whatever their feelings about the law and its agents, they cannot have been totally opposed to the idea of invoking the law to prosecute thefts of private property — or else, again, they need not have made use of it at all. By making use of the law in this way, they showed an acceptance of its basic legitimacy as applied to themselves and their affairs.

This does not necessarily invalidate Thompson's assertion (though he offers very little evidence to support it) since he was writing about the late eighteenth century, when property offences were still capital; probably, at a time when the law could still take life for property offences, it would be an unpopular action to set the machinery of the law in motion. But by the 1830s one does not find that 'popular odium' attached to Black Country workingmen who initiate prosecutions. (True the professional 'common informer' was still an unpopular figure, but he does not appear very frequently by the 1830s.)

There were some areas in which the working class, on the whole, did show dislike for, and distrust of, the law and its agents — for instance, the initial working-class hostility to the 'New Police'. In the 1830s and 1840s, the popular Black Country attitude towards fights and assaults remained basically that there was no need to call in the law in such matters, and the parish constables received very little help in their efforts to break up and put a stop to the frequent fights.[68] And there was widespread popular acceptance among the Black Country working class of the right of workers and local inhabitants to take coal, metal, tools and parts from the coal and iron works.[69] But when it came to property stolen from themselves, the Black Country working class was prepared to prosecute. It may be that many of them did not prosecute for offences against themselves — there is no way of knowing of how many this may have been true; nor can one find out whether there was a basic difference in terms of 'respectability' and general attitude between those who were prepared to prosecute and those who were not. What is clear from Table 13(a) and (b) is that there was a large number of workingmen who did prosecute for thefts from themselves, and that the working-class prosecutor was a common, and not an exceptional figure in the courts of the Black Country. This indicates that the Black Country working class of this period accepted important areas of the legitimacy of the criminal law. They valued their rights to such little private property as they had, and when these were infringed, they accepted that the infringements should be dealt with through the machinery of the law rather than by the informal use of violence and forcible repossession of the property.

Generally, the working-class attitude to the law and its agents seems to have been a complex one: opposed to some laws which cut across community-sanctioned values – e.g. the Game Laws, or the idea that taking waste coal was theft – and to some aspects of the police; but not totally opposed in principle to laws which protected private property; prepared to sympathise with some people who broke the law, especially against the rich and powerful, but also to prosecute those who took property belonging to other members of the working class. It also seems to be true that in the early part of the nineteenth century, offences which had formerly been punished by informal communal action were increasingly being handed over to the authorities and formally prosecuted. As one witness to the Select Committee on Criminal Commitments put it:

> I think one reason we may give for the increase of Crime, or the greater exhibition of it to public view, is the seizure and delivery to the Police of all those who commit offences, that are styled offences at all. I remember in former days, persons were taken and pumped upon, or something of that sort; but now they are handed over to the Police, and tried on it.[70]

This development was probably linked to the extension (outlined above) of the scope of the system of reimbursement for prosecution.

The evidence strongly suggests that there was no working-class disinclination to prosecute for property offences by the 1830s. The extension of reimbursement for prosecutors and witnesses between 1752 and 1826 probably brought a large number of potential working-class prosecutors into the formal system of prosecution. But the fact that the system still involved financial difficulties for the poorer prosecutors, even by the 1850s, would certainly have deterred a number of working-class victims from prosecuting. We recall the Wolverhampton example (cited earlier, p.114) where, in 1856-7, only one of fifty-nine thefts from dwelling-houses by lodgers had been cleared up, because 'the persons complaining being of the working classes, have no means to pay the officers' expenses to go in pursuit'. It remained much easier to prosecute if you had money to spare for the purpose.

IV

Two important modifications to the prosecution system which has been outlined here took place during our period.

The first was the establishment of the 'New Police' forces. The parish constables had always played some part in prosecutions, and where the magistrate could find no individual willing or able to prosecute a case, he would sometimes bind over a constable to do so. The 'New Police' forces began to do this more regularly and systematically. The Staffordshire county force saw themselves explicitly as filling the gap caused by the absence of any form of public prosecutor.[71] This was, in fact, to be the line of development of all English police forces to the modern situation in which most normal prosecutions are brought by the police.

Table 13(c) shows the Staffordshire police in 1847 handling nearly 30 per cent of the prosecutions. This proportion gradually increased — evidence given to the 1855 Select Committee refers to the Staffordshire police conducting a large proportion of all prosecutions.[72] But this development was slow — by 1860, the Staffordshire police still seem to have been handling less than half of all Black Country prosecutions.[73]

This development slowly transferred the cost of prosecutions from individual prosecutors to the police. It also slowly improved the quality of preparation of the cases brought to court. The police had the organisation, experience, money and time to collect the necessary witnesses, prepare a thorough case, retain regular solicitors and brief counsel. They were also better equipped than a private prosecutor to decide whether a particular case should be proceeded with, and whether the evidence was strong enough to enable it to proceed with a chance of success. The result was a gradual rise in the ratio of convictions to committals for trial — fewer acquittals on trial and fewer Bills thrown out by Grand Juries. This can be shown by comparing the Black Country figures for two six-year periods before and after the establishment of the police forces:

Table 14   Outcome of Black Country Trials Before and After Establishment of Police Forces

			Percentage		
Period	Guilty	Not Guilty	No True Bill	Other*	Total
1835-40	67	23	9	1	100
1850-55	75	18	6	1	100

* Includes those found insane, those who turned Queen's evidence, those who did not appear for their trials, etc.

The second important modification was a change in the law on some aspects of criminal procedure. As the law stood in the 1840s, every theft of any piece of property, no matter how small or trivial, was a form of larceny; hence it was a felony, and could only be tried on indictment at Quarter Sessions or Assizes. As the totals of charges tried on indictment mounted steadily in the 1820s and 1830s, increasing criticism was levelled against this anomaly. It was common for a man to be committed for trial for stealing an article worth 6d or 1s. He would have to spend three months in gaol awaiting trial; prosecutor and witnesses would have to be brought to the county town for the trial, involving great expense. These trials would take up a large part of the time and trouble of the Sessions or Assizes, at the expense of more serious crimes; and at the end, the offender, if found guilty, would only be sentenced to about two weeks' imprisonment. Even if the accused pleaded guilty, he would still have to wait in custody for one to three months for the Sessions or Assizes before he could be formally convicted; by this time, his spell in gaol would probably have amounted to more than the normal sentence for that offence. For instance, Catherine Cross pleaded guilty to stealing fifty pounds weight of coal in November 1850; she was kept in gaol from 7 November until she came up for trial at the beginning of January 1851. Here she was given the merely nominal sentence of seven days' imprisonment in view of the two months she had already had in gaol, awaiting trial.[74]

Criticism centred on a number of specific points. First was the disproportionate cost to the county — it could easily cost £10 for the prosecution, plus another £20 in maintaining the accused in gaol awaiting trial, to prosecute for a theft of the value of 6d. Secondly, there was the fear of contamination of first offenders — it was pointed out by a number of persons that first offenders, especially juveniles, committed to gaol for long periods to await trial for such a trivial offence, were often corrupted by the experienced criminals whom they met there, with the result that the lengthy prosecution of the petty offence (which, if speedily punished, might not have been repeated) led them on to a full career of crime. Thirdly, many prosecutors were deterred from prosecuting by the expense, time and trouble which a full prosecution at Sessions or Assizes involved, and preferred to let the charge drop. As a remedy, many magistrates and law reformers had been advocating for some time that Justices of the Peace sitting in pairs in Petty Sessions (i.e. without a jury) in their own Petty Sessional districts, once or twice a week, should have the power to try summarily larcenies committed by juveniles, and petty larcenies committed by persons of any age.[75]

In 1847, Parliament took the first steps in this direction, by passing the Juvenile Offenders' Act (JOA) 1847 (10 and 11 Vict., c. 82), which allowed summary trial of persons aged under fourteen accused of simple larceny. The Act also restricted the punishment which could be imposed to three months' imprisonment, with or without hard labour, and allowed the Justices as an alternative to discharge the juveniles without punishment, or have them whipped, instead of imprisoning them. In 1850, the age limit for juveniles was raised to sixteen by the second Juvenile Offenders' Act (13 and 14 Vict., c. 37). In 1855 came the much more important (quantitatively) and long-awaited Act covering all petty theft offenders — the Criminal Justice Act (CJA) (18 and 19 Vict., c. 126). This Act enabled two JPs in Petty Sessions to try summarily cases involving thefts of under the value of 5s, if the accused agreed to a summary trial, and thefts of 5s or more, if the accused pleaded guilty; it limited the penalties to a maximum sentence of three months' hard labour for thefts of under 5s, and six months' hard labour for thefts of 5s and over.

The CJA offered great advantages to the parties concerned. The trial would take place in the town of the Petty Sessional district in which the offence took place, which would be within a radius of at most three miles from the place of the offence — this would remove the transport and accommodation problems and delays involved in having to go to the county town. The trial could be held immediately, or within a week of the commission of the offence — again obviating the delays inherent in a Sessions or Assizes trial; this would mean that the accused did not have to spend those months in goal awaiting trial, and the prosecutor did not have the long delay before his case came to trial. It was easier for prosecutor and witnesses to get to the Petty Sessions for the trial, and the proceedings were much shorter, less elaborate and less expensive than a Sessions or Assize trial, not requiring an elaborate indictment, or the use of Grand or Petty Juries. And it removed the previously existing anomaly whereby, even if the accused pleaded guilty, he and the prosecutor and witnesses still had to go to the Assizes or Sessions and wait for their case to come up there, before sentence could be pronounced. Both prosecutor and accused could get advantages from the CJA, the former saving time, trouble and money, and the latter being dealt with much more swiftly, and being sure that the sentence which could be imposed was limited. So it is not surprising that most of those accused of thefts of under 5s elected, after 1855, to be tried summarily, while large numbers of those who pleaded guilty were also dealt with in this way.

However, it is important to note the effect which the CJA (and, to a lesser extent, the JOA) had on the number of such prosecutions brought, not merely for what is demonstrated about the effect of these Acts, but also for the light which is thrown on the working of the whole prosecution system before and after 1855. The effect of the CJA and the JOA was not simply to transfer to the Petty Sessions those larcenies which had previously been tried at Quarter Sessions (because of their petty nature, it was extremely unusual for one of these small larcenies to be tried at Assizes), but also to *increase by a vast extent the number of such larcenies which were tried at all.* This can be seen very clearly if one looks at the figures of trials for indictable larcenies for Staffordshire Quarter Sessions before and after 1855 (Table 15).[76] (It is important to note that these simple larcenies still remained felonies and indictable offences in law, nor was their legal definition or scope changed in any way; the JOA and CJA simply provided machinery whereby they *might* be tried summarily; the Acts did not change them into summary offences, nor lessen their seriousness as offences.)

Table 15 shows clearly the great increase in the number of larcenies tried after 1855, this increase coming in the enormous numbers tried under the CJA, and, to a lesser extent, under the JOA. The table also shows that the CJA did achieve its aim of relieving the pressure of cases on Quarter Sessions — from 1855 to 1856, the number of larcenies tried at Quarter Sessions was halved. But this reduction in the cases tried at Quarter Sessions was far more than matched by the numbers tried under the CJA; by 1858, the Quarter Sessions larceny trials were down to 110 from 368 in 1855, but the CJA convictions were up to 688 in that same year. In other words, the CJA did not simply enable men who were going to prosecute anyway to do so more easily, but it also encouraged and brought out men who would not have prosecuted at all at Quarter Sessions or Assizes before the passing of the CJA, but who were prepared to prosecute under the easier conditions established by the CJA.

The vast scale of this increase (doubling the number of larcenies prosecuted) suggests that before the passing of the CJA there had existed a large pool of potential prosecutors — people against whom thefts had been committed which they had not prosecuted. The fact that they now took advantage of the CJA to prosecute, strongly reinforces the idea that the main deterrent to their prosecuting before had been the time, trouble and expense involved. The CJA now enabled

Table 15   Larcenies Tried from the Staffordshire Black Country 1835-60

Year	Tried at QS	Tried and Convicted under CJA*	Tried and Convicted under JOA*	Total
1835	141	0	0	141
1836	168	0	0	168
1837	216	0	0	216
1838	252	0	0	252
1839	275	0	0	275
1840	290	0	0	290
1841	353	0	0	353
1842	430	0	0	430
1843	334	0	0	334
1844	295	0	0	295
1845	241	0	0	241
1846	319	0	0	319
1847	389	0	17	406
1848	371	0	33	404
1849	348	0	43	391
1850	377	0	42	419
1851	366	0	39	405
1852	307	0	53	360
1853	386	0	38	424
1854	399	0	35	434
1855	368	88	58	514
1856	185	381	88	654
1857	124	660	141	925
1858	110	688	148	946
1859	150	545	159	854
1860	125	574	120	819

* These figures are for *convictions* only, not for all *committals* to trial, because only the convictions are recorded; this means that these figures are in fact a slight *under*statement of the numbers tried under the CJA and JOA.

Source: Compiled from the sources listed in Appendix I.

them to prosecute cheaply, quickly and in their own district, and as a result the number of prosecutors coming forward doubled. This result bore out what those who had been urging the passage of something like the CJA had hoped would occur. P.B. Purnell predicted in 1836 that granting summary jurisdiction for these cases would save prosecutors and witnesses much time when prosecuting small larcenies,

> . . .the accumulation of which cases causes an attendance of six or seven days at the assizes, and of three or four at the quarter sessions. . .Nothing would more conduce to the encouragement of prosecutions for minor offences, of which, notwithstanding the number at assizes and quarter sessions, not one half, I should say, of those where convictions would be certain, are brought forward, in consequence of the fear of not receiving adequate remuneration for the trouble, and of the irksomeness, inconvenience, and almost certain loss, in attending to prosecute at the county town.[77]

Finally, one should stress that the prosecution system which has been discussed in this chapter was one in which the figures of committals to trial could be influenced by changes within that system as well as by the number of criminal acts committed. There is no doubt that the number of committals to trial increased dramatically from 1805 to the 1820s, and yet again in the 1830s and 1840s; but at least part of this increase was an artificial inflation of the figures by increased prosecution, brought on by the increased reimbursement to prosecutors enacted by the 1818 and 1826 Acts, and perhaps also by the repeal of most of the capital statutes for property offences in the 1820s and early 1830s. As early as 1828, this point was recognised when the Select Committee on Criminal Commitments reported:

> Your Committee have much satisfaction in stating their confirmed opinion that the great part of the increase in the number of Criminal Commitments arises from other causes than the increase of Crime. Offences which were formerly either passed over entirely, or were visited with a summary chastisement on the spot, are now made occasions of commitment to gaol and regular trial.
> . . .[The Criminal Justice Act 1826] and other Acts not necessary to mention have tended to fill the Prisons without any positive increase of Crime. The Magistrates likewise are more ready to commit than they used to be.[78]

And not only changes in the system for reimbursing prosecutors, but also the whole way in which the prosecution system operated, had an important effect on who ended up in court and for what offences. This must be borne in mind in the next four chapters, in which the Black Country figures of committals to trial are examined in detail.

Notes

1. F.W. Maitland, *Justice and Police* (London 1885), p.141 (italics in the original). This is still technically the position in England and Wales today, though in practice the police take most of the responsibility for the prosecutions now – see R.M. Jackson, *Enforcing the Law* (Pelican edn., Harmondsworth 1972, pp.82-8).
2. Details of the case set out here are taken from the depositions, the recognisances to prosecute and give evidence (both in SRO Q/SB E. 1842), and the report of the trial in *SA* 8 January 1842. Details of the procedure generally are drawn from the depositions, recognisances and newspaper reports of a large number of Black Country cases for 1835-60, especially for the years 1836 and 1842, but including a number in the 1850s. A good outline of the whole process of prosecution, committal and trial in the nineteenth century can be found in Maitland, *Justice and Police,* pp.118-73.
3. For details on the difference between indictable and summary offences, see Appendix II.
4. Table of Returns for Mining District for December 1845-February 1846, February-May 1846, September-November 1847, in C.C. Reports to QS (SRO Q/SB Ea. 1846, M. 1846, E. 1848). The proportions here are calculated as proportions of those offences which came before the magistrates and could, if they had been regarded as serious enough, have been committed for trial. This includes larcenies, robberies, assaults, riots etc., but *excludes* those offences which could only have been tried summarily, such as vagrancy, drunkenness, offences against the licensing laws, etc.
5. Theft of items worth only a few pence was still larceny and hence a felony to be tried on indictment – 'The judges had determined that if a person stole a piece of paper, the value of which could not be estimated by the smallest coin in the realm, yet that offence was still a felony' (Charge to Grand Jury, QS E. 1848, in *SA* 8 January 1848). This point was repeatedly made by the Chairman of Quarter Sessions in his Grand Jury Charges – see reports of Grand Jury Charges in *SA* 9 January 1836, 12 March 1836, 4 January 1845, 21 October 1848, 18 October 1851.
6. See section on Industrial Thefts, in ch.6.
7. Ibid.
8. All Grand Jury Charges were fully reported by the local press; some of the more thoughtful and substantial ones were printed in pamphlet or book form – e.g. M.D. Hill, *The Repression of Crime* (London 1857), a collection, with additional comments and articles, of his Grand Jury Charges as Recorder of Birmingham.
9. Maitland, *Justice and Police,* p.137. There are detailed descriptions of the procedure to be followed by Grand Juries in, e.g. the Charges to the Grand Jury at Staffs. QS M. 1835, M. 1839, and M. 1840, all reported in the relevant issues of the *SA.*
10. Maitland, op.cit., p.139; Jackson, *Enforcing,* p.96.
11. Lists of Assize Grand Juries in *SA* 1835-60; Maitland, op.cit., p.185.
12. Based on the analysis of cases made to determine the proportion in which counsel were employed (see note 16 below). It is a minimum figure, because the plea was not recorded in a number of the shorter newspaper reports of

cases, and those cases which the newspapers were likely not to report or to report in barest outline, were likely to be those in which 'Guilty' pleas were made — the less serious offences, in which there was no serious legal contest worth reporting.

13. B. Abel-Smith and R. Stevens, *Lawyers and the Courts* (London 1967), p.30; Charge to Worcs. Grand Jury, *WH* 26 October 1836; petition to Parliament by the JPs of Worcs. urging rejection of the Bill (WRO Q/SB M. 1836); Hill, *Repression of Crime*, pp.38-40.

14. See *RC on County Rates* (2nd Report) (1836), pp.1-383; *First Report of Select Committee on Public Prosecutors*, P.P. 1854-5, XII (481), pp.3-309. A good description of the life and practices of a barrister on the Oxford Circuit is found in A.C. Plowden, *Grain or Chaff? The Autobiography of a Police Magistrate* (London 1903).

15. *RC on County Rates* (2nd Report) (1836), pp.22-3; *SC on Public Prosecutors* (1st Report) (1855), pp.117, 164, 219; Plowden, op.cit., pp.122, 164-5; Abel-Smith and Stevens, *Lawyers*, p.32.

16. Derived from the newspaper reports of Black Country cases tried before a jury of Staffs. QS and Ass. during 1842. The newspaper reports are very full, and virtually every case in the Calendars for that year is mentioned in the newspapers. However, some are only mentioned in the barest outline; these have been excluded because of the insufficient detail on the conduct of the cases; excluded, too, are cases for which the Grand Jury found no True Bill, and which therefore never went for trial. This leaves 350 cases for analysis, 263 larceny and 87 non-larceny.

17. Larceny cases made up 70-80 per cent of all indictable offences tried — see ch.5.

18. See the examples cited below, pp.121-2, in which the Chillington Association for the Prosecution of Felons felt it unnecessary to employ a solicitor and barrister for the prosecution of two straightforward cases of theft of hay and coal.

19. Tobias, *Crime*, p.267.

20. Maitland, *Justice and Police*, p.86.

21. H. Pelling, *Popular Politics and Society in Late Victorian Britain* (London 1968), p.63; R.M. Jackson, *The Machinery of Justice in England* (Cambridge 1964), p.276; W.R. Cornish, *The Jury* (Pelican edn., Harmondsworth 1970), pp.25-8.

22. Maitland, *Justice and Police*, p.166.

23. List of jurors and their occupations for the petty juries at Staffs. QS Mich. 1836 (SRO Q/SB. 24).

24. Lists of Grand Jurors and their occupations for Staffs. QS Mich. 1836 (SRO Q/SBm 24), E. Adj. 1845 *(SA* 15 March 1845), Ea. 1851 *(SA* 12 April 1851), M. 1851 *(SA* 5 July 1851), M. Adj. 1851 *(SA* 26 July 1851).

25. Jackson, *Enforcing*, p.100; Abel-Smith and Stevens, *Lawyers*, p.150; J.F. Stephen, *A History of the Criminal Law in England* (London 1883, reprinted by Burt Franklin, New York) 3 vols., vol.1, p.441.

26. Hill, *Repression of Crime*, pp.5, 19; *SC on Public Prosecutors* (1st Report) (1855), pp.21, 172, 221; (2nd Report), P.P. 1856, VII (206), pp.347-84.

27. Stephen, *History*, vol.1, pp.303-4.

28. See e.g. the case of David Martin, in *SA* 1 July 1848, report of QS.

29. *SA* 16 January 1847, report of QS.

30. *SA* 11 March 1837, report of QS; 2 July 1842, report of QS; 9 April 1842, report of QS; 19 March 1836, report of Ass.

31. See, for an example of a failure of the prosecutor to turn up, the case of Sarah Charles *(SA* 9 January 1836, report of QS), and for failure of witnesses

to turn up, the case of Anthony Moran *(SA* 1 July 1848, report of QS).

32. Stephen, *History,* vol.1, pp.283-6; Tobias, *Crime,* p.266; Charge to Grand Jury, *SA* 18 October 1851.

33. E. Melling (ed.), *Kentish Sources, vol. VI: Crime and Punishment* (Maidstone 1969). For more detail on this point, see Appendix II.

34. Maitland, *Justice and Police,* p.171. Occasionally the High Court could grant a new trial for a misdemeanour, but not for a felony. Very rarely, an appeal could be made to the Court of Appeal and House of Lords on the grounds of 'error apparent on the record', but these were only in exceptional cases, involving important issues of law, and would require vast sums of money for legal expenses; besides, such an appeal could only be made on a technical point of procedure, not on the question of verdict or sentence.

35. Discretion to record sentences of death instead of pronouncing them was given to judges by the Judgement of Death Act 1823 (4 Geo. IV, c. 48) (Radzinowicz, *History,* vol.4, p.342).

36. *SA* 22 March 1851, report of Ass.

37. A. de Tocqueville, *Journeys to England and Ireland* (1835; ed. J.P. Mayer, London 1958), p.63.

38. See e.g. *SC on the State of the Police of the Metropolis* (2nd Report) P.P. 1817, VII (484), pp.321-562; *SC on Criminal Commitments* (2nd Report) (1828); *SC on Public Prosecutors* 1st Report (1855) and 2nd Report (1856); and scattered evidence relating to Black Country cases in newspaper reports of trials and statements of magistrates and police officers.

39. This point was especially stressed by tradesmen giving evidence to the *SC on Criminal Laws* (1819).

40. The total expenses involved in a prosecution are well set out in *RC on County Rates* (1836), pp.15-17.

41. For a detailed description of the operation of these rewards 'to which the odious appellation of Blood-money has been given', see *SC on Police of Metropolis* (2nd Report) (1817), from which this quotation comes, p.323, and Radzinowicz, *History,* vol.2, pp.33-163.

42. *SC on Police of Metropolis* (2nd Report) (1817), p.325.

43. These stages by which the law on reimbursement was changed are set out in *RC on County Rates* (1836), pp.5-6; see also Radzinowicz, *History,* vol.1, p.573, vol.2, pp.76-8, vol.3, p.82, vol.4, pp.224-6.

44. *RC on County Rates* (1836), pp.12-13, 45, 61, 165, 167, 170, 177, 188, 206-8, 211; *RC on Constabulary Force* (1839), pp.89-109; *SC on Police* (2nd Report) (1853), p.228.

45. MWWC Report of Wolverhampton Watch Committee to Borough Council (December 1857) incorporating printed Returns by Chief Constable for July-December 1856 and 1857. (Italics added).

46. *RC on County Rates* (1836), pp.44, 61, 177. See also *SC on Police* (2nd Report) (1853), p.270. *RC on Constabulary Force* (1839) which drew on the evidence given to the Commissioners on County Rates, put it thus: [The victim of an offence] who has already suffered loss, having in prospect the trouble of a pursuit and a trial (for which the usual allowance of expenses will frequently compensate very inadequately the pecuniary loss by attendances) — having moreover, as a consequence of giving information, the prospect of the certain loss of any chance of the recovery of the property stolen, will not, for the bare satisfaction of rendering service to the public, which has failed to protect him, willingly incur these additions to the inconvenience already sustained. (p.97.)

47. e.g. John Hall brought a prosecution against his sister and her lover for theft of £7 from his box; but at the trial he 'appeared to have a very accommodating

memory, as he recollected very little of the matter. The consequence was that the prisoners were acquitted and the Court refused to allow the prosecutor his expenses'. *(SA* 5 July 1851, report of QS).

48. Hill, *Repression of Crime,* p.5; *RC on County Rates* (1836); *SC on Criminal Commitments* (1828); *SC on Public Prosecutors* (1st and 2nd Reports) (1855 and 1856).

49. *RC on Constabulary Force* (1839), p.99.

50. *SC on Public Prosecutors* (1st and 2nd Reports) (1855 and 1856). The reports contain a particularly large amount of information on the system operating in Staffs., which was singled out for criticism of its prosecution practices.

51. Ibid. (2nd Report), p.349.

52. Ibid. (1st Report), p.19.

53. Ibid., p.39; see also the evidence of Captain Hatton, Chief Constable of Staffs. pp.115-18, 123; James Hemp, pp.88-92; J.H. Preston, pp.106-14.

54. The best list of such associations is the table in the Appendix to the County Rates Report, which lists all associations in existence between 1832 and 1836; even this probably *under*estimates their numbers, since it does not include, for example, the Chillington Association, established in the 1820s and active until 1859 *(RC on County Rates,* Appendix C, pp.37a-45a); *RC on Constabulary Force* (1839), p.97.

55. This list is only partial, and is compiled from the table in the *RC on County Rates,* local directories, local newspapers and local histories.

56. In the following discussion of associations, the Chillington minutes (SRO D590/741) are the chief source, supplemented by the information on associations in the Parliamentary Papers and in miscellaneous local sources.

57. The same close co-operation was used in the parts of Kesteven in Lincolnshire, which also relied on parish constables and local associations for detection and apprehension of offenders *(SC on Police* (2nd Report) (1853), p.234.)

58. SRO D590/741 – Accounts for year ending April 1830; reports of Committee Meeting 30 April 1849 and Annual General Meeting 22 May 1849 (italics added to the quotation).

59. *RC on County Rates* (1836), Appendix C, pp.37a-45a. For 1830-4, the Wednesbury Association brought two prosecutions at Assizes and four at Quarter Sessions; for the Assize prosecutions they received £32 in allowance, and paid out another £38; for the Sessions prosecutions they received £18 and paid out another £39.

60. Ibid., p.47.

61. SRO D590/741; *RC on County Rates,* Appendix C, pp.42a-43a.

62. Ibid., p.47; *RC on Constabulary Force* (1839), p.97.

63. *SC on Police* (2nd Report) (1853), pp.233-41, quotation p.240.

64. These offences are discussed in detail in chs. 6, 7 and 8.

65. This point is discussed in the discussion of larcenies in ch.6.

66. See Tobias, *Crime,* p.262.

67. Thompson, *Making of the English Working Class,* pp.64, 66. See also his article '"Rough Music": Le Charivari Anglais', *Annales: Economies, Sociétés, Civilisations* (mars-avril 1972), pp.285-312.

68. There is much material illustrating this point in Freeman, *Stories and Sketches.* See also the 'Old Potter's' *My Life as a Child.*

69. See the Industrial Thefts section, ch.6.

70. *SC on Criminal Commitments* (1828), p.422. G.R. Porter similarly pointed out that much of the apparent increase in crime was due to an increase in official action taken to deal with crime – in former periods, the offences existed but were not formally punished by law: 'The pickpocket, for example, who should be detected in the commission of his offence, was dragged by the mob to the nearest pump, half drowned, and then allowed to depart' *(Progress*

of the Nation, p.641).

71. See evidence of Captain Hatton to *SC on Public Prosecutors* (1st Report) (1855), pp.115-18.

72. Ibid., pp.38-9, 106-14, 115-18.

73. In a sample of thirty Black Country prosecutions in the standard returns made to the Chief Constable in 1862, only seven are brought by policemen and twenty-three by private individuals (SRO Q/APr 8). But these returns are evidence of an increasing concern on the part of the police to be kept informed of all prosecutions and to exert some control over them. These returns had been made regularly since the 1840s *(SC on Public Prosecutors* (1st Report) (1855), p.116).

74. *SA* 4 January 1851, report of QS.

75. Evidence and recommendations on these points are most fully set out in the Report and Minutes of Evidence of the *SC on Criminal Commitments and Convictions* (2nd Report) (1828) – see *passim.* and especially the recommendations, pp.427-31, and the evidence of Sir John Eardley Wilmot, pp.444-9. See also *RC on County Rates* (1836), pp.66-70, 193, 200, 202, 216-19. The Chairman of Staffs. QS repeatedly called, in his Grand Jury Charges, for legislation to allow such offences to be tried summarily – see the Charges reported in *SA* 9 January 1836, 12 March 1836, 4 January 1845, 1 July 1848, 5 July 1851.

76. This table is compiled from the sources listed in Appendix I. Only the Staffs. part of the Black Country is used here, because only the Staffs. records for the CJA and JOA convictions are available. Extensive work among the individual CJA and JOA cases confirms that they are exactly the same sort of offence which, before the passage of these Acts, was being tried at Sessions and Assizes; there is no change in the *quality or nature* of the offences being prosecuted – only in their *quantity.*

77. *RC on County Rates* (1836), p.217.

78. *SC on Criminal Commitments* (1828), p.422; see also Porter, *Progress of the Nation,* pp.641-3.

5 THE OFFENDERS — NUMBERS, TRENDS AND CHARACTERISTICS

In the case of the whole kingdom, however, and especially of the [manufacturing and mining] districts above pointed out, it would appear that a rapid progress in material civilization, without a proportionate moral advancement, has thrown new and more frequent incentives to disorder among the people at large, which produce their worst effects on the recoil of each wave of industrial prosperity, amidst those classes whose moral ties to the existing framework of society are feeblest and least felt and understood, and to many to whom socialism or any other destructive theory would appear as consistent with their well-being, as the most cherished axioms of political science, or even the words of Christian truth itself.
(Joseph Fletcher, 'Moral and Educational Statistics of England and Wales', *JSSL*, 12 (1849), p.171.)

We can now examine the Black Country figures of committals to trial, bearing in mind that the last three chapters have shown the need for caution in interpreting these figures.[1]

The first point which emerges clearly is that the committals were overwhelmingly for offences against property (see Table 16). Taking the period 1835-60 as a whole, nearly 80 per cent of the committals were for larcenies of some sort; in any given year during that period, the lowest to which the percentage of larcenies falls is 63.2 per cent (in 1835), and it rises as high as 87.8 per cent (in 1857). This is similar to the modern situation where larcenies still comprise nearly three-quarters of all indictable offences.[2]

Other property offences — those committed with violence, plus receiving and embezzlement — comprised another 8 per cent. Offences against property with violence reached their peak in 1843 when they made up 10.1 per cent of total Black Country committals. The fraud and forgery group were 3.8 per cent over the period as a whole; their peak was 6.7 per cent in 1853.

Offences against the person (homicides, assaults, sexual offences) reached their highest percentage (9.4 per cent) in 1852. Committals for public order offences naturally fluctuated markedly from year to

Table 16   Total Committals to Trial for Indictable Offences, for the Black Country 1835-60, Divided into Categories of Offence[3]

	Offence Category	No.	Percentage
(1)	Larceny	17,410	78.9
(2)	Offences against property committed with violence (robbery, housebreaking)	1,216	5.5
(3)	Receiving stolen goods	343	1.6
(4)	Embezzlement	230	1.0
(5)	Fraud, forgery, currency offences	841	3.8
(6)	Offences against the person	1,225	5.6
(7)	Riot and public order offences	598	2.7
(8)	Malicious damage or injury	75	0.3
(9)	Other	134	0.6
TOTAL		22,072	100.0

year; in 1842, that year of great distress and disturbance, they soared to 14.4 per cent of the total. Malicious damage and miscellaneous offences were always a minute proportion.

The trends in committals for the five largest categories of offence[4] can be graphed. To control the effect of the increase of population, the committals for each year are expressed as a ratio per 100,000 of the population of the area for that year.[5] (Figure 1 (a) and (b) — these are on different scales because the total committals and the larceny committals are of an overwhelmingly greater magnitude than the other categories.)

What can we make of these trends in committals? We cannot assume that any increase automatically reflects an increase in unlawful acts committed. But we can try to isolate the effect of administrative factors on these figures. If the introduction of a police force has an effect, it is likely to be to cause an increase in the figures over the early years of the force, as more arrests are made. In the longer term, it might be expected to cause a decrease in committals, but this could only come after the force had become established as an efficient agency at preventing crime — which was not the case with the Black Country forces for most of our period. So we could expect the effect, if any, of the establishment of the police to lie in the direction of increasing the committal figures. Similarly, the changes in prosecution discussed in the last chapter could be expected to produce only a steady increase

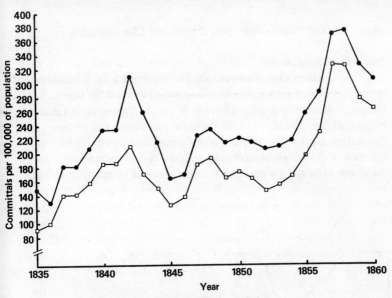

Fig. I (a) Black Country committals to trial 1835–1860, expressed as a ratio per 100,000 of population.

- ● Total committals per 100,000 of population
- □ Larceny committals per 100,000 of population

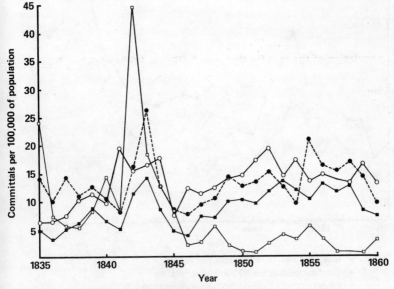

- ○ Offences against the person
- ● Offences against property with violence
- ■ Fraud, forgery and currency offences
- □ Riots and public order

Fig. I (b) Black Country committals to trial 1835–1860, expressed as a ratio per 100,000 of population.

over a fairly long period.

These administrative factors cannot be responsible for a decrease in the figures; nor for short-term changes such as a sudden sharp increase followed by a sharp decrease. When the figures show a pattern of cyclical fluctuation — as with the total committals and larceny committals until 1849 — we can make some cautious inferences from the trends. These figures have been graphed against an index of economic activity[6] for the Black Country for our period (Figure 2).

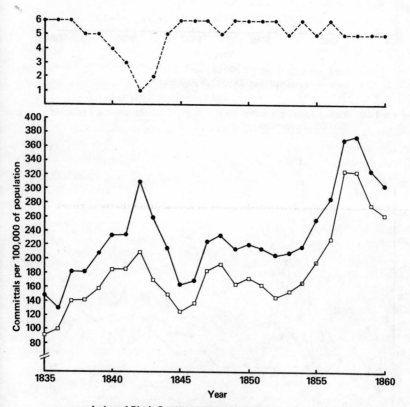

- Index of Black Country economic activity
- Total committals per 100,000 of population
- Larceny committals per 100,000 of population

Fig. 2   Black Country committal rates 1835-1860.

The graph falls into two periods, showing different patterns of correlation: (1) 1835-49; (2) 1850-60.

(1) 1835-49

For this period, we see a clear tendency towards an inverse correlation of economic activity and crime committals. This is particularly marked between 1837 and 1845. As the economy moved down into the depression of 1840-3, so the committal figures moved upwards. The depression reached its trough in 1842, the year in which unemployment was at its worst and when the Black Country was racked by strikes and disturbances; in the same year, the committal figures reached their peak. As economic activity moved upward again to full employment by 1845, so the committal figures declined. With the depression of 1848, the committal figures again move up to a peak and then decline as prosperity returns.

How much does this tell us about trends in illegal acts in these years? This cycle could not be produced by administrative factors, such as the police or prosecution procedures. It must represent (albeit at some remove)[7] an actual fluctuation in these years in the number of crimes committed, especially of property thefts which make up 80 per cent of the total.

This pattern of increases and decreases over this period might conceivably not reflect fluctuations in crimes being committed, but be due to a greater and lesser willingness of prosecutors to prosecute — if property owners were particularly strict in prosecuting thefts in times of depression, but less so in times of prosperity. What evidence is there on this point?

There is evidence that some of the large coal and iron masters favoured a tough policy on prosecution during the 1842 depression and strikes; but this applies mainly to protecting their works against strikers and rioters, not to prosecuting thefts.[8] On the other hand, the forces of authority (constables, troops, special constables) were directed by the county magistrates (who were then predominantly landed gentry and not coal and iron masters); they found their resources barely adequate in 1842 to cope with the strikes and riots, let alone to set out deliberately to arrest and prosecute more property offenders than usual.[9] Many magistrates and landowners seem to have taken the view that in times of 'distress' and disorder, the authorities should look *more* leniently than usual on small property offences.

So changes in strictness of prosecution alone cannot explain the cyclical pattern of committals correlated with the level of economic

activity. The pattern seems to show that property offences did increase
in times of distress. This suggests that at least some of those who stole
did so, not as a regular practice, but for occasional relief in times of
hardship. This adds some support, at a local level, for the conclusions
reached by Macnab and by Gatrell and Hadden in their national studies;
and goes against Tobias's view that 'there is little ground to think that
the immediate pressure of want was a major cause of adult crime, or
that cyclical changes in this pressure altered its level'.[10]

(2) 1850-60

For the years 1850-60, however, the pattern has clearly changed; there
is no longer a visible correlation between the committals and the
economic index. The dip in the economic index may explain some of
the climb in committals for 1852-4; but how can one explain the steady
steep climb in committals after 1854, to a peak in 1858 and levels in
1859 and 1860 which are higher than all previous levels except 1842?

There is no economic explanation for this dramatic rise, nor other
social factors at this time which could account for it; nor do
contemporary writings suggest any feeling that the community was
subjected to a sudden increase in offences at this point. The rise is, in
fact, simply a rise in the *number of prosecutions brought,* not in the
number of illegal acts being committed – it reflects the effect,
discussed in the last chapter, of the Juvenile Offenders Acts (JOA) of
1847 and 1850 and, much more important, of the Criminal Justice Act
(CJA) of 1855. As that discussion brought out, the great increase in
prosecutions was due to the greater ease and convenience of prosecution
established by these Acts.

The fact that such a marked rise in committals could come about
as the result of a change in the prosecution procedure rather than in
the level of illegal activity, emphasises the need for caution in
interpreting the relationship of the numbers of committals to the
number of illegal acts. When the number of committals fluctuates
sharply, as with the figures for 1835-49, it is reasonable to interpret
the movement of the figures and the direction of that movement as
reflecting movement in the level of acts committed (in the absence of
evidence of other factors which could account for these movements);
but it would be unwise to see the *numbers* of committals as telling
much about the actual *numbers* of illegal acts. The figures are useful as
indicating *trends,* in illegal acts, or in the practices of prosecutors, or in
some other factor, as the particular circumstances may indicate; but
they are at a considerable remove from the actual numbers of offences

committed.

The figures, then, show us a picture of 'official crime' which rose from 150 committals per 100,000 of population in 1835, to a peak of 375 committals per 100,000 in 1858. The increase is of two sorts: a short-term increase, presumably reflecting an actual increase in illegal acts in bad economic years, which disappears in the good years; and a long-term increase attributable to changes in the system of prosecution and trial. The years 1836 (good economic year) and 1842 (bad economic year) were picked for detailed study of the individual cases from the depositions, recognisances and newspaper reports; in addition, selected Sessions and Assizes from 1847, 1848, 1851, 1855 and 1858 have been taken for detailed study from newspaper reports and recognisances;[11] these sources are drawn upon in the next three chapters for the study of particular offences. These show that it is only the offences of larceny and riot that are significantly affected in numbers by the year and the economic conditions. With the other offences, the sorts and number (proportional to population) of unlawful acts do not alter significantly from year to year.

The next three chapters look in detail at the different categories of offence, and the circumstances and people involved in them. In the remainder of this chapter, the general characteristics of all the people committed to trial, the offences for which they were tried, and how they were disposed of, are discussed.

The Offenders

(1) Sex

In all, 22,074 persons from the Black Country were tried for indictable offences; of these, 16,407 were male and 5,667 female (Table 17).

As one might expect, the proportion of female accused is highest for larceny, receiving stolen goods, and fraud and currency offences — acts which require no physical strength for their commission — and lowest for those involving force or violence. (The tiny female proportion of those accused of embezzlement presumably reflects the fact that females were unlikely to be appointed to the positions of trust from which embezzlement was possible.)

In general, Table 17 shows that men were committed to trial in a ratio of 3 to 1 over women. It also shows that 90 per cent of the female committals were for larceny. In fact, the more minor the larceny, the greater seems to have been the proportion of female participation — the figures for convictions under the Criminal Justice

Table 17   Black Country Committals to Trial 1835-60, Divided
According to Category of Offence and Sex of the Accused

Offence Category	Male		Female		Total	
	No.	%	No.	%	No.	%
Larceny	12,329	70.8	5,081	29.2	17,410	100
Receiving stolen goods	234	68.2	109	31.8	343	100
Embezzlement	223	97.0	7	3.0	230	100
Fraud, forgery, currency offences	672	79.9	169	20.1	841	100
Offences against property with violence	1,142	93.8	75	6.2	1,217	100
Offences against the person	1,090	88.9	136	11.1	1,226	100
Riot and public order offences	540	90.3	58	9.7	598	100
Malicious damage	72	96.0	3	4.0	75	100
Other	105	78.4	29	21.6	134	100
TOTAL	16,407	74.3	5,667	25.7	22,074	100

Act (minor larcenies only) for 1855-60 show that 35 per cent were female.

This general male-female ratio of 3:1 is of interest, differing markedly from the situation today, where this sex ratio in indictable offences is about 7:1[12] Why there is this marked difference in male and female rates at all is 'one of the unsolved mysteries of criminology'[13] and very little has been written which seriously approaches this topic.[14] The best explanation would seem to involve the difference in strength and skills between males and females, and the different roles which males and females perform in our society; men, being the breadwinners, have more economic pressure on them to break the law, and more opportunity to do so, in their daily life and work outside the home. But one still has to explain why there has been a change from the nineteenth century to the present day. It is not conceivable that this is due to any change in the respective strengths of males and females.

Perhaps the change has come in the economic pressure on women. The economic situation of women trying to run a household in mid-nineteenth century England could often be a desperate one, with no form of welfare assistance available except the New Poor Law. This

would be particularly the case with widows and single women who,
if they could not find employment and wanted to avoid the workhouse,
might try theft as an alternative. Certainly, most female offences were
larcenies – the category of crime most obviously associated with
economic distress. On the other hand, graphing the male and female
larceny committals for 1835-49 separately against the economic index
shows a very clear inverse correlation for the male committals, but no
clear link with the economic conditions for the female committals.
This point must be left inconclusive.

And one must not forget that women also figured in some quantity
in offences other than larceny, as Table 17 shows. Some types of
theft – for example, by prostitutes from their clients – were entirely
a female domain; and in some types of robbery, the female acted as
bait to lure men into situations where they could be robbed by a male
accomplice. Where women were involved in robberies or assaults, they
do not seem to have been notably less violent or more pacific than their
male accomplices, though they did lack the male crude physical strength.
Some contemporaries claimed to discern, with horror, the emergence
in the large towns of a breed of aggressive, violent, drunken, lawless
women, as prone as their menfolk to crime and disorder. The
Irishwoman in an English town, it was said, would be found alongside
the Irishmen in communal brawls and crowd assaults on the police. An
episode in Walsall in 1859 shows some of this:

> Four Irish men and two women, who had been creating a disturbance
> in a lane, were ordered by the Police to leave. They refused, swearing
> at the Police, and one woman called on the others to 'fetch pokers
> to split the b——s skulls'. Pokers were fetched, and two policemen
> injured. Police reinforcements came, but the Irish retreated to a
> house which they barred. The Police broke into it, but were there
> attacked by 20-30 Irish men and women, armed with colliers' pikes,
> fire-irons, bludgeons and candlesticks. Three more policemen were
> injured, and they had to retreat again. When they finally returned
> with a stronger force, only the woman who had called for the pokers
> was there, and she was arrested, but the rest could not be found.[15]

This episode is fairly typical of the urban brawl or riot of that period,
and reminds us of a side of female crime which must not be overlooked.

Nineteenth-century commentators on crime drew attention to this
differing sex ratio in crime, mostly because they were disturbed that
the female rate was as high as 1:3 to the male crime rate; this was seen

as a product of 'the collection of large masses of population in crowded cities' and of female industrial labour, since the female crime rate was higher in cities and industrial areas than in agricultural areas; and female criminals, though fewer in number than male, were regarded as morally worse and more hardened criminals than the men.[16] A late nineteenth-century commentator saw women's lower crime rate as springing from the fact that:

> they are better morally. . .the duties of maternity have perpetually kept alive a certain number of unselfish instincts; these instincts have become part and parcel of woman's natural inheritance, and, as a result of possessing them to a larger extent than man, she is less disposed to crime. . .[Another important cause is their] want of physical power.
> . . .The proportion of female crime in a community is also to a very considerable extent determined by the social condition of women. In all countries where social habits and customs constrain women to lead retiring and secluded lives the number of female criminals descends to a minimum. . .On the other hand, in all countries where women are accustomed to share largely the active work of life with men, female crime has a distinct tendency to reach its maximum. . . The more women are driven to enter upon the economic struggle for life the more criminal they will become.

And he went on to suggest that as female emancipation, from their traditional role caring for the home and children, increased, so female crime would increase.[17] Certainly, most Black Country girls worked from the age of nine, which may have contributed to their higher crime rate. But growing female employment and emancipation in the twentieth century do not seem to have necessarily led to growing female crime.[18]

The female contribution to specific offences will be dealt with in the following chapters. But it should be noted here that female larcenies were not limited to shoplifting. Women were prominent in stealing items of clothing and food from shops and stalls; but were also prominent in taking articles from houses (usually done by domestic servants), and in thefts from the person; and they actually *outnumbered* the men in the people charged with thefts of coal from collieries.

The next three categories to be discussed, concern information listed in the calendars about the age, degree of education and occupation of each offender. These raise the question of how reliable the evaluation and recording of such information was likely to be, and how much weight can be placed on conclusions based on such information. Gatrell and Hadden warn that this information is 'probably the least reliable material in the official records. The standards and methods of classification on the part of prison officials and police were quite unsystematic, and in some cases there is no guarantee that they did not vary both regionally and over a period of years'.[19] However, they were considering the *national* totals listed in the criminal tables, over a long period of time. The problem with a regional study, over a shorter period of time, is much less – there are many opportunities to check the accuracy of the information against details available on individual cases, and the problem of regional variation in the classification does not apply. Even if the information is shown to be imperfect, it may still, if handled with sufficient care, be used to give approximate patterns of what the situation was.

The Black Country material, when tested in this way, appears adequate to allow general statements to be made on the basis of that material. The proportions occupied by each category from year to year do not vary much, and there are no sudden sharp increases or decreases; this suggests that the classification did not alter significantly from year to year, and that roughly the same methods of classification were being used over the whole period. The facts of individual cases, as reported in depositions or newspapers, tally with their classifications as listed in the calendars. However, there are differences in the possible adequacy of each of the categories and each should be discussed separately.

Age. Tobias claims that the age listings are unreliable because compulsory registration of births was not introduced until 1836, and there would therefore be no way of checking an offender's age. The authorities would be dependent on the accused giving his own age correctly, and, Tobias claims, 'prisoners would overstate or understate their age' in order to gain advantages for themselves.[20]

But this does not mean that the figures are useless; even if ages were misstated on a large scale, it is unlikely that the prisoner would claim for himself more than a few years either side of his real age – one would not find a thirty-five-year-old claiming to be fifteen, nor a twelve-year-old to be twenty-five; his appearance would belie the claim. The greatest effect that this could have in a table analysing age groups of a large number of offenders over several years would be to push the totals to slightly higher or slightly lower age groups than was in fact the case. Since it is hard to see what advantage the average offender might expect to gain by claiming that he was *older* than he really was (except in the age group over fifty, which was a very small proportion), the chances are that this would, if anything, push the totals to slightly lower age groups and increase the number recorded as juveniles (since they might hope for more lenient treatment as juveniles). But the ages recorded for the Black Country accused seem to have been consistent; cases followed up in which an individual appeared in court on a number of occasions over a period of years show that the age claimed on each occasion was consistent with the age claimed at the other appearances. And the newspapers regularly recorded their impression of the accused's age from his appearance and this generally coincides with the age given in the calendar. We can conclude that the age figures can be used, at least in tables which give a broad outline of the age structure of offenders, though not for highly detailed statistical analysis; at worst, the age tables can be expected to show a slightly lower age structure than was in fact the case and to overstate the proportion of juvenile offenders.

Degree of education. This classification was made by the prison chaplains and its adequacy may well have varied over time and between different prisons. But the categories used for classification are sufficiently large and loose for it to be unlikely that there was serious distortion of the true position in the results obtained. Once again, they can be used to give a general outline of the situation.

Occupation. This is perhaps the most difficult of the categories to use but potentially one of the most useful. Gatrell and Hadden state that

> the least reliable material of this kind relates to prisoners' occupations. . .The Criminal Registrar himself pointed out in 1857 that 'as it would be desirous (for prisoners) to claim some honest employment, the numbers classed as in employment would probably be overstated'.

And Tobias claims that

> a new arrival in prison would describe himself as of whatever occupation was most convenient for the particular prison. Many would declare themselves to be painters in order to have a chance of the most favoured work.[21]

Obviously, there is some validity in these points and a professional criminal would be unlikely to give that as his occupation or to say that he had no occupation.

However, once again, this sort of material is more easily checked in a local than a national study. In many of the Black Country cases the evidence, as reported in the newspapers, bears out the accused's claim about his occupation. There was a very large number of cases of industrial theft — in these the evidence of both prosecution and defence witnesses made it clear that the accused worked as an employee in the particular colliery, factory, workshop, etc. There were many cases of theft or robbery which followed on from a group of men drinking together and in these cases the prosecutor would often testify that the man, or men, who robbed him were workmates of his. The accused often called as a witness to his character his employer, who would testify to the job held by the accused. Where the accused's occupation is mentioned in a deposition or newspaper report and can be checked against a calendar listing of his occupation, the results tally reasonably well in most cases.

However, this does not mean that everyone who was tried for an offence was employed at the time he committed the offence, nor that the description of the occupation is always precise and fully accurate. Many described their occupations as 'labourer' — a very general category and one which does not preclude the possibility that the man concerned had simply taken on a few casual labouring jobs on some occasions, without it being his regular occupation.

But even if one could successfully pretend to be a labourer, it would have been more difficult for an offender from one of the smaller Black Country towns with their close-knit communities, falsely to pose as a miner at his preliminary examination, when it would be well known to most people in the town which people were, and were not, miners; much the same would apply to people claiming to be ironworkers, nailers, boatmen, etc.

These are the predominant categories of offenders who emerge from the Black Country — labourers, miners, nailers, ironworkers, boatmen; even if Tobias is right in general terms, it is hard to see how claiming to be one of these occupations could be expected to *save* one from manual labour in prison — the reverse seems true. It can be taken as the case that most of the people claiming a certain occupation when appearing in court had at least practised, or did practise, that occupation for some time. And even if that amorphous category 'labourer' did contain a number of people who did not strictly deserve that occupational description because they hardly ever worked at a job, it none the less gives an idea of the social class from which they come. Used in fairly broad, general categories, over fairly long periods of time, the occupation data can be useful in conveying the approximate proportions occupied by particular occupational and social groups among the offenders.

The general conclusion then, is that these data on offenders are imperfect and not sufficiently 'hard' to merit detailed and minute analysis; but that, within reasonable limits, they convey useful and usable information about the offenders.

(2) Education

One view commonly held by those concerned with crime and the law in the nineteenth century was that crime was a product of the lack of education and could best be checked in its growth by the spread of education. Time and again this view was expressed by judges, magistrates, prison chaplains, law reformers, statistical investigators and educational reformers. For instance, Baron Watson concluded an address to the Worcestershire Grand Jury by urging his hearers to promote 'education among their poorer neighbours', which would help to check the high crime rate in the Dudley area since it would 'result in elevating the people of Dudley to be an honest, industrious and respectable class'.[22]

In this remark Watson was simply echoing what had become a common view from the 1820s onwards, articulated very forcefully by those who espoused this cause. Proponents of wider provision of education took it up strongly, not least because it provided an answer to those who objected to increased education on the grounds of expense; if it could be shown that increasing education diminished crime, it could be said that it actually saved the country money. For instance, Joseph Bentley, who was employed by Pigot & Sons in compiling their commercial directories, investigated the Manchester Sunday schools in 1833 and became interested in the connection between crime and lack of education; in 1838 he published *The State of Education Contrasted with the State of Crime,* and in 1842, *Education as It Is, Ought to Be and Might Be.* So concerned was he with this topic that when he compiled and published his monumental six-volume directory for Worcestershire, between 1840 and 1842, he added a seventh volume containing

> such an account of the State of Education and Crime as was never
> before compiled for any district, in any age or country,

in which he purported to show that crime was least in those areas of
Worcestershire with the highest number of schools per head of
population, and greatest in those with the lowest ratio of schools to
people.[23]

It was with a view to testing this sort of thesis that the statistical
investigator, G.R. Porter, successfully induced the Home Office to
collect statistics on this point; from 1835 the degree of instruction of
every accused person was to be listed in the Calendar of persons for
trial. At first this was listed on a tripartite scale: those who could
neither read nor write, those who could read only; and those who
could read and write. This was felt to be too clumsy and was changed
in 1836 into: neither read nor write; read and write imperfectly; read
and write well; and those who had received a superior degree of
education. And this was eventually broadened to a five-point scale:
neither read nor write; read only; read and write imperfectly; read and
write well; and superior education. This information is therefore
available in the Calendars and the Home Office tables from 1835
onwards. The 1835 scale is probably too crude to be used; and the
1836 assessment was apparently unreliable because those responsible
were not yet used to carrying out the assessments;[24] but the information
can be used for 1837 onwards and it has been compiled for those
committed to trial in the Black Country between 1837 and 1855[25]
(see Table 18).

The investigators of the Statistical Society of London eagerly took
up these figures, and claimed that their early investigations confirmed
their thesis that education tended to repress crime, while its absence
tended to encourage it; G.R. Porter was in no doubt about it, and
flatly stated:

> The most cursory glance at these figures must carry conviction to
> every mind that instruction has power to restrain men from the
> commission of crimes.[26]

A number of the other early statistical investigators suggested the same conclusion.[27] But more detailed investigations during the 1840s, as the figures of crime both increased and decreased, would not sustain the simple thesis that education, at any rate as measured by the test of mere literacy, was the key factor controlling the amount of crime committed.[28]

However, this did not daunt those advancing the view that education was the answer to the crime rate, since they had always maintained that education meant far more than mere literacy and involved a sound inculcation of religion. Baron Gurney, addressing a Staffordshire Grand Jury in 1840, urged them to do what they could to prevent crime by helping to provide more education for the young of the working class,

> not merely to teach them to read and write, for education falls far short of its purpose when it includes those objects only; but to give them a good moral, and more important still, a sound religious education; to teach them their duty to society and above all, their duty to God.[29]

R.W. Rawson distinguished education from mere instruction:

> Education may be said to consist of that moral, combined with intellectual, training, by which the mind is taught to discern, and the heart is led to feel, the great object for which man is created, and the duties which he is called upon to fulfil in this stage of his existence. Instruction, in its broadest and complete sense, is merely the intellectual training, by means of which the mind acquires the power of discerning and correctly appreciating things and persons, and the faculty of reasoning upon the facts observed. There is, also, a narrower meaning frequently ascribed to the term 'instruction' by which it is limited to an initiation in the arts of reading and writing etc. It is obvious that in either of these senses instruction is insufficient of itself to repress criminal passions, which are not the result of any action of the mind, but spring from the secret impulses of the heart. . .Religion is the only sound basis of education.[30]

This view that the aim of any useful education must be the instilling of sound Christian principles underlay the proposals of all the investigators, reformers, magistrates, judges and prison chaplains who considered education in relation to crime. So Joseph Fletcher, the most thorough investigator of the relationship between crime and education through the official statistics, was able to advance intact the thesis that education tended to repress crime, even when his figures failed to show the expected relationship between literacy and crime; he accounted for this by stating that education varied in quality, and where literacy was instilled without it leading to 'Christian knowledge and advancement', this would not have the good effect of 'education' in repressing crime.[31] This offered an escape from inconvenient statistical conclusions; though it was not made clear how the amount of 'Christian knowledge and advancement' was to be measured, if it was still to be measured statistically and if the literacy figures were inadequate for this purpose.[32]

But most people who held this view did not need to convince themselves with this sort of sophistry. Certainly there seemed to be *prima facie* evidence in the figures themselves which showed the vast majority of the prison population to be illiterate or only barely literate in the 1840s and 1850s. Those who held this view were probably sincere in their advocacy of education as the remedy; but it is noticeable that they often put it forward in answer to the suggestion that crime might be caused by poverty or by fluctuations in employment and prosperity. This suggestion could be refuted by the assertion that lack of education and drinking were, in fact, the main causes of crime. This view was particularly put forward by prison chaplains, and was eagerly taken up by others.[33] It was used as an answer to those who charged that much crime was a product of the structure of society and could be diminished by social reforms; the answer was that the working class must be educated to a sound 'Christian knowledge' and acceptance of society as it stood. As Lord Chief Justice Tindal said in his charge to the Grand Jury at the Special Assize at which Staffordshire men were tried for their parts in the riots arising out of the Chartist-influenced strike of August-September 1842,

> the effectual, and only effectual, method of counteracting the attempts of wicked and designing men to undermine the principles

of the lower classes, and to render them discontented with the established institutions of their country, is the diffusion of sound religious knowledge (in which there can be no excess) amongst those classes who are the most exposed to their attempts.[34]

Tindal was here referring to a number of men being tried for 'political' offences rather than 'normal' crime, but his prescription is identical to that advanced as a cure for 'normal' crime. A sound Christian education would reconcile the working classes to the existing order, and work against all forms of disorder, whether Chartist-inspired subversion, strikes and riots, or 'normal' crime.

It has been a central contention of this study that nothing useful can be said about a monolithic entity labelled 'crime'; the same applies to the idea of 'education' as a remedy for 'crime'. However, it is of interest to list the literacy rating of Black Country people committed to trial, and to compare them with the information on the literacy of the Black Country population as a whole (Table 18).

This can be compared with Table 19 giving the available statistics on literacy in the Black Country in this period. These are derived from the figures given in the annual reports of the Registrar-General from 1839 onwards, taken from the marriage registers. From the 1750s onwards, it had been compulsory for all persons marrying to sign the

Table 18   Degree of Instruction of Those Committed for Trial from the Black Country 1837-55

| Years | (1) | (2) | (3) | (4) | (5) | |
	N	R only	RW Imp.	RW Well	Sup.	Total
1837	32.6	17.4	37.7	11.8	0.5	100.0
1838-40	33.9	26.7	28.4	10.5	0.5	100.0
1841-43	35.4	28.2	26.3	9.5	0.6	100.0
1844-46	39.3	30.7	21.8	7.5	0.7	100.0
1847-49	37.5	28.1	28.7	5.2	0.5	100.0
1850-52	40.0	28.0	26.1	5.1	0.8	100.0
1853-55	40.9	22.4	31.7	4.7	0.3	100.0

Above sub-columns (1)-(5) is the heading: Percentages

N = Neither read nor write;   R only = Read only;   RW Imp. = Read and Write Imperfectly;   RW Well = Read and Write Well;   Sup. = Superior Education register, and the Registrar-General collected the figures annually, showing what proportion of signatures was in writing and what proportion was signed with a mark. From these returns, rough tables of literacy for each area and the country as a whole could be constructed. The Registrar-General pointed out that the average age of people marrying was twenty-five, so this test would not show the state of literacy of children and young persons at that particular moment, but it would give an idea of the state of education about fifteen years before; nor does the test cover those people who did not marry formally. He also pointed out that a number of people who could write very badly might not attempt a proper signature, but take the simpler course of using a mark; on the other hand, a number of the signatures which did come in were of a very rough and clumsy nature, suggesting that those who signed were not very used to writing.[35] The figures do at least provide a useful guide to the relative states of literacy in various parts of the country, and to changes over time. Unfortunately, the figures are broken down into registration districts (giving the actual districts making up the Black Country) only for the years 1841-6, and from 1855 onwards; for the rest of the period, the information is given on a county basis only, and is therefore listed in Table 19 for Staffordshire and Worcestershire.

A number of points emerge from these two tables. Firstly, it is clear that both Staffordshire and Worcestershire throughout this period had

Table 19 Percentage of People Signing the Marriage Register with Marks 1838-58

Years	Black Country		Staffs.		Worcs.		England	
	Men	Women	Men	Women	Men	Women	Men	Women
June 1838-41	—	—	44.0	61.0	46.3	61.0	33.0	49.3
Jan.-Dec. 1841-43	51.8	67.9	41.4	57.7	43.8	57.7	32.5	48.5
1844-46	55.6	71.2	45.2	60.8	48.0	61.3		
1847-49	—	—	45.6	60.1	38.3	49.3		
1850-52	—	—	45.3	60.4	35.8	46.8		
1853-55	48.9	62.5	45.4	59.0	33.9	42.5	29.0	41.0
1856-58	49.4	62.0	43.2	55.6	33.8	40.3		

The figures were compiled for the year ending June, from 1838 to June 1841; from December 1841, they were compiled for the year ending December.

illiteracy rates (using this to refer only to people unable to write) for both men and women above the average rate for England as a whole. Furthermore, the Black Country area itself had illiteracy rates considerably higher still than those for the counties of Staffordshire and Worcestershire. This impression is borne out by the surveys which were done of education and the provision of schooling in the Black Country in the 1840s; these show that about half of the children of the Black Country working class had no schooling of any sort, and that there was a high degree of illiteracy and ignorance even among those who had received some teaching in a Sunday school or even a short period in a day school.[36] The Statistical Society investigators into West Bromwich education in 1837 interviewed the town's 2,193 working-class families who had children living with them; of these, 1,428 children were over the age of fourteen. These 1,428 were tested for literacy and it was found that:

> 27.2 per cent could read and write;
> 39.8 per cent could read only;
> 33.0 per cent could neither read nor write.

– an indication of a high degree of illiteracy among even the younger people of the town.[37]

Secondly, one can compare the degree of instruction of those committed for trial with the general standard of literacy in the area. Since the marriage register test is a test of being able to write one's name, people who could read but not write, or who could write very badly and with great difficulty, would be included in the 'illiterate' total of those signing with a mark. The comparable figure in Table 18 to put against this percentage would be a combination of columns (1) and (2) – those who can neither read nor write and those who can read only. This shows that there was a higher degree of illiteracy among those committed to trial than among the population as a whole (bearing in mind that three-quarters of the accused were male) – but not very much higher, even by the mid-1850s. The criminal offenders of the area were slightly less literate and less educated than the population of the area, but not very much less; certainly not enough to sustain the thesis that their delinquency was directly attributable to their want of adequate education. And if one takes the West Bromwich survey of 1837 (above) and compares it with the figures for 1837 in Table 18, one finds that 50 per cent of those sitting in gaol could read and write, whereas this was true of only 27 per cent of the West Bromwich children over the age of fourteen. Certainly, Table 18 shows that those tried for criminal offences in the Black Country were not a literate or well-educated lot; the percentage who could read and write well is small, and progressively diminishes from 1837 onwards; while the proportion with a superior education is minute. But then, they came predominantly from the working classes, in an area where the working classes were ill-provided with facilities for education.

(3) Age

Age was another factor which was felt to be a key to the criminal problem. From the early 1800s, concern was expressed about the rapid growth of juvenile crime within the general rise in crime figures, and about the need for special treatment for juvenile offenders to prevent them growing up into hardened criminals. This sort of concern led to the passing of the Juvenile Offenders Acts of 1847 and 1850 (allowing summary trial of minor larcenies committed by juveniles), and the institution in the 1850s of Reformatory schools (for juveniles sentenced to imprisonment) and Industrial schools (for children who had committed less serious offences or who lived in such circumstances as made it likely that they would become criminals).[38]

This study is not specifically concerned with juvenile delinquency and the treatment of juvenile offenders – for details on these issues, see the works cited by Tobias and Eade. But Table 20 sets out the age structure of those coming before the courts in the Black Country. This is done for the period 1835-55, since age figures are not available for those tried under the CJA after 1855, and the absence of this very large number of people from the analysis would distort it.

Table 20 shows that the peak age for offenders was the years 18-21, closely followed by 22-3; these six years between them provided 30-35 per cent of all the accused in each year. Ages 24-40 provided another 36-40 per cent. The term 'juvenile' in the nineteenth century technically referred to someone under the age of sixteen, and in this sense only between 6 per cent and 11 per cent of Black Country indictable offences was 'juvenile crime'; but 'juvenile' was also often used to refer to people up to the age of eighteen or even twenty, and in this sense a substantial proportion of Black Country indictable committals was for 'juvenile crime', the years 16-19 furnishing about 20 per cent. Note how the proportion of persons aged twelve or thirteen more than doubles after 1846; this shows the effect of the Juvenile Offenders Act of 1847 which allowed summary trial of persons under the age of fourteen charged with simple larceny, and which

Table 20   Ages of Those Committed to Trial in the Black Country
1835-55

	Percentages						
Age	1835-7	1838-40	1841-3	1844-6	1847-9	1850-2	1853-5
5-11	1.2	1.1	0.6	1.7	0.5	0.4	0.8
12, 13	1.8	2.7	1.5	2.6	5.7	5.4	4.3
14, 15	4.9	4.7	4.6	5.4	4.4	4.9	3.9
16, 17	8.0	8.5	8.2	8.0	8.4	7.6	6.7
18, 19	12.6	12.4	11.0	11.5	13.2	10.7	11.6
20, 21	13.5	12.0	10.7	11.2	9.8	11.4	11.0
22, 23	11.3	10.1	10.8	10.3	10.3	9.5	8.9
24, 25	8.2	9.4	8.5	7.3	8.0	8.1	7.1
26, 27	7.1	6.1	7.4	6.3	6.4	5.3	6.2
28, 29	5.7	4.4	5.6	5.1	4.5	4.9	5.7
30, 31	4.4	4.5	5.7	5.0	5.0	5.3	6.6
32, 33	2.8	3.1	3.5	4.1	3.8	3.7	3.1
34, 35	3.4	2.7	4.0	4.2	3.1	4.0	4.0
36-40	5.8	6.7	5.9	5.8	6.0	6.7	8.7
41-50	5.6	6.4	7.5	7.0	7.3	7.8	7.1
51-60	2.8	3.3	3.4	2.4	2.5	3.3	3.2
Over 60	0.9	1.9	1.1	2.1	1.1	1.0	1.1
Total	100.0	100.0	100.0	100.0	100.0	100.0	100.0
No.	1,134	1,676	2,374	1,735	2,197	2,164	2,369

Table 21   Age Distribution of Black Country Population of the Age
of Five and Over, 1851

Age	% of Population
5- 9	14.6
10-14	13.2
15-19	11.7
20-24	11.7
25-29	10.2
30-34	8.5
35-39	7.2
40-49	10.6
50-59	6.6
60 and over	5.7
TOTAL	100.0

Source: 1851 Census.

clearly stimulated increased prosecution of such offences (in the same way as the Criminal Justice Act did for all minor larcenies after 1855).

Table 20 can be compared with Table 21, setting out the age structure of the Black Country population. They are not directly comparable at all points, since the census gave the totals in five-year blocks, but a general comparison can be made. This shows that the age-group 5-13 is, as one might expect, under-represented in the criminal figures relative to their proportion in the population as a whole; the groups 14-19, 20-25, and 26-30 are all over-represented, with by far the largest surplus being in the 20-25 group; the 31-40 group is just slightly under-represented in the court figures, the 41-50 group is substantially more under-represented, and the over fifties, naturally, form a much smaller proportion of the offenders than they do of the population. The key 'criminal decade' in age terms was from the age of sixteen to twenty-five – they provided over 50 per cent of committals in the 1830s and 45 per cent in the 1850s.

One final point can be made from Table 20. Tobias strongly disputes the point that distress caused by the cyclical fluctuations in the economy had an important effect on the level of criminal activity. He states that discussion of 'the effect of want on the entry into crime of the honest poor must again be divided, this time on the basis of age'. The adult poor did not move to criminal acts in bad times; any such increase which did come about would generally have come from previously honest juveniles 'entering the criminal class', especially in those towns where there was little demand for juvenile labour.[39] Gatrell and Hadden refute this thesis on the basis of their figures, and conclude

> At *no* period does the incidence of juvenile crime appear to have been of sufficient quantitative importance to account alone either for the long-term trends or for the short-term fluctuations in criminal activity.[40]

Table 20 lends support to the Gatrell and Hadden conclusion. For the depression years of 1841-3, when the committals increased dramatically, Table 20 shows that there was no increase in the proportion occupied by juveniles, but rather a slight decrease, and a noticeable increase in the proportion of those aged 26-40. If this does indeed reflect an increase in criminal activity during the period of distress (as, it has been argued, it does – even if at a distance), then it is an increase in adult crime, carried out by people in their late twenties

and thirties. It was not only juveniles who might find themselves
suddenly out of work, or unable to cope, turning to illegal activity to
supplement their incomes in times when jobs and money were short;
in depression years in the Black Country many adults found themselves
in this position. Tobias states that 'on the whole honest people
remained honest despite appalling suffering and often great
temptation'.[41] He does not define who he means by 'honest people'
but, if the statement is not simply tautologous, it must refer to the
whole class of 'the adult poor' under discussion in that paragraph. He
offers no evidence for this generalisation other than a statement in the
Chadwick papers, and there is evidence in the Black Country (discussed
in the following chapter) that the 'adult poor' did not refrain *en masse*
from taking property unlawfully in times of depression, and that the
distinction between a 'criminal class' and the 'adult poor' was much
less clear-cut than Tobias implies.

(4) Occupation

Information on the occupation of the accused was not listed in all
Calendars until 1854; so the Staffordshire Calendars do not contain
any indication of the accused's occupation before 1854. In the
Worcestershire Calendars, this information is given from the 1830s
onwards; but, because a number of the Worcestershire Calendars are
missing for 1835-8, reliable tables on occupations can only be compiled
for 1839 onwards. And when analysing the occupation of all offenders,
one must end the analysis at 1855 because after that date the vast
majority of larceny offenders were dealt with under the Criminal
Justice Act, and there is no information on the occupation of the
people dealt with under the CJA (see Appendix I for details). The
occupational breakdown is set out in Table 22. (Dudley has been taken
from the Black Country Worcestershire towns as the largest one, and
the one best suited to serve as a rough model for the whole area; the
years 1845 and 1847 have been omitted, as too high a proportion of
the occupations of the Dudley accused is not available for those two
years.)

These figures can be compared with the occupational structure of
the Black Country and Dudley populations. There is no full
occupational breakdown of the whole Black Country population
available for this period; but a good idea can be gained from the
occupational breakdown of males of the age of twenty and above, in
the 1851 Census (Table 23). This can only be a rough guide, since a
substantial number of both the people committed to trial and of those

Table 22 Occupation of Persons Committed to Trial, from Dudley for 1839-44, 1846 and 1848-55, and from the Black Country as a Whole 1854-5

| | | Percentages | | |
| | | Dudley | | Black Country |
Occupation	1839-43	1844, 46, 48-50	1851-5	1854-5
Unskilled and partly-skilled manual workers:				
Miners (coal, iron, limestone)	21.6	26.2	25.6	12.6
Labourers (all types)	24.3	29.0	30.6	44.3
Unskilled ironworkers	6.9	3.6	2.3	2.1
Other unskilled factory workers	3.4	2.4	2.1	2.0
Nailers	7.4	7.6	4.2	1.9
Chain, anchor makers	2.1	2.9	2.9	1.0
Unskilled building workers	0.5	0.7	0.5	0.4
Boatmen	3.2	3.6	4.2	5.0
Servants (domestic and other)	0.3	0.0	1.3	2.2
Other unskilled manual workers	3.2	1.7	2.3	3.1
	72.9	77.7	76.0	74.6
Skilled manual workers and retail trades:				
Smiths and other metalwork craftsmen	4.2	5.7	3.4	4.7
Artisans	8.7	6.0	8.1	6.1
Skilled ironworkers	2.1	1.7	1.8	3.3
Glassworkers	2.4	0.9	1.3	0.5
Other skilled factory workers	1.6	0.9	1.6	2.3
Leatherworkers	0.5	0.7	0.5	0.3
Skilled building workers	0.5	0.7	0.8	1.2
Retail trades	4.8	3.6	5.0	4.4
	24.8	20.2	22.5	22.8
Upper and middle classes:				
Clerical workers	1.0	0.0	0.5	1.1
Professions	0.3	0.0	0.0	0.2
Farmers	0.0	0.0	0.0	0.1
Other	1.0	2.1	1.0	1.2
No occupation	0.0	0.0	0.0	0.0
TOTAL	100.0	100.0	100.0	100.0
Number	379	420	383	1,412
No. for which occupation was not listed	133	151	185	275

Table 23   Occupations in the Town of Dudley and in the Black Country 1851

Occupation	Black Country Males 20 and over	Dudley Males 10 and over
Unskilled and partly-skilled manual workers:	%	%
Miners (coal, iron, limestone)	19	23
Labourers (all types)	13	10
Unskilled ironworkers (approx.)	9	5
Other unskilled factory workers (approx.)	1	1
Nailers	5	7
Chain, anchor makers	1	0.4
Unskilled building workers	1	1
Boatmen	1	1
Servants (domestic and other)	1	1
Other unskilled manual workers	3	3
	54	52.4
Skilled manual workers and retail trades:		
Smiths and other metalwork crafts	9	5
Artisans	9	7
Skilled ironworkers (approx.)	7	6
Glassworkers	1	1
Other skilled factory workers (approx.)	1	1
Leatherworkers	1	1
Skilled building workers	3	2
Retail trades	5	7
	36	30
Employed in agriculture and animal breeding (exc. proprietors)	1	0.5
Army, police (exc. officers)	0.5	0.3
Upper and middle classes:		
Landowners, gentry, army officers	0.3	0.1
Professional men	1	1
Commercial and financial men	1	2
Farmers	1	0.2
Clerical workers	1	0.5
Others	2	2
TOTAL employed	97.8	89
Not employed (dependants, scholars, paupers, vagrants, no stated occupation)	2.2	11
TOTAL	100.0	100.0
Number	101,192	13,987

Note: The Dudley Census figures give the breakdown for all males of all ages; from the total of all males (19,273) has been deducted the numbers given in the census for Dudley boys aged 0-9 (5,286), on the assumption that none of these would have been employed, giving the total for employed males aged 10 and over of 13,987.

employed in the local industries, was under the age of twenty. But an occupational breakdown for those under the age of twenty is available only for the towns of Wolverhampton and Dudley, not for all the registration districts making up the Black Country; the analysis can therefore be performed more fully for Dudley but not for the whole Black Country. The Dudley table naturally has a much larger proportion of persons not employed, since it includes boys aged 10-20, a substantial number of whom were not employed. The Black Country breakdown for males over twenty gives the rough proportions of the occupational groups in the population as a whole. The occupational breakdown for women over twenty is not listed here, because a woman's employment was seldom recorded in the Calendar of prisoners awaiting trial; they were usually described simply as 'wife', 'widow', 'spinster', etc.

A number of points must be noted about Table 23. The census abstracts do not give any clear distinction between skilled and unskilled, for either ironworkers or factory workers in general. They simply list the number of people involved in the industry; the division into skilled and unskilled is an *estimate* of their likely proportions. Table 23 gives only the rough proportions occupied by each group, for comparative purposes. Black Country and Dudley figures in Table 22 differ in some respects, notably in their respective proportions of miners, labourers and nailers; this is, in part, attributable to the different proportions which these occupations comprised of their respective populations, as Table 23 shows. In their broad conclusions, these occupation figures do not differ much – if one takes miners and labourers together, they amount to about 55 per cent of committals for each of the three Dudley periods and for the Black Country; and the proportion occupied by unskilled and skilled manual workers as groups remains much the same.

Treating the figures with some caution, one can draw some broad conclusions. The unskilled manual workers are clearly over-represented in the committals figures – slightly more than half the male population, they made up about three-quarters of those tried for offences. Another 20-25 per cent of those tried for offences was made up of skilled manual workers and persons engaged or employed in retail trades – slightly less than the proportion they occupied of the population. The remaining classes of the population contributed only a minute fraction of the committals in any period. As many commentators stressed at the time, it was mostly the working classes from whom the offenders came.

Men who gave their occupation as 'labourers' made up the largest group of offenders. However, this is the vaguest of all occupational categories; probably it is a catch-all category whose occupants ranged from genuine agricultural and industrial labourers, to men who had no job or worked only occasionally but could claim to be a 'labourer' since that required no particular skill. Effectively, we must take this category as meaning nothing more specific than 'unskilled manual worker'.

One group which stands out in its number of committals relative to its proportion of the population is the canal boatmen; they were no more than 1 per cent of the populations of Dudley or the Black Country, yet they account for 3-5 per cent of the committals. The Black Country was crisscrossed with a large number of canals and, given the extent of mining and industrial activity in the area, the canals played a vital part in its economic life. Large amounts of coal and metal were carried in canal barges around the Black Country itself, and outside the area — most large coal and iron firms had their own wharves on the canals for this purpose; while raw materials and other goods were likewise brought into the area on the canals. This offered the boatmen good opportunities, during the long journeys, to remove articles from the unprotected cargoes they were carrying; their opportunities to pilfer were similar to those of workmen in a factory, warehousemen or dockers. Boatmen made up 5 per cent of Black Country and Dudley larceny committals, and there must have been many more who were not caught and prosecuted for their thefts. They also comprised about 4 per cent of committals for robbery and housebreaking.[42]

(5) Place

The towns of the Black Country in which the offences were committed are listed in Table 24, with the proportion of total committals coming from each town or parish. It is immediately apparent that a disproportionately large proportion of prosecuted crime came from the two largest towns, Wolverhampton and Dudley; with about 23 per cent of the population between them, they regularly supplied 35-40 per cent of the committals to trial. Conversely, areas without concentrated population centres supplied a considerably smaller proportion of committals than their proportion of population; Sedgley, Tipton, Kingswinford, and Rowley Regis — all of them parishes covering wide areas with large populations, but without any large towns — together comprised about 25 per cent of the population, but supplied only 13-17 per cent of the committals.

Table 24   Proportion of Persons Committed to Trial from Each Black Country Town or Parish 1835-55

| Town or Parish | Percentages | | | | | | | |
| | Committals | | | | Population | | | |
	1835-40	1841-5	1846-50	1851-5	1831	1841	1851	1861
Wolverhampton	26.7	22.1	24.3	24.3	11.7	12.4	13.3	12.9
Dudley	13.9	14.5	16.3	14.5	11.1	10.6	10.1	9.5
Walsall	9.9	5.5	8.2	7.1	6.8	6.8	6.9	8.0
West Bromwich	8.7	9.0	6.0	7.9	7.3	8.9	9.2	8.8
Bilston	4.7	6.5	8.2	6.2	6.9	6.9	6.3	5.1
Sedgley	4.1	5.5	4.1	3.7	9.7	8.5	7.9	7.7
Tipton	3.9	3.5	4.7	4.9	7.1	6.4	6.6	6.1
Kingswinford	4.4	6.7	5.5	4.1	7.2	7.6	7.3	7.2
Rowley Regis	1.0	2.0	1.5	1.6	3.5	3.8	3.8	4.2
Halesowen and Oldbury	4.1	4.5	4.2	5.2	4.4	4.4	4.9	4.9
Wednesbury	3.8	2.5	2.6	5.0	4.0	4.0	3.8	4.6
Smethwick and Harborne	1.5	1.3	2.0	2.6	2.0	2.3	2.9	3.6
Darlaston	1.2	2.7	1.3	1.4	3.1	2.8	2.8	2.7
Willenhall	2.5	1.8	3.1	3.3	2.8	3.0	3.2	3.6
Amblecote	0.2	0.3	0.2	0.4	0.6	0.5	0.6	0.6
Cradley	0.0	0.3	0.2	0.3	1.0	0.9	0.9	0.9
Stourbridge	2.3	3.1	2.2	1.1	2.9	2.5	2.2	1.9
Handsworth	2.1	2.1	2.3	1.7	2.3	2.1	2.1	2.4
Wednesfield	1.2	1.3	0.7	1.4	0.9	1.1	1.3	1.8
Oldswinford and the Lye	2.1	2.5	1.6	2.4	3.1	2.9	2.6	2.4
Tettenhall	1.4	1.8	0.7	0.7	1.2	1.1	0.9	0.8
Bentley	0.2	0.2	0.1	0.0	0.0	0.1	0.1	0.1
Great Barr	0.1	0.3	0.0	0.2	0.4	0.4	0.3	0.2
TOTAL	100.0	100.0	100.0	100.0	100.0	100.0	100.0	100.0
Number	2,899	3,648	3,546	3,926				

Note: The figures are not listed beyond 1855 because of the absence of the CJA data for Walsall and the Worcestershire areas.

There are two reasons why the committals were markedly higher in the large towns. Firstly, it is likely that proportionately more offences were committed in the large towns than in smaller places. The existence in large towns of considerable amounts of commercial, manufacturing and personal wealth and easy accessibility to a wide range of goods, offered easy opportunities for crime, especially for theft. The simultaneous existence, in close proximity to the wealth and goods, of poor slum populations provided a potential group to take advantage of these opportunities. Also, life in the streets of the slums and in the numerous drink-shops of the large towns was conducive to the assaults and brawls which formed a part of the committals. And services such as prostitution, and the attendant thefts and robberies, were only available on any substantial scale in large towns like Wolverhampton and Dudley. Secondly, as chapter 3 showed, the large towns tended to be better policed and therefore a higher proportion of offenders was arrested and sent for trial than was the case in the non-urban areas.

(6) Verdict and Sentence

As was mentioned in chapter 4, the proportion of persons committed to trial which was found guilty, increased gradually over this period from about 68 per cent to about 75 per cent. Table 25 sets out the verdicts on those committed to trial. The JOA and CJA figures have been excluded from this table, as they recorded convictions only; for this reason, the table does not go beyond 1855.

Table 25   Verdicts on Persons Committed to Trial from the Black Country 1835-55

Years	Guilty	Not Guilty	Percentages No True Bill (Grand Jury)	Other*		Total
					%	No.
1835-40	67.6	22.3	9.0	1.1	100.0	2,897
1841-45	68.9	22.7	7.4	1.0	100.0	3,644
1846-50	69.9	20.5	7.9	1.7	100.0	3,540
1851-55	74.5	18.4	5.8	1.3	100.0	3,927

*Includes those who were found insane, turned Queen's evidence, did not appear for their trials, whose prosecutor did not turn up to prosecute, etc.

Table 26 sets out the sentences imposed on those found guilty. Imprisonment was by far the commonest form of punishment; even in 1835-40 it accounted for 75 per cent of the sentences imposed and its use increased as the period went on. Imprisonment took place in the Stafford County Goal or House of Correction; it was usually accompanied by hard labour and often involved a short spell of solitary confinement. The great effect which the CJA had on prosecutions for minor larcenies can be seen in the column for 1856-60, which shows a sudden 250 per cent increase in the proportion imprisoned for less than one month. This increase comes entirely in persons prosecuted under the CJA and JOA for minor larcenies, and given short sentences – usually fourteen days.

Death sentences were, by 1835, only being carried out for murder; in other cases where the offence was theoretically capital, the judge would 'record' a death sentence which would automatically be commuted to a term of transportation. Even where the death sentence was 'confirmed' by the judge, meaning that he intended the sentence to be carried out, the Home Secretary could still intervene and reprieve the convicted person. In fact, the death sentence was 'confirmed, in thirteen Black Country cases over this period but was only executed in four of those cases. Those whose death sentences were commuted were generally sentenced to long terms of transportation.

Persons sentenced to transportation terms of ten years or more were almost always sent to Australia, but many of those sentenced to a term of seven years (the commonest transportation sentence) spent a number of years imprisoned in a hulk in England, and were then released in England without ever going overseas. In 1853, a term of four years' penal servitude in one of the new convict prisons being built in England was substituted for the seven-year transportation sentence and transportation was gradually phased out; but the longer transportation sentences were retained, to be used for offenders whom the judges or magistrates felt to be particularly hardened, dangerous and anti-social. All transportation was finally abolished in 1867. Longer terms of penal servitude were increasingly brought in to replace the previous terms of transportation, as can be seen in the columns for 1851-5 and 1856-60.[43]

Another penal innovation of the 1850s was the Reformatory school (given statutory recognition and powers in 1854, though private Reformatories had existed before this time), for offenders under the age of sixteen. The magistrate wishing to make use of Reformatory facilities for a juvenile offender had first to sentence the juvenile to a minimum period of two weeks in prison, and could then commit him

Table 26   Sentences Imposed on those Found Guilty of Indictable
Offences in the Black Country 1835-60

Sentence	Percentages				
	1835-40	1841-5	1846-50	1851-5	1856-60
Imprisonment:					
Less than 1 month	8.4	8.1	10.8	10.9	25.2
1-3 months	36.8	38.8	42.2	38.7	34.2
4-6 months	19.7	21.0	20.9	24.1	13.9
7-12 months	8.8	8.9	8.6	12.8	9.1
More than 12 months	2.1	2.5	1.1	1.3	2.2
TOTAL Imprisonment	75.8	79.3	83.6	87.8	84.6
Transportation:					
7 years	12.0	8.2	8.1	3.9	0.0
10-15 years	4.6	8.9	5.0	1.9	0.2
16-30 years	0.1	0.2	0.0	0.0	0.0
Life	1.5	0.7	0.3	0.3	0.04
TOTAL Transportation	18.2	18.0	13.4	6.1	0.2
Penal Servitude:					
3-4 years				3.2	4.4
5-9 years				0.7	2.4
10-20 years					0.9
Life					0.1
TOTAL Penal Servitude				3.9	7.8
Death:					
Recorded	1.6	0.2	0.2	0.5	0.2
Confirmed	0.1	0.1	0.1	0.1	0.02
TOTAL Death	1.7	0.3	0.3	0.6	0.2
Fine:	1.4	0.5	0.7	0.8	3.7
Bound Over	2.5	1.9	1.1	0.1	0.4
Committed to Reformatory				0.1	1.7
Privately Whipped	0.4	0.0	0.9	0.6	1.4
TOTAL	100.0	100.0	100.0	100.0	100.0
Number	1,993	2,545	2,649	3,261	4,238

for 2-5 years to a privately-run Reformatory which had been licensed
by the Home Secretary.[44] As Table 26 shows, the Staffordshire and
Worcestershire magistrates made use of Reformatories for juvenile

offenders from the start. Another form of punishment used for
juveniles and young males was private whipping. Public and private
whipping of women had been abolished in 1820, and there are no
instances in this Black Country sample of public whipping of males;
but private whipping was used on young male offenders, both as a
punishment in itself, in place of imprisonment, and as an additional
punishment to be imposed on top of a prison sentence.

Use of whipping increased in the late 1850s, when it was imposed
instead of prison sentences on juveniles convicted under the JOA.

The other forms of minor punishment were fines and binding over.
As Table 26 shows, fines were not widely used, though their use
increased sharply in the 1850s, when many juveniles convicted under
the JOA were fined. Binding over was a process whereby the magistrate
would require the offender and/or two others to enter a recognisance
for a sum of money of £10-£100 that the offender would keep the
peace for a certain length of time. If he was again convicted within that
period, the recognisance would be forfeited. It was a convenient device
for magistrates to use, particularly in minor cases of riot or assault.

Larceny, the commonest category of offence, was normally punished
with imprisonment for a first offence. But a third conviction – and in
the 1830s even a second conviction – for larceny often resulted in a
sentence of transportation if the magistrate or judge felt that the
circumstances showed the prisoner to be a hardened or persistent
offender; nor was the prisoner's youth any bar to such a sentence. For
instance, in 1840, Rachel Lunn, aged twelve, stole twenty-eight yards
of printed cotton, valued at 8s, and was sentenced to seven years'
transportation; Richard Carr and Joseph Rotton, aged thirteen and
fourteen respectively, stole a bat worth 5s from a shop and were each
given seven years' transportation. In 1842, Joseph Shaw stole sixty
yards of ribbon from a shop and 'showed by his conduct that he was
a common thief'; James Clarke, aged twenty-five, stole 3lb veal and 1lb
butter – they each received seven years' transportation.[45] The majority
of the more serious offences involving violence (burglary, robbery,
homicides, assaults involving wounding, rape) were punished by
transportation or a 'recorded' death sentence (which amounted to a
sentence of transportation), or later, penal servitude. Since the death
sentence was carried out on only four occasions in these twenty-six
years in the Black Country, transportation (with penal servitude, from
1853) was effectively the most severe penalty normally imposed. Table
26 shows a clear relaxation, over this period, in the imposition of this
penalty – from 20 per cent in 1835-40 to 8 per cent by 1855-60.

Notes

1. The evidence presented in this and the following three chapters is based on the data compiled from Quarter Sessions and Assize records for the Black Country for 1835-60. The compilation of these data, and their nature and quality, are discussed in Appendix I.
2. H. Jones, *Crime in a Changing Society* (Harmondsworth 1969), p.21.
3. The offence categories used here are a modified version of the categories used by Redgrave, the Criminal Registrar, in his presentation of the annual criminal statistics from 1834 onwards. His six categories were: (1) Offences against the person; (2) Offences against property committed with violence; (3) Offences against property committed without violence; (4) Malicious offences against property; (5) Forgery and offences against the currency; (6) Other (including treason, perjury, riot). Redgrave's groups (2) and (4) have been kept as they were to become groups (2) and (8) in Table 16. Redgrave's group (3) has been split up so as to bring out the importance of larceny as an offence, and two separate groups created for receiving stolen goods and embezzlement. Fraud has also been taken out of Redgrave's group (3) and placed in group (5) of the table together with forgery and currency offences. Assault on police officers has been removed from Redgrave's group (1) and added to riot and public order offences to make up group (7) of the Table. Group (9) of the Table is the same as Redgrave's group (6), except that public order offences have been removed from it; it includes treason and perjury.
4. The other four categories are too small to register at all noticeably on a graph.
5. The population for each year is calculated on the basis of the 1831, 1841, 1851 and 1861 Census tables for the Black Country. Assuming a roughly constant rate of increase throughout each decade, the actual increase during each decade was divided by ten and spread evenly over the decade.
6. The index of Black Country economic activity is derived from Barnsby, 'Standard of Living', pp.220-39, and from his Ph.D thesis 'Social Conditions' from which the article is taken. The index is based on reports of mines and factory inspectors, boards of guardians, chambers of commerce, local newspapers, reports of the Amalgamated Society of Engineers for 1856 onwards, and T.E. Lones, *The History of Mining in the Black Country* (1898), which records the state of economic activity in mining for 1815-98. It is a six-point index, in which 1 represents the lowest point (the equivalent of only one day's work per week) and 6 the highest point (equivalent of six days' work, full employment).
7. It is not argued that the *numbers* of committals represent directly the *numbers* of illegal acts being committed, but simply that the *movements* in the numbers of committals in this period reflect roughly the same *movements* in the numbers of illegal acts. Committals are always an imperfect indicator of the numbers of illegal acts committed, and there are always the distorting effects of the prosecution system at work; but for 1835-49 there are no significant changes in the system which would have interfered so strongly as to cause the movements in committals to be unrelated to movements in the numbers of illegal acts being committed. It is argued below that this position changed in the 1850s.
8. See the letters by large coal and iron masters to the local magistrates, Lord Lieutenant, and Home Office and the replies, in 1841-2 (PRO HO 45/42, 51 and 260; HO 41/16 and 17; TLB).
9. Ibid.
10. Tobias, *Crime*, pp.180-2; Macnab, 'Aspects'; Gatrell and Hadden, 'Criminal Statistics'.

11. See Appendix I.
12. Wootton, *Crime and the Criminal Law*, p.5; Jones, *Crime in a Changing Society*, p.21.
13. Jones, op.cit., p.21.
14. See F. Heidensohn, 'The deviance of women: a critique and an enquiry', *British Journal of Sociology*, 19 (1968), pp.160-75; Wootton, *Crime and the Criminal Law* and *Social Science and Social Pathology* (London 1959), pp.30-32; H. Mannheim, *Comparative Criminology* (London 1965), 2 vols., vol.2, pp.690-708.
15. *SA* 29 January 1859.
16. *JSSL*, 1 (1838), p.326, and 2 (1839), pp.91, 325-6, 343; Porter, *Progress of the Nation*, p.642; Tobias, *Crime*, p.104; W.D. Morrison, *Crime and its Causes* (London 1891), pp.151-2; J. Bentley, *Bentley's Ancient and Modern History of Worcestershire. . .with such an account of the State of Education and Crime. . .* (Birmingham 1842), pp.133, 142, 146; *MC* 'Labour and the Poor', 3 January 1850.
17. Morrison, *Crime and its Causes*, pp.152-9.
18. *Children's Employment Commission* (1843), pp.561-738; Wootton, *Crime and the Criminal Law*, p.8.
19. Gatrell and Hadden, 'Criminal Statistics', p.379.
20. Tobias, *Crime*, pp.15, 21-2.
21. Ibid., p.22; Gatrell and Hadden, op.cit., p.379.
22. *WH* 6 March 1858, report of Ass. See also Charges to Staffs. Grand Juries in *SA* 15 March 1851 and 12 March 1859.
23. J. Bentley, *Bentley's History, Directory and Statistics of Worcestershire* (Birmingham 1840-42), 7 vols.
24. R.W. Rawson, 'Enquiry into the Condition of Criminal Offenders in England and Wales with respect to Education', *JSSL*, 3 (1840), p.333.
25. The figures for 1855-60 have not been used because by then the majority of indictable offences were being tried summarily under the CJA, and information on the accused's literacy is not available for any of the CJA cases.
26. Porter, *Progress of the Nation*, p.657, and *JSSL*, 10 (1847), pp.316-44.
27. Rawson, 'Enquiry'; Rev. W. Russell, 'Statistics of Crime in England and Wales for the Years 1842, 1843, and 1844', *JSSL*, 9 (1848), pp.223-76; F.G.P. Neison, 'Statistics of Crime in England and Wales for the Years 1834-44', *JSSL*, 11 (1848), pp.140-65.
28. J. Fletcher, 'Progress of Crime in the United Kingdom', *JSSL*, 6 (1843), pp.218-40; S. Redgrave (Criminal Registrar), 'Criminal Tables for the Year 1845 – England and Wales', *JSSL*, 9 (1846), pp.177-83; J. Fletcher, 'Moral and Educational Statistics of England and Wales' – a series of articles under this title: *JSSL*, 10 (1847), pp.193-233, 11 (1848), pp.344-66, 12 (1849), pp.151-76 and 189-335.
29. *WC* 18 March 1840, Report of Ass. See also Erskine, J.: Education is necessary to check the growth of crime; 'I do not mean that education which consists in mere reading and writing – as that may confer the power of doing more evil than good – but all education, to be of any value, must be based on religion.' (*SA* 16 March 1839, report of Ass.) and Hill J.: 'But what an infinitesimal portion of education does the mere ability to read and write constitute! In order to make education a social blessing as it ought to be, it must fashion the heart as well as instruct the head. Can that man be expected to honour the Queen, or obey the laws, who has not been taught and who does not fear God?' (*SA* 24 July 1858, report of Ass.).
30. Rawson, 'Enquiry', p.331.
31. Fletcher, 'Moral and Educational Statistics' (1848), p.349.

32. For a full examination of the statistical investigators and the moral preconceptions which they brought to their supposedly 'objective' studies of criminal and educational statistics, see Michael J. Cullen, *The Statistical Movement in Early Victorian Britain* (Hassocks, Sussex 1975).

33. See Rev. J. Clay (Chaplain of Preston Gaol), 'Intoxication a Source of Crime', *JSSL*, 1 (1838), pp.124-5, 'Criminal Statistics of Preston', *JSSL*, 2 (1839), pp.84-103, 'On the Effects of Good or Bad Times on Committals to Prison', *JSSL*, 18 (1855), pp.74-9; Report of Chaplain of Stafford County Prison to Quarter Sessions October 1855 (*SA* 20 October 1855); Staffs. Ass. Grand Jury Charges: *SA* 24 July 1858 and 12 March 1859.

34. *SA* 1 October 1842, report of Special Assize.

35. See the Registrar-General's discussion of these points in his first three annual reports.

36. *Children's Employment Commission* (1843); *Midland Mining Commission* (1843), pp.cxliv-clvi; 'Report on the State of Education among the Working Classes in West Bromwich', *JSSL*, 2 (1839), pp.375-7; 'Education in the Mining and Manufacturing District of South Staffordshire', *JSSL*, 10 (1847), pp.234-42; Barnsby 'Social Conditions', ch.6.

37. 'Report on the State of Education. . .', pp.375-7.

38. For examples of this concern, see the evidence of Sir John Eardley Wilmot to *SC on Criminal Commitments* (1828), pp.444-9; articles in *JSSL*, 1 (1838), p.235, and 2 (1839), pp.86-102 and 326-32; Report to Staffs. QS of Committee appointed to enquire into the best means of checking the growth of Juvenile Crime and promoting the reformation of Juvenile Offenders (SRO Q/SB E. 1851; discussion of this report in *SA* 4 January 1851). Tobias, *Crime,* contains much information on juvenile crime and nineteenth-century opinions about juvenile offenders; see also S. Eade, 'The Reclaimers: A Study of the Reformatory Movement in England and Wales 1846-1893', Australian National Univ. Ph.D thesis 1976.

39. Tobias, *Crime,* pp.181-3.

40. Gatrell and Hadden, 'Criminal Statistics', p.383 (their emphasis).

41. Tobias, op.cit., p.182.

42. On the social and 'moral' condition of the canal boatmen in this period, see H. Hanson, *The Canal Boatmen 1760-1914* (Manchester 1975).

43. On transportation and penal servitude, see Shaw, *Convicts and the Colonies,* and L. Robson, *The Convict Settlers of Australia* (Melbourne 1965).

44. On Reformatories, see Hill, *Repression,* pp.335-6; Eade, 'The Reclaimers'.

45. SRO Q/SB Ea. 1840; Q/SPcl Ea. and M. 1842; *SA 2* and 9 July, report of QS.

6 PROPERTY OFFENDERS (1) — LARCENIES

Security of life and limb was never greater. Property, it is true, is not equally safe; but even here there are not any large proportion of offences which reach to the ruin of the person against whom the offence is committed, or to subject property in general to any very serious risks.

The most usual, numerous and troublesome crimes consist of stealing from the house or the person, goods which are easily transported, and may be quickly converted into money.
(*2nd Report from SC on Criminal Commitments and Convictions,*
P.P. 1828, VI (545), p.423.)

This chapter and the following one discuss offences against property committed without violence — Larceny; Embezzlement; Receiving Stolen Goods; Fraud, Forgery and Currency Offences — the offences which together accounted for 85 per cent of indictable committals over the whole period. This chapter discusses the various types of larceny.

Larceny was by far the largest of these categories of offence, accounting alone for almost 80 per cent of all committals to trial. Larceny was legally defined in 1825 as:

. . .a feloniously and fraudulently taking and carrying away by any person, the goods of another, above the value of 12d; if the goods taken are under the value of 12d it is then *petty* larceny.[1]

It covered all forms of theft in which there were no aggravating circumstances.

Until the early nineteenth century, virtually all forms of grand larceny (above 12d in value) were capital offences; only petty larceny and a few forms of grand larceny were non-capital — and they too were felonies, punishable by transportation, whipping or a fine.[2] The Larceny Act 1808 (48 Geo. III c.129) was the first statute to begin the repeal of the eighteenth-century capital code, abolishing capital punishment for larceny from the person (picking pockets). Thereafter, a number of statutes reduced the number of capital larceny offences. Most important was the Larceny Act 1827 (7 and 8 Geo. IV, c.29), which abolished the distinction between grand and petty larceny, made simple larceny a single offence punishable by imprisonment or transportation, and left only two capital larcenies – larceny in a dwelling-house of property worth £5 or more, and larceny of horses, sheep or cattle. The death sentence for these two offences was abolished and replaced by a mandatory sentence of transportation for life, by the Punishment of Death Act 1832 (2 and 3 Will. IV, c.62). So, by 1835, larcenies were no longer capital offences and were punishable only by imprisonment, transportation or fines. Larceny was a felony and was therefore triable only at Quarter Sessions or Assizes; an 1827 Act (7 and 8 Geo. IV, c. 29) transferred to summary jurisdiction the offences of stealing goods from a wrecked vessel, stealing deer, hares, wild animals, trees, shrubs, etc. But with these unimportant exceptions, all other larcenies were triable and tried only at Quarter Sessions and Assizes. This remained the position until the passing of the Juvenile Offenders Act (JOA) of 1847 and 1850, and the Criminal Justice Act (CJA) of 1855.

Examination of the Black Country records shows that the majority of the larcenies for which people were tried were thefts of not very large amounts or of not very important articles. Over the whole period 1835-60, the larcenies divided as follows (Table 27):

Table 27   Black Country Larceny Committals 1835-60 Divided into Categories

Category of Larceny	Committed for Trial	
	No.	%
Industrial thefts	4,904	28.2
Larceny of clothing	2,996	17.2
Larceny of food or drink	1,438	8.3
Larceny from the person	1,304	7.5
Larceny of small domestic animals	925	5.3
Larceny of large domestic animals	331	1.9
Larceny of timber and fodder	321	1.8
Other simple larcenies	5,191	29.8
TOTAL	17,410	100.0

Note: The distinction of categories in this table has been made on the basis of articles stolen, except for one category – larceny from the person – which involves particular skills and modes of operation different in kind from the other types of larceny listed here. Apart from this, the categories have been drawn in terms of the articles stolen, and aggravating features – e.g. larceny by a servant – have not been noted for the purposes of this classification.

Table 27 shows that the largest distinct categories are industrial thefts and thefts of items of clothing. The detailed evidence on the facts of cases for 1836, 1842 and other years[3] makes it clear that the value of the goods involved in these categories and in 'other simple larcenies' was usually very small.

The sentences imposed for all types of larceny are set out in Table 28.

A number of points emerge from Table 28. In the 1830s, larceny, though no longer a capital offence, could still be punished severely — nearly 20 per cent of the sentences in 1835-40 are of transportation. It was common for a second conviction for larceny to be regarded as grounds for a transportation sentence. Secondly, the effect of the CJA and JOA on sentencing can be seen in the great increase in sentences of

Table 28   Sentences Imposed for all Black Country Larcenies 1835-60

Sentence	Percentage				
	1835-40	1841-7	1848-54	1855-60	1835-60
Imprisonment:					
Less than 1 month	9.8	10.7	11.7	28.2	17.0
1-3 months	41.9	44.8	45.9	39.3	42.8
4-6 months	21.4	21.1	23.2	13.5	19.1
7-12 months	6.5	6.5	6.9	5.8	6.4
More than 12 months	0.9	0.3	0.3	0.9	0.6
Transportation:					
7 years	14.0	9.4	5.9	—	5.7
10-15 years	3.7	6.7	2.4	0.1	2.7
Life	1.2	—	—	—	0.2
Penal Servitude:					
3-4 years	—	—	1.5	3.2	1.6
5-9 years	—	—	0.1	1.3	0.5
10-15 years	—	—	—	0.2	0.1
Other:					
Reformatory	—	—	0.0	1.7	0.6
Fine	0.1	0.2	0.5	4.1	1.6
Bound over	—	0.3	0.5	0.1	0.2
Privately whipped	0.5	0.0	1.1	1.6	0.9
TOTAL	100.0	100.0	100.0	100.0	100.0

n = 1,545 n = 2,636 n = 3,287 n = 4,061 n = 11,529

under one month after 1855 (all of which come from CJA and JOA cases), and in the increase in whippings and fines as punishments (mostly imposed in the JOA cases). Thirdly, a clear move towards a more lenient sentencing policy can be seen over the period as a whole: in 1835-40 19 per cent were transported and 73 per cent received prison terms of six months or less; in 1855-60 the combined transportation and penal servitude sentences amounted to under 5 per cent, while prison terms of six months or less took care of 81 per cent and 7 per cent were fined, sent to Reformatory, whipped or bound over. Throughout the period, of course, prison sentences of six months or less comprised the vast majority of larceny sentences; over half of all larceny sentences were always imprisonment for three months or under.

The different categories of larceny, as set out in Table 27, are now considered separately – their typical form, the offenders, and their importance within the Black Country.

(A) Industrial Thefts

This category comprises thefts of amounts of coal, of pieces of metal, and of tools, machine parts and manufactures from a place of work. Virtually every theft of coal was from a colliery, pit bank, ironworks, canal boat or canal wharf; most metal thefts were from collieries, ironworks, metal workshops or canal boats; and most thefts of tools etc. were from collieries, ironworks, workshops or factories.

Together, these made up *more than one in four* (28.2 per cent) of *all committals for larceny* over the period 1835-60, and *more than one in five* (22.2 per cent) of *all committals for all types of offence* over this period. It is worth stressing this point since figures of committals for these offences played a large part in swelling the totals of committals for all offences – those totals which led many contemporaries to talk of a swelling wave of 'crime and lawlessness'. But when one examines the industrial thefts, the growth in their number of committals is shown to stem from the expansion of large-scale capitalist mining and manufacturing production and, importantly, the attitudes and practices of employers.

Typical examples of these offences, taken from the courts:

Coal

(1) Edward Morgan, an engineer working at Baldwin's Bovereaux Iron Works in Bilston, was seen to take two large pieces of coal in the course of a night's work, and place them in an adjoining field; he

was seen doing this by Andrew Dawes, a filler working in the same furnaces, and Dawes went for the local parish constable and gave Morgan in charge. Dawes stressed in his evidence that, although Morgan worked at Baldwin's works, 'no-one is allowed to carry away Coal from the Works'.[4]

(2) Mary Ann Whatmore, aged 23, took a basket of coals from the colliery of Messrs Bagnall and Davis in Tipton; she had no particular connection with the colliery, and was seen taking the coals by James Sheldon, a waggoner, who gave evidence against her.[5]

(3) Thomas Skelding and Thomas Whitehouse jumped on a canal boat while it was in a lock, and threw about 500 lbs of coal off the boat onto the canal side, and then jumped off onto the canal side themselves. Here they were accosted by a Tipton police constable, who asked if the coal belonged to them; one of them said that it represented his allowance from the pit, and the other said that he had had a few lumps given to him. The constable arrested them; and Skelding then admitted that they had taken it from the boat.[6]

Metal

(4) George Plant and Thomas Lees were both labourers at the Pumphouse Colliery of Messrs James and William Bagnall at West Bromwich. Lees was seen by another labourer breaking up some iron, putting it in a hole and covering it up; later, Lees came and took the iron and wheeled it away in a barrow, helped by Plant. The labourer told Mr Bagnall, who called the police; they arrested the two men and found that the iron had been sold to a dealer in wrought and cast iron, from whom it was recovered.[7]

(5) Benjamin Scriven, a chainmaker, was charged with stealing a bundle of iron for chainmaking from the workshop of his employer, John Parkes, a Kingswinford master chainmaker. Scriven took the iron to the workshop of another chainmaker and sold it to him; the iron was found in the other workshop and identified by Parkes.[8]

(6) William Aston was seen by a puddler employed in the ironworks of James Solly, Tipton ironmaster, throwing four pigs of iron (140 lbs) from Solly's canal wharf into Aston's boat. Edwin Cartwright, who was in the boat, was covering the pigs with cinders. The puddler called his master, a watchman stopped and searched the boat, and both Aston and Cartwright were prosecuted.[9]

Tools, Parts, etc.

(7) James Gutteridge went to Messrs Bagnall's Iron Works in West

Bromwich and asked for work. He was left in the engine house there for a while by himself, and, after he went, it was found that the two pairs of brasses from the engine had gone. The parish constable was brought in, and Gutteridge admitted taking the brasses and showed where he had hidden them.[10]

(8) Jeremiah Cocklin, a labourer at the steel works of Richard Edwards in Stourbridge, worked with a sledge hammer there. One day, after the men had left, the hammer was found to be gone. Cocklin was seen with the hammer in his possession, and a search revealed it in his home; he was prosecuted.[11]

(9) James Picken and William Hobley, apprentices to a latchmaker, aged 16 and 13 respectively, stole a number of latches from the shop while he was out; they were seen by his wife, who took back the latches and told her husband when he returned.[12]

Coal was often taken by an employee during or immediately after working hours, but more often it was taken by someone from outside the colliery. Most of those who took coal from outside were women — unlike almost all other offences and other types of larceny, women made up a clear majority (62.5 per cent) of those charged with stealing coal over the period. Most of these women were not employees of the places from which they took the coal;[13] a substantial minority (about 40 per cent) of coal thefts *was* by employees.

With metal thefts, the clear majority (about 65 per cent) *was* committed by employees, though a few were done by outsiders. The stolen metal was usually disposed of by selling it to other metal workers or to metal dealers or marine store dealers, who were numerous in the Black Country. It was also easy for a piece of metal to be melted down or turned into another form, since forges and furnaces existed in large numbers and were very accessible all over the area; apart from the furnaces available in factories and workshops, there were the forges of the domestic workers such as the nailers and chainmakers.

Most of the thefts of tools, machine parts, manufactures, etc. were committed by employees from their places of work.[14]

In most of these cases, the accused was caught by a watchman of the works, or was seen and reported by a fellow-employee. In all of these cases, the value of the items taken was very small — coal worth 6d, metal or tools worth a few shillings. And the prosecution, being private, was brought by the coal and iron master himself (acting through an agent or employee in the case of the large firms).

One might well ask why the coal and iron masters went to the trouble and expense of prosecuting thefts of such tiny value. This point is discussed in more detail below; but one can note here that this is an attitude of the employers which only developed in the early nineteenth century as they tried to stamp out traditional ideas about people's right to help themselves to pieces of coal and metal. But popular local attitudes continued to regard the taking of these things, especially of coal, as a natural right.

In many of the coal-stealing cases the defence was advanced that the accused was entitled to take the coal. Miners were indeed allowed a coal allowance which formed a regular part of their wages, and their wives or female relatives were entitled to take it on their behalf; the allowance was: for a married man, one ton of coal per twenty-four completed turns of work; for a single man, one ton per forty-eight completed turns.[15]

But there was also much discarded coal – slag and low-grade stuff, commercially unsaleable but still able to be burnt, even if inefficiently – which was dumped in heaps at the pit mouths, and which was taken by people needing fuel, especially women. As the *Morning Chronicle* correspondent described it:

> A more miserable class even than the bankswomen [women who work at a pit mouth] are the poor creatures who come out to pick coal from the rubbish heaps at the pit mouth. Sometimes they are suffered to make their black gleaning in peace – but at other times, perhaps if the buttie or the doggie [subcontractor and foreman in charge of working the pit] happen to be not in the best of humours, they are given in charge, and hurried off to gaol for stealing coals. 'I go to pick at the pitheaps', said one poor woman to me. 'It's the only way I can get fuel to keep me from starving these cold nights; but I must be very careful, and not go too near the shaft. There were two poor creatures committed to Stafford gaol last week for stealing coal, and they were only just picking out a few bits from what the pit people threw away for rubbish.'[16]

People such as the 'two poor creatures' mentioned here would end up at Quarter Sessions, facing a charge of larceny. Following Peel's Act of 1827, and until the Criminal Justice Act of 1855, all such larcenies, if they were prosecuted at all, had to be prosecuted on indictment at Quarter Sessions, even though the value of the property taken might amount to no more than a few pence – as was frequently the case in these coal-stealing prosecutions. The Chairman of the Staffordshire

Quarter Sessions repeatedly pointed out this anomaly in his charges to
Grand Juries during these years, but also pointed out that as the law
stood, this could not be helped, unless Parliament passed an Act to
enable such small thefts to be tried summarily (as the Criminal Justice
Act eventually did.)[17]

Popular Black Country attitudes continued to view the taking of
coal as a legitimate perquisite. After all, the district produced vast
quantities of coal, brought out of the ground by miners at considerable
danger to themselves; their coal allowance was a traditionally
recognised part of their real wages, and the amount to be taken was
not always strictly construed. Similarly, the 'black gleaning' of the
coal tips was seen as analogous to agricultural gleaning – a traditional
right of the poor to the inferior leavings. The coalowners and legal
authorities battled hard to convince the local populace that taking coal
was wrong and was prohibited by law. As Mr Justice Cresswell
indignantly noted when sentencing Phoebe Price for this offence:

> His Lordship observed that coal stealing was so common an offence
> as almost to induce the belief that some persons were not aware
> that it was a crime; they were very much deceived; it was quite as
> criminal to steal coal as anything else.[18]

And Twemlow, Chairman of Staffordshire Quarter Sessions, repeatedly
warned the Grand Juries against discharging the prisoner simply on the
grounds that it was only a small amount of coal or iron which had been
taken –

> the amount of property stolen did not alter the offence, as however
> small the value, the party was equally guilty of stealing, or larceny.[19]

There was similarly a large amount of popular legitimation for the
taking of metal or tools from the place of work – such items taken
from the employer were fair game for all employees, and the other
employees would not interfere. Such legitimation was not universal –
in a number of cases, the theft was reported to management or the
police by a fellow-employee. But there is much evidence that it was
common for nineteenth-century employees, especially in the metal
industries, to take materials for their own use; workers in workshops
and factories would take such materials themselves and accept the right
of their fellow-workers to do so.[20] The general population seems to
have shared this attitude of legitimation – for instance, the arrest of

five men charged with stealing iron set off a riot against the authorities in Walsall in 1832. The rioting continued for three days, and was only suppressed after the Riot Act had been read twice, many special constables had been sworn in, and a number of people arrested. The prosecutor then declined to prosecute, presumably deterred by this outburst.[21]

We might expect a large number of industrial thefts in an area with large and increasing opportunities for such thefts – the numbers of pits, ironworks, workshops and factories were increasing throughout this period and large amounts of coal and iron were transported by canal boat, offering easy opportunities for theft. The Chairman of Quarter Sessions pointed this out:

> It seemed that a great deal of property of that kind [iron sleepers, rails, quantities of iron] was allowed to lie exposed in the neighbourhood of coal pits, and the proprietors permitting it to remain in that exposed state, offered an inducement to persons to take it away.[22]

It is not surprising that workmen in these industries took coal, metal and tools for themselves. Modern studies stress that 'whipping' or 'knocking off' such items is standard practice among workers in industry.[23] This had been common practice in English trades and industries at least as far back as the eighteenth century, when each trade had its own traditional 'perk' to be taken by the workmen:

> In some industries there was a tradition that the workers should have a share of the product of their labour. Both the coal-hewers of the north and the coal-meters of the Thames received by custom an allowance of fuel; and ironworks and other establishments that used coal often supplied it on special terms to their workers. The mates of the West Indiamen had a right to the sweepings of sugar and coffee from the hold of the ship; the gangsmen and coopers established a claim to the drainings of molasses and spilt sugar on the floor of the warehouse; and the labourers in the corn ships believed themselves to be similarly entitled to the grain that had been removed as samples. At the Royal Yards, the shipwrights were allowed to take for firewood the chips that fell from the axe, and their womenfolk were permitted to do the gleaning. In each case the workers saw to it that the crumbs from the master's table were ample. Casks were handled not too gently; sacks were liable to

burst open; shipwrights took care that their wives did not go short of firewood. *The line of demarcation between the extension of established right and barefaced robbery is difficult to draw.* . . Yarn spinners, and weavers had ample opportunities of purloining material and of disposing of it by sale. . .Industrial concerns had to take special precautions to avoid losses of fuel from the wagons and from the stocks at the works.[24]

Modern studies point out that acts of this sort are not regarded by those who commit them as being in any serious sense wrong; and even if the people concerned agree that theft in general is wrong, they will distinguish such 'knocking off' as falling into a different category.[25] The Black Country coal and metal stealing cases show a similar popular distinction between legitimate 'taking' and illegitimate 'stealing'.

The interesting question is not why industrial thefts took place — they can be regarded as practically an automatic feature of such an industrial set-up — but why so many prosecutions were brought for these offences.

It must be stressed that the figures which have been tabulated in this chapter are for cases which appeared in court. In order for someone to appear, it would be necessary that all the following stages should have been gone through: (1) the person takes the article from his place of work (or from the pit mouth, in the case of much coal stealing); (2) he or she is seen by a workmate, superior or watchman in the act, or is suspected of stealing and found with the article; (3) he is reported to the manager, or handed over to the watchman or a constable; (4) the management (or perhaps, though much less frequently, the police) decides to prosecute him for this; (5) the magistrate before whom the preliminary enquiry is held, commits him to trial. If any of these stages after the first was not carried out, the man or woman did not appear in court.

We can be certain that the number of these offences which appeared in court was very much smaller than the number which took place. To look at stage (2), for instance, it has been noted that thefts of this sort were regarded by many as a legitimate 'perk' from the employer; in this atmosphere, there would be many cases in which the employee taking something for himself would be only one of a whole group doing so; even where the other employees were not taking things themselves, there would be a disinclination in many cases to report a fellow-worker to the management.

A crucial decision comes at stage (4), where the employer decides whether or not to prosecute those thefts which are reported to him. This would not have been an automatic decision. As has been described, the system of prosecution depended heavily on individual initiative, and no penalty or moral obloquy would attach to a failure to prosecute. The value of the articles stolen was usually very small. If the prosecution was successful, the employer could expect the man to be sent to prison for a short period (between one week and three months); if it was unsuccessful, it might cost him money, and would certainly take up time and trouble. The employer would have to balance the possible moral and deterrent effects of a successful prosecution on that employee and all other employees against the time and expense, the small value of the article taken, the fact that conviction would mean the loss of that employee's services for the length of his prison term and perhaps ultimately his discharge from the employer's service, the possible bad effect that such a prosecution would have on relations with the workforce in general, etc.

In modern firms, in which pilfering of this sort is still common, there is a tendency for managements to overlook much of the taking of articles of small value, where they will accept the employees' own definition of this as 'perks' rather than theft. A study of businesses in Reading found that most employers drew a distinction between 'reasonable pilfering', which was expected and tolerated, and 'theft', which was not; but even 'theft' was punished far more frequently by dismissal than by prosecution. The commonest criterion used as the dividing line between 'pilfering' and 'theft' was the monetary value of the goods taken; of the ninety firms who gave an answer to the question of where the dividing line came, one-third said that taking became 'theft' when the value of the goods taken was over £1.[26] This study also found that most cases in which an employee was found committing theft from the firm were not prosecuted; in the great majority of the cases which *were* prosecuted, the police had already been called in; this suggests that they were prosecuted either because they were relatively serious offences, or because there was strong pressure from the police to go through with the prosecution. When left to themselves, the firms clearly preferred not to prosecute, preferring rather to punish the man themselves, usually by dismissal. The commonest reasons advanced for not prosecuting were 'Case not serious enough', 'Not worth the publicity/unpleasantness/against policy', and 'Because he was a decent worker, decent chap, etc.' This was not simply due to the employer's humanity; Martin points out that not prosecuting saves the employer time, trouble and possible unfavourable publicity; where the value involved is small, he may well feel it unnecessary to invoke the full force of the law.[27]

One might expect, then, that nineteenth-century employers would similarly have made as little formal use of the criminal law as possible, would have overlooked the 'pilfering' and 'perks', and would have punished larger thefts by fines and dismissal. In the early eighteenth century, the average employer seems to have tolerated the taking of 'perks'. But from the later eighteenth century, with the growth in scale of manufacturing industry, putting out industries, and mining, employers began increasingly to view 'perks' as a problem to be rooted out. They were able to secure the passage of statutes defining the taking of 'perks' as a form of embezzlement or theft; and by the 1790s prosecutions for such acts, instituted by employers or groups of employers, began to increase.[28]

By the 1830s such prosecutions were already fairly common, and they increased steadily, in absolute numbers and as a proportion of all prosecutions, through to the 1860s (see Table 29). The prosecutions were for items of small value – even allowing for the difference in money values in the 1830s, 6d worth of coal or one shilling's worth of iron are not significant amounts. Why then did the coal and iron masters go to the trouble and expense of prosecuting these offences?

One answer lies in the commonness of this type of offence; this came into conflict with the increasing emphasis of the employers on the need to rationalise the costs of production and impose stricter definition of, and control over, the employer's property. As Twemlow put it, in a Grand Jury charge:

> The cases in question [coal stealing] were sent from the southern division of the county [the Black Country], and were sent not by poor people who had had their coal heaps robbed, but by the great ironmasters of the county, who found it necessary, for the protection of their property, that such offences should not be allowed to go unobserved and unpunished. The persons charged had taken, they would probably find, but small pieces of coal, yet by the system being pursued, it would amount to a great quantity by the end of the week. He understood that the quantity thus stolen from some of the masters amounted to some tons. . .There were also several cases of stealing iron, the value of which was perhaps but a few pence, and to these cases the same remarks would apply.[29]

As far as the coal and iron masters were concerned, each theft, however small in itself, represented only one of many such thefts, amounting in aggregate to large losses. Each person caught, prosecuted and punished, however small his own theft was, might serve to deter many potential further offenders from such thefts.

In the eighteenth century, when the scale of the enterprise and the size of the workforce were generally much smaller, employers could remain on relatively close and easy terms with their employees; they did not feel the need to define property rights so sharply, nor to invoke the law in enforcing discipline and security of property in their works.[30] In the twentieth century, with a general corpus of management skills more firmly established, has come the realisation that rigid enforcement of the laws governing theft against employees may be counterproductive; to prosecute for taking articles of small value might cost the firm far more than the value of the articles, not only in terms of the time and trouble involved in the actual process of prosecution, but also in terms of the goodwill and morale of the employees. But by the mid-nineteenth century, this modern position had not yet been worked out; the Industrial Revolution, with its growth in the range and extent of goods produced, transported and displayed, had resulted in stricter attention being paid to enforcement of the letter of the law. Prosecution had been made easier and cheaper, and the manufacturers took advantage of this to emphasise the need to enforce a strict definition of property rights, and to try to eradicate the still lingering notions about traditional communal rights and legitimate 'perks'.

This is the greatest significance of the rash of industrial theft prosecutions. They mark an offensive by the employers designed to eliminate popular ideas about the legitimate taking of property, which the employers now wanted to be clearly defined as unlawful and liable to be punished. This offensive continued to gather momentum; over the period 1835-60, there was a continual and marked increase in industrial theft prosecutions – in absolute numbers, as a ratio per 100,000 of population, and as a percentage of all prosecutions brought for any indictable offence and of all larceny prosecutions brought (Table 29).

Such a dramatic increase – in 1835, 34 prosecutions, less than 14 per 100,000 and less than one-tenth of all indictable prosecutions; in 1860, 478 prosecutions, 103 per 100,000 and one-third of all indictable prosecutions – cannot be explained purely in terms of an increase in actual industrial thefts committed. Between 1835 and 1860 there was an increase in the number and size of collieries and ironworks, which would have meant more property in those works exposed to more

Table 29   Black Country Industrial Theft Prosecutions 1835-60

| Year | | Industrial Theft Prosecutions | | |
	No.	As % of Larcenies	As % of Total Prosecutions	Per 100,000 of Population
1835	34	14.9	9.4	13.9
1836	44	17.4	13.3	17.4
1837	58	15.8	12.2	21.6
1838	64	16.8	13.1	23.8
1839	87	19.7	15.0	31.4
1840	105	19.9	15.6	36.8
1841	109	20.0	15.8	37.2
1842	150	23.5	16.0	49.8
1843	142	26.6	17.7	45.9
1844	125	25.9	18.2	39.3
1845	78	19.0	14.8	23.9
1846	105	22.9	18.4	31.4
1847	155	24.5	20.2	45.3
1848	171	25.1	20.6	48.8
1849	109	18.3	14.2	30.4
1850	171	26.7	21.1	46.7
1851	124	20.3	15.3	33.1
1852	122	21.6	15.3	31.7
1853	150	24.2	18.1	38.0
1854	168	24.6	19.0	41.5
1855	238	29.3	22.3	57.4
1856	332	34.0	27.3	78.3
1857	492	34.8	30.6	113.3
1858	559	38.9	33.5	125.9
1859	534	42.3	36.1	117.6
1860	478	39.3	33.7	103.0

employees, leading to increased thefts – but the increase in such works was not on a scale anywhere near to being able to account for the enormous increase shown in Table 29.

Most of the increase lies not in the thefts themselves but in increased prosecution by the employers. This shows a continuation and intensification of the campaign to deter and stamp out the taking of 'perks'. The power of the employers to pursue this campaign was greatly assisted by two developments during the period 1835-60.

First, during the period 1836-60, there was a marked change in the social composition of the men making up the Black Country magistracy. Before 1836, this magistracy had been dominated by members of the landed aristocracy and gentry. From 1836 onwards, coal and iron masters began to be appointed to the Bench in growing numbers until, in the 1850s, they were the dominant group on the Bench of the Black Country.[31] Over exactly the same period, the number of industrial theft prosecutions increased markedly. It was predominantly the large coal and iron masters who brought these prosecutions (see below, pp.192-5) and it was these same men who were being appointed as magistrates.

In the typical case, the prosecutor, ironmaster A who was also a JP, brought the accused, his employee, for preliminary examination before another magistrate, ironmaster B. This situation probably increased the chances that such a case would be committed for trial. Some of the older landowning magistrates were prepared to take a fairly lenient attitude towards the assertion of popular rights to 'perks', and were disinclined to commit a man for trial at Quarter Sessions for stealing only 6d worth of coal; they might instead discharge him at the preliminary examination. But the new ironmaster-magistrates were determined to stamp out the belief in traditional rights and 'perks'; such men were themselves bringing large numbers of such prosecutions for thefts from their own works; they looked with favour on these prosecutions brought by other coal and iron masters and freely committed such cases for trial.

The second, very important, development was the implementation of the Criminal Justice Act (CJA) of 1855 allowing summary trial of these indictable thefts of small value. Table 29 shows a sharp increase in the figures in 1855 and a marked continual increase in the years following. This reflects the fact that the CJA made prosecution much easier, cheaper and quicker for the prosecutor, and thus encouraged prosecutors to bring prosecutions in cases which they might otherwise have allowed to drop. This applied all the more strongly to industrial theft prosecutions, since cases tried under the CJA were heard by two local JPs. By the 1850s, almost all the JPs in the inner manufacturing areas of the Black Country were coal and iron masters, who could be expected to look sympathetically on prosecutions brought by their fellow ironmaster-magistrates. (The figures for the CJA are for *convictions* only – i.e. they slightly *under*state the number of prosecutions brought.)

One can look a little more closely at the coal and iron masters as prosecutors of industrial thefts. The name of the prosecutor has been noted for 2,298 of these industrial theft prosecutions.[32] For the whole period, 318 prosecutors are listed; they can be broken down into groups according to the number of industrial theft prosecutions they brought (Table 30).

Table 30 shows that not all employers prosecuted on the same scale for industrial theft. The power in the prosecutions lay with relatively few prosecutors – 26 of those 318 prosecutors (Groups 3, 4 and 5) together brought nearly 60 per cent of all the prosecutions.

The makeup of these groups can be analysed. The people in Group 1 mostly brought only one prosecution each; the maximum was three. The majority here were small coal and iron masters, ironfounders and metal workshop masters; this group also covers some diverse individuals and firms who prosecuted once; but it does also include a few *large* coal and iron firms.

Group 2 comprises almost entirely coal and iron masters – mostly the larger ones; there is also one glass manufacturer (the large and important firm of Chance Bros.), one edge tool manufacturer, four railway companies, one canal company, and two landowners (one of them with important coal and iron interests). Groups 3, 4 and 5 are all composed entirely of large and important coal and iron firms.

In all these groups, and especially in Groups 3, 4 and 5, the decision to prosecute lies in the hands of the coal and iron masters. It is not surprising that the large coal and iron masters prosecuted more frequently than the small workshop employers. The large coal and iron firms owned a number of works, spread over a number of areas; each works was on a much larger scale than a workshop, employing hundreds

Table 30   Black Country Prosecutors for Industrial Thefts 1835-60

Group	No. of Prosecutions per Prosecutor	No. of Prosecutors	Total Prosecutions Brought by Each Group
1	1- 3	219	341
2	4- 20	73	599
3	20- 50	17	516
4	50- 90	6	407
5	90-180	3	435
TOTAL		318	2,298

of men and exposing large quantities of property to the workmen; the problems of control and surveillance would obviously be far greater than in a workshop. One would expect these firms to suffer more from depredation, and hence to prosecute more frequently.

However, the difference in the numbers of prosecutions brought cannot be explained solely in terms of the respective sizes of the firms involved. Certainly, the three prosecutors making up Group 5 were all very large coal and iron concerns. They were, respectively: the vast integrated coal and iron concern of the Earl of Dudley;[33] the Chillington Iron Co. of John Barker and his two sons George and Thomas; and the firm of W. & J.S. Sparrow.[34] And of the six firms making up Group 4, five (John Bagnall & Sons, Philip Williams & Co., the New British Iron Co., Samuel Holden Blackwell, and Thomas & Isaac Badger) were top-ranking coal and iron firms.

But size and importance of the firm alone do not explain the large number of prosecutions. All the large prosecutors are top coal and iron firms, but not all the top coal and iron firms are among the greatest prosecutors. Of the large Black Country coal and iron firms listed by G.C. Allen,[35] five come into Groups 4 and 5, one (Benjamin Gibbons) falls into Group 3, three (the British Iron Co., G.B. Thorneycroft & Co., and Barrows & Hall) are found in Group 2, and the other two (N. Hingley & Sons, and John Bradley & Co.) do not feature as prosecutors at all. A large firm such as Lloyds is found in Group 3, and a number of other large firms, such as those of James Foster, Addenbrooks and the glassmakers Chance Bros. who were among the largest employers in the Black Country, are found only in Group 2; firms such as the steel manufacturers Isaac Jenks, the engineering firm Thomas Perry & Sons, and the large Patent Shaft & Axletree Co. are all found in Group 1.[36]

These were all large firms with a number of works and many employees, and it is inherently unlikely that one firm would suffer significantly more thefts by its employees than another. There must be some other reason to explain this disparity in the numbers of prosecutions – why in the same period the Barkers' Chillington Iron Co. brought 175 prosecutions for industrial theft, while Lloyds brought forty-five, Thorneycrofts brought eleven, the Patent Shaft & Axletree Co. brought only one, and N. Hingley and Sons brought none. The answer must lie in the different policies of the proprietors of these firms towards prosecution for industrial thefts. The employers of Group 5 evidently had a policy of prosecuting for such thefts where those of Group 1 would presumably use other forms of sanctions or overlook the offence.

One can suggest some possible reasons for these differences in policy by looking at the three firms in Group 5. First of these was the firm W. & J.S. Sparrow. The presiding influence here was William Hanbury Sparrow himself and, to a lesser extent, his son William Mander Sparrow and his nephew John Sparrow who took over the running of the firm after William Hanbury's death in the 1860s. Over the whole period 1835-60, Sparrow instituted 120 prosecutions for industrial thefts in the Black Country, as well as an equally large number in the North Staffordshire Potteries, where he also had a number of coal and iron works.

Secondly, the Dudley estates recorded 140 industrial theft prosecutions in 1835-60; here the dominant influence was that of Richard Smith, from 1836 agent to the trustees of the Earl of Dudley's estates, and from 1845 agent to Lord Ward (Earl of Dudley after 1860). Smith's reorganisation and efficient administration of the large Dudley estates and mineral resources, both through leasing out coal and iron mines on a royalty basis and through direct coal mining and iron manufacture undertaken by the estate, built up the Dudley estates to make the Earl the seventh richest peer in England. Smith not only administered the mineral resources of the estate but also acted as Lord Ward's political and administrative agent, through whom Ward exercised a total dominance and political stranglehold over the town of Dudley, and considerable influence over the rest of the Black Country.[37]

Finally, John Barker was an ironmaster who with two others built up a very large ironworks at Chillington near Wolverhampton which, after his death in 1852, was run by his sons Thomas and George; he was a prominent Liberal and Dissenter, among the first of the ironmasters to be appointed High Sheriff of Staffordshire. His firm brought the largest number of industrial theft prosecutions – no less than 175, and all of these in the period 1844-60.[38]

Evidence relating to these three firms and their policy on prosecutions is fragmentary, and is stronger for Sparrow and the Dudley estates than for Barker, but it suggests that the frequent prosecutions came in those coal and iron works where relations between employer and employee were bad. Sparrow certainly enjoyed a bad reputation as an employer – he was notorious for openly and unashamedly using truck in the payment of his workmen, and his name was cited as a bad employer during miners' strikes.[39] The Dudley estate was also resented, in some respects, as a bad employer; true, it did not use truck and was prepared to support campaigns against truck payments, but it employed 'butties' to run its mines, was prominent in enforcing wage-cuts which led to strikes, and was criticised for not using its enormous economic, social and political power in the area to improve the shocking safety conditions in the local coal-pits. Richard Smith himself was personally unpopular for the amount of power he wielded and the way in which he exercised it.[40] There is no comparable information which can be found for Barker, though he was publicly shown to use truck payments in 1842.[41]

One feature shared by all the firms in Group 5, almost all in Group 4, and most of those in Group 3 is that their proprietors and managers were appointed as magistrates in the late 1830s, 1840s or 1850s. This brought them considerable influence and importance and, it has been suggested, may well have been related to their increased number of prosecutions and committals to trial for industrial thefts.

Finally, it is of some interest to note that the nine firms making up Groups 4 and 5 together were responsible for at least 842 industrial theft prosecutions between 1835 and 1860 – about 4 per cent of *all indictable prosecutions brought for any offence* in the Black Country in this period. The coal and iron masters were the main employers of the area; they also came to dominate the magistracy with its important judicial and administrative powers; and here we see the power which a few of them exercised within the legal system as prosecutors, as well.

The sentences imposed on those convicted of industrial thefts were generally not very heavy. About 90 per cent were given prison sentences, 70 per cent being prison sentences of three months or less. About 8 per cent were transported in the 1830s and early 1840s, and a decreasing proportion thereafter. The increased numbers convicted under the CJA after 1855 were either fined or given prison terms of less than one month.[42]

(B) Thefts of Items of Clothing

This was a common type of theft; typical examples:

(1) Sarah Smith went into the pawnshop of Abel Hartill, a Willenhall pawnbroker, to redeem a pledge. A few hours after she had left, Hartill found a shirt and waistcoat missing from his stock; he went to John Atkins, another Willenhall pawnbroker, told him what had been taken, and that he suspected Smith of having taken them. Shortly thereafter, Smith brought the waistcoat to Atkins to pledge it, and she was given in custody.[43]

(2) James Holsby lodged in the same house in Wolverhampton as

George Bagley. One day he suddenly left the house without notice, taking with him a pair of shoes, a pair of trousers, a velvet jacket, and a pair of razors in a case, all belonging to Bagley. Holsby pledged the trousers with a pawnbroker in Wolverhampton, and was subsequently arrested in Stafford by a police officer, with the jacket on his back, and in his pocket the pawn ticket for the trousers and the case with the pair of razors.[44]

Typical places from which articles of clothing were stolen were: a shop (pawnbroker's, or a clothing shop or stall); a house or room in which the accused had been lodging (or, in a few cases, had been employed as a servant); a pub (usually the clothing taken was a hat or coat); or from inside a house, an outhouse or a washing line by some outsider.

Theft of clothing was very common, as the number of prosecutions suggests. Clothes were easy to get at, easy to carry away, and relatively difficult for the owner to identify with certainty. They were not generally of great value in themselves, but were very easy to dispose of – being worn by the thief or his immediate family, or being easily pawned or sold.

The prosecutions for this offence are certainly only a fraction of the number of such thefts which actually took place. Clothing could be too easily taken and disposed of for the system of prosecution to work with any greater precision. This can be seen from those cases which did reach the courts – a number of these rely on a more or less fortuitous finding and identification of the person responsible, in order to recover the property and prosecute the offender. If an article of one's clothing was stolen, there was no point in telling the constable unless one had at least some idea of the name, appearance or whereabouts of the person who might have taken it.

For example, Ann Manley took a pair of boots from John Whitehead's kitchen and was seen by Whitehead's servant doing so; two months later she was seen in a beershop by a Bilston parish constable, who recognised her on the strength of the servant's description and arrested her. Peter Whitfield, from Bilston, had a bundle of clothes taken from him while in a Wolverhampton pub. Suspecting that they had been taken by Jane Young, he searched around Wolverhampton until he eventually found her in another pub and had her arrested.[45]

There must have been many such incidents which never reached the courts at all because of the difficulty and inconvenience of first finding the culprit and then producing sufficient evidence for a prosecution.

Even many of the cases which got to Quarter Sessions failed there for lack of evidence.

But it is clear that many of the Black Country towns were small and cohesive enough for the old police system to function fairly well. Since pawning was a common form of disposal of stolen clothes, a visit to the pawnshop could often produce the stolen items and a name or description of the person who pawned them; if they had not yet been pawned, a warning to watch for certain articles being brought in could result in the thief being caught. And a number of people *were* caught by the victim or a constable doing the rounds of the pubs or putting out the offender's name or description.

The examples cited so far all come from the 1830s or early 1840s, when the Black Country police system still consisted almost entirely of parish constables supplemented by a few night watches. By the 1850s the position had changed somewhat, as the 'New Police' forces increased in size and scope; but, as chapter 3 showed, even the 'New Police' were stretched in their manpower and resources, and had to continue the 'Parish constable' *modus operandi* for large areas of the Black Country. Recovery of stolen clothes was not something to which the police gave high priority, so the burden of finding and identifying the thief and the property remained mainly on the victim.

People disappearing from lodging-houses, pubs or shops after a theft were not easy to trace, and even the 'New Police' were disinclined to follow up such cases.[46] Even if the offender was found, many victims were more interested in recovering their property than in prosecuting; some prosecutors in cases which came to court made it clear that they had only prosecuted because it was the only way they could recover the property.

Commonest prosecutors for clothing theft were small tradesmen or artisans in the clothing trades – clothes dealers, hatters, drapers, shoemakers, tailors, pawnbrokers. A fairly large number of labourers, miners and boatmen also prosecuted for thefts of their clothes, and a number of widows and spinsters who took in lodgers or let out rooms.

Of those charged with this offence, about 75 per cent were unskilled manual workers, especially labourers and miners.[47] The typical clothing theft was committed by a miner or labourer against a small clothing retailer or against the family of another unskilled worker.

How far was this a crime committed by professional thieves? Most of those accused of clothing thefts are recorded as having an occupation; but they might also have stolen clothes and other articles fairly regularly to supplement their income. The sentences imposed on clothes thieves are fairly heavy, with a high proportion receiving transportation.[48] This suggests a fairly high rate of previous convictions among those convicted of clothing thefts; larcenies (other than of horses or cattle) were seldom punished by transportation for a first offence.[49] The fact that police or prosecutors were fairly easily able to lay their hands on those whom they thought responsible, suggests that some of those prosecuted for clothing thefts were 'known' to the authorities. Comments made in sentencing some of the clothing thieves suggest a view from the Bench of the prisoners as known bad characters.[50]

The evidence suggests that many of the clothing thefts were committed by people who stole regularly, while also having occupations at which they worked at least part of the time. These were the people who stole from shops, pubs, and private houses – the clothing thefts by absconding lodgers and servants seem to be more irregular and unplanned. Those who stole regularly while also being employed were the 'hardened' ones who received the heavier sentences. But they can hardly be called 'professional thieves', since stealing clothing was not particularly lucrative. They were rather neither 'honest poor' nor 'criminal class', but an important third category – people in employment who supplemented their income with thefts.

Finally, as has been noted, the cases which reached court were probably only the tip of the iceberg. Tradesmen prosecuted such thefts frequently, despite the cost and inconvenience, because it was in their interests to go to some trouble to deter such thefts. But for workers and their families, many clothing thefts must have gone legally unpunished because of the difficulty of prosecuting unless the culprit could be easily and quickly found. Even if he were found, there may have been many cases in which he was punished by immediate rough summary justice dealt out by the victim rather than by a full legal prosecution. But it is important to note that there still *was* a fairly large number of prosecutions for clothing thefts brought by working-class victims. Unlike industrial thefts, there was no attitude of popular legitimation of clothing thefts – which, of course, harmed not the wealthy coal and iron masters but the working class individual and family.

(C) Thefts of Food and Drink, Timber, Fodder, etc., and Small Domestic Animals

These made up another large group of thefts; typical examples:

(1) John Morgan went into the butcher's shop of Thomas Jones in Wolverhampton. He was seen by Jones' brother to walk up and down the shop, without buying any meat. Suspecting him, Jones continued to watch him, and saw him take a chawl of pork from the counter, put it under his frock, and walk out of the shop. Jones followed and caught him, and Morgan claimed that a woman had bought the chawl and asked him to take it home for her.[51]

(2) William Sheldon, a farmer in Handsworth, had a potato patch 200 yards from his house, which he found was being frequently plundered while a canal was being built in the vicinity. The farmers of the area paid the local constable, Richard Aston, and a labourer, Thomas Mills, to watch at night, and to see if they could find the thieves. They were led to some deserted buildings where John Hardy, a canal builder, and some others were, where a sack of potatoes was found. Hardy was arrested, and admitted that he had taken them from a field; he took Aston to the field, which was Sheldon's patch.[52]

(3) John Burford, a farmer near Bilston, kept fowls in a locked shed next to his house. One morning he found that the shed's lock had been broken with a collier's pick and two fowls and a duck taken. He knew of the existence of a 'gang of thieves, which for a long time has infested the neighbourhood of Tipton', especially robbing fowl roosts, and knew that Isiah (or Isaac) Green was a member of this gang. So he looked for Green, and found him in a pigsty, plucking two fowls. The fowls, being plucked, could not be identified, but Burford identified the duck as his. Green was found guilty, and, 'there being no redeeming quality in the prisoner's character', he was sentenced to seven years' transportation.[53]

Most frequent of the food thefts was the theft from shop or market stall; as in example (1), meat, cheese, bread or butter was taken from the shop or stall. Usually the customer bought, or pretended to look at, some other item, while slipping the stolen food under his or her coat or cloak; sometimes they would suddenly seize the food and run off.

In some cases, the accused had been employed in the shop from which he took the food. For example, Humphrey Roberts was employed by Joshua Hall, butcher in West Bromwich. Hall had to leave his shop for a short time, and left Roberts in charge; when he returned, he found Roberts gone and noticed that several pounds had been cut off a piece of beef. He went and looked for Roberts, and found him with the beef in his possession.[54] Generally, the thefts of food from shops and stalls are similar in their details to the thefts of clothing from shops and stalls; food and clothing were the commonest articles sold in shops in the 1840s and 1850s, and both could be easily taken and disposed of.

Example (2) is a pattern fairly frequently encountered – crops taken from a farmer or householder; timber or fodder taken from farmers, householders or dealers. Potatoes were the commonest vegetable taken from the fields, and sometimes turnips; occasionally grain or other stored foodstuffs were taken from a barn or storehouse.

Farmers and smallholders were apt to get very sensitive to the dangers of their fields being raided by marauding 'vagrants' or migrant workers. In example (2) the canal workers were immediately suspected by all the farmers of being responsible for the depredations; whenever canal workers – and later railway workers – were employed in the vicinity, farmers and property owners were apt to get nervous and ask for special police protection for their property. For instance, when the South Staffordshire Railway Co. were building a line through Rushall Parish, the farmers asked the local JP to swear in a special constable to guard their property; their depositions stress the thefts, trespassing and damage committed by the navvies – 'The first week they came into the neighbourhood I lost a couple of ducks'; the several hundred navvies 'are frequently about my premises in the night; they pull my Straw places about', etc. Similar complaints were made about navvies constructing a canal branch near Pelsall at the same time.[55] Presumably the farmers had good grounds for these suspicions, as the lives and conditions of navvies were known to be conducive to such 'living off the country'.[56] But navvies were not the only such offenders; in many cases which reached the court, the accused had been temporary workers employed by the prosecutor to pick the vegetables, who had kept some for themselves, or had returned after the picking was over to help themselves.

Other food thefts involved small quantities taken from people's houses – usually by servants or employees. A few cases concern containers of drink taken from warehouses, boats or railway depots by employees. And there are a few cases in which labourers prosecute for theft of their bundles of lunch – stolen while they were at work or on the road.

Example (3) typifies the theft of small domestic animals – mostly poultry, but also sometimes rabbits or pigeons; virtually all of them were thefts of the animals from their fowl-roost, shed or hutch. All of these animals could, of course, be eaten, though the pigeons were kept by their owners for recreation and not food.

Theft of food is the example most often used to illustrate a crime committed through hunger. How far was this true of the people committing these thefts? A sizable proportion of these thefts was clearly *not* committed on impulse by starving people, and showed deliberate planning. The thefts of food from shops, like those of clothing, bear all the hallmarks of being planned jobs. Like the clothing thieves, many of the food shoplifters seem to have been people who were employed, but who also stole fairly regularly; like the clothing shoplifters again, a large proportion of them had previous convictions and received transportation sentences. Poultry thieves were given transportation in an even higher proportion suggesting a large number of prior offenders among them.[57]

The occupations of these offenders were very similar to those of the people charged with clothing thefts – over 75 per cent were from the unskilled and semi-skilled working class, mostly miners and labourers.

The typical prosecutor in the food thefts was a small shopkeeper, or a farmer or householder with a vegetable patch. The motive for prosecution seems to have been the general hope of deterring other potential offenders, rather than of recovering the specific item, since the value of the items stolen was always very small.

William Cobbett commented adversely on this habit of prosecuting for the theft of a few inexpensive vegetables. While riding through Gloucestershire, he came upon a group of people chasing an old man, 'a *poor* man', for stealing cabbages 'out of Mr Glover, the hatter's garden'.

'What!' (Cobbett reports himself saying) 'do you call that *stealing*; and would you punish a man, a poor man, and therefore, in all likelihood, a hungry man too, and moreover an old man; do you set up a hue-and-cry after, and would you punish a man for taking a few cabbages, when that Holy Bible. . .teaches you that the hungry man may, without committing any offence at all, go into his neighbour's vineyard and eat his fill of grapes, one bunch of which is worth a sack-full of cabbages?'

'Yes; but he is a very bad character.'

'Why, my friend, very poor and starved people are apt to be "bad characters"; but the Bible, in both Testaments, commands us to be merciful to the poor, to feed the hungry, to have compassion on the aged; and it makes no exception as to the 'character' of the parties.'

And he remarks that in the United States it would be unheard of to prosecute someone for taking part of a growing crop for his own use.[58]

Cobbett here rightly stresses the way in which prosecutions were determined by the growers of the crops, who always had the option not to prosecute. Farmers were among the keenest prosecutors of such thefts of crops; this can be seen, not only in the examples cited above, but also in the Associations for the Prosecution of Felons, which were largely made up of farmers and concerned themselves with prosecutions for thefts of crops.[59] And shopkeepers formed the backbone of the movement which pressed, between 1800 and 1830, for repeal of the death penalty for stealing from shops and the substitution of less severe penalties more efficiently enforced; the theory was that lesser penalties enforced uniformly were preferable as a deterrent to the death penalty enforced unevenly, its terror mitigated by frequent pardons and refusals of juries to convict.[60]

The prosecutors for the theft of small animals included a large number of farmers, but the majority were ordinary householders who kept poultry, pigeons or rabbits — miners were particularly common among these, also some labourers, metal craftsmen and publicans, and there were a few butchers for whom the animals were part of their trade. Pigeon fancying was a common Black Country working-class recreation, and fowls were kept wherever possible to supplement the family income and diet. Theft of poultry and pigeons was one of those areas in which miners and labourers brought prosecutions themselves.

Freeman mentions how common fowl-stealing was in the Bilston area in the 1830s and 1840s, but suggests that it was not treated very seriously by the men affected, and was punished by informal, rather than formal legal sanctions:

> In those days fowl stealing was regarded by many as nothing worse than a rude practical joke, and amongst themselves the fraternity practised a crude sort of justice. When a man found that during the night his chicken pen had been cleared of his roosters, he 'hearkened out' as the old phrase has it, made up his mind who was the thief and raided his pen.[61]

If this is correct, and most poultry thefts from workingmen *were* remedied by this form of self-help, then the number of cases which reached the courts would represent only a small fraction of the total incidence of such cases. Freeman may be right in his description of these forms of self-helping punishment and compensation; but a substantial number of workingmen undoubtedly *did* prosecute formally for this offence.

Freeman suggests here that taking poultry from one's neighbour was a common practice of Black Country workingmen at this time. But in two other passages, he suggests that there was a more identifiable group of poultry thieves, and he names two Bilston inns at which the poultry thieves used to gather to plan their raids.[62] The heavy sentences on many poultry thieves suggests that many of them had previous convictions and were seen by the courts as 'bad characters'.

The evidence on both offenders and prosecutors for poultry thefts suggests that these thefts took place among the miners and labourers themselves. Probably the number of these cases which got to court was only a small proportion of the total thefts. Unless the thief was caught in the act, it would be difficult to find him, and even more difficult to identify the stolen birds – particularly if the thief had already plucked them, as Isiah Green had done in example (3).

In the extract from Cobbett given above (p.201), he stressed hunger as the cause of theft of food. How much light can we throw on this point? In a few cases, the accused gave as a reason for his stealing food the hunger of himself or his family – for instance, Thomas Hunt in 1848, year of depression and unemployment, pleaded guilty to stealing 7 lb of cheese from a shop; he said in mitigation that he and his family were starving; 'The parish would afford him no relief, and he had been obliged to sell his bed to purchase bread; and had nothing to lie on but straw.'[63] This instance is a pathetic and probably genuine one. But hunger was an obvious justification for an accused to raise in mitigation of his stealing food; the surprising fact is not that it was raised as a defence, but how *infrequently* it was raised as a defence – suggesting that the majority of the cases prosecuted were not of people who had been forced to steal through desperate want.

The shoplifting instances do not seem to have sprung from the immediate pressure of want; most indicate careful planning before the offender entered the shop. But some of them may have been provoked by the sight of the food displayed and a spur-of-the-moment decision to take it – this is particularly true for open stalls in markets. Many nineteenth-century observers noted and condemned the way in which shopkeepers invited theft by the way in which they displayed their goods. Matthew Davenport Hill, Recorder of Birmingham, in 1845 criticised

the pernicious habit indulged in by the shopkeepers of this town, in common with those of other places, who persist in exposing their wares at their shop-doors. Many a child has been led into overpowering temptation by this practice.[64]

One or two of the cases in court support the idea that the accused was suddenly tempted by the opportunity offered to him, seized the item and ran off. But most of the cases indicate that most of those who stole food from shops were like those who stole clothing from shops – people employed regularly or casually, who stole on a reasonably regular basis to supplement their incomes. It is notable that in virtually all these cases which came to court, the actual food taken was found and identified, even when it involved a search of the accused's lodgings – showing that the food was not taken for immediate consumption.

On the other hand, in cases where growing vegetables were taken, they seem to have often been for immediate consumption. Navvies took them to supplement their irregular supplies; and some thefts were by labourers who felt they had some right to the vegetables. For example, Martin Meighan, Patrick McGovern and Michael Connolly were hired by Robert Corgan, a farmer, to bag his potatoes; they were found taking potatoes, and pointed out in their defence that they were allowed to take six of the largest potatoes each night they had worked. This was admitted by Corgan, and the only question was whether they had taken more than they were entitled to.[65] Similarly, Humphrey Roberts, charged with taking meat from his employer, a butcher, claimed that he was often paid in stale meat instead of cash, and that he had done no more than take some of his wages for himself.[66]

It may also be significant that there was an abnormally large number of prosecutions for thefts of food in the Quarter Sessions of January 1842; these people had been arrested in November and December 1841, and this increase may reflect some people pushed into theft by the effect of a hard winter during a depression. Some of those charged at these Sessions *did* claim that they stole the food because of distress – but, as was mentioned above, this was the obvious excuse to put forward once one had been caught; one cannot take it as proving that distress was the cause of the thefts. A reasonable conclusion seems to be that want and immediate distress *did* play a part in provoking some of the thefts of food, but that a large number – certainly a majority of those which reached the courts – seem not to have sprung directly from the immediate pressure of hunger.

(D) Theft of Large Domestic Animals

This covers thefts of horses, cattle and sheep. It was treated far more seriously than other larcenies in terms of the penalties imposed, and the value of the property stolen was much greater than in other larcenies. These thefts, especially horse stealing, had always been regarded as very serious offences; in the eighteenth century they were capital offences, and this (together with stealing in a dwelling-house to the value of £5 or more) was the last type of larceny for which the death penalty was repealed, in 1832; even then it was replaced, initially, by a mandatory sentence of transportation for life.

This offence came up relatively infrequently from the Black Country – only 331 such cases between 1835 and 1860; one would expect such an offence to be less common in an industrialised area than in an agricultural one. But there was still a fair amount of sheep stealing from farms on the edge of the Black Country (thefts of cattle were far less common); and horses, of course, were used and valued in the towns as well as on farms.

In the typical sheep-stealing offence, the sheep was taken from the farmer's field during the night and immediately killed for the meat. In most of the cases in which sheep stealers were prosecuted, the prosecutor relied on identifying the meat or the skin to prove that it had been stolen from him. Much of the sheep stealing was done by people similar to those involved in stealing farmers' crops, or poultry – unskilled workers, casual labourers, navvies – in order to supplement their diet. There were also some professional gangs of sheep stealers who took large numbers of sheep, and sold them live or sold their meat. But most of the men who ended up in court (and, in effect, all of them *were* men – only six of the 331 prosecuted for all large animal thefts in these twenty-six years were women) were more amateurish about it, and were found with the stolen meat in their lodgings, the carcass of the sheep having been clumsily cut up.

Horse-stealing offences were more varied; horses were taken from a farmer's field at night or from where they were tied up outside a house or inn or from stables; some were taken while they were being sold at a market or fair, the alleged purchaser mounting the horse to try it out and then simply riding off without paying for it. The motive behind the stealing seems to have varied considerably, too: often the horse was ridden to another town and sold as soon as possible; sometimes the thief kept it for his own use.

At times, the theft seems to have been just a high-spirited prank to take an illicit joyride, in the manner of some modern teenage motor-car thefts. This last would seem to be an incredible risk to take for a bit of fun in view of the harsh penalties which the offence carried, but some prisoners did make this claim in their defence. For example, William Smith, aged twenty-four, took a pony which had been left at the door of a house in which its owner was visiting. He was chased on a borrowed horse and caught. His defence was that 'it was a lark'; the jury presumably accepted this, since they acquitted him.[67]

But many more of the horse thefts were committed by professional thieves, often members of gangs, with previous convictions. The courts tended to be severe with large animal stealers. Some sheep stealers were imprisoned; but, in the 1830s, all horse thieves were transported, most for very long terms. In the 1840s and 1850s, the proportion being given transportation or penal servitude gradually declined; but over the period as a whole, half of the men convicted of this offence were transported. Fourteen per cent of all the convicts sent to Australia went for theft of large animals.[68]

Probably, with this offence, wherever a culprit was found he was prosecuted. It may have been difficult to identify, for instance, the meat of a sheep which had been killed (as a number of the cases suggest), and some stolen horses may have proved difficult to trace and find. But it is most unlikely that, once the stolen animals and likely culprits were found, the prosecutors would have held back from prosecuting, as was the case with some larcenies of smaller articles or animals. For one thing, the value of a horse or a sheep was substantial enough to make it important to try to recover the stolen animal by means of an investigation and prosecution. For another thing, the men from whom the animals were stolen tended to be farmers or butchers, or men who could afford to keep and ride horses — substantial men who could afford to pay for the investigations and prosecution. One can see, for instance, how much emphasis the Associations for Prosecution placed on investigating and prosecuting thefts of horses and sheep; the Chillington Association's system of rewards and patrols was primarily directed towards this end. Not all horse-stealing prosecutions were brought by men in comfortable financial circumstances — some of the horses were stolen from carters, horse-dealers or boatmen, for whom the horse was an integral part of their occupation; but the importance of the horse to their livelihoods ensured that these people, too, followed up and prosecuted all such cases keenly.

These offences were relatively infrequent in an area like the Black

Country but, because of the value of the animals, the frequent involvement of gangs in the thefts and the harsh penalties attached to conviction, it was regarded as an important offence, and was much discussed by magistrates, judges, policemen and police reformers as an indication of the state of law and order in an area. Breaking up a sheep-stealing gang, or a decline in the number of animal thefts was often cited by police forces or constables as an indication of their efficiency. The popular attitude towards it seems to have been that it was a serious offence; except for the few cases of youths taking horses for 'joyrides', there is no indication of a casual attitude of tolerance towards this offence, such as was seen in the case of poultry thefts.

(E) Thefts from the Person

This category includes the offence which was taken as typifying professional crime and the criminals of the cities — picking pockets. When contemporary writers talked about the state of crime in the cities and discussed whether it was increasing or decreasing, it was the crimes which struck at the safety of person and property in the streets — robbery and picking pockets — to which they most often referred.[69] In the most famous literary representation of nineteenth-century London crime, Fagin is the master and instructor of a gang of pickpockets. But not all of those tried for larceny from the person were professional pickpockets. Three typical examples show the three main forms taken by the offence, as prosecuted in the courts:

(1) William Bottwood, a servant employed by a gentleman in Albrighton, Shropshire, was sent to Wolverhampton on business. When his business was over, he went into a liquor shop, where he picked up a young prostitute. He went home with her, had intercourse with her, and paid her 2/6. He then found that his money, £17 17s was missing. She said she would look for it, and Bottwood, who admitted to being a little drunk at the time, let her go, only to find that she had vanished from the house. He then called in a policeman, who arrested a girl answering to the name which Bottwood gave. But his identification of her was tentative, and his evidence shaky, and the indictment was thrown out by the Grand Jury.[70]

(2) Mary Burkin was selling butter and eggs in Wolverhampton market. Mary Ann Joyce and Ellen Riley came up to her and asked her about prices. While Riley was haggling with her, Joyce got behind her and took her purse without her noticing; the two then left without

buying anything. They were arrested later that day on another
charge of pocket-picking, and Burkin's purse was found on them.
They were both found guilty and transported for seven years.[71]

(3) John Toy, a boatman, was drinking in a beer shop with John
Woodham and Thomas Jones. He became drunk and fell asleep, and
was awoken by Woodham trying to get his hand into his breeches
pocket. He found his money and three handkerchiefs gone; Jones
had one of his handkerchiefs. He asked Woodham for his money
back, but did not get it, so he called in the constable. Woodham was
found guilty and transported for ten years; Jones was acquitted.[72]

Example (1), theft by a prostitute or a woman offering sexual
intercourse, recurs again and again; unlike this example, the woman
was often convicted and transported. Typically, this would involve a
man from out of town coming into one of the large towns (usually
Wolverhampton), and either being picked up by a woman in a pub, or
directly visiting a brothel. This would usually take place in
Wolverhampton or Dudley, as only these two towns possessed a large
number of brothels and prostitutes; there were very few prostitutes
to be found in the other towns of the Black Country.[73]

Usually, the woman would take the money or articles from the
man's clothes after he had undressed for intercourse, or while she was
sitting on his lap in the pub; sometimes a male accomplice would come
in and take the money with threats of violence. The woman obviously
reckoned on the fact that the embarrassment of admitting that they
had been with a prostitute would prevent many of the men pressing an
investigation and prosecution. Furthermore, if they were arrested, the
women could always claim that they had not taken the money, but
that it had been given to them as payment for intercourse.[74] The fear
of embarrassment among the victims was clearly strong; even of those
cases which got as far as the courts, a number of policemen testified
that they had had to argue very hard to persuade the victims to carry
through the prosecutions; victims called in the police to recover the
stolen property, but then often wanted to drop the prosecution at that
point. The Chief Constable of Wolverhampton reported that there had
been thirty-eight such offences reported, and only eighteen brought to
justice, and noted: 'Chiefly committed in brothels. Complainants
generally drunk – and following day decline to prosecute.'[75]

Even when the cases did get to court, the embarrassing nature of
the case often induced Grand Juries to 'ignore' the indictment. The
Chairman of the Staffordshire Quarter Sessions noted in many charges

to Grand Juries that such cases frequently came to court from
Wolverhampton; he referred to the embarrassment of himself and Grand
Juries in such cases at the fact that the prosecutor should have shown
himself to be immoral, imprudent, and thereby in some respects,
deserving of his fate. He euphemistically described the problem of

> those cases in which women were charged with robbing men under
> particular circumstances. Men leaving public-houses at night, not
> quite sober, met with women of the town by whom they were
> induced to accompany them for a purpose he need not mention,
> and the women took the opportunity of robbing them of their
> money. Grand juries sometimes threw out the bills in these cases,
> with a feeling natural, perhaps, to most men, that those men robbed
> under these peculiar circumstances deserved to be robbed, and that
> the county ought not to be called upon to pay for the prosecution
> of the offenders.

In another charge, he told the Grand Jury that

> it was a matter of surprise that men were not ashamed of bringing
> them [cases of robbery in brothels] to the Sessions.

But he also stressed that Grand Juries were too apt to use this as a
reason for throwing out the Bill altogether, which meant that the
women were able to get away with such acts unpunished; he
recommended

> that if the felony were clearly made out, that it was better for the
> jury to discard all extraneous considerations in such cases, and
> return a true bill, for it was too much to say that women were to
> be allowed to go about lying in wait for drunken men for the
> purpose of robbing them with impunity.[76]

But a number of these prosecutions were thrown out by the Grand
Jury or found not guilty by the jury. Grand Juries and juries evidently
felt that prosecutors in such cases had by their conduct contributed to
their own loss. In addition, the evidence in such cases was often
shaky – the prosecutor had to be able to identify the woman
positively, and to testify firmly that he had had his money when he
joined the woman and had missed it immediately afterwards; a good
defence counsel could play on the man's drunkenness and lust in order

to discredit his evidence. So, probably many such cases never found their way to court. On the other hand, the fact that the sums stolen were often large (in excess of £10) probably would have meant that the victims pushed hard at least for an investigation and a chance to recover the money. When the victims did press charges, the police or parish constables seem to have been able to lay their hands on the prostitutes fairly easily.

Example (2) typifies the professional pickpocket at work in the street, the market or any crowded public place. An enormous amount was written in nineteenth-century books, pamphlets, periodicals and reports about the craft skills of experienced pickpockets, derived from the confessions of convicted thieves or the investigations of journalists like Mayhew.[77] Description of these techniques and practices has been fully covered in Mayhew and in recent books on nineteenth-century crime,[78] and is not dealt with in any detail here; the Black Country cases show themselves to be less dramatic and colourful than some of the London incidents and revelations, but they reveal similar techniques in use. The cases show the accused picking pockets in public places – the street, the pub, the market, fairs and wakes, the racecourse, and removing wallets, watches, handkerchiefs. Usually they operated in pairs, one picking the pocket, the other being used to distract the victim's attention or to dispose of the stolen articles before they could be found on the person of the actual thief. It is noteworthy that here was an area of crime in which women and young boys were prominent; Binny noted that young boys were trained to the skill from an early age, and that 'the most dexterous pickpockets generally average from twenty to thirty-five years of age'.[79]

Example (3) is of a different sort and was usually not the work of a professional criminal; but it is as common in the courts as either of the other two. The facts of these cases are monotonously simple: The victim and the accused (and sometimes some others) would be drinking together in a pub or in someone's house; the victim would become drunk and fall asleep, and awake to find his money and/or other possessions taken from his pocket; or be awakened by feeling a hand inside his pocket. This was the commonest set of facts repeated in case after case. On some occasions, the victim would take off his jacket and lay it down and find, when he retrieved it, that his money was gone from the pocket; quite often, this would happen when the victim took part in a sparring match in the yard of the pub – an incident which seems to have occurred frequently. For instance:

> Benjamin Guy was drinking in a pub with Charles Kitson; Guy took
> off his coat and went outside to spar with a friend, and during his
> absence, his money was taken, presumably by Kitson.
>
> Luke Wilkes was in a beershop with John Bennett; Bennett
> induced Wilkes to spar with another man, and, while Wilkes was
> taking off his smock for this purpose, his money and tobacco-box
> were taken from his pocket.[80]

Sometimes the prosecution seems to spring out of what began as some
form of practical joke which grew more serious when the 'joker' refused
to return the property. For instance,

> John Dawkins had been drinking with Thomas Roper and two others;
> being drunk, he feigned sleep to avoid having to drink any more;
> Roper came up to him while he was apparently asleep, and took a
> crown-piece out of his pocket, saying 'Now we'll go and have some
> more drink'. Dawkins assumed this was done as a joke, and so took
> no action until much later in the evening, when he asked Roper to
> return the crown, but Roper denied that he had taken it. Dawkins
> brought the prosecution in order to get it back.

Similarly,

> William Brookes got into a quarrel with his brother at a club feast
> held at a pub. He was pulling his hand out of his pocket in a hurry,
> in order to start fighting his brother, when he pulled out and dropped
> a sovereign. Phoebe Downing picked it up off the floor; Brookes
> asked for it, and she said: 'I'll give it you when the bother is over'.
> Brookes pulled off his waistcoat and coat, which had six half-crowns
> in the pockets and put them on the table. After the fight, he found
> the sovereign and the half-crowns missing, and the prisoner gone.
> At the trial, the jury announced: 'They found the prisoner (Downing)
> guilty, but thought it a bit of a drunken frolic.' The Chairman would
> not accept that verdict — they must find her either guilty or not
> guilty; they then found her guilty, but recommended her to mercy.[81]

These cases are clearly not the work of professional criminals, unlike
the other two types of theft from the person. In most of these cases,
the men with whom the victim was drinking were friends or associates
of his, often men with whom he worked. The circumstances suggest
that the theft sprang from a sudden realisation of the opportunity

offered by the companion being drunk and having money on his person.
There are a few of these cases in which the offender seems deliberately
to have decoyed his victim into this state of drunkenness in order to
rob him, but most of them show no premeditation of this sort; and, as
the examples show, there was only a thin borderline between the crude
practical joke and a criminal offence. Because of the normal
circumstances of such a prosecution – relying heavily on the testimony
of a prosecutor who was admittedly drunk at the time of the offence –
the prosecution case could be easily shaken, and acquittals were
frequent.

Taking the three types together, this was a category in which female
offenders were prominent – 500 (38.3 per cent) of the 1,304 people
prosecuted for this category during 1835-60, were women or girls. In
terms of the three types of case, those accused of type (1) were,
naturally, always women; those accused of type (2) were often women;
those accused of type (3) were very seldom women.

Severe sentences, often involving transportation, were imposed on
those convicted of types (1) and (2) – thefts by prostitutes and by
pickpockets; but the type (3) thefts were usually punished by only
light prison sentences.[82] Judges and magistrates were keen to inflict
strong penalties on those who were clearly professional pickpockets or
thieves. For instance:

Two women picked up a man who had come to Wolverhampton to
sell a horse, got him to buy them drinks, and then robbed him as
they came out of the pub; when he tried to chase them, several men
came out and knocked him down, to help the women escape. 'The
learned Chairman in passing sentence [on the two women], remarked
that not only were they abandoned women, but it was evident they
were connected with a gang of thieves, and had therefore become
very dangerous to society' and ordered them both to be transported
for seven years.[83]

Victims of the pickpockets included all sorts of people, and cannot be
classified into any pattern. But victims of thefts by prostitutes were
usually tradesmen, farmers or their servants, from out of town. And in
type (3) thefts, the victims were unskilled workers – labourers, miners,
navvies, boatmen; and the offenders came from the same social and
occupational group. This was a type of theft which took place within
the unskilled working class, in the setting of the pub, and usually
among people who knew and worked with each other. You could

expect such thefts in a basically poor and rough community, particularly on pay-night; but it is noteworthy that the victims should so often have brought formal prosecutions rather than taking matters into their own hands — for instance, having the offender beaten up and the property retrieved. Such a remedy might have been impracticable if the victim was an old man or if the theft had been committed by a number of men; but it must have been a possible remedy in many cases. Probably this informal justice *was* meted out on a number of such occasions. But it remains significant that workingmen prosecuted formally as often as they did for this offence — indicating that many of them were prepared to work through official procedures to obtain restitution and retribution in such cases.

(F) Other Simple Larcenies

Finally, we can briefly discuss the larcenies which do not fall into the categories already discussed. These include thefts of money, watches and handkerchiefs (except where taken from the person), and of domestic utensils and appliances from houses and canal boats.

Commonest prosecutors were retail tradesmen; then came unskilled and semi-skilled workers, especially labourers, miners and ironworkers prosecuting for thefts of money, watches and small articles from their homes and places of work. Once again it is notable how many unskilled workers were prepared to prosecute formally for such offences. Sometimes this meant prosecuting a workmate or companion:

> Richard Richards, a miner, put his watch and shirt inside his hat, while working in the pit. While he was working, the watch was taken by Richard Jones, a miner working in the same pit; Jones pawned the watch. Richards prosecuted Jones for this; Jones was convicted and, since he had a previous conviction, was transported.[84]

Offenders, once again, were about 75 per cent unskilled and semi-skilled workers, particularly labourers and miners.[85] The typical offence which came to court is one where one unskilled worker stole from another worker, or stole from a small retailer. Sentences imposed follow much the same pattern as those imposed for all types of larceny (see Table 28).

Notes

1. W. Robinson, *The Magistrate's Pocket-book* (London 1825), p.189; emphasis in original.

2. Radzinowicz, *History*, vol.1, pp.632-3.

3. See Appendix I. A large number of examples are cited in this and the following two chapters, taken from newspaper reports of cases and from the depositions of witnesses found in QS bundles. Quarter Sessions is cited as QS, Assizes as Ass; particular Sessions are abbreviated as follows: Epiphany – E.; Easter – Ea.; Midsummer (sometimes called Translation) – M.; Michaelmas – Mich.; any Adjourned Sessions – the addition of 'Adj.' (e.g. Epiphany Adjourned Sessions – E. Adj.)

4. SRO Q/SB E. 1842.

5. SRO Q/SB M. 1842.

6. SRO Q/SB E. 1842.

7. SRO Q/RCc 1 1859.

8. SRO Q/SB E. 1842

9. SRO Q/RCc 1 1856.

10. SRO Q/SB E. 1842.

11. SRO Q/SB Mich. 1836.

12. SRO Q/SB M. 1836.

13. Women had never worked underground in Black Country coal mines, and the collieries employed them only in relatively small numbers at the pit mouths, emptying coal from the skips into waggons (*MC* 'Labour and the Poor', 3 January 1850; *Midland Mining Commission* (1843), p.xxxi; *Children's Employment Commission* (Mines) (1842), pp.11-12.)

14. For the occupations of those charged with stealing coal, metal and parts etc., see my D.Phil thesis 'Crime and Authority in the Black Country 1835-60; a study of prosecuted offences and law-enforcement in an industrialising area' (unpublished, Oxford Univ., 1974), Table 32, p.296.

15. Freeman, *Stories and Sketches*, p.223; *MC* 'Labour and the Poor', 3 January 1850; Barnsby, 'Social Conditions', p.36; Faucher, *Etudes*, p.92.

16. *MC* 'Labour and the Poor', 3 January 1850.

17. See e.g. Charges to Grand Jury at Staffs. QS: E. 1836, E. Adj. 1836, E. 1845, E. 1848, M. 1848, M. 1851 – all fully reported in *SA* reports of those QS.

18. *SA* 19 March 1842, report of Ass. Similarly, William Martin, employed as a furnace-man by the large Dudley iron firm, Grazebrooks, admitted 'taking but not stealing' 1 cwt of coal. 'The Court did not see any distinction between the taking and stealing the coal, as the prisoner was not authorised to take it; he then pleaded guilty to the charge as alleged, and [the barrister] who prosecuted, said he could not recommend him to the merciful consideration of the Court as the prosecutors were plundered by their workmen in this way to a serious extent, and it was necessary to make an example.' (*Worc. Chron.*, 15 April 1840, report of QS).

19. *SA* 5 July 1851, report of QS; see also Staffs. Grand Jury Charges E. and E. Adj. 1836, E. 1845, E. and M. 1848.

20. Raphael Samuel, ' "Cabbage": Industrial Theft in 19th century Warwickshire', unpublished paper presented to National Deviancy Conference April 1973; and abstract of his paper 'Industrial Crime in the 19th Century', *Bulletin of the Society for the Study of Labour History*, 25 (autumn 1972), p.7; see also the chapter on Manchester in Faucher, *Etudes*.

21. Willmore, *History of Walsall*, pp.422-3.

22. *SA* 9 January 1847, report of QS.

23. See W.G. Carson and P. Wiles (ed.), *Crime and Delinquency in Britain*

(London 1971), pp.85, 101.

24. T.S. Ashton, *An Economic History of England: The Eighteenth Century* (London 1955), pp.208-9 (italics added). See similar point about the traditional perks of the workmen in various eighteenth-century trades in abstract of paper by P. Linebaugh on crime and social control in eighteenth-century England, in *Bulletin of Society for Study of Labour History,* 25 (autumn 1972), p.13.

25. Carson and Wiles, *Crime and Delinquency,* p.102.

26. J.P. Martin, *Offenders as Employees* (London 1962), pp.114-19.

27. Ibid., pp.84-106.

28. Ashton, *Economic History,* pp.210-11; Linebaugh abstract in *Bulletin* (autumn 1972), pp.11-15; S. Pollard, *The Genesis of Modern Management* (Harmondsworth 1968), pp.46-7.

29. *SA* 5 July 1851, report of QS.

30. See Pollard, *Genesis.*

31. For a full discussion of this important change and its effects on the administration of justice and maintenance of order in the Black Country, see D. Philips, 'The Black Country Magistracy 1835-60; a changing local élite and the exercise of its power', *Midland History* (spring 1976). The terms 'magistrate', 'Justice of the Peace', 'Justice', and 'JP' are synonymous; collectively they were referred to as the 'Bench', 'magistracy' or 'Commission of the Peace'.

32. These could not be evenly noted throughout the 1835-60 period: for 1835-43, the name of the prosecutor has been missed in a large number of cases, but has still been noted for 288 of them; for 1844-54, every prosecutor has been noted – a total of 868; and for 1855-60, the names of most prosecutors (with a few small gaps) have been noted – a total of 1,142.

33. These interests had belonged to the Ward family, who were Viscounts Dudley and Barons Ward; in 1827, John William Ward, 9th Baron Ward and 4th Viscount Dudley, was created 1st Earl of Dudley. When he died in 1833, without a direct heir, his second cousin Rev. William Humble Ward succeeded him as 10th Baron Ward, but the earldom and viscountcy became extinct. However, the bulk of the Earl's estate went to William Humble's son, William (1817-1885), and was held in trust for him until he turned twenty-eight in 1845. Rev. William Humble Ward, the 10th Baron, died in 1835, and his son William became the 11th Baron Ward. The Dudley estates were administered for Lord Ward by trustees until 1845 when he took them over himself; in 1860, the earldom and viscountcy of Dudley were revived and Lord Ward became 2nd Earl of Dudley. Thus, the title of the owner of the estates and works, and hence of the prosecutor for industrial thefts, changes from 'Trustees of the Earl of Dudley' to 'Lord Ward' to 'the Earl of Dudley'; for convenience, they will be referred to simply as 'the Dudley estates'. (See *DNB,* 'John William Ward, 1st Earl of Dudley'; Raybould, *The Economic Emergence of the Black Country* and 'The Development and Organization of Lord Dudley's Mineral Estates 1774-1845', *Ec. Hist. Rev.,* 2nd series XXI (1968), pp.529-44; R.P. Fereday, 'The Career of Richard Smith' (Keele Univ. MA thesis 1969).

34. On the Barkers and Sparrows, see Griffiths, *Guide to Iron Trade,* pp.56-9.

35. Allen, *Economic Development,* pp.146-50.

36. For details on all these firms, see Griffiths, *Guide to Iron Trade.*

37. On the economic aspects of Smith's activities as agent, see Fereday, 'Career of Richard Smith' and Raybould, *Economic Emergence* and 'Development and Organization'. On the exercise of political, social and administrative influence, see Fereday, 'Career', p.124, and C.F.G. Clarke, *Curiosities of*

Dudley and the Black Country (Birmingham 1881), which gives a very full description of political struggles and influence in Dudley between 1820 and 1860, and makes clear the overwhelming influence of 'Dudley Castle'; see also Barnsby, 'Social Conditions', p.348. A good part of the political power lay in the fact that most of the influential coal and iron masters in and around Dudley leased their mines and ironworks on a royalty basis from the Dudley estates, and hence were vulnerable to Lord Ward's economic and political pressure. The most active of the trustees of the Earl of Dudley's estate had been Lord Hatherton, and Smith, as agent, worked very closely with him. When Hatherton became Lord Lieutenant of Staffordshire in 1854, this co-operation continued; he appointed both Smith and his son Frederick JPs for Staffs., and relied on Smith as a close adviser for appointments to the magistracy and for political strategy in Staffs. (HC 5/5/1 to 6).

38. On Barker, see reports of two dinners given for and by him, on the occasion of his becoming High Sheriff; the speeches contain some biographical information (*SA* 15 March 1851). See also A.G. Cumberland, 'Protestant Nonconformity in the Black Country 1662-1851' (Birmingham Univ. MA thesis 1951), pp.120-1.

39. Truck payment was a notable and greatly disliked feature of Black Country working-class life; discontent over truck played a major part in precipitating the large miners' strikes of 1842 and the 1850s (*Midland Mining Commission* (1843); PRO HO 45/O.S. 260 Dartmouth to Graham 4 August 1842; HO 45/O.S. 6378 Hogg to H.O. 23 December 1857). During the 1842 strike, Sparrow openly declared that he used truck payment (*Midland Mining Commission,* p.ci). Freeman mentions a Bilston gang of burglars in the 1830s who enjoyed considerable popular support because they specialised in burgling truck shops, which the workmen regarded as a form of robbery forced on them; Sparrow's shop was a particular target (*Stories and Sketches,* pp.120-1). The great 1842 strike began in June with a turnout of men at Sparrow's Longton colliery, brought on by a wage cut. In May 1843, the Longton colliers struck again against a wage cut, and the Chief Constable reported to the Home Secretary that 'Mr Sparrow in whose employment the men were is much censured for not paying as much wages as the other proprietors, notwithstanding he has threatened a further reduction'. (quoted in R.F. Wearmouth, *Some Working-Class Movements of the Nineteenth Century* (London 1948), p.241). See also *Midland Mining Commission,* p.51, and PRO HO 45/O.S. 260, Talbot to Graham 4 February 1842.

40. See Fereday, 'Career of Richard Smith', pp.128-9; Barnsby, 'Social Conditions', p.348; Davies and Hyde, *Dudley and the Black Country,* pp.30-32, 39-40, 57-61. The 'butty' system – by which the mineowner subcontracted the working of his pits to a 'butty' or 'chartermaster' – was a strong grievance of the miners, as it was felt to conduce to exploitation, low wages and irregular payment of their wages (*Midland Mining Commission*), pp.xxxiii-xlvii. During the long and bitter, but non-violent, miners' strike of August-October 1858, the Staffs. Chief Constable wrote to the Lord Lieutenant advising that Richard Smith should not attend a meeting of magistrates called to discuss the strike since 'the *strongest feeling* exists *against* him and I think it unsafe that he should be from home after dark'. (HC 5/6/2 Hogg to Hatherton 3 October 1858; emphasis in original). Raybould calls Lord Ward's relationship with his employees and tenants 'benevolent and paternalistic' (*Economic Emergence,* pp.239-40), but he cannot cite much evidence of this except the payment of pensions to miners, and the refusal to use truck; he mentions nothing about the well-attested resentment of Dudley Castle dominance of the local politics of Dudley and its surrounding area, nor about the strength of feeling expressed

during the miners' strikes.

41. *WC* 27 April, 4 May, 11 May 1842.
42. See Philips thesis, Table 34, p.321.
43. SRO Q/SB E. 1842.
44. SRO Q/SB E. 1842.
45. SRO Q/SB E. 1842, E.Adj. 1836.
46. See Wolverhampton Chief Constable's Report, quoted in ch.4, p.114.
47. See Philips thesis, Table 35, p.327.
48. Ibid., Table 36, p.329.
49. Robson notes that transportation was imposed as a penalty for larceny generally only when it followed a previous conviction; and he notes of his sample transported for theft of clothing that most of them had previous convictions. (*Convict Settlers*, pp.36-7, 53-4.)
50. e.g. John Jones and William Smith: 'It appeared there were several indictments against the prisoners, who, though only 15, were such notorious characters as to call for the sentence of *seven years' transportation.*' (*WC* 15 January 1836, report of Staffs. QS E. 1836; emphasis in original.) Thomas Davis was given twelve months in the Penitentiary as he was aged thirteen and 'was well known to be connected with bad characters'; Thomas Belfield, aged thirty-six, convicted on two counts of stealing clothes, was given seven years' transportation, as 'the Court knowing the prisoner's habits to be very bad, decided to send him out of the country.' (*SA* 22 October 1836, report of QS.)
51. SRO Q/SB E. 1842.
52. SRO Q/SB E. 1842.
53. *SA* 9 April 1836, report of QS.
54. SRO Q/SB E. Adj. 1836.
55. HC 5/6/1 Clerk to Justices of West Bromwich, Wednesbury and Walsall Division to Hatherton 16 and 25 July 1855. See also SRO Q/SBm 24 Leics. Clerk of the Peace to Staffs. Clerk of the Peace 15 March 1838, enclosing a petition from farmers asking the JPs to appoint a police force because the farmers fear that the employment of large bodies of men to construct a railway through their area 'may endanger the Peace of the District and the property must necessarily be exposed in the neighbouring fields'.
56. See T. Coleman, *The Railway Navvies* (London 1965), ch.6; Chesney, *Victorian Underworld,* pp.40-5.
57. See Philips thesis, Tables 37 and 38, pp.336, 345; see also R.A. Westcott, 'Shoplifting and Law Enforcement: A Consideration of Social Factors Affecting both Shoplifting and the Initiation of Legal Proceedings Consequent to the Offence' (London Univ. M.Phil thesis 1971-72), ch.1.
58. W. Cobbett, *Rural Rides* (Everyman edn. London 1941), pp.102-3, emphasis in original; cf. the Chartist J.R. Stephens who, in public speeches in 1838, proclaimed that it was no crime to steal from the well-stocked larders and cellars of the rich (R.G. Gammage, *History of the Chartist Movement 1837-1854* (1854; New York 1969), p.92).
59. See ch.4.
60. See evidence of London tradesmen to *SC on Criminal Laws* (1819).
61. Freeman, *Stories and Sketches,* p.195.
62. Ibid., pp.123, 195.
63. *SA* 1 July 1848, report of QS.
64. Hill, *Repression of Crime,* p.75; see also *SC on Criminal Laws* (1819), p.50; Westcott, 'Shoplifting', p.44; Tobias, *Crime,* p.288.
65. SRO Q/SB E. 1842.
66. SRO Q/SB E. Adj. 1836.

67. *SA* 12 March 1842, report of Ass.
68. See Philips thesis, Table 39, p.353; Robson, *Convict Settlers*, p.47.
69. See the numerous sources cited in Tobias, *Crime*, pp.38, 111-112, 124-30; and the examples given in Robson, *Convict Settlers*, pp.31-2, 35, 39.
70. SRO Q/SB E. 1842; *SA* 15 January 1842.
71. *SA* 5 and 12 July 1851, report of QS.
72. SRO Q/SB E. 1842; *SA* 8 January 1842.
73. *Children's Employment Commission* (1843), pp.571, 612, 622, 625, 640; *Midland Mining Commission* (1843), p.xlvi.
74. As Elizabeth Mason did, when charged with stealing £9 7s from a 72-year-old man. She had got him to buy her a few beers and bread and cheese, and then later pushed him down in the road and took his money. She claimed in defence that he had given her the money for 'improper intercourse'. She was not believed, and was transported for ten years. (*SA* 23 July 1842.)
75. MWWC Return of Offences 1 July-31 December 1856 and 1 July-18 December 1857.
76. *SA* 19 May 1855, 15 March 1845, and 20 October 1855. See also *SA* 8 January 1842 and *SA* 4 July 1840.
77. For some of these sources and descriptions, see *RC on Police* (1839), Appendix 6; John Binny, 'Thieves and Swindlers' in Mayhew, *London Labour*, vol.4, pp.303-10; M. McIntosh, 'Changes in the Organisation of Thieving', in Cohen, *Images of Deviance*, pp.98-133; Tobias, *Crime*, pp.111-12, 124-30; Chesney, *Victorian Underworld*, pp.130-9; J. Hall, *Theft, Law and Society* (New York 1952), pp.70-6.
78. Binny, op.cit., in Mayhew, *London Labour*, vol.4; Tobias, *Crime;* Chesney, *Victorian Underworld.*
79. Binny, op.cit., pp.304, 308.
80. *SA* 5 and 12 July 1851, report of QS; SRO Q/SB E. 1842 and *SA* 8 and 15 January 1842, report of QS.
81. *SA* 5 and 12 July 1851, report of QS; SRO Q/SB E. 1836 and *SA* 9 and 12 January 1836, report of QS.
82. See Philips thesis, Table 40, p.364.
83. *SA* 1 July 1848, report of QS.
84. SRO Q/SB E. 1835.
85. See Philips thesis, Table 41, p.368.

7 PROPERTY OFFENDERS (2) — RECEIVING, EMBEZZLEMENT, FRAUD AND CURRENCY OFFENCES

When we look to the number of common thieves prowling over the metropolis — the thousands living daily on beggary, prostitution, and crime — we naturally expect to find extensive machineries for the receiving of stolen property. These receivers are to be found in different grades of society, from the keeper of the miserable low lodging-houses and dolly shops in Petticoat Lane, Rosemary Lane, and Spitalfields, in the East-end, and Dudley Street and Drury Lane in the West-end of the metropolis, to the pawnbroker in Cheapside, the Strand, and Fleet Street, and the opulent Jews of Houndsditch and its vicinity, whose coffers are said to be overflowing with gold. (John Binny, 'Thieves and Swindlers', in Henry Mayhew, *London Labour and the London Poor,* vol.4, p.373.)

Receiving Stolen Property

This category of offence was similar and related to larceny, but was legally distinct; it can be treated separately, because it often involves a different class of offender.

The charge itself would be couched in the form: 'AB did receive into his possession [description of the stolen property] knowing that it had been stolen'. The knowledge that it had been stolen was an essential ingredient in the legal definition of the offence, and had to be proved; but the offence will be referred to, for convenience, simply as 'receiving'. The charge of receiving was used to cover two distinct types of cases: (1) full-time receivers of stolen property — 'fences', who made a business of buying stolen property from thieves, and selling it on a large scale; (2) persons on whom the police or prosecutors found stolen property, but for whom they were unable to prove the taking of the property with felonious intent (an essential legal element of a larceny prosecution), so the alternative charge was brought of receiving stolen property. Cases of this second type involve situations exactly similar to those dealt with in the section on Larceny, and will therefore not be dealt with again here; this section will deal only with the full-time receiver or 'fence'.

The receiver figures prominently in nineteenth-century writing on

crime, both fact and fiction: Fagin, in *Oliver Twist,* was a large-scale
receiver, and Dickens is supposed to have modelled him, at least
partially, on the notorious London 'fence' of the period, Ikey Solomons;
while the best-known English criminal of the eighteenth century had
been Jonathan Wild, a receiver and criminal entrepreneur on an
enormous scale.[1] But, in addition to these large-scale fences, there was
a very much larger number of small-scale receivers — pawnbrokers and
second-hand dealers of various sorts — buying stolen articles of small
intrinsic value from those who had stolen them. The really large fences
were only able to flourish in a metropolis with a large criminal
underworld like London, or perhaps the largest provincial cities,
Manchester or Birmingham; in a less metropolitan area like the Black
Country there is no mention in the contemporary literature of any
large-scale fences in operation, and certainly none ever appeared in
court from there in the period under consideration. There may have
been some large fences in Birmingham providing an outlet for some
Black Country stolen goods, but most of the day-to-day receiving of
stolen goods took place within the Black Country itself on a much
smaller scale.

As the previous chapter showed, the commonest articles stolen in
the Black Country (apart from money) were clothes, food, coal, metal,
handkerchiefs, watches, and household appliances and utensils. The
most usual way of disposing of the articles was by selling or pledging
them to pawnbrokers, second-hand dealers, marine store dealers, or
occasionally publicans or beer-house keepers. Clothes, sheets and
blankets, watches, handkerchiefs, ornaments and utensils were most
commonly disposed of to a pawnbroker. Most pawnbrokers stated, of
course, that they had not known at the time that the property in
question was stolen; there are even some cases in which pawnbrokers,
being suspicious of the origins of an article, themselves notified the
police or constable and initiated the accused's arrest. But on the whole,
pawnbrokers made it a rule not to enquire too closely into the
antecedents of a pledged article. After all, the pawnshop was at this
time the sole means of raising a loan for most of the working class, and
many articles were pledged and re-pledged in order to raise money when
it was needed;[2] the pawnbroker's living depended on his not being too
inquisitive about the origins of his clients' pledged articles. But many
pawnbrokers were suspected of receiving stolen property, not merely
unwittingly, but deliberately and regularly. The problem for the
authorities was to prove this.

Until the end of the seventeenth century, receiving stolen property had not been a crime; by a 1692 Act, a receiver became an accessory to the felony of the larceny itself; and one of Peel's Acts (7 and 8 Geo. IV, c.29) in 1827, made it a felony to be convicted of receiving stolen goods, even if the actual thief who had stolen the goods had not been convicted.[3]

But in order for the prosecution to succeed, it was necessary to prove that: (a) the property was stolen, (b) the accused received the property, (c) he knew at the time that it had been stolen. Since the parties to such a transaction were usually only the thief and the receiver, it was hard to get testimony against the receiver which would convict him; merely receiving the property without the guilty knowledge was not sufficient.[4] Thus, although a large number of pawnbrokers were suspected of being receivers, relatively few could be prosecuted, and fewer still convicted.

As well as pawnbrokers, dealers in second-hand goods, especially clothing, were thought to be receivers, their trade offering an ideal cover for the activity; stolen clothes and handkerchiefs could be disposed of to them as well as to pawnbrokers. Even more important in the Black Country were the marine store dealers, who dealt in scrap metal; much of the stolen metal in the Black Country found its way to them where it could be easily melted down to an unidentifiable form. Matthew Davenport Hill pointed out how widespread this was in Birmingham, where 'our staple manufactures are in metals'; in the hands of these dealers, stolen 'metallic wares are soon made by the melting-pot to change their form, and thus to defy identification', and Hill called for a system of licensing for marine store dealers, which would make them record all purchases of metal with a note of the name and address of the person selling it.[5] Finally, some goods — food, game, various articles — were disposed of to the keepers of 'flash-houses' or low drinking-houses.

The agencies of the law tended to take a strong line against receivers — in words, at least, if not always in deeds — because of the generally-held view that receivers were one of the chief forces behind professional crime, fostering and encouraging young criminals and disposing of their loot. 'The truth. . .of the proverb, that 'were there no receivers, there would be no thieves', is made obvious.'[6] But they were not particularly successful in trying to bring all receivers to justice, mostly because of the difficulty, mentioned above, of obtaining sufficient evidence against them. In all, 343 prosecutions for receiving were brought in the Black Country in the period 1835-60; but, of these, over half were people who had been charged with receiving because there was insufficient evidence to support a larceny charge. And half of these were acquitted at the trial – only 174 of the 343 were found guilty.

When they were convicted, the courts tended to be relatively severe on the full-time fences, as the figures for transportation and penal servitude show (Table 31). But quite a high proportion of those convicted received prison sentences; many of these were people convicted of receiving as an alternative to a charge of larceny; some of them are also those pawnbrokers, marine store dealers, or beerhouse keepers who received and disposed of stolen goods, but on a relatively small scale.

Table 31   Sentences Imposed on those Convicted of Receiving Stolen Property in the Black Country 1835-60

Sentence	Percentage 1835-60
Imprisonment	
Less than 1 month	1.7
1-3 months	19.5
4-6 months	26.4
7-12 months	27.6
More than 12 months	2.9
Transportation	
7 years	10.9
10-15 years	5.7
Life	1.2
Penal Servitude	
3-4 years	3.5
5-9 years	0.6
TOTAL	100.0
	n = 174

Embezzlement

Embezzlement is 'the crime of a servant appropriating to his own use the money or goods received by him on account of his master'; to satisfy the legal ingredients of the offence, the accused must be the servant of the prosecutor, must be authorised to receive money or goods on his master's account, and must have received money or goods on that account and appropriated it to his own use.[7]

There were 230 prosecutions for this offence in the Black Country in the period 1835-60. The typical circumstances are very simple, and usually involve fairly small sums of money. For instance:

Henry Aldridge was employed by William Harrison, a Walsall lime master. He delivered a load of lime to a Mr Labon, took the money for it (£1 19s 5d), and made out a receipt. But Aldridge kept the money, which he admitted when Harrison tried to find out why he had not yet been paid for that load.[8]

Benjamin Elwell was employed by Daniel Hughes, a brickmaker, to sell bricks and receive the money. Hughes could not write, but could understand figures, and the usual practice when the prisoner paid him any money, was to put a cross against the sum received. On a number of occasions, he told Elwell to collect the £13 12s owing from George Jones, a local ironmaster, but Elwell always made some excuse to avoid doing so. Eventually, Hughes himself went to Jones' office, and found that Elwell had collected the money and given a receipt some time before, and kept the money.[9]

Thomas Bird, coal merchant, employed Thomas Pool to sell coals for him at a wharf on the Birmingham and Liverpool Canal. On Friday 12th November, Pool was sent to the wharf which had nearly two tons of coal; by Monday 15th, all the coal was gone. Bird tracked down two loads which had been sold by Pool for 12s and 3s respectively; but Pool had disappeared with the money. Bird got the Constable of Brewood to find Pool, who admitted taking the money, which he had spent.[10]

These were the typical embezzlement cases in the Black Country. A number of embezzlements were carried out by accountant clerks or other clerical staff concerned with keeping accounts; but there were no dramatically large defalcations of really large sums of money, such as one might find in an important commercial and financial centre. The occupations of the accused show, not surprisingly, that the great majority of these offences were committed by men employed in a clerical or retail capacity, usually men with a better than average education and standard of literacy. In fact, the very way in which embezzlement was defined legally meant that it could only be committed by men employed in some position of trust, and not simply by any employee. There is an illustration of this, as well as of the excessive insistence on the technical strictness of the rules of criminal procedure which was remarked on in chapter 4, in this case:

John Jones was tried for embezzling £3 from his employer. 'On the first question being put to the prosecutor, it became clear that the prisoner was a *labourer,* and was not employed in such a capacity as would render him answerable under the indictment.' The Judge then directed an acquittal.[11]

Embezzlement seems to have been a totally male crime — of the 230 persons prosecuted, 223 were male — presumably a reflection of the scarcity of occasions on which women were placed in a position of trust from which this offence could be committed.

Embezzlements of large sums of money were punished by transportation or penal servitude; but (see Table 32) many of the Black Country embezzlement cases, which concerned much smaller amounts, were punished by simple imprisonment.

One final point should be made about embezzlement. It was noted, in the section on industrial thefts in the last chapter, that it was the practice in most eighteenth-century trades for workers to take part of the raw material for their own use; this was particularly the case among domestic outworkers and, where employers prosecuted this practice,

Table 32   Sentences Imposed on those Convicted of Embezzlement in the Black Country 1835-60

Sentence	Percentage 1835-60
Imprisonment	
Less than 1 month	3.1
1-3 months	32.1
4-6 months	30.8
7-12 months	17.9
More than 12 months	2.5
Transportation	
7 years	6.2
10-15 years	2.5
Penal Servitude	
3-4 years	3.1
5-9 years	1.2
Fine	0.6
TOTAL	100.0
	n = 162

they generally prosecuted it as *embezzlement* of the raw material.[12]
By the 1830s, use of the term 'embezzlement' to cover this sort of
taking had died away. Such taking was still prosecuted – as we have
seen, the rate of prosecutions was in fact greatly stepped up – but
now the prosecutions were brought for larceny and not for
embezzlement.

Presumably, this owes something to the fact that much of the
outwork system had been replaced by work in factories and workshops,
so that the element of trust involved in putting out the raw material to
the outworkers (on which the embezzlement charge could be founded)
was removed. But probably more important was the fact that the
development of the industrial system and the concentration in factories
and workshops simplified the legal position on ownership and theft of
raw material; there was no longer the legal problem which outwork
posed, that while the *ownership* of the raw material remained with the
master, the *possession* was with the outworker. Once all the material
was worked up within the factory or workshop, this legal confusion
disappeared. As larceny prosecutions were becoming much more
common and easier to bring, employers naturally prosecuted for
larceny in these cases. And it was only in 1799 that a statute made it
a criminal offence (rather than a civil wrong) for a servant to convert to
his own use money or goods received from a third person for his
master.[13] So the category of embezzlement which developed in the
nineteenth century covered a different subject matter from the offence
of that name in the eighteenth century.

Fraud, Forgery and Currency Offences

This group covers offences involving deception and betrayal of trust
(which have some similarity to the embezzlement offences discussed
above) and offences involving the manufacture and passing off of
counterfeit currency, notes and coins.

(A) Fraud

Overwhelmingly the commonest form in which this offence was found
in the Black Country was 'obtaining property by false pretences'.
There were 395 prosecutions for this offence in the period 1835-60,
of a total of 418 prosecutions for all types of fraud. Obtaining
property by false pretences was similar in its effects to larceny – the
victim was dishonestly deprived of some property – but it was legally
very different. It had not even existed as a proper legal offence until
the end of the eighteenth century,[14] and it differed from larceny in

the way in which the property was obtained; the victim's property was not taken secretly by the offender, but was given to him as a result of some false pretence made by him.[15] And, unlike larceny, it was not a felony but a misdemeanour.

Typical examples of these cases:

Stephen Waring was a bricklayer, employed by John Calloway, a builder. John Underhill, a butcher, for whom Calloway had built two houses, knew Waring as Calloway's employee. Waring came to Underhill and said that Calloway wanted Underhill to send him £2 — one sovereign, and 20s in silver — because people at his house needed change. Underhill gave him the money. Calloway had given Waring no authority or instructions to borrow the money.[16]

George Richmond agreed to pay John Wright, a Birmingham corn factor, 31s for twelve quarters of barley. The barley was delivered to him a few days after; he gave his name to the waggoner who delivered the barley, as 'Richards', said he lived at Wednesbury, and promised to pay for the barley the next time Wright was in Wednesbury. These statements were false, and Wright never received his money. But, at the trial, Mr. Justice Cresswell said that the barley had not been delivered in consequence of any false pretences used at Birmingham; the only false representation had been made to the waggoner who delivered it, which was a different case, and removed it from the scope of the relevant statute. Richmond was therefore discharged.[17]

The courts varied in their treatment of people found guilty of this offence. People who had previous convictions for such an act, and educated people who held responsible positions from which they had committed the offence, tended to get fairly long prison sentences or transportation; but the majority of cases were treated as no more serious than the analogous larceny cases (see Table 33).

Analysis of the occupations available for the accused (for all of the Black Country for 1854-60, and for Dudley for 1839-60) shows that just over half were unskilled and semi-skilled manual workers — labourers were the biggest group, as usual, followed by miners, and some way behind both of these, unskilled ironworkers and nailers. Just under 20 per cent were skilled manual workers (artisans, skilled metal workers, skilled building workers), and 10-20 per cent were in retail trade. This shows a much lower proportion of unskilled manual workers than is the case for larceny offences, where 70-80 per cent of

Table 33   Sentences Imposed on those Convicted of Fraud in the
            Black Country 1835-60

Sentence	Percentage 1835-60
Imprisonment	
Less than 1 month	6.2
1-3 months	43.6
4-6 months	27.5
7-12 months	13.4
More than 12 months	2.8
Transportation	
7 years	4.1
Penal Servitude	
3-4 years	0.7
5-9 years	0.3
Reformatory	0.7
Fine	0.7
TOTAL	100.0
	n = 291

the accused were unskilled workers. Obtaining by false pretences
generally required more planning than did a simple larceny, and was a
more subtle operation; it was important for the offender to put across
a sufficiently plausible and respectable appearance for the victim to
believe the false pretence being advanced.

This was the sort of offence at which one could grow adept with
practice, and many of those charged with it seem to have moved
around the Black Country and its environs, practising this sort of
fraud wherever they could succeed with it. For instance, Simeon
Walters, aged twenty-one, was tried at the Epiphany (January) Sessions
in 1842 for having, in December 1841, obtained groceries by false
pretences from the tommy shop of the coal and ironmaster, William
Hanbury Sparrow. Walters and his wife had gone to the shop and
claimed to be coming for goods to the amount of 10s which was
standing to the credit of William Lavender, a furnaceman employed
by Sparrow. They took the groceries away and kept them, having had
no authority from Lavender to go and collect them. Walters was given
one month's imprisonment for this; but at the Spring Assizes (March)
1842, he was back in court, charged with fraudulently altering an order

for delivery of goods. This time he was sentenced to two years' hard labour.[18]

The other forms of fraud practised in the Black Country were essentially similar to obtaining by false pretences and were concerned with acquiring relatively small sums of money or credit. There were no spectacular frauds involving hundreds of pounds; they were small frauds to obtain money, goods, or credit. For some people it seems to have been the equivalent of a 'moonlight flit' from lodgings leaving the rent unpaid, resolving the problems of debt by failing to pay; for others, like Walters, it seems to have been an easy way to get money or goods — provided one moved from town to town fairly frequently, one could probably keep it up for some time; others, particularly employees in the position of Waring, seem simply to have yielded to the temptation which their position offered in order to get some easy money.

(B) Forgery and Currency Offences

These concern essentially the same subject matter. Forgery was usually a case of forging banknotes, cheques or promissory notes; currency offences covered coining, and uttering forged coins or banknotes.

Birmingham and its surrounding area were notorious for coining and forgery; Binny stated that most | forged Bank of England notes in London came from Birmingham, while coining was rendered easy in the area by the large amount of metalworking carried out there, which provided both the materials and the skill for manufacturing false coins.[19] Freeman suggested that the prevalence of coining activity in the Black Country stemmed from the fact that the early ironmasters, such as John Wilkinson, had, when there was a shortage of currency in the late eighteenth century and early nineteenth century, manufactured their own metal tokens, with which they paid their workmen and which were accepted as valid currency by the shops of the area. After this practice had ceased, he suggested, some of the local inhabitants carried on this sort of procedure in order to make false coins.[20]

However, over the period 1835-60, only thirty prosecutions for forgery and nine prosecutions for coining were brought from the Black Country. Forgery and coining were probably offences which were not engaged in on a large scale, and they were certainly difficult offences for which to obtain a conviction. To secure a conviction, it was necessary for the prosecution to show that the accused had possession of moulds and equipment for coining, presses for forging, or forged notes or coins. Forgers and large-scale coiners were usually careful to work in secret and well-protected places, in which they had sufficient opportunity to destroy the incriminating evidence before it could be seized.[21] But there is much evidence of the production of counterfeit coin and notes in the fact that, between 1835 and 1860, 384 prosecutions were brought for possessing or uttering counterfeit coin or notes. 'Uttering' was the charge which was brought against people caught passing off bad coin or forged notes in shops or pubs; 'possession' was used as a charge against suspected forgers found in possession of bad coin or notes, but with no proof that they had actually been the manufacturers; most of these prosecutions were for uttering. The number of prosecutions for uttering suggests that there was a large amount of bad money circulating in the Black Country, most of it probably made in the area. To sustain a prosecution for uttering, it was necessary to show only that the accused uttered the money and that he knew at the time that it was bad.

Typical cases involving these offences:

Forgery

Thomas Brittle was charged with forging and issuing an order for eleven shillings, in the name of his employer. Brittle pleaded guilty, and his employer asked for mercy for him, holding that he had not intended ultimately to defraud him.[22]

Coining

From information received, a superintendent and two officers of the Birmingham police force raided a house in West Bromwich, where they found Thomas and Susannah Davis, James Field, and Thomas Williams present. In the house, they found, in all, fourteen counterfeit shillings, one of which Thomas Davis was caught trying to hide. In an outhouse, they found a spoon with a mixture of tin and lead in it, hidden in a stack of coals; in the roof of the house, they found a pair of moulds for the manufacture of counterfeit shillings, wrapped in a rag. The metal and the moulds were clearly used for the manufacture of the bad coins. Susannah Davis was discharged from the indictment by the Grand Jury, but Thomas Davis, Field, and Williams were all found guilty, and each was given fifteen years' transportation.[23]

Uttering – Notes

John Evans, a horse-dealer, went to a Wolverhampton beer-shop and gave the keeper, John Gould, a £5 Bank of England note in payment of a 2s 4½d debt which he owed him; Gould gave him

£4 17s 7½d in change. Gould subsequently discovered that the note was a forgery, and that Evans had given a similar note and received change, in payment to a Walsall pub. He then informed the police. Evans was found guilty and was sentenced to seven years' transportation.[24]

Thomas Swift Cooper came into the shop of Charles Butler in Wolverhampton and bought some beef, costing 6s 8d. He offered a note for £5 issued by Messrs Arkwright's bank at Wirksworth (Derbyshire), in payment. Butler suspected the note, and took it across to the local bank to check it. The bank cashier said it was a forgery, and came with Butler into the shop, where he asked Cooper where he had got the note. Cooper tried to grab the note back, but Butler called a police officer and had him arrested. It was shown that he had bought meat from a butcher in Bilston, also with a forged £5 note. He was found guilty, and sentenced to fifteen years' transportation.[25]

Uttering – Coins

John Williams, a collier, offered a crown piece in payment for ale in a Sedgley inn, but the landlady refused to take it. His companion paid for that ale, and the two then left the inn and went to a beerhouse about a quarter of a mile away. The landlord of the inn followed them and saw Williams tender the same crown piece in payment; he then had them arrested. Williams was found to have another three counterfeit crown pieces on his person. Williams pleaded guilty and was given twelve months' imprisonment.[26]

The forgery prosecutions were mostly for forgery of cheques, promissory notes or legal documents; there were few prosecutions for forging banknotes. It is clear that there was a large number of forged banknotes circulating in the Black Country, but forging notes required relatively sophisticated skills and equipment, and probably most of this was taking place in Birmingham rather than the Black Country. There certainly was a good deal of passing forged banknotes.

The banking situation might have contributed to this – until the 1844 Bank Charter Act, all country banks could issue their own notes, and even after 1844 those banks which had already been issuing notes could continue doing so until amalgamation with another bank.[27] So the circulation contained a number of notes issued by different country banks circulating together with Bank of England notes. It might be expected that the task of passing off forged notes would be made easier by the use as currency of so many different types of banknote, originating from a number of different sources. But Binny observed, in 1861, that forgeries of country banknotes were more difficult and therefore less common:

> There are also forged notes of provincial banks, but these are not so numerous as those of the Bank of England. The provincial banks have generally colours and engine-turned engraving on their notes. Some have a portion of the note pink, green, or other colours, more difficult and expensive to forge than the Bank of England note, which is on plain paper with an elaborate water-mark.[28]

The solicitor to the Association of London Bankers likewise made this point; asked, in 1854, 'Does the circulation of provincial notes increase the number of forgeries in the country?' he replied, 'Hardly so. The forgery of country bank-notes is very rare; a few cases have occasionally occurred, but they are very few.'[29]

In the Black Country cases, forged notes which were uttered were more usually Bank of England notes than the notes of a local bank. Since 1826, the issue of banknotes of value under £5 had been prohibited, so the only notes circulating were for £5 or more. It was £5 notes, then, which were forged and uttered, with the result that the typical incident in which a forged note was uttered was in payment for some small amount, from which a large amount in good money could be gained in change.

Coining as an operation was a good deal easier than forging notes, requiring only very simple equipment. Binny gave his readers a full description of the process in 1861:

> Take a shilling, or other sterling coin, scour it well with soap and water; dry it, and then grease it with suet or tallow; partly wipe this off, but not wholly. Take some plaster of Paris, and make a collar either of paper or tin. Pour the plaster of Paris on the piece of coin in the collar or band round it. Leave it until it sets or hardens, when the impression will be made. You turn it up and the piece sticks in the mould. Turn the reverse side, and you take a similar impression from it; then you have the mould complete. You put the pieces of the mould together, and then pare it. You make a channel in order to pour the metal into it in a state of fusion, having the neck of the channel as small as possible. . .You make claws to the mould, so that it will stick together while you pour the metal into it. . .When

you have your coin cast, there is a 'gat', or piece of refuse metal, sticks to it. You pare this off with a pair of scissors or a knife. . . then you file the edges of the coin to perfect the 'knerling'. [The coin is now of a bluish colour, and needs silvering.] You get a galvanic battery with nitric acid and sulphuric acid, a mixture of each diluted in water to a certain strength. You then get some cyanide and attach a copper wire to a screw of the battery. Immerse that in the cyanide of silver when the process of electro-plating commences. [Thereafter] get a little lampblack and oil, and make it into a sort of composition, 'slumming' the coin with it. This takes the bright colour away, and makes it fit for circulation. . . Counterfeit coin is generally made of Britannia metal spoons and other ingredients. . .[30]

This meant that coining was well within the reach of most people with an inclination towards it; as Binny said:

Counterfeit coin is manufactured by various classes of people — costermongers, mechanics, tailors, and others — and is generally confined to the lower classes of various ages.[31]

It was easy for such people to make their moulds and go to work with little elaborate preparation or equipment. For instance:

David Foster came to stay in a Walsall lodging-house. On the third day, the woman in charge saw him making a mould with something like flour, and putting it to bake by the fire. She asked what it was for, and was told it was for making 'cocks and shollars'. The next day he was doing it again. She went and told a policeman, who arrested Foster. Foster dropped and broke the mould, but large enough pieces were left to show that it was a mould for coining. The policeman also found a counterfeit shilling, some soft white metal such as was used in counterfeit coins, and chalk for making moulds which would make an impression on soft metal.[32]

Foster's case shows how a coiner could set up even in temporary lodgings, with little space or specialised equipment. But there were also cases, such as that cited earlier, in which a whole group of coiners operated from one house or special hideout.

There were fewer prosecutions for coining than for forgery, but there was certainly a good deal of bad coin in circulation in the

Black Country, and there were considerably more prosecutions for
uttering bad coin than for uttering counterfeit notes. Most of these
coins were uttered in pubs or beerhouses, sometimes in shops.

Forgery and currency offences were severely regarded and treated
by the law. Until 1832, they had been capital offences; after the
Forgery Act and Coinage Offences Act, both of 1832, capital
punishment was abolished for all forgery and coinage offences, except
forgery of wills and of powers of attorney for transfer of government
stock; the death penalty was abolished for these latter two cases by
the Forgery Act of 1837. In fact, the last execution for forgery took
place in 1829, and during the 1820s very few of the death sentences
for forgery had been carried out. But commutation of the death
sentence still involved heavy sentences of transportation. The majority
of those convicted of forgery or coining in the 1830s and 1840s were
given sentences of transportation. Even after 1853, when transportation
was being phased out, two men from the Black Country in 1857 were
given terms of transportation of fifteen and ten years respectively, the
one for forging names to insurance policies, and the other for uttering
two forged £5 notes.

Table 34 shows the high proportion transported among those
convicted of coining or forgery. Even after the death penalty had been
abolished for forgery, it took some time before the courts imposed any
other sentence for this offence but transportation – the prison
sentences listed in the 'Forgery' column were all imposed after 1846;
before that, it was only transportation.

The case is somewhat different for uttering forged notes or bad
coins. These divide into about 90 per cent uttering coins, and 10 per
cent uttering notes. The punishment for uttering forged banknotes was
invariably harsher than for uttering bad coins. Virtually all of those
who had uttered banknotes received transportation or penal servitude,
while most of those caught passing bad coins received shorter prison
sentences. This was because the forging of banknotes was regarded as
a very serious offence and one dangerous to the public, and those
who passed forged banknotes were seen as closely connected with
those engaged in forging them. Since banknotes did not exist below
the value of £5, the average Black Countryman was unlikely to acquire
a forged banknote by accident; and the attempt to pass such notes
was therefore seen as a deliberate and planned activity. On the other
hand, bad coins circulated commonly as sixpences, shillings, and
half-crowns, and there was a good chance of acquiring one innocently
in one's normal business. Even where the court held that the person

Table 34   Sentences Imposed on those Convicted of Forgery and
Currency Offences in the Black Country 1835-60

Sentence	Percentages		
Imprisonment	Forgery	Coining	Uttering
Less than 1 month			1.3
1-3 months	5.9		3.5
4-6 months	11.8		30.2
7-12 months	35.3	28.6	50.9
More than 12 months			4.4
Transportation			
7 years	23.5		3.1
10-15 years	17.6	71.4	2.5
Life			0.6
Penal Servitude			
3-4 years	5.9		1.3
5-9 years			0.6
10-15 years			1.3
Other			
Reformatory			0.3
TOTAL	100.0	100.0	100.0
	n = 17	n = 7	n = 318

passing the coin clearly knew it to be bad at the time, it could be
understood, and to some extent excused, if someone received a bad
coin and determined to pass it off onto someone else. In any event,
passing off a bad sixpence or shilling did very much less damage to
the recipient and to the public than did the passing of a number of
forged £5 notes. So sentences for uttering bad coins were relatively
lighter.

But whenever the Court had reason to suspect that the accused
habitually passed bad coins (as shown by previous convictions, or
by large quantities of bad coin found on the accused's person or in
his lodgings), there would be a tendency to impose transportation.
Underlying the attitude towards the uttering of forged notes seems to
have been the assumption that this was part of habitual activity, and
the connection of the act of uttering with the act of forgery itself
was invoked to justify the stiff sentences. For instance, in passing
sentence on two men who had uttered forged £5 Bank of England

notes, in 1851, the Judge

> . . .remarked that within his recollection, and probably not more
> than twenty years ago, persons found guilty of the offences of
> which they (the prisoners) had been convicted, were consigned to
> the hands of the hangman, and forfeited their lives on the scaffold.
> He rejoiced that such was not now the law of the country; but
> still the crime was regarded as one of a serious character, and a
> severe punishment was still awarded.[33]

He sentenced them to seven and ten years' transportation respectively.
Although they had been convicted only of *uttering* the notes, the
judge is clearly here linking them with the act of forgery itself, in
justifying the severity of the sentence imposed.

Such evidence as there is, suggests that most of those convicted
of forging banknotes were full-time criminals specialising in this sort
of work; but this offence, as has been said, was relatively rare in the
Black Country. Those convicted of forging orders, bills, cheques or
notes of their employers or of others, tended to be clerks or other
white-collar workers, using their education and position for this
purpose — but, again, there were too few of these in the Black Country
sample for any generalisation to be more than suggestive. Among the
coiners, one could find serious people devoted to it full-time, like the
three West Bromwich people in the one example cited, or they might
be doing coining more casually, like David Foster in the other coining
example; because of the simplicity of the coining process, anyone with
any knowledge of metalworking could easily take it up. But nine
prosecutions for coining over twenty-six years is too few for one to be
able to make any clear representation of the 'typical coiner'; perhaps
more important is the very fact that there were only nine such
prosecutions.

Of those charged with uttering counterfeit coins and notes, the
occupation information shows that about 50 per cent were labourers,
miners and other unskilled manual workers. One-quarter were artisans
or other skilled workers, and just under 10 per cent were in a retail
trade. Ten per cent are also listed in the Calendars as having 'no
occupation', an unusually high proportion for this classification; many
of these may have been full-time criminals.

The prosecutor, in cases of forgery and coining, was the Royal
Mint, who briefed counsel to conduct such prosecutions. In cases of
uttering, it seems usually to have been the local constable or police

who brought the prosecution. Forgery and coining are among the few cases which were publicly prosecuted by the Government or its agencies in this period.

Notes

1. On receivers, their methods of operation, and the law relating to them, see Binny, 'Thieves and Swindlers', pp.373-5; McIntosh, 'Changes in Organisation', pp.109-16; Tobias, *Crime*, pp.117-24, 173, 266; Robson, *Convict Settlers*, pp.31-2, 66-7; Radzinowicz, *History*, vol.2; Hill, *Repression of Crime*, pp.66-70; Hall, *Theft, Law and Society*, pp.70-5.
2. *MC* 'Labour and the Poor', 7 January 1850.
3. Radzinowicz, *History*, vol.1, p.575; Hall, *Theft, Law and Society*, pp.52-8.
4. See Hill, *Repression of Crime*, pp.66-7; Charge to Staffs. Grand Jury in *SA* 2 July 1842.
5. Hill, op.cit., pp.69-70. See also 'Outline of duties. . .etc. . .of Wolverhampton Police' (1863, in WCL), p.26, which explicitly instructs detectives on the force to visit pawnbrokers and marine store dealers if there is reason to suspect that they have received stolen property.
6. Hill, op.cit., p.67.
7. Binny, 'Thieves and Swindlers', p.383; Charge to Staffs. Grand Jury in *SA* 1 December 1855.
8. *SA* 23 July 1836, report of QS.
9. *SA* 12 March 1842, report of QS.
10. SRO Q/SB E. 1842.
11. *SA* 23 and 30 July 1842, report of Ass.
12. Pollard, *Genesis*, pp.45-6; Hall, *Theft, Law and Society*, pp.39, 65.
13. Hall, op.cit., pp.37-40, 65-6.
14. Ibid., pp.45-52.
15. See Charge to Staffs. Grand Jury in *SA* 2 July 1842.
16. SRO Q/SB E. 1842.
17. *SA* 12 and 19 March 1842, report of Ass.
18. SRO Q/SB E. 1842; *SA* 12 and 19 March 1842.
19. Binny, 'Thieves and Swindlers', pp.377-83; Hill, *Repression of Crime*, pp.42-8; Tobias, *Crime*, pp.173-4, 225, 229-30.
20. Freeman, *Stories and Sketches*, p.213.
21. Tobias, *Crime*, p.174; Binny, 'Thieves and Swindlers', pp.378-80. Freeman mentions a Bilston family who set up a workshop for coining in a disused coal pit (*Stories and Sketches*, p.214).
22. *SA* 15 and 22 March 1851, report of Ass.
23. *SA* 23 and 30 July 1842, report of Ass.
24. *SA* 15 and 22 March 1851, report of Ass.
25. *SA* 23 and 30 July 1842, report of Ass.
26. *SA* 20 October 1855, report of QS.
27. See A. Feaveryear, *The Pound Sterling* (London 1963), chs. IX, X.
28. Binny, 'Thieves and Swindlers', p.380.
29. Questionnaire, quoted in full, in Hill, *Repression of Crime*, pp.44-5.
30. Binny, op.cit., pp.377-8.
31. Ibid., p.378.
32. *SA* 23 and 30 July 1836, report of Ass.
33. *SA* 15 and 22 March 1851, report of Ass.

8 VIOLENT OFFENDERS

Without pretending to any great exactness on this subject, it may be inferred that the whole quantity of crime is greater in proportion to the population in England than in France; but that of offences against the person there are more, both in proportion to the whole number of offences, and to the population in France, than in England. The general conclusion from this and other facts seems to be that crowded towns and flourishing manufactures tend to increase depredations on property, and to diminish acts of violence against the person. (*Report from SC on Criminal Commitments and Convictions* (1828), p.437.)

This chapter deals with those offences, against the person or against property, in the commission of which some element of violence or force was involved — offences against property committed with violence (robbery, breaking and entering, poaching while armed); all forms of offence against the person (homicides, assaults involving wounding, less serious assaults, sexual assaults); riots, breaches of the peace and public disturbances; and malicious damage to animals, machinery or other property (Table 35).

Table 35   Black Country Committals to Trial for Violent Offences 1835-60

Offence	No.	%
Breaking and entering	714	22.9
Robbery	487	15.7
Poaching while armed	16	0.5
Homicides	353	11.3
Assaults	499	16.0
Sexual offences	345	11.1
Other violence to the person	28	0.9
Riots and public disturbances	598	19.2
Malicious damage	75	2.4
TOTAL	3,115	100.0

These were the offences which most nineteenth-century commentators had in mind when they talked about crime and whether it was increasing; today, too, when people talk about 'real crime', it is usually some form of robbery, breaking and entering, or serious assault which they have in mind. These were the offences which struck most directly at the safety of the person and of property, in the streets and in the home. These were the crimes which, it was feared, could lead to a 'breakdown of society' and a reversion to anarchy and barbarism.

It has already been shown that a mere increase in the total number of committals to trial was not necessarily an accurate indicator of what was happening to these violent offences, since (apart from the influence of changes in prosecution) about 75 per cent of the figures are made up of larceny committals. The violent offences listed here constituted 14 per cent only of the total Black Country committals, and the proportion was much the same for the rest of the country. There was a debate, among those who held that crime was increasing, as to whether it was increasing in this area of violent offences or only in that of property offences. The majority view seems to have been that the increase was in property offences only. But there were those such as the Frenchman Faucher, and a writer in *Blackwood's* in 1818, who held that 'atrocious' and violent crimes were increasing in England.[1]

Now to examine each category of Black Country violent crime:

(A) Breaking and Entering

This category covers breaking and entering houses, shops, offices and warehouses, and stealing therein; also burglary of such places. Breaking and entering and burglary are essentially the same act, but legally burglary is distinguished by being a different offence, and meriting a more severe punishment. Burglary was the offence of breaking and entering during the hours of darkness, and (after Peel's Act of 1827 – 7 and 8 Geo. IV, c. 29) it was limited to breaking into a dwelling-house itself. Any breaking into the dwelling-house by day, or breaking into any outhouse or outbuilding not directly connected to the dwelling-house, or into a shop or warehouse, constituted the legally less serious offence of housebreaking or breaking and entering. Burglary was regarded as the more serious because, by taking place in the dwelling-house at night, it thereby put the inhabitants of the house 'in fear'. The essential point which distinguished burglary and housebreaking from mere larceny in a dwelling-house was the act of breaking into the house.[2] Breaking and entering was commonly dealt with at Quarter

Sessions, and burglary at Assizes; from 1842 onwards, burglary could only be tried at Assizes.

There were 714 Black Country prosecutions for breaking and entering or burglary between 1835 and 1860. Typical examples:

(1) Samuel Thompson, a publican, went to bed, having fastened all doors and windows in his house. At about 2.30 a.m. his two sons were disturbed by noises downstairs; they went down and found three men in the kitchen. The men went out of the back door, and the sons followed and attacked them. The three men each had thick bludgeons, at least one of them tipped with iron, and fought with the two sons. The one son, John Thompson, was injured, but he held on to one of the men, William Phillips, and shouted 'Murder'. The other two men climbed over a wall, but Phillips shouted 'Come back! there are only two, and we can beat them yet.' They came back and struck with their sticks over the wall, which was a low one. Then Samuel Thompson, having heard the noise, came up, and the two ran away. Phillips was the only one of the three burglars to be caught; he was found guilty, and the Judge *recorded a sentence of death.* He announced that he had decided to recommend clemency to the King, because all the violence used had been while trying to escape, and not in order to further the purpose of burgling the house. So the death sentence was not in fact carried out, but Phillips was transported for life.[3]

(2) David Reynolds and his wife went to bed at about 2 a.m. At about 4.30, they were disturbed by a noise downstairs; they went down, and found that the house had been broken into, and some beef, pork, bread, and cheese taken. They reported this to the local constable, and two days later, he searched the house of Richard Bennett, where he found a piece of beef and a marrow bone, which Mrs. Reynolds identified. Bennett said he had not taken the articles himself, but had been given them by his brother. He was found guilty and sentenced to ten years' transportation.[4]

(3) John Reeves, a West Bromwich coachsmith, went off to work during the day, and returned, with his wife, to his house at about 8 p.m. They found the front door broken open. They went in, and a strange dog attacked Reeves; he backed away from the dog, and sent his wife to fetch a poker and candle; with the poker, he killed the dog. He went into the kitchen, and there found John Blackham, who had broken into the house. They struggled, and Reeves sent someone to fetch the constable, but the constable was

not at home. Reeves and his brother then put Blackham out of the door, and he lay in the road for about ten minutes in a stupefied state. People gathered around; someone said: 'Give him a good thrashing and let him go.' Blackham asked Reeves if he would be satisfied with that, but Reeves said no. A little later, Blackham tried to run away, but Reeves caught him again. Looking for somewhere to shut him up, Reeves took him to the workhouse, but the Governor would not take him in. Later, Reeves finally found the constable, and got him to take Blackham into custody.[5]

(4) John and Samuel Flatley, bricklayers, broke into the dwelling-house of John Beardsmore, while he was out during the day, and took a ham, a bag, and thirty pairs of boots. They were caught, and the property found on them; they were found guilty, and given two years' penal servitude each.[6]

(5) Onesimus Jones, a nailer, broke into the warehouse of Messrs Pargeter, nailmasters of Stourbridge, by making a hole in the roof, and stole 240 lbs. of nails. Next day, he offered the nails for sale. The man to whom he sold them, having heard about the break-in at Pargeters, became suspicious, and told the constable. After some time, Jones was caught by the constable, and the stolen nails identified.[7]

These examples cover the common and important types of burglary, housebreaking, or breaking into a shop or warehouse.

Example (1) is the extreme case of burglary committed with violence, in which the idea of the householders being 'put in fear' by the men who break into the house was literally put into effect. It is clear in this case that Phillips and his companions had come armed with bludgeons, expecting to be able to fight their way out of any trouble, if they were found. They were a gang of burglars, who might well have relied on committing a series of burglaries in order to support themselves.

This was the sort of case which judges and writers on crime loved to cite, to illustrate the increase in crime and insecurity of life and property, and to stress the need for severe sentences for convicted burglars. Burglary touched a deep chord of fear and anxiety, violating the most deeply cherished beliefs about the sanctity of an Englishman's home. It was disturbing to have to fear that one's property, and perhaps one's very life, might not be safe while one was sleeping in one's own house. M.D. Hill set out this anxiety clearly in a Grand Jury charge on the subject of a Birmingham burglary, in which the burglars had severely injured the householder. He could remember, Hill said,

> no parallel instance of a crime so audacious, or one which must inevitably have diffused such dismay (not to say terror) throughout your vast population. That one of your townsmen, roused from his sleep by the invasion of his peaceful dwelling in the dead of night, should, when he meets with the burglars, inspire them with no fear – that he should be the pursued instead of the pursuer, and should have to defend his life against their murderous violence. . .is a most disastrous and humiliating event – an event which imperatively calls on every man among us. . .to spare no effort which may tend to restore to the inhabitants that feeling of personal security formerly enjoyed by them in its fullest extent, but now so rudely shaken.

And he went on to propose a highly controversial scheme whereby men known to have been convicted of crimes should, after their release, have the onus of proof thrust upon them to prove that they earned their living by honest means; in default of such proof, they should be able to be imprisoned again without being convicted of any specific new crime.[8] To such extreme measures would the fears aroused by burglary push even a self-professed Liberal penal reformer like Hill.

Until 1837, death remained the penalty for burglary (though usually commuted to transportation, as in example (1)). The Burglary Act 1837 (7 Will. IV and 1 Vict., c. 86) abolished the death penalty for all types of burglary, except burglary of a dwelling-house accompanied by an attempt to murder or wound the inmates. The death penalty for this latter category was abolished in 1861 (24 and 25 Vict., c. 100), but no executions for burglary had been carried out since the 1830s.[9]

However, although example (1) represented the 'ideal type' of burglary for judges and commentators, statistically it was not the typical Black Country burglary, which was far more frequently like example (2). Small quantities of food or clothes were by far the commonest items taken when houses were burgled. Nor was the sort of violence which characterised example (1) typical of the burglary cases; in most cases, the burglars either accomplished the job without being disturbed and were arrested with the stolen property later, or they were caught by the householder or a police officer and gave themselves up without a fight. Violence, as used by Phillips and his associates, did occur in some burglaries, but it was not the norm – at least, in those cases of burglary which came to court.

Most Black Country burglaries were not large-scale, planned operations against rich town or country houses; they were incursions into the houses of tradesmen and artisans, and occasionally of unskilled labourers. The haul was usually a few pieces of food or clothing – which suggests that it would have been difficult for their perpetrators to have been professional burglars existing purely on the fruits of their raids. Like most of the larceny offenders, they must have had some other form of livelihood as well.

Dickens vividly imprinted on the image of this period, for his contemporaries and for ourselves, the threatening figure of Bill Sikes, the professional burglar who plans large jobs at regular intervals and lives solely by his haul from these burglaries. Tobias accepts Sikes unquestioningly as an accurate model of the burglar of this period.[10] But he is certainly not an accurate model of the typical Black Country burglar who appeared in court. It may be that London, in this as in many other respects, was markedly different from the Black Country, and that its large population and large number of wealthy houses made possible a class of professional burglars who lived solely off the proceeds of regular, planned, large-scale burglaries. It is also possible that the police were failing to arrest the skilled professional burglars in the Black Country, and that those appearing in court were merely the less skilled amateurs of the trade. But it is more likely that the burglars who appeared in court *were* representative of the Black Country burglars; it is unwise for historians to rely heavily for objective evidence on a novelist like Dickens, who was not producing documentary reportage but was concerned to dramatise situations and characters for fictional purposes.[11]

Examples (3) and (4) are examples of breaking and entering a house during the day while the owner was absent. Once again, the first example contains a dramatic set of facts, but the second is closer to the usual case of breaking and entering. Here again, the usual articles taken were food and clothing from the houses of tradesmen, artisans and a few miners or labourers, usually while they were away at work.

The Chief Constable of Wolverhampton, in 1858, reported twenty-seven burglaries, for which ten people had been prosecuted, and noted: 'Entrance chiefly effected by the cellar approaches being left insecure.' He reported fourteen cases of housebreaking and larceny, of which one had been prosecuted, and noted: 'Left unprotected. – Occupiers out at work.' He also noted that it was common for burglaries and break-ins to take place on Sunday evenings, while families were away at church services.[12] This second note indicates that the numbers prosecuted fo for breaking and entering offences fell far short of the number of break-ins committed. As with most of the larcenies, the conclusion seems to be that only a fraction — probably under half — of the burglars and housebreakers were in fact brought to court (though, of course one man or group might be responsible for a whole series of break-ins).

Breaking and entering was not treated as severely as burglary, the death penalty for housebreaking having been abolished in 1833. And the general sentences passed for breaking and entering were less severe than those for burglary (Table 36), since it lacked that element of putting householders 'in fear' by night.

Example (3) is also interesting for the light it throws on the issue referred to in chapters 4 and 6 — the problem for the victim of finding and apprehending the offender, and getting him into police custody. This incident took place in 1836, when West Bromwich had only four parish constables for the town with a population of nearly 21,000. It shows how difficult it could be for the victim even if he had caught and subdued the offender; if the constable happened not to be at home when he was sent for, there was no other legal machinery to hand. We also see here people advocating immediate informal punishment for the housebreaker — 'Give him a good thrashing and let him go'. This may well have been all that did happen when some housebreakers were caught. Reeves seems to have been unusually persistent in not settling for this but continuing his search for some place to lock up his prisoner — even to the extent of trying to put him in the workhouse!

Finally, example (5) is typical of the cases of breaking and entering into shops, offices, warehouses. Most of these involved breaking in in order to steal pieces of metal or articles of metal manufacture similar to the items stolen in industrial thefts. Nails or nailmaking iron were very commonly taken.

In some cases, the break-ins were connected with the violence and hostility which characterised the frequent industrial disputes in the nailmaking industry. For instance:

Samuel Round was tried for breaking and entering the nail shop of Reuben Pearson, and stealing fifty pounds of rod iron from it. Pearson's shop had been broken into and the iron and an apron were found by a policeman in Round's house. But Round called in his defence the leader and a member of the South Staffordshire Nailers' Union, of which he was a member, and they testified that Round had honestly bought the iron and apron. Pearson was not a member of the union, and the cross-examination of the two union witnesses suggested that threats had been made by members of the union to cut Pearson's bellows for refusing to join the union and their strike. The jury did not believe the union witnesses, and found Round guilty. It was then announced that Round had four previous convictions — two for assault, and two for felony, one of these being stealing iron. He was given seven years' transportation.[13]

Table 36   Black Country Sentences for Burglary and Breaking and Entering 1835-60

Sentence	Percentage	
	Burglary	Breaking and Entering
Imprisonment:		
Less than 1 month		0.4
1-3 months	5.4	9.1
4-6 months	11.3	20.7
7-12 months	24.4	28.4
More than 12 months	5.0	5.6
TOTAL Imprisonment	46.1	64.2
Transportation:		
7 years	4.1	10.9
10-15 years	26.7	11.9
Life	6.3	
Penal Servitude:		
3-4 years	5.0	8.8
5-9 years	5.9	2.8
10-15 years	0.9	0.7
Death Recorded	5.0	
TOTAL Transportation and Penal Servitude	53.9	35.1
Bound over		0.7
TOTAL	100.0	100.0
	n = 221	n = 285

This incident took place in November 1846, during a Black Country nailers' strike. Cutting bellows had long been the method by which the nailers enforced their demands on non-union nailers or blacklegs, and they were to be used again in the bitter nailers' strikes and lockouts of 1859-60.[14] It would seem that the main reason for breaking into Pearson's shop was to cut his bellows, in order to bring him in line with the union and the strike. But it also seems clear that Round had taken advantage of this in order to take some rod iron and an apron for himself at the same time – and his previous convictions suggest that he had done this before. Similarly, in 1860, a nailer named George Vanes, who was one of those convicted of cutting bellows during the 1860 lockout, was shown to have a previous conviction for burglary in 1855.[15]

This does not mean that all the nailers who resorted to cutting bellows did so as a cover for stealing – on the contrary, bellows-cutting was the main weapon which the nailers' unions could use in order to enforce a strike, and they used it as a bargaining counter against the nailmasters. But it does suggest that the borderline was not clear between social/industrial/political crime on the one hand, and 'ordinary' crime on the other. The primary purpose was to enforce a stoppage and deter blacklegging, but this was not going to stop some individuals benefiting themselves at the same time. There was nothing in the nailers' feelings towards the nailmasters or blackleg nailers to make them scrupulous in their attitude towards private property. The previous sections on industrial theft, thefts of clothing and thefts of food have suggested that these offences were mostly carried out, not by professionals, but by people who worked at jobs but had low and precarious incomes, and therefore enriched themselves where and when they could. Nailers figure prominently among those charged with larcenies of all sorts and it is understandable that, in the course of advancing the cause of the united nailers, some of them should also have advanced the cause of themselves.

The occupation data show that about 25 per cent of those charged with all breaking and entering offences gave their occupations as miners; 19 per cent were labourers; 6 per cent nailers; and other unskilled manual workers made up another 16 per cent. Skilled manual workers made up another 27 per cent – with skilled ironworkers such as puddlers particularly prominent, and artisans and metalworking craftsmen also fairly numerous. A miner's pick was the tool commonly used in breaking open outhouses, or breaking open a door in a house during the day. Not surprisingly, breaking and entering was almost a totally male crime – of the 714 persons prosecuted, 668 were male, and only 46 female.

(B) Robbery

Robbery is the offence of 'the felonious taking of money or goods of any value from the person of another, or in his presence, against his will, by violence or putting him in fear. . .The scope of the law of robbery – like that of burglary – largely depended on the construction put upon it by the courts, especially on the elements of violence and fear.'[16] Basically, robbery consisted of the act of taking someone's possessions from him, by the use or threat of violence; it was the violence which was the aggravating factor distinguishing robbery from mere larceny from the person. Robbery generally took place on the streets; with burglary, it was the crime most apt to give rise to fears of a breakdown of law and order – in the late eighteenth century, highway robberies by highwaymen and footpads caused considerable alarm; in the 1860s, a wave of reported garrottings (in which the victim was seized around the head and his throat squeezed to keep him still while he was robbed) in London caused a panic, and flogging was introduced as a penalty for those found guilty of this offence. (In both its method of operation and the reaction of the public and authorities, garrotting resembles 'mugging' in the 1970s.)

There were 487 prosecutions for robbery in the Black Country in this period. They took place mostly on the streets of the towns and the roads between towns, mostly when the victims were returning home at night. Typical examples:

(1) John Rutter, a saddler, who lived at Dudley Port, was going home from Walsall at about 10 p.m. He went a little way on the road, and then went across the fields. In the second field, he was attacked by four men. One of them, John Yates, hit him hard five times on the head with a life preserver, and knocked him down; while he was down, the men robbed him of £1 and a silk handkerchief. The men then left, and he managed to get to a nearby pub, and then to a police officer and a surgeon. He was severely injured, and had lost much blood from wounds on the scalp. A policeman arrested the four men, and Rutter identified them; one turned Queen's evidence, and gave evidence against the other three, who were tried. All three were found guilty; two were sentenced to twelve months imprisonment with hard labour; for Yates, who had struck the blows that did the damage, the Judge recorded a sentence of death,

but said that he would recommend that he be transported for seven years.[17]

(2) John Roahan, a labourer, was walking through Carribee Island, the Irish slum quarter of Wolverhampton, and passed three men, Patrick Tunney, Thomas M'Donnell, and John M'Keon. Tunney then came up and knocked him down, and M'Donnell held him there, while M'Keon rifled his pockets, taking a purse containing 5s 6d. The three then went into a house a little way down the street, and Roahan went to the police station. He returned with two constables to the house, and found the three men there. The purse was found on M'Keon, and Tunney admitted knocking Roahan down. The three were found guilty, and were each sentenced to ten years' transportation.[18]

(3) John Clough, a miner, was in a pub on 'reckoning (pay) night' until about 1 a.m. While he was there, Thomas Gilbert, whom he knew well, came into the pub, but left before Clough did. Clough left the pub, and went along the street; Gilbert came up to him, with Thomas Cotterell, whom he also knew well. Cotterell knocked Clough down, and Gilbert kicked him while on the ground. Gilbert took 2s 6d. (all the money he had) from Clough's pocket. Clough's cries awakened a man, who shouted out of the window: 'Lads, binne you ashamed of yourselves?' Cotterell ran away, and Gilbert kicked Clough several more times, and then ran away.[19]

(4) John Beddow had been paid his wages in a pub in Walsall, and stayed there until late. Also in the pub were Charles Biddle, and George and John Reeves. When Beddow left the pub, they were still there, but they overtook him outside; one put his hands over Beddow's face, another held his arms, and the third cut off his pocket containing one sovereign. During this time, he got a distinct view of the face of John Reeves. All three were found guilty, and the judge recorded a sentence of death on all of them, with the understanding that it would be commuted.[20]

(5) Enoch Hodgetts, a boy, was walking back from Wolverhampton to Willenhall on a Saturday night at about 10.30, with his father a little way ahead of him and his mother a little behind. He was carrying a handkerchief, gown, and a pair of trousers in a bundle. John Hodgkins came up and offered him a penny to show him the road to Wednesfield. Hodgkins seized the bundle, wrested it from Enoch Hodgetts, and ran off. Enoch called his father, and, a few days later, the Willenhall constable searched Hodgkins' lodgings and found the trousers and gown there. Hodgkins was found guilty and

given one month's hard labour.[21]

These examples show that there were at least two different types of robbery: technically, all robbery involved violence, but in some cases the violence was only what was needed in order to seize the property from the victim; in others there was a good deal of violence inflicted on the victim in addition to what was necessary to effect the robbery. In examples (1) and (3), there was clearly violence above and beyond that necessary to carry out the robbery; in (2) and (4) the violence was only what was necessary in order to rob the man; and in (5) there was no real violence, but only the use of force in order to seize the bundle.

Examples (1) and (2) are the archetypal instances of highway robbery, in which the victim is robbed by people whom he has not seen before, while on the road or fields between towns at night, or in the rough quarters of a town like Wolverhampton. These were crimes which struck at people's safety in the streets, an important point at a time when a large part of the population had to rely on walking long distances through the streets at night in order to get to and from places. This same point is seen in (5) in which the Hodgkins family were walking home from Wolverhampton to Willenhall, a distance of about three miles; Rutter's proposed journey, in (1), would have been close to ten miles.

This sort of robbery therefore tended to be punished very severely. Until 1837, all forms of robbery were capital; the 1837 Act (7 Will. IV and 1 Vict. c. 87) abolished the death sentence for all forms of robbery, except where it was accompanied by serious violence. An 1841 Act (4 and 5 Vict., c. 56) abolished death for even this case. But even before 1837, the death sentence had usually only been recorded, and transportation remained the usual punishment for people convicted of serious robberies. Robberies of the sort represented by example (1) were common in the Black Country on the roads between towns.[22] Example (5) also took place on the open road; here, it was the absence of any real violence which led the judge to impose such a light sentence, though he warned the accused that he was being treated lightly because it was a first offence; if he repeated the offence, he would be transported.

But even more common than the set of facts exemplified by example (1) are those represented in examples (3) and (4); this was by far the commonest way in which robberies in the Black Country took place. The facts of these cases are monotonously simple, and very similar to that category of larceny from the person which involved the victim and the offender drinking together during the time in which the theft took place. The difference, in this case, is that the robbery would take place in the road, after the victim had left the pub, and would often involve a fair degree of violence.

In all these cases, the victim was robbed after he had left the pub late at night. In some cases, the robbers would be people who did not know that the victim would be passing that way, but who were simply waiting for someone to come along — but these were relatively few. Much more common was the case in which the robbers were in the pub with the victim, left the pub just before him, and lay in wait for him; or left the pub just after him, and caught up with him. These cases happened most frequently on the nights when the victim had just been paid — often in the pub itself — so that the robbers knew that he would have money on his person. In a surprisingly large number of cases, the victim knew the robbers personally from before, either as workmates, or as people whom he knew in the town or the pub; probably this number is so high in the cases which came to court because the fact that the victim knew the robbers personally made it easier for him to get an arrest, identification and committal to trial. In a number of these cases, it was the fact that the robbers knew the victim personally that gave them inside knowledge that he was carrying sufficient money to make a robbery worthwhile.

There is no doubt about the prominent part played by the pub in the stories of these robberies. This is presumably because most robberies took place late at night, and the most usual reason for people being on their way home alone, on foot, late at night was that they were returning from the pub. The other common circumstance for being on the road late at night was when people were returning from one town to another, and this was also a frequent situation in which robberies took place. But the pub had the advantages of offering the robbers a place in which they could keep warm and drink while watching their prospective victim until he set out for home (which seems usually not to have been before about 1 a.m.), and of ensuring that the victim would probably be at least slightly drunk by the time they accosted him, making it easy to surprise him and knock him down. Judges, magistrates, criminal reformers and temperance advocates were not slow to draw the moral of the connection of this sort of crime with drink; for instance, Baron Watson, at a Worcestershire Assizes, observed that

. . .although in the county of Worcester generally the state of morals and the small amount of crime evinced the good conduct of the population, yet in one district of the county — the coal and mining neighbourhood of Dudley — a very large proportion of the offences against the laws occurred. . .Nearly all the cases to which he had alluded (chiefly highway robbery) happened in this way. The lower class of people resorted to public-houses and beer-houses, and on coming out at night, some one was followed, knocked down, and robbed. That was the general feature of nearly all those cases, which showed a very loose and depraved state of morals at Dudley and the neighbourhood. It seemed probable that the bulk of these cases originated in the facilities for crime afforded by the beer-houses.[23]

Robbery, particularly when accompanied by violence inflicting injuries, naturally caused concern about people's safety in the streets; whenever it was thought to be on the increase, there were moves to stamp it out by more severe punishments. For instance, the Judge, in sentencing two men for highway robbery with violence in July 1842, remarked that robbery was greatly increasing in Staffordshire, and must be put down by terror of punishment. He considered transporting them for life and ended by giving them each sentences of twenty-one years' transportation — an abnormally long sentence.[24]

However, we must note that, although violence was freely used in these robberies, murderous weapons were seldom employed for the task. In virtually all the robberies in the Black Country, the most dangerous weapon used was a life-preserver, a cudgel or a stick; more often it was simply parts of their bodies which were used — fists, arms (for seizing and pinioning people from behind) and feet (kicking them once they were down on the ground). Certainly, these weapons could inflict serious injuries, and even death could result from being beaten over the head with a loaded cudgel or being kicked in the head repeatedly by a man wearing heavy boots. But it is noticeable that the robbers did not arm themselves with specifically lethal weapons for the task. It is difficult to discover any cases in which the robbers were armed with knives — a particularly noteworthy fact in view of the prevalence of knife-carrying in the area (see pp.263-6 below), and the use of firearms for this purpose was so rare, that the occasion of the one case of this sort which has been found, called forth a surprised comment from the *Staffordshire Advertiser*. In this case, three men had stopped the victim on a canal towing path, and one had produced two pistols and threatened to shoot him if he did not give up his money.

This was so unusual an event that the newspaper expressed its surprise
that one should still come across cases of this sort which 'partook of
the character of the Turpin school of highwaymen'.[25] But in the
overwhelming majority of robberies which appeared in court, the
weapons used had been fists or some sort of stick. This is an important
qualification to bear in mind — the facts of the robbery cases show
that this was a rough society, in which considerable violence might be
encountered in the streets, enough to cause alarm in the minds of
'respectable' citizens. But they did not have to fear murderous assault —
the danger was of being beaten up, perhaps severely, but not of being
knifed or shot. There were no powerful, well-armed gangs of robbers
prowling the Black Country roads.

Most of those tried for this offence, as with burglary, were miners,
labourers, nailers, chainmakers, and skilled iron or metal workers
(Table 37), who took to robbery when the opportunity presented
itself. One of the points which emerges most clearly from the
numerous cases involving men being robbed after leaving the pub, is
the absence of long-term planning, the relatively casual way in which
the two or three men decided on a potential victim, and carried out the
robbery soon after that.

Table 37   Occupation of Those Charged with Robbery — from Black
Country as a Whole 1854-60, and from Dudley 1839-60

Occupation	Percentage	
	Black Country 1854-60	Dudley 1839-60
Miner	42.2	48.9
Labourer	18.6	12.0
Nailer, chainmaker	5.6	8.7
Boatman	2.5	6.5
Other unskilled manual worker	2.5	6.5
Skilled metal worker	13.6	7.6
Other skilled manual worker	6.2	7.6
Other	4.4	2.2
No occupation	4.4	0.0
TOTAL	100.0	100.0
TOTAL number whose occupation is known	161	92
Occupation not available	33	24

Like breaking and entering, robbery was overwhelmingly a male offence — of the 487 accused of it, only 29 were women. Robbery and burglary were both offences normally requiring male strength for their commission — particularly since most of the violence in the robbery cases was inflicted by naked fists. Women, as we have seen, tended to go rather for the more subtle practice of stealing, without violence, from drunk men whom they had lured by the promise of intercourse.

Sentences for robbery were severe, 60 per cent being transportation or penal servitude (Table 38). There was a trend towards slightly less severe sentences over the period: in the 1830s, virtually every robbery punishment was a recorded death sentence or transportation, and it was only in the 1850s that prison sentences of less than twelve months were imposed for robbery.

Table 38   Black Country Robbery Sentences 1835-60

Sentence	Percentage
Imprisonment	
Less than 1 month	0.4
1-3 months	4.0
4-6 months	12.7
7-12 months	15.6
More than 12 months	6.9
TOTAL Imprisonment	39.6
Transportation	
7 years	8.4
10-15 years	14.6
Life	1.1
Penal Servitude	
3-4 years	12.3
5-9 years	8.7
10-15 years	0.7
Death Recorded	14.6
TOTAL Transportation and Penal Servitude	60.4
TOTAL	100.0

n = 275

(C) Poaching While Armed

This is only a small category. Poaching itself — the offence of taking game which is declared protected from being taken without permission — was not an offence which featured at Quarter Sessions or Assizes. Game Law offences were tried summarily by two Justices of the Peace sitting in Petty Sessions — this gave rise to the notorious situation in which the landowner whose game had been taken, sat, as JP, in judgement over the man accused of poaching.[26] The penalties which the Justices in Petty Sessions could impose were limited to fines or prison terms of up to three months. However, if the poaching was done by night, and if the men involved were armed and had previous poaching convictions, they could be committed for trial at Quarter Sessions or Assizes.

Poaching was not very important in the Black Country, and only sixteen cases of this sort came up to Quarter Sessions over the whole period 1835-60. So the evidence on this offence is thin; what there is suggests that these indictable prosecutions involved poaching gangs who became involved in armed battles with groups of gamekeepers. This offence had been a capital one under the eighteenth-century Waltham Black Act, but that Act was repealed in 1823.[27] These sixteen Black Country cases received much milder treatment. All sixteen were men, and fifteen of them were convicted. Only two of those were transported — for seven years each; ten were imprisoned for 7 to 12 months; and the remaining three got prison terms of 4 to 6 months.

(D) Homicides

This category covers the legal offences of murder and manslaughter, and also the offences connected with infanticide. The difference between murder and manslaughter turns on the presence of absence of 'malice aforethought'. Murder was defined thus, in the early nineteenth century:

> Murder, in the sense in which it is now understood, is the voluntarily killing any person. . .under the king's peace, of malice prepense or aforethought either express or implied by law.[28]

A modern definition brings out the meaning of 'malice aforethought':

> Murder is unlawful homicide with 'malice aforethought'. Malice

aforethought consists of an intention on the part of the accused:

1. To kill another human being within the Queen's peace; or
2. To do grievous bodily harm to another human being within the Queen's peace.

...The presence of malice aforethought distinguished the...
capital felony of murder from the less culpable forms of unlawful
homicide which came to be known as manslaughter [which was
non-capital, while murder was capital throughout the 19th century].
...Malice aforethought does not always imply an intention to kill...
It might have been 'express', 'implied', or 'constructive'.[29]

It was the jury who decided whether malice aforethought had been
present or not, and they often downgraded a charge by bringing in a
verdict of guilty of manslaughter on an accused who had initially been
charged with murder.

Examples of these offences:

Murder

(1) One night four men, Joseph Wilkes, James Wilkes, Thomas Boswell,
and George Giles, together broke into the house of Matthew Adams,
a wealthy man aged between seventy and eighty years. Adams heard
them and seized a fork in the pantry, to use against them. Joseph
Wilkes struck him with a hammer, a blow which killed him. The
noise was heard in adjoining houses, and a number of people saw
the four men. They were also found to have a pistol with them.
Joseph Wilkes, who was aged seventeen and was a farm servant, was
found guilty of murder, sentenced to death, and was executed three
weeks later. The other three were found not guilty of murder, since
it was Joseph Wilkes who had struck the blow, but were found
guilty of burglary. James Wilkes and Thomas Boswell were to be
transported for life, and Giles for fifteen years.[30]

(2) Reuben Curtis was found, early one Sunday morning, in a jacky pit,
suspended by a hook over the hot water that was flowing into it
from a nearby engine. He was taken out, gasped once or twice, and
died; cause of death was established as his having been suspended,
head downwards, over the vapour arising from the water. The jacky
pit was so narrow at the surface that it was impossible that he could
have fallen into it by accident; and injuries on his body showed that
violence had been used to put him there. Indicted for the murder
were Ann Curtis, the dead man's wife who had not lived with him
for some time, George Clarke, the man with whom she was living,

and William Cowell. One witness described seeing these three knock Curtis down and put him in the pit. But he had not originally told the authorities of this (he claimed that Clarke had terrorised him into silence), and his testimony contained a number of contradictory points and was unsupported by the evidence of any other witness. The judge, in summing up, said there was no doubt that Curtis had been murdered, but there was only the one witness to connect the accused to the deed.

'The jury, after a short consultation, returned a verdict to the effect that they considered the evidence insufficient to fix the guilt of murder on any of the prisoners; but they had unfavourable suspicions of them. Under the direction of his Lordship a verdict of not guilty was recorded.'[31]

Manslaughter

(3) Thomas Wilkes and Thomas Clewitt were having a fight in front of a fairly large crowd. At the end of the first round, they fell, and while they were struggling on the ground, Joseph Foster tried to pull Clewitt from under Wilkes. When they stood up, Wilkes' brother, Edward Wilkes, being angry, went to a nearby house, and returned with a bar of iron, with which he struck Foster twice on the top of the head. Foster fell, and subsequently (45 days later) died. The surgeons found that the blows had caused his death. Edward Wilkes was tried for murder, but the jury found him not guilty of murder, and guilty of manslaughter.[32]

(4) Joseph Beddesford, Peter Perry and Frederick Sambrook were in a pub together, relations between them being friendly. Later that night, Beddesford and Sambrook had a long fight, for over an hour, in the course of which Beddesford knocked Sambrook down a number of times; each time, Perry picked him up again, and sent him back into the fight; the last time he was knocked onto a pile of stones. Afterwards, the three of them went off together in friendly spirits. But two days later, Sambrook died of an inflammation of his abdomen, caused by his injuries. Beddesford and Perry were charged with manslaughter, Beddesford as principal and Perry as accessory. Both were found guilty, and they were sentenced to one month's imprisonment each.[33]

(5) James Sumner was an engineer at a coal pit, in charge of the winding engine by which men descended into, and came up from the pit. He had to replace the old block of the engine with a new one, but put the new one in sideways by accident. The result was

that, when the skip was going down the pit, it went too fast and the chain came off the drum barrel, and fell down the shaft, on top of the miner in the skip, Daniel Sneyd, killing him. The judge stated that *gross negligence* was necessary to convict of manslaughter in such a case; this mistake could be made without gross negligence, and the evidence seemed to show that th..t was the case. He therefore directed an acquittal.[34]

Infanticide

(6) Mary Weston, a domestic servant aged 19, was charged with the murder of her illegitimate child. She had woken the fellow servant with whom she shared a room, told her that she was in labour, and asked for her help. The other servant was alarmed, and, instead of helping, left the room. While she was out, Weston gave birth to a child which the other servant heard cry three times — a proof that it had been born alive. Weston put the child in an earthenware vessel, and took it to a churchyard, where she intended to bury it, but found the ground too hard. She was charged with the murder of the child, or, alternatively, concealing its birth. The judge said that the facts did not support either charge; even if the child was born alive and was alive when placed in the vessel, there was no proof that she *knew* it was alive. She was in a very nervous state, having been abandoned by the father, and feeling herself in alarming circumstances; she could not be proved to have known that the child was alive. Nor could she be charged with concealing the birth, since she had told her fellow-servant about it and about the burial. So the judge directed an acquittal.[35]

Examples (1) and (2) are clear cases of murder, in which there was not only a death, but also a clear intention on the part of whoever carried out the act, to inflict the injuries with the clear possibility that they might result in serious bodily harm or death. In example (1), it was the fact that the accused had gone to the house armed, expecting to use force and possibly even to kill in order to carry out their burglary, that constituted the necessary element of malice aforethought for a murder charge to be upheld.

Murder is one of those crimes for which it is difficult to give typical examples — each case must be taken as unique. What does stand out in the Black Country is the small number of people who were convicted of murder; between 1835 and 1860, only eight people were so convicted; fifty-six people were *indicted* for murder, but forty-eight of those were found guilty of manslaughter or acquitted completely. Of the eight convicted of murder, seven had the genuine death sentence pronounced (as opposed to a 'recorded' death sentence routinely commuted to transportation); the other one (a woman) had the death sentence recorded. The death sentence was carried out for four of these seven – all men (one of them was Wilkes in example (1)). The other three were reprieved by the Home Secretary – two were women, and there was a strong disinclination to execute women;[36] the third was found guilty of murdering his wife, but the jury gave a strong recommendation to mercy; the judge sentenced him to death, but passed on the jury's recommendation, and the Home Secretary ordered him to be reprieved on the ground of insanity, and detained during Her Majesty's pleasure.

These four executions were the only capital sentences put into effect in the Black Country between 1835 and 1860. For a period of twenty-six years, and an area with a population of over 200,000 at the start, and 470,000 by the end, this is a low incidence of murders and executions. And it is likely that this reflects the true position as regards murders in the area, since the murder rate is one of those areas in which, criminologists suggest, the official rate is very close to the 'real' rate; whatever may be the case in regard to the theft of various articles, a dead body is something which is noticeable and difficult to explain away.[37] Most of the prosecutions for murder and manslaughter were initiated by coroners' juries bringing in verdicts of murder or manslaughter against particular people, against whom the indictment was then prepared. So the Black Country court figures suggest a rough society with a degree of personal violence, but not a society in which the criminal violence generally extended to the taking of life. The chance of being killed in an accident in a mine or factory was much greater, for most of the population.

Examples (3) and (4) are examples of the standard charge of manslaughter in which the accused caused the death of the victim, but it was held to have been done without malice aforethought. In the case of example (3), the jury seems to have felt that Wilkes did not intend to kill or very seriously injure Foster; and, though Foster's death seems to have resulted from the injuries, it followed sufficiently long afterwards not to constitute the sort of direct link between the action and the death usually established in a murder case. In (4), Beddesford and Perry were never even charged with murder, since, although they were clearly responsible for Sambrook's death, the act was not done with the intention or expectation that it would lead to his death; his death due to his injuries was an unforeseen event. In these cases, the courts were punishing a form of homicide which could not be allowed to take place unchecked, and had to be punished and deterred, but which none the less was not culpable in the same degree of seriousness as murder.

Example (5) introduces a different sort of manslaughter charge, which was very common in the Black Country. People died frequently in accidents — most commonly falls, explosions, or accidents to the winding gear and skips, in the mines,[38] but also railway or factory accidents — and an inquest would be held on the bodies. If the coroner's jury returned a verdict of manslaughter against a particular person, the coroner could commit him to trial on that charge. The result was that a number of engineers in charge of pit winding gear and other lesser mine officials, factory foremen, or employees of railway or omnibus companies, found themselves in court facing manslaughter charges resulting from alleged negligent behaviour on their part.

In almost every case, they were not convicted; in many cases, the bill was thrown out by the Grand Jury;[39] in others, it appeared in court only for the judge to dismiss it immediately on the grounds that there was no prosecution case for the accused to answer. In those cases which did come to trial, the judges took their stand on the doctrine that gross negligence was necessary in order to constitute grounds to support a manslaughter charge, and they resisted as far as possible imputing any degree of responsibility for the deaths, to the engineers, foremen, etc. In this they showed themselves staunch upholders of the dominant individualist ideas of the time; if workmen were injured or killed in industrial accidents, the responsibility had to rest with the individual affected and not be transferred to the employer or superior workman.

Example (5) gives one instance of a judge following this doctrine. In another case, there was a serious railway accident involving fourteen deaths, and the railway guard was charged with manslaughter. Baron Bramwell, a notable Victorian judicial upholder of *laissez-faire,* made it clear in his address to the Grand Jury that the guard should not be held legally responsible for this; the Grand Jury threw out the fourteen Bills of indictment, and, to make sure of clearing the guard, Bramwell had the prosecution formally continued, without any evidence being presented, so that the petty jury found the guard not guilty on all counts as well.[40] In another case, the child of a labourer had been burned and application was made to one of the relieving officers of the Poor Law Union for a note to give to the parish doctor; the relieving officer refused, and the child died. The coroner's jury indicted the relieving officer, but the judge directed a discharge on the grounds that a public officer could be indicted for neglect if he neglected to perform an act which his office obliged him to perform,

> but a mere mistake or indiscretion in the performance of a duty was not a punishable offence.[41]

In another case in which an engineer was charged with failing to slow down the engine in time, as a result of which three men were killed, the defence counsel raised the objection that the actual accident had taken place once the skip had come up out of the pit, while the indictment charged it as happening in the pit. Mr Justice Patten accepted this objection.

> In directing the prisoner to be discharged, he said he did not much regret the result of this case, as the prisoner was not the only man to blame in the matter; the banksman had also been guilty of very great neglect. He expressed an opinion that owners of collieries ought to consult some experienced railway engineers, in order to introduce some more efficient system of working the machinery in connection with mining operations, and to prevent the deaths which so frequently occurred through the negligence of servants.[42]

The judges repeatedly made it clear that they were not going to hold employers and superior employees vicariously liable in criminal law for the deaths of employees in accidents. One can only conclude that these indictments continued to come from the coroners' juries more as a form of protest at the frequency of such fatal accidents and at the lack of a strong law forcing employers to take adequate safety precautions, than in the belief that the people indicted would actually be convicted.[43]

Apart from the cases involving accidents of this type, most of the manslaughter cases arose from fights of some sort. Fights of the type encountered in examples (3) and (4) were common, held outside the pub, in the street or in a patch of waste ground, usually with some sort of crowd around the fighters. Boxing was a favourite Black Country working-class sport; many of the fights were simply to settle bets or challenges, others were provoked by quarrels. They were fought with fists only, and to a rough sort of code, though it was a long way from the Queensberry Rules, and there were no boxing gloves used.[44]

People were frequently hurt in these fights, and on a number of occasions, killed. For instance, James Smith had quarrelled at work with Thomas Bartholomew; they went to a piece of waste ground to fight, and after about twelve rounds, Bartholomew died from a blow which ruptured his stomach. Smith and the man who had acted as his second, William Yates, were tried for murder, and found guilty of manslaughter, with a recommendation to mercy. 'The learned judge said if he did not show mercy he should not do justice. . .It was a fair fight, but death in any fight was manslaughter. He saw that they were very sorry.' Since they had already been nine months in prison awaiting trial, he sentenced them to only five days' imprisonment each.[45]

In some cases, people were killed in the more formal (though illegal) prizefights, held for money stakes, which were also very popular and frequently held in the Black Country; in such cases, the men who acted as seconds, referee, and timekeepers were often indicted for manslaughter.[46] There were also cases of death inflicted during faction fights and communal brawls, such as the one in which five Irishmen killed another Irishman in a fight arising out of some feud. In other cases, death resulted from the accused suddenly striking the victim with some implement during a quarrel — as when Wilkes struck Foster with an iron bar in example (3); or where two boys of fourteen were playing in the sand and began fighting, and the one threw a large rock at the other, which killed him; or where a man, having been thrown out of a girl's room by her uncle, hit him over the head with a stick and killed him.[47]

These sorts of cases reinforce the point already made in the section on robbery — this was a rough society, in which violence and physical combat could be and were often encountered; but it was not a notably homicidal society. The manslaughter cases do not show a free use of lethal weapons, nor much evidence of intention or willingness to kill on the part of the offenders; at most, they show a somewhat callous disregard for the possible consequences of a blow over the head or punches in the stomach (as well as the callous disregard shown in the area of precautions against accident in mines, factories, and transport).

In all, over the period 1835-60, there were 258 indictments for manslaughter and 110 convictions (a number of these convictions were of people originally indicted for murder). Sentences for manslaughter were not severe by comparison with other violent offences. None was sentenced to death, and only twelve of the 110 received transportation or penal servitude — four of them for life. The vast majority were imprisoned, most for six months or less; seven were fined or bound over.

Altogether, 258 manslaughter indictments (which, remember, include a number of industrial accidents) and 110 convictions, plus fifty-six indictments and eight convictions for murder, does not add up to a very formidable catalogue of illegal homicides for an industrial area of that size and population over a period of twenty-six years.

There is one final form of homicide to be dealt with, and that is infanticide, as shown in example (6). The facts in this sort of case were usually that a young woman, often a domestic servant, would have an illegitimate baby, and would try to dispose of it as soon as possible, in order to avoid being landed with the burden and stigma of the child. There were several possibilities in such cases; if the girl and one or two close friends could keep the birth a secret, they could dispose of the child (by leaving it somewhere to die, drowning, or burying it) without anyone knowing whose child it was. Alternatively, even if the birth had become known, if it could take place in secret, it could be hoped that the child might be stillborn, or claimed that it *was* stillborn, and it could then be taken away and buried. Hence, the alternative and lesser charge was that of 'concealing the birth of a child', since the concealment made it impossible to prove whether or not the child was born alive. The most usual charge used against girls in this position was this one of concealing the birth.

However, it is noticeable that, since the law at this time made no special provision for mothers who committed such an act under these conditions of mental stress and disturbance, judges and juries invariably took a sympathetic and lenient attitude towards women charged with this offence; they did their best to make up, through their rulings and verdicts, for the defects in the state of the law which rendered it harsher than it should be. This was easy to do in these cases. The evidence was usually (by the nature of things) scanty and inconclusive; in a situation in which the woman might genuinely have believed that the baby was stillborn, or where the baby might well have died of its own accord, judges and juries were ready to give the woman the benefit of the doubt wherever possible. The result was that, in more than half the cases, the women were acquitted; of thirty-nine women charged with infanticide or concealing the birth of an infant between 1835 and 1860, only 15 were found guilty. The sentences were imprisonment only — three received sentences of between seven and twelve months; four were jailed for between four and six months; six were sentenced to between one and three months; and two received sentences of less than a month.

(E) Assaults

Technically speaking, what is normally referred to as an assault is, in strict legal terminology, the offence of battery:

> A person is guilty of an assault if he unlawfully displays force against another in such a way that he creates in the mind of that other the belief that force is about to be used against him, provided he intended to create such belief.
>
> A person is guilty of battery if he intentionally uses unlawful force against another.
>
> An assault or battery which is not accompanied by aggravating circumstances is. . .a 'common assault'.[48]

However, this section employs the term 'assault' in its commonly understood sense of the use of unlawful force against another.

'Common assaults' — that is, assaults involving no aggravating circumstances — did not as a rule come before the Quarter Sessions and Assizes. All assaults were misdemeanours, and most common assaults which came to court were tried summarily by justices in petty sessions; the usual punishment for them was a small fine, or being bound over to keep the peace. These were the not very serious cases in which husbands or wives hit each other, neighbours came to blows, drinking companions or workmates fought each other, people brawled in the streets or public places — in each case, without any serious injuries being inflicted.

Of course, many cases of what were technically assault and battery never came before a magistrate at all. We have already mentioned the frequency of fights among the Black Country working class; unless serious injuries had been inflicted on one of the combatants, it was most unusual for a prosecution for assault to follow such a fight, even though it technically constituted an assault. Nor did cases of blows exchanged between husband and wife, neighbours, workmates, or drinking companions (in which injuries were not inflicted) normally come to court, unless one of the parties brought the prosecution out of malice or to satisfy a grievance; often, in such a case, the two parties involved would each bring a charge of assault against the other. Such cases kept the justices in petty sessions busy, but usually sprang from trivial situations. The case of Eliza Price illustrates these points:

Eliza Price, a seven-month-pregnant woman went to give evidence

at the Kingswinford Petty Sessions on behalf of a female neighbour,
who was charged with having assaulted and threatened Joseph
Newey, a common informer — and therefore a man disliked and
despised by most of the local population. While Mrs Price was
passing through the crowded room in which the Sessions was held,
Newey tried to push past her; she resisted, and struck Newey in the
side; he then pushed her violently in the bosom. Next day, she
obtained a summons against Newey for assault, from the magistrates
at Wordsley, about two miles from Kingswinford; this case was
heard three days later, and Newey was fined and bound over to
keep the peace towards Mrs Price, by the Wordsley magistrates
But on the same day on which this occurred, Newey obtained from
the Kingswinford magistrate a summons against Mrs Price for being
abusive to him and having struck him. He managed to get her
arrested and locked up under this summons, though she was
subsequently discharged by the Kingswinford magistrates when they
heard of Newey's conviction at Wordsley.[49]

Some cases of common assault *did* come to Quarter Sessions and
Assizes, but these involved more serious circumstances. Also, a number
of persons indicted for rape or aggravated assault were convicted of
only common assault. *All* forms of *aggravated* assault were tried on
indictment — that is, assaults which involved unlawful wounding, and
the infliction of grievous bodily harm either with or without a weapon.
Examples of the assaults which did come before the courts on
indictment:

(1) Sarah Fennell kept furnished lodgings which she let to James
Thomas and his wife Jane. One morning, Fennell and Jane Thomas
had an argument about a teapot. Fennell grabbed Jane's hair, threw
her on the bed, and hit her with some implement. Jane shouted and
help came. Fennell was found guilty of assault, and given one
month with hard labour.[50]

(2) William Whitehouse, James Hart, and Jethro Duley were all at a
dog fight, at a place in Darlaston, at about one o'clock one Sunday
morning. Duley and Whitehouse quarrelled and began a fist fight;
after they had had two rounds of this fight, Duley began sparring
with Hart. Whitehouse came up behind Duley and cut him with a
knife, laying open his face from his ear to the corner of his mouth.
Whitehouse and Hart were charged with maliciously cutting Duley
with intent to do him grievous bodily harm; Hart was acquitted,

and Whitehouse found guilty and given nine months' hard labour.[51]

(3) Francis Lowe had been engaged to the daughter of Thomas Phillips, a Willenhall blacksmith, but, as a result of Phillips' objections, the engagement was broken off. One evening, Lowe came to Phillips' house, hoping to get to see the girl and change her mind. Phillips came to the door and told Lowe to go away. Lowe refused, and they started fighting, in the course of which Lowe drew a knife, with which he wounded Phillips in the ear and hand. Lowe was found guilty of cutting and wounding with intent to do grievous bodily harm, and given six months' imprisonment.[52]

(4) At 11.30 one evening, Benjamin Hayes and another man came to the house of Samuel Jukes, a beer-seller, and asked for a pint of beer. Jukes refused, as it was past closing time; Hayes became abusive, so Jukes pushed them both out of doors. Hayes struck Jukes on the shoulder; Jukes hit Hayes in the face and knocked him down, and then went inside and locked the door. Hayes then went around to the kitchen door and accused Jukes of having robbed him of two silk handkerchiefs. Jukes went out again, and was stabbed four times in the face by Hayes, with a moulder's trowel. Hayes then ran off, but Jukes caught him and charged him with cutting and wounding.[53]

(5) John Waterhouse and Daniel M'Iver were hawkers who had known each other for years. They met in Wolverhampton, both being there on business, and went to a large number of pubs together, as a result of which both became very drunk. A quarrel arose, in the course of which Waterhouse stabbed M'Iver a number of times with a pocket knife, and inflicted some serious wounds. He was charged with cutting and wounding with intent to do grievous bodily harm, but the jury found him guilty of common assault only, and recommended him to mercy; M'Iver joined in this plea for mercy, and it was pointed out that Waterhouse had been drunk at the time, had been in prison for eight months awaiting trial, and had a previously good character. The judge announced that these factors reduced the punishment necessary, and sentenced him to nine months.[54]

(6) William Taylor, a Willenhall policeman, saw Thomas Pumford, at about 11 p.m., urinating in the street. He told him not to do it; Pumford replied: 'Damn your eyes, mind your own business.' Taylor then ordered Pumford to tell him his name. Pumford produced and opened a clasp-knife, with a blade about four inches long and pointed at the end, and struck at Taylor. Taylor defended himself with his staff, but was stabbed in the thigh. He shouted

'Murder', and people came up and helped him overpower Pumford. The wound was a fairly serious one, near his groin. Pumford was found guilty of cutting and wounding, with a recommendation to mercy by the jury. In pronouncing sentence, 'His Lordship having alluded to the *un-English practice* of using the knife in cases of quarrels, as requiring to be put down by the strong arm of the law, sentenced the prisoner to be imprisoned twelve months to hard labour.'[55]

(7) Edward Bridgwater fired two pistols at Job Prime during a quarrel. He was indicted for attempted murder; but the Grand Jury found a Bill for common assault only. He pleaded guilty to this charge. The Judge cautioned him to guard in future against giving way to his violent temper, and bound him over to keep the peace for twelve months, on his own recognisance of £100, and two sureties bound in £50 each.[56]

(8) James Millington lived together with a woman. She then threw him out, and would not let him return. Millington saw her in a pub with another man. She and the other man left the pub at about 11 p.m. Millington followed her down the street, grabbed her, and cut her throat and chin with a knife. He was found guilty of attempted murder, and a death sentence recorded, commuted to transportation.[57]

These examples show the range of assault cases which came before a jury. We can note the use of a knife (or a similar sharpened implement) in most of these cases; in some cases grievous bodily harm was inflicted by a group of persons using their fists and feet, but commonly it was a knife that was used. Example (7) is a case in which pistols were used, but the use of firearms was rare. Stabbing, and cutting and wounding, were the common forms which aggravated assault took, and the knife was the normal weapon.

The judge talked, in example (6), of the 'un-English practice of using the knife in cases of quarrels'. He may well have believed it to be an 'un-English practice', as the upper and middle classes generally seem to have believed that the use of knives in assaults was something reserved for the less civilised foreigners. But most workingmen carried knives (usually clasp knives of some sort), which they used for cutting tobacco, cheese or bread, whittling sticks, etc., and which were easily turned into weapons once a quarrel or a fight began. We are not here talking of gangs of youths in their teens or early twenties, carrying knives for use in fights explicitly, but of men, often in their thirties (see Table 39), who carried knives routinely and sometimes used them in fights.

Many of these aggravated assaults, like the thefts from the person and robberies, took place among acquaintances or friends. A quarrel took place while in the pub or watching some public spectacle, a knife was drawn and the wound inflicted. This was a very common pattern. Also common was the assault which took place between lodgers and the landlord or landlady, as in example (1), following disputes about the rent, furniture, utensils, behaviour in the lodgings, etc. Other cases indicate an element of revenge — on the father who would not let his daughter marry the man, as in (3); on the woman who had thrown him out, as in (8); on the beer-seller who would not serve the late customers and threw them out, as in (4); and, one commonly encountered in the 1840s and early 1850s, on a policeman. Example (5) shows Thomas Pumford stabbing the policeman who tried to interfere with his behaviour. A similar case is that of William Frost, who was drinking in a liquor shop, and got into a quarrel. The proprietor tried to get him to leave, and called in a policeman, George Corden, to enforce this. Frost refused to leave, and told Corden he would 'pay him off for it', whereupon Corden tried to arrest him. Frost resisted and stabbed Corden twice with a knife.[58] These could not be said to be instances of any articulate or organised opposition to the police, but they are signs of a resentment of the police by a part of the population, who were prepared to use their knives against them.

In all, over the period 1835-60, there were 322 indictments for common assault, and thirty-four for attempted murder or shooting at a person. The highest number of committals in any one year for all forms of aggravated assault (including attempted murder) was thirty-three in 1852 — a ratio of 8.6 per 100,000 of population. Viewed in overall perspective, this does not suggest a notably violent society.

Not surprisingly, these offences were predominantly a male enterprise — of 356 persons tried for aggravated assaults, only forty were women, and of the 143 tried for common assaults, six were women. The ages of those charged with assaults (Table 39) show that it was not youths of under twenty-one who were responsible for most of this violence. This can be contrasted with the modern position in Britain where

...the age-group most given to violence [is] that of 'young adults' between seventeen and twenty-one, with 'young persons' between 14 and 17 a bad second.[59]

Table 39   Ages of Those Tried on Indictment for Assaults from the
Black Country 1835-60

Age	Percentage		
	Common Assault	Assault with Intent to do Grievous Bodily Harm	Attempted Murder, Shooting at
0-17	4.1	2.3	3.3
18-23	31.2	34.7	40.0
24-30	25.4	34.0	40.0
31-40	19.7	16.3	6.7
41-50	9.8	10.0	10.0
Over 50	9.8	2.7	0.0
TOTAL	100.0	100.0	100.0
	n = 122	n = 300	n = 30
Age not given	21	22	4

Sentences for assaults are set out in Table 40.

We can note that the common assaults were punished by only imprisonment, a fine or being bound over. Remembering that these were only the more serious common assaults which reached Quarter Sessions or Assizes (the more routine ones being dealt with summarily), these are not heavy sentences when compared with those for larceny (Table 28). This was a society which normally punished attacks on private property more severely than attacks on the person.

Table 40   Sentences Imposed for Black Country Common and
Aggravated Assaults 1835-60

Sentence	Percentage	
	Aggravated Assault	Common Assault
Imprisonment:		
Less than 1 month	0.4	6.0
1-3 months	18.0	25.6
4-6 months	21.9	20.5
7-12 months	29.8	17.1
More than 12 months	10.5	8.6
TOTAL Imprisonment	80.6	77.8
Transportation:		
7 years	1.3	
10-15 years	5.7	
Life	0.4	
Penal Servitude:		
3-4 years	2.7	
5-9 years	1.8	
10-15 years	3.1	
Death Recorded:	2.2	
TOTAL Transportation and Penal Servitude	17.2	
Other:		
Fine		17.1
Bound over	2.2	5.1
TOTAL	100.0	100.0
	n = 228	n = 117

Note: The figures for aggravated assault combine the figures for assault with
intent to do grievous bodily harm, with those for shooting at a person with
intent to wound, and attempted murder.

(F) Sexual Offences

This category covers rape, assaults with intent to rape, and other sexual offences such as buggery (the term normally used to describe cases of intercourse of men with animals, but also sometimes used to cover homosexual relations between men — 'perpetrating the abominable crime of buggery with each other').[60]

In the rape cases which came to court, the facts are straightforward; most concern attempts to rape girls under the age of sixteen (often, indeed, under the age of ten). In many of these cases, where the rape itself was difficult to prove, the jury would convict simply for an assault with intent to rape, or for common assault. Relatively little information is available on the circumstances of most of the rape cases, since the newspapers seldom published much detail on the cases, presumably feeling that the facts were often improper,[61] and perhaps wanting not to inflict avoidable embarrassment on the young girls who had been the victims.

This reticence of the newspapers is even more marked in their reporting of cases of buggery. There was at least one of these cases a year from the Black Country, but the local newspapers would never even print the charge itself, let alone the details. The Assize Calendars would phrase the charge as one of 'unlawfully committing an unnatural offence with a cow' or 'feloniously and carnally knowing an ass'. But the newspapers would hesitate even to print as much as this. For instance, Thomas Dobson was indicted (according to the Calendar) for 'feloniously and carnally knowing an ass'; the *Staffordshire Advertiser,* however, simply reported that Dobson was accused of a 'felony of an infamous description', and stated that the facts of this case were of a description not fit to be published at length. William Roberts, charged with the same offence, was reported to have been 'indicted for an unnatural offence'.[62]

Buggery was not numerically an important offence — there were only twenty-five committals for intercourse with animals, and five for homosexual intercourse between men, over the whole period — but some points about it can be noted. First, it carried a very serious penalty — that of having a sentence of death recorded against the man convicted. Secondly, it was an offence for which it was fairly difficult to obtain a conviction; of twenty-five men committed for intercourse with animals, only ten were found guilty, the others being discharged by the Grand Jury or acquitted by the jury. The ten found guilty all had a sentence of death recorded against them, which was commuted to transportation for life. Sexual intercourse with animals is not a common crime in the courts, though modern research indicates that it is a fairly common practice in rural areas.[63] Even in an area like the Black Country, there were enough domestic animals available for it to be practised; probably the number committed to trial and convicted was only a tiny fraction of those committing such acts. The high rate of acquittals suggests the difficulties of convicting for this offence. Evidence was naturally difficult to obtain, since the 'victim' was a dumb animal; prosecution would have to rely on the evidence of a third party — and most people going in for buggery would probably try to ensure that they did so in private. The newspapers' reticence on the details of these cases leaves us only able to speculate, but it seems likely that juries were reluctant to convict for such an offence which did not cause harm to any other human being and which carried such a severe penalty. Probably Grand Juries and juries gave the accused the benefit of the doubt and acquitted him wherever possible, unless the evidence against him was overwhelming.

In the rape cases, there were 287 committals for rape or assaults with intent to rape, and 161 convictions for rape or assault. Penalties were fairly severe (Table 41).

(G) Riots and Public Order Offences

The Black Country indictments for riot and public disturbances over the period 1835-60 can be divided into two broad categories, which will be briefly discussed here: (1) large-scale political and industrial disturbances; and (2) small-scale communal disturbances, such as crowd assaults on policemen, disturbances in public places and street brawls.[64] There were 123 indictments for the first category, and 447 for the second.

(1) Large-scale political and industrial disturbances[65]

Basically, there were six such disturbances or disturbed situations in the Black Country over this period. The first came in 1835, when there were election riots; in the riot in Wolverhampton during the May 1835 by-election, troops were called in and fired on the crowd, wounding four people.[66] In August 1840, a large crowd attacked and broke up a Tory dinner which was being held, in defence of the Corn Laws and the Established Church, in a marquee in Bilston market-place. The crowd inflicted injuries on the twelve members of the Offlow Police Force guarding the marquee and on some of the Tory dignitaries.[67]

Table 41   Black Country Sentences for Rape or Assault with Intent
            to Rape 1835-60

Sentence	Percentage
Imprisonment	
Less than 1 month	0.6
1-3 months	4.3
4-6 months	13.7
7-12 months	26.7
More than 12 months	22.4
TOTAL Imprisonment	67.7
Transportation	
7 years	0.0
10-15 years	7.4
Life	10.6
Penal Servitude	
3-4 years	1.9
5-9 years	4.3
10-15 years	1.9
Life	1.9
Death Recorded	2.5
TOTAL Transportation and Penal Servitude	30.5
Other	
Fine	1.2
Bound over	0.6
TOTAL	100.0
	n = 161

In August-September 1842 came the most serious disturbances of the whole period, growing out of the miners' strike which began in August and was the first of the Chartist-associated 'Plug Plot' stoppages and disturbances which convulsed most of the industrial north and midlands at that time.[68] The disturbances were most violent in the North Staffordshire Potteries, but the Black Country also experienced its share of violence. In the Black Country, the strike led to clashes between bands of strikers trying to enforce a total closure of pits on the one hand, and on the other, detachments of troops, yeomanry and special constables. For a few weeks the authorities had great difficulty coping with the extent of the disturbance and the number of people involved, especially since they had no police force and the national authorities' resources were stretched thin by the simultaneous disturbances over most of the industrial north and midlands.[69] On a number of occasions, magistrates read publicly the proclamation from the Riot Act of 1715 ordering the crowds to disperse — this was the procedure (generally called simply 'reading the Riot Act') which entitled the authorities to use force to put down a riotous situation; the fact that the Riot Act was read a number of times is an indication of the extent of the disturbances.[70]

Once the strike was over and order restored, the Government appointed a Special Commission of Assize for Staffordshire to try the people arrested during the strike. The Commission tried 276 people for riot and associated activities — 232 from the Potteries and forty-four from the Black Country. In addition, Black Countrymen were tried at the Staffordshire, Worcestershire and Shropshire Quarter Sessions in October 1842 for public order offences arising from the strike.[71] These disturbances, as we have seen, were directly responsible for inducing Staffordshire Quarter Sessions to set up a county police force.[72]

After 1842, the area experienced relative political and industrial peace until 1855 when another miners' strike set off another disturbance. By this time, however, not only was Chartism effectively dead as a national mass movement, but the Staffordshire county police force was functioning efficiently in suppressing disorders. In March 1855, a crowd of 3,000 striking miners armed with sticks and stones was dispersed, within an hour, by a force of thirty county police armed with cutlasses and truncheons; thereafter the police prevented any serious rioting taking place.[73] In 1857 and 1858 came two more miners' strikes in the area, which provoked fears of widespread disturbances, but which passed off without any major violence — due apparently to the increased efficiency of the police as a riot-control force and to the greater organisation and restraint shown by the strikers.[74]

Finally, in July 1858 there was a riot in Wolverhampton when a large crowd of Wolverhampton Irish broke up a lecture given by the itinerant anti-Catholic lecturer who called himself 'Baron de Camin'. The Mayor of Wolverhampton read the Riot Act, the police charged and dispersed the crowd; two people were arrested and one of them indicted.[75]

(2) Small-scale communal disturbances

Political and industrial issues of some importance can be seen at work
in the large-scale riots; the communal disturbances, however, were
much more mundane affairs. Typical examples:

> Two policemen in Tipton arrested a man for being drunk and
> incapable of taking care of himself. A man named John Langford
> came up and tried to rescue the drunk, and to push one of the
> policemen into the canal. Langford was fended off by the two
> policemen, but he later returned with six other young men, and
> they attacked the one policeman violently; a large crowd gathered,
> stones were thrown, and the drunk was rescued from the policemen.
> The policemen were unable to do anything about it at the time, but
> they recognised the seven men responsible, and subsequently
> arrested them. They were all charged with assaulting a policeman
> in the execution of his duty; all pleaded guilty, and they were bound
> over on recognisances of £10 each to keep the peace.[76]
>
> Joseph Phillips and his brother were taking to the pound three
> horses which had broken into Phillips' garden and damaged his
> vegetables. On the way, they were stopped by a crowd of fifty to
> sixty people, armed with sticks and bludgeons, led by Benjamin
> Wyley, owner of one of the horses. Wyley demanded that his horse
> be returned to him; Phillips and his brother refused, and were then
> attacked by the crowd with sticks and stones. Both Phillips and his
> brother were injured; witnesses testified that there was much
> fighting and shouting, and, one witness said, 'It was as much like
> a riot as any thing he ever seed.' Phillips charged Wyley and another
> man with riot and assault; the other man was acquitted, and Wyley
> was convicted and fined £5.[77]

Similar prosecutions for riot involved crowd disorders at prizefights,
mass attempts to resist eviction from houses, and street brawls. Those
convicted of taking part were generally punished by fines, binding
over, or imprisonment for three months or less. In addition to the
people indicted for these disturbances, many people were also tried
summarily for less serious offences arising from public disturbances.

Indictable prosecutions for these communal disturbances were far
more frequent in the period 1835-45 than in the subsequent years
1846-60 (Table 42). This suggests the impact of the new police forces
in curbing such disturbances — after initially provoking what was

probably an increase in such disorders (especially in assaults on the police) in their first few years 1843-5, when they were new and unpopular and were being used to suppress rowdy popular sports and recreations.[78] It also suggests a general decline in public disorderliness of the Black Country population. It is perhaps significant that from 1856 onwards, most of those prosecuted for these communal disturbances bear Irish names. This was the period when Irish immigration into the Black Country was making itself most felt. The police found in the Irish a natural target for their attentions, and the Irish reciprocated with attacks on the police; in addition, the Irish in the large towns were known for brawls, both amongst themselves and against the non-Irish of their immediate vicinity. This Irish prominence in prosecutions for disorder seems to highlight the relative orderliness which seems to characterise the native English inhabitants of the area by the late 1850s.

Generally, we can summarise the trends from these two categories of riot over this period. The large-scale riots show political or industrial grievances, but in a relatively crude and unsophisticated form. They also show the Black Country as a relatively stable and peaceful area during this period. The disturbances never really threatened the structure of authority of the area; the most serious disturbance was that of 1842, which was primarily an industrial conflict — it frightened the authorities by its wide and rapid spread, its solid support and its Chartist links, but it represented no threat of insurrection or serious upheaval.

We can also see the improvement over this period in the law-enforcement forces available for suppressing public disorders; by the late 1850s, the authorities could use the police forces to cope with disorders with much greater ease than had been the case in the 1830s.

Finally, there seems to be a definite trend away from violence and public disorder over this whole period. This trend can be seen in the large-scale disturbances where the crowds of strikers or protesters became more organised and less violent. It can also be seen in the communal disorders where there was a marked decline in indictable prosecutions at the same time as the new police forces were imposing a higher standard of public order on the area.

For those convicted of riot offences, the sentences imposed varied enormously, depending on the nature of the riot and the seriousness with which the authorities viewed it. At the one extreme, five men convicted at the Special Assize for riot and cutting and wounding a special constable during the events of the 1842 strike, were transported

Table 42   Black Country Indictments for Public Order Offences
              1835-60

| Year | No. of Indictments | |
	Large Political/Industrial	Small Communal
1835	23 (Election riots)	35
1836		18
1837		15
1838		14
1839		24
1840	8 (Bilston riot)	34
1841		25
1842	83 (Strike and riots)	52
1843		48
1844		41
1845		26
1846		5
1847		7
1848		20
1849		5
1850		4
1851		3
1852		11
1853		14
1854		9
1855	8 (Strike and riot)	13
1856		13
1857		1
1858	1 ('De Camin' riot)	3
1859		1
1860		6
TOTAL	123	447

for life; at the other extreme, many people convicted of communal
disturbances were merely fined small amounts or bound over.

(H) Malicious Damage

Associated to some extent with public order offences come those

involving malicious damage — arson, malicious damage to machinery or
other property, and malicious injury to animals. This was an infrequent
Black Country offence — only eighty-one committals over the period
1835-60, of which seventeen were for arson, thirty-five for damaging
machinery, nine for damage to other property, and twenty for malicious
injury to animals.

'Malicious' damage of this sort has a long history of association
with early trade union activity and labourers' protest activities. Burning
ricks and maiming cattle were traditional ways for the labourer to strike
at the farmer; destruction of machinery in mines and manufacturing
trades was an early way of enforcing strikes and bringing the employer
to negotiation; while in labourers' movements like the 'Captain Swing'
disturbances of 1830, rick-burning was combined with destruction of
agricultural machinery.[79] One can look for evidence of similar
motivation in the malicious damage cases which came before the courts
from the Black Country.

Throughout this period, the authorities were concerned at the
possibility of arson or damage being used as part of a wider campaign.
For instance, during the miners' strike of 1855, in which the strikers
rioted in Bilston, the Chief Constable reported daily to the Lord
Lieutenant on the tense situation. Three days after the riot, he
reported that the ricks of Mr Fletcher, landlord of the George Hotel
in Walsall, had been burned down, and voiced his suspicion that this
was deliberate incendiarism, committed because the Walsall Yeomanry
troop had been allowed to assemble at the George Hotel on the evenings
of the two days following the riot. He subsequently reported that the
fire seemed to have no connection at all with the riot or the Yeomanry;
but the idea that the fire might have been connected with the riot and
the authorities' reaction had been a possibility which had immediately
suggested itself to the Chief Constable.[80]

Only one type of Black Country malicious damage case was clearly
connected with trade union or protest activities. The nailmaking and
chainmaking of the area were both carried on as outwork trades. Trade
unions and strikes in these industries were difficult to organise because
of the dispersed nature of the workplaces and workers; the nailers and
chainmakers therefore resorted to machine-breaking — cutting the
bellows of blackleg workers — in order to enforce solidarity. This
damage to a small but vital piece of equipment would force the affected
nailer or chainmaker to stop work.

The nailers' earnings and standard of living had been falling steadily
since the 1830s, as a result of machine competition. This imparted a

growing element of desperation and violence to the strikes and lockouts in which they were involved during the 1850s. During these episodes, and especially during the long and bitter strikes and lockouts of 1858-60, the nailers cut the bellows of blacklegs and non-union members, and made some attacks on the shops of nailmasters. The chainmakers' strikes were smaller in scale and less bitter, but they too used the tactic of bellows-cutting.

Of the thirty-five Black Country committals for malicious damage to machinery or equipment, seventeen are for bellows-cutting; a few of these come from nailers' strikes of the 1840s, but most come from 1859-60, when the coincidence of a chainmakers' strike with the nailers' lockout led to a rash of such incidents, to which the authorities reacted with alarm and a number of prosecutions.[81] The judges punished these offences severely, and took the opportunity to deliver their views on trade unions and the use of militant tactics to enforce strikes. Mr Justice Byles

> first severely condemned the conduct of the violent members of trades' unions, and then told the jury that if they convicted the prisoner of this crime, he should pass a very severe sentence.[82]

Baron Bramwell, in sentencing a nailer to one year's imprisonment with hard labour for bellows-cutting,

> made some very severe strictures upon trades unions and strikes. He said no society or union had a right to make rules as to the manner in which others should conduct themselves. These unions were mischievous in the extreme, they were against the interests of the workmen themselves, against public opinion, and would not be tolerated in this country. These crimes were committed in a dirty sneaking manner, and were deserving of the strongest reprobation.[83]

This crude type of 'wrecking' was the only weapon the nailers could bring to bear on their masters, and it proved of little ultimate avail; the nailmasters' lockout of 1859-60 broke the union of the horsenailmakers, which had been the strongest of the nailers' associations.[84]

In none of the other cases of malicious damage which came to court can one discover overt motive and organisation behind the acts. The cases of arson were mostly against cornricks, with one or two against buildings, but they were infrequent and unconnected. The same is true of the malicious injuries to animals — mostly injuring or killing horses; they were random and infrequent.

The cases of damage to property involved railways and mines. The railway companies prosecuted a few people for throwing stones at trains or piling stones on the rails to damage the trains; these were generally the work of boys and were infrequent. Coalowners prosecuted a few people for damaging mines by leading water into them or filling the shafts with stones.

Finally, there were some instances of damage to machinery — factory machinery or steam engines in factories or mines. Some of the damage to steam engines seems to have been simply the result of people stealing working parts from the engines, which, as we have seen, was a common practice in factories and collieries. But in some cases the damage was deliberate; for example:

> Ebenezer Dollar, Edward Elwell, and James Millington, all aged 13, entered Bradley's Ironworks in Tipton, at about midnight. They were seen to throw pieces of iron into the driving wheel of the machinery, which brought it to a stop, and they were arrested.[85]

The deposition does not make it clear, but it seems to be the case that all three were employed in the ironworks. Certainly in some of the other cases of damage to machinery, those responsible were employees working in that factory or colliery. Once again, these were isolated cases — there are no signs of any concerted campaign of industrial sabotage. The Black Country cases are too few, and the information available on them too meagre, to enable one to attribute any coherent motives to these instances. And one should perhaps be cautious in attempting to attribute such motives too easily — Dollar and Millington, in the example cited above, were both subsequently transported for theft; they may have broken into the ironworks in order to steal, and have damaged the machinery simply out of pique at not finding any worthwhile property to take.

Notes

1. Faucher, *Etudes,* pp.75-7; *Blackwood's Edinburgh Magazine* (1818), p.76, quoted in Tobias, *Crime,* p.134.
2. Radzinowicz, *History,* vol.1, pp.582-3, 634-5.
3. *SA* 12 and 19 March 1836, report of Ass.

4. *SA* 12 and 19 March 1842, report of Ass.
5. SRO Q/SB Ea. 1836.
6. *WC* 7 July 1858, report of Worcs. QS.
7. *SA* 22 and 29 October 1836, report of QS.
8. Hill, *Repression of Crime*, pp.146-231, quotation at p.151. See also Radzinowicz, *History*, vol.1, pp.41-4.
9. Radzinowicz, *History*, vol.4, pp.320-1, 330, 341.
10. Charles Dickens, *Oliver Twist* (London 1837-9; Penguin edn. 1970), chs.19, 22. Tobias, *Crime*, p.69; other references to Sikes, Fagin and the Artful Dodger as accurate examples of nineteenth-century criminals and their ways are found on pp.14, 69, 73, 97, 103, 110, 118, 124, 128-9, 246, 285.
11. See Anne Mozley, 'A Religious Novel', *Blackwood's Edinburgh Magazine*, XCIX (1866), pp.275-6. She argues that 'when a future generation judges us by Mr. Dickens's animated pictures of life, or by the works of such lesser luminaries as Charles Reade or Wilkie Collins, on the ground of their universal acceptance', they will be in danger of getting a distorted picture − 'regard their works as being really what they profess to be − pictures of English social life − and how grotesque, distorted and absolutely and ridiculously improbable one and all are!' Novelists' evidence will always be suspect in this area 'taking into account the universal attraction of the exceptional over the commonplace'.See also P. Collins, *Dickens and Crime* (London 1965).
12. MWWC 18 and 31 December 1857.
13. *SA* 9 and 16 January 1847, report of QS.
14. See pp.276-7 below.
15. PRO Assizes 5, Worcs. Winter Assize 1860. Vane's previous conviction was at Worcs. Summer Assizes 1855.
16. Radzinowicz, *History*, vol.1, p.367.
17. *SA* 15 and 22 March 1851, report of Ass.
18. Ibid.
19. *SA* 23 and 30 July 1842, report of Ass.
20. *SA* 23 and 30 July 1836, report of Ass.
21. *SA* 23 and 30 July 1842, report of Ass.
22. Freeman cites a case of a family known as the 'Three Turpins' who were notorious footpads, robbing people on the roads around Bilston, until eventually they were caught and transported (*Stories and Sketches*, p.215).
23. *WH* 6 March 1858, report of Ass. The theme that robbery, and indeed most crimes, were caused by drink, was one very frequently advanced by nineteenth-century commentators. See e.g. Tobias, *Crime*, pp.210-14; Hill, *Repression of Crime*, pp.109, 372-438. On this theme in the Black Country specifically, see Bentley, *Directory of Worcestershire*, vol.VII, pp.132-42; and numerous of the Grand Jury Charges between 1835 and 1860. Harrison very briefly comments on this view (*Drink and the Victorians*, pp.69, 77, 84).
24. *SA* 23 and 30 July 1842, report of Ass.
25. *SA* 15 and 22 March 1851, report of Ass. Firearms were, of course, relatively expensive and difficult for the average Black Countryman to get hold of.
26. For an impressive examination of the workings of the Game Laws in the late eighteenth century, in the Cannock Chase area adjacent to the Black Country, see D. Hay, 'Poaching and the Game Laws on Cannock Chase', in D. Hay, P. Linebaugh and E.P. Thompson (eds.), *Albion's Fatal Tree* (London 1975), pp.189-253.
27. Radzinowicz, *History*, vol.1, pp.49-79.
28. E.H. East, *A Treatise of the Pleas of the Crown*, 2 vols. (1803), vol.1, p.214, cited in ibid., p.629.
29. R. Cross and P.A. Jones, *An Introduction to Criminal Law* (6th edn., London

1968), pp.129-30.

30. *SA* 12 and 19 March, 19 April 1842, reports of Ass. and of execution of Wilkes. Ironically, although the other three escaped the legal death penalty, their punishment effectively became one of death for two of them very soon after. All three were transported on the 'Waterloo' which sailed for Van Diemen's Land, but sank off the Cape of Good Hope with the loss of most of the convicts aboard. Both Boswell and Giles were drowned; James Wilkes was among the few convicts who survived to reach Van Diemen's Land safely. (PRO HO 11/13 Convict Transportation Registers; Tasmanian State Archives CON 33/30 Convict Conduct Register, and CON 14/18 Indents of Male Convicts).

31. *SA* 15 and 22 March 1851, report of Ass.

32. *SA* 12 and 19 March 1836, report of Ass.

33. *SA* 12 and 19 March 1842, report of Ass.

34. *SA* 15 and 22 March 1851, report of Ass.

35. *SA* 12 and 19 March 1842, report of Ass.

36. Since 1843, only 13.3 per cent of the women sentenced to death for murder in England and Wales have been executed, as compared with 58.6 per cent of the men; the rest of the women have been reprieved by the Home Secretary of the time. (P. Wilson, *Murderess* (London 1971), pp.9-10, 178-81).

37. Sellin, 'The Significance of the Records of Crime', p.495.

38. In this period, the Black Country had by far the highest death rate of any mining area in Britain, particularly from roof falls in the mines (P.E.H. Hair, 'Mortality from Violence in British Coal Mines 1800-1850', *Ec. Hist. Rev.*, XXI (1968), pp.545-61).

39. E.g. after a gas explosion at Messrs Underhills' colliery in Bloxwich in which two men were killed, the coroner's jury returned a verdict of manslaughter against the ground bailiff of the colliery, on the grounds that he had neglected to provide adequate ventilation for the mine. The Grand Jury threw out this indictment (*SA* 23 July 1859, report of Ass.).

40. *SA* 4 December 1858, report of Ass. Bramwell maintained that: 'People had better be taught prudence by suffering from the want of it.' (Quoted in Burn, *Age of Equipoise*, p.103; Burn cites other illustrations of Bramwell's strongly individualist views on pp.68-9, 102.)

41. *SA* 31 July 1858, report of Ass.

42. *SA* 15 and 22 March 1851, report of Ass.

43. See O. MacDonagh, 'Coal Mines Regulation: the First Decade 1842-1852', in R. Robson (ed.), *Ideas and Institutions of Victorian Britain* (London 1967), pp.58-86; B. Lewis, *Coal Mining in the Eighteenth and Nineteenth Centuries* (London 1971), chs. 3-4.

44. Freeman, *Stories and Sketches*, pp.29, 71, 88, 222; *When I Was a Child, by an Old Potter*, pp.31-2.

45. *SA* 15 and 22 March 1851, report of Ass.

46. 'There was no doubt that prize fights were altogether illegal, just as much so with regard to the persons who attended them, as to those who fought. If all these persons went out to see these men strike each other, they were all guilty of an assault. There was no distinction between those who concurred in the act and those who fought.' If one of the fighters was killed in the fight, then all who attended the fight were equally guilty of manslaughter. 'If they encouraged by their presence the persons who were fighting. . .they were guilty of the offence in law.' (Chairman's charge to Grand Jury, quoting the opinions of Patteson and Littledale JJ., in *SA* 9 January 1836).

47. *SA* 15 and 22 March 1851, report of Ass.; 12 and 19 March 1836, report of Ass.

48. Cross and Jones, *Introduction to Criminal Law,* p.155.
49. *Case of Eliza Price,* P.P. 1845, XXVII, pp.249-50.
50. *WH* 9 and 16 March 1856, report of Ass.
51. *SA* 23 and 30 July 1842, report of Ass.
52. *SA* 15 and 22 March 1851, report of Ass.
53. *SA* 12 and 19 March 1836, report of Ass.
54. *SA* 15 and 22 March 1851, report of Ass.
55. Ibid. (italics added).
56. *SA* 12 and 19 March 1842, report of Ass.
57. *WH* 9 and 16 March 1856, report of Ass.
58. *SA* 15 and 22 March 1851, report of Ass.
59. N. Walker, *Crime and Punishment in Britain* (Edinburgh 1968), p.20.
60. Phrase used to describe the charge against Samuel Adderley and Henry Travis (WSL Assize Calendars, spring 1846).
61. The newspapers usually referred to the rape itself simply as 'a felonious assault' or 'assault with a criminal intent' on the woman or girl involved; they seldom gave much detail of the circumstances surrounding the alleged rape, and covered the actual act of rape itself with some phrase such as 'the prisoner then committed the offence charged in the indictment'. The medical evidence relating to the rape and the condition of the victim was always omitted from the report.
62. *SA* 23 and 30 July 1842, report of Ass., and 15 and 22 March 1851, report of Ass.; WSL Assize Calendars, summer 1842 and spring 1851.
63. A.C. Kinsey, W.C. Pomeroy and C.E. Martin, *Sexual Behaviour in the Human Male* (Philadelphia 1953), pp.667-75.
64. For a detailed examination of all the Black Country public order offences in this period, see D. Philips, 'Riots and Public Order in the Black Country 1835-60', in J. Stevenson and R. Quinault (eds.), *Popular Protest and Public Order* (London 1974), pp.141-80.
65. The riots are only dealt with briefly here; for details on their events and causes, see ibid.
66. See ibid., pp.149-51; *SA* 30 May, 6 June 1835; PRO HO 41/12.
67. Philips, 'Riots and Public Order', pp.152-3; *SA* 8 and 15 August 1840, 31 October 1840; SRO Q/SB M. 1840.
68. See F. Mather, 'The General Strike of 1842', in Stevenson and Quinault, op.cit., pp.115-40.
69. See PRO HO 45/260; HO 41/16 and 17; Mather, 'General Strike' and *Public Order,* pp.15-16, 228-31.
70. The main events of the riots, and the basic grievances underlying the strike are set out in the report of the Commission of Inquiry into these disturbances – the *Midland Mining Commission* (1843).
71. WSL Assize Calendars, Special Assize October 1842; QS Calendars for Staffs., Worcs., and Salop. Mich. 1842; *SA* 30 July-10 September, 1-22 October 1842.
72. See ch.3.
73. Philips, 'Riots and Public Order', pp.158-9; HC 5/6/1 Hatton to Hatherton 3 March and 25 March 1855.
74. Philips, 'Riots and Public Order', pp.160-2; PRO HO 45/O.S. 6378 November-December 1857, August-October 1858; HC 5/6/2 January 1858, August-October 1858.
75. Philips, 'Riots and Public Order', p.164; *WC* 30 June, 7 July 1858; *SA* 3 July 1858; HC 5/6/2 Mayor of Wolverhampton to Hatherton 5 July 1858; PRO HO 41/20 Walpole to Mayor of Wolverhampton 2 and 6 July 1858.
76. SRO Q/SB Mich. 1840; *SA* 24 October 1840.
77. *SA* 31 October 1835, report of QS.

78. See ch.3, pp.84-7.
79. See G. Rudé, *The Crowd in History* (New York 1964); E.J. Hobsbawm, 'The Machine Breakers', in his *Labouring Men* (London 1964); E.J. Hobsbawm and G. Rudé, *Captain Swing* (London 1969, Penguin edn. 1973).
80. HC 5/6/1 Hatton to Datherton 26 and 30 March 1855.
81. Worcs. Assizes spring and winter 1860, Staffs. Assizes spring and summer 1860; Barnsby, 'Working-Class Movement', pp.346-8.
82. *SA* 23 and 30 July 1859, report of Ass.
83. *Worcs. Chron.*, 14 March 1860, report of Ass.
84. Allen, *Industrial Development,* p.171.
85. SRO Q/SB Mich. 1840.

9 CONCLUSIONS

> . . .the people of the country in general, and even those who appear
> to be the worst disposed, do feel that there is a power and supremacy
> in the law, to which they are ready to yield obedience.
> (Lord John Russell, speech in Parliament, August 1839).

We opened this book with some quotations from observers in the 1830s
and 1840s about the frightening increase in crime which they had
witnessed from the beginning of the century. We are now in a position
to try to assess the validity of their fears. Generally, the evidence we
have dealt with casts doubt on the usefulness or even the validity of
using a blunt concept such as 'increasing crime'. Certainly, recorded
crime increased from the beginning of the nineteenth century, but this,
we have seen, was closely related to changes in police and prosecution.
'Crime' and the measurement of crime are too elastic as concepts to be
easily quantified. It must always be borne in mind that what was
criminal was what the authorities defined as criminal, and what was
prosecuted as such. In the Black Country between 1835 and 1860,
75-80 per cent of indictable prosecutions were for larcenies, and the
majority of those were thefts of articles or amounts of small value.
For an industrial area like the Black Country, industrial thefts made
up an important and increasing proportion of indictable prosecutions —
yet their dramatic increase was mainly due to an increase in prosecution
by manufacturers for such acts, rather than to an increase in the acts
themselves. By far the largest increase in the Black Country figures of
prosecutions over this period came as a result of the Criminal Justice
Act of 1855, which made prosecution easier but did not affect the
number of illegal acts being committed. On the other hand, the figures
do show a probable increase in thefts in depression years such as 1842.
But it is more useful, in this instance, to talk specifically about
'property offences' or 'larcenies' increasing, rather than to use that
vague and all-embracing term 'crime'.

Of the criminal acts which came to court, the Black Country
evidence shows that they were overwhelmingly not violent crime.
There were very few murders committed, and relatively few serious
assaults; robberies and burglaries, though often accompanied by the
use of force, seldom included murderous or maiming attacks on the

victims. There is much evidence that it was a rough society, but little to show that people feared for their lives, or felt themselves unable to use the roads at night. There was roughness, much fighting, much casual violence, but little lethal violence and serious injury. Unless most of the Black Country homicides and serious assaults never reached the courts — which is unlikely — the court cases show that there was relatively little danger of criminal violence and death for the inhabitants.

The other type of violence which had alarmed commentators in the 1830s and 1840s was political and industrial violence — the threat of strikes, riots and insurrections. These certainly existed in the Black Country — the threat of public disorder was constantly in the forefront of the minds of the authorities in the 1830s and 1840s, and the establishment and early development of the Staffordshire county police force stemmed largely from this fear. Yet, when all the Black Country disorders of this period are considered together, they never posed a really serious threat to the authorities and the institutions of society; nor do they show evidence of notably rebellious or disorderly tendencies in the working class of the area. By the 1850s, violence in public disorders seems to have been decreasing. It was not a particularly orderly society, but it was not a markedly violent and disorderly one. The concern of the authorities had shifted, by the 1850s, from a fear of crime as part of a general social and political threat to the existing society and its institutions, to a view of crime as a normal problem inherent in industrial society, to be dealt with on a normal day-to-day basis by preventive, detective and penal measures.

Engels and Alison had predicted that a growing crime rate might lead to class war and ultimately to social breakdown in England; even Porter had feared that this was a possibility. The Black Country evidence shows that these fears, though understandable in the political climate of the 1830s and 1840s, were exaggerated in terms of contemporary criminal activity. The evidence never suggests a society in danger of disintegrating under the strain; nor does it suggest that the maintenance of law and order was on the verge of breaking down at any point in the period under consideration. The authorities were stretched at times and, during periods like the 1842 strikes and riots, some of the magistrates panicked and overstated the degree of danger facing them. But even at those times, the Lords Lieutenant and Home Secretary seem to have kept their heads, and always appeared confident that they could control the situation. In the area of 'normal' crime, judges and Chairmen of Quarter Sessions often expressed their alarm and dissatisfaction at the growth of crime, in their Grand Jury Charges, but there is no hint in their words or actions that they felt themselves or the authorities unable to cope with the situation. Basically they knew, as the newspaper reports of cases show, that most of the population accepted the legitimacy of the criminal law as it affected them; many would try to break it and evade the consequences but they would not deny its legitimacy and try to set up an alternative moral and social code in opposition to the criminal law. The reasons for this must go deeper than simply the physical repression of disorder and illegal activities, since, as we have seen, the forces of law enforcement were never very strong in the area and were certainly never numerically strong enough to coerce the population into obedience. The system of law enforcement and the administration of the criminal law could only have worked with the active co-operation or the passive acquiescence of the mass of the population — and the evidence suggests that the authorities received at least this passive acquiescence. The relatively peaceful, orderly and law-abiding Englishman seems to have been a reality by the 1850s already.

The evidence on prosecution shows that, despite the financial difficulties involved, the working class made considerable use of the system of prosecution, predominantly to prosecute property offences committed against themselves — which suggests considerable acceptance on their part of the legitimacy of the law, and of the correctness of proceeding through legal channels to deal with offences of which they were the victims. The working-class attitude towards the law was a complex one: there is evidence of working-class distrust of, and hostility towards, the early police forces. There was also considerable resentment of the ways in which the law worked in favour of the propertied classes — the use of the police forces to break strikes; the fact that the prosecution system imposed a burden on any potential prosecutor and made it difficult for those with low incomes to bring their cases to court; the fact that the large coal and iron masters were able to make use of the Master and Servant Act of 1823 to break strikes by their miners, and were able to evade the provisions of the Truck Act of 1831 which outlawed the payment of wages in goods instead of in cash, while taking their places on the county Bench where they played an important role in the local dispensing of law and order. But there is no evidence of working-class opposition to the legal system as a whole, or to the whole system of property rights entrenched by that system; on the contrary, the evidence suggests, through the frequency of working-class prosecutions for property thefts, that they accepted the legitimacy of the system, and supported it by invoking the law in defence of their own property. The extraordinarily orderly and constitutional nature of the English working class, which was noted by a number of foreign observers in their political activities, seems to have characterised their attitude to the everyday legal system as well.

An area on which the nature of the evidence makes it difficult to say anything precise is the question of whether there were any links between 'political' activities which fell foul of the law (such as strikes and riots), and 'normal' criminal acts; also whether there is much evidence of a wider social purpose behind any of the offences committed. The evidence is very scanty here and it is difficult to say much. There is the odd case in which a 'social' claim was made for the criminal act — such as the gang of burglars who burgled only the unpopular tommy shops of the ironmasters, or people who claimed that they had stolen food in order to feed themselves or their families in times of distress; this latter claim, we saw, was made surprisingly infrequently considering how easy a justification it offers, and there is no way of knowing how valid or typical these claims were. These cases remain isolated, individual examples.

In the area of 'political' offences, Hobsbawm and Rudé have suggested that one must sharply differentiate persons involved in, and convicted for, such offences, from persons convicted for 'normal' criminal activities; E.P. Thompson, on the other hand, has strongly denied that any such line can be drawn between '"nice" social crime and "nasty" antisocial crime', and contends that those who took part in 'social' and 'political' offences often took part in 'normal' criminal activities as well.[1] Again the Black Country evidence is too scanty to give a clear answer: there are the two cases of nailers (cited in chapter 8) who took part in cutting the bellows of blacklegs as part of their union activities, but also had convictions for burglary and theft. But a few isolated examples cannot tell us how representative these cases were. We cannot tell, from the evidence, whether the crowds of rioting miners, ironworkers and nailers include miners, ironworkers and nailers who also appeared in court for 'normal' criminal activities, or whether these groups were totally separate. Certainly, for those people who were tried for riot, previous criminal records were not mentioned in court (and we can assume that, had they existed, they would certainly have been mentioned); but, even if the leaders in riots were not men with 'normal' criminal convictions, this does not rule out the possibility that among the men taking part in the riots were others who also committed 'normal' criminal acts. The most that can be

concluded is a verdict of 'non-proven': there is no substantial evidence
of links between persons engaged in 'normal' criminal activities and
those engaged in 'political' activities; nor are there visible indications
of social purpose, still less of the individualistic waging of the class war,
behind most 'normal' criminal acts.

Were most crimes committed by a professional 'criminal class'?
The evidence of the Black Country suggests this was not the case.
Perhaps 10 per cent of the offences we have dealt with were committed
by professional burglars, professional pickpockets, experienced thieves.
But the great majority of offences seem to have been committed by
people who were not full-time criminals, who worked at jobs normally,
but also stole articles on some occasions, or became involved in a fight
or a robbery; what is noticeable is the casualness and lack of
professional planning in these instances. This is not to say that all the
working class and the poor habitually broke the law — there may well
have been a distinction between the 'honest' and 'dishonest' poor; but
most of those who appeared in court from the Black Country were
from the working class, and only a small proportion of them seem to
have been full-time criminals. The overall impression left of criminal
activity in the Black Country is of small amounts of property taken
by poor men and women, of thefts, robberies or burglaries carried out
with little planning against victims without large amounts of property
to be taken. Essentially, it is an undramatic picture. The picture which
Tobias gives of crime in nineteenth-century industrial England is a
much more dramatic one, in which a professional 'criminal class' and
the rookeries and flash-houses play central roles. This may have been
true for London; but London was a very large and rich city, which
probably could support a large professional criminal class. London,
though comprising a large and important segment of the population of
England, was very different from the industrial towns and areas; the
Black Country gives us a picture of an industrial area in the early
Victorian period. And probably the basic facts of crime and law
enforcement in most industrial areas in the period were closer to those
of the Black Country than to those of London — prosaic and
undramatic, involving small amounts being stolen, squalid robberies,
burglaries and assaults, in which roughness was common but not fatal
violence, and in which the items taken were usually small amounts of
coal, metal, clothing, food, money or personal possessions.

In the eighteenth century, the English criminal law had the
reputation of being particularly harsh towards property offences — of
the more than 200 capital offences on the statute book, the vast

majority were for property offences. By the period 1835-60, capital
punishment had been repealed for property offences; but the criminal
law still showed a tendency to deal more strictly with offences against
property than with those against the person. About 90 per cent of all
the indictable offences dealt with by the courts were property offences;
the smallest larcenies were indictable offences, and were dealt with by
Quarter Sessions, whereas minor assaults were dealt with summarily or
not at all. Even of those assaults which reached Quarter Sessions or
Assizes, all common assaults were punished by only prison sentences,
fines, or binding over; even for serious aggravated assaults, 80 per cent
of the sentences were prison sentences and only 15 per cent sentences
of transportation or penal servitude. For larceny, on the other hand,
a third conviction (and often, a second conviction) ensured a
transportation sentence in the 1830s, and often in the 1840s as well.
True, murder was punished severely, as were burglary and robbery,
where force or violence was associated with the taking of property;
but assaults unaccompanied by taking property — even serious assaults
and some cases of manslaughter — were treated relatively more
leniently.

Recent work on English nineteenth-century social history has
helped to build up a steadily growing picture of working-class life in
the period. The view from the courts presented in this study adds
detail on one facet of that picture — it is certainly not a complete and
rounded picture of working-class life which emerges from the details
of prosecuted illegal acts, but it is a vivid picture nonetheless. Most
of the activities of the working class — at work, at home, and in
recreation — are reflected, even though in a distorting mirror, in setting
out the patterns of lawbreaking and law enforcement of the area. The
drinking habits of the working class, their attitudes and behaviour at
the workplace, their traditional sports and recreations, the way in
which the police and parish constables operated and their relationship
to the population around them, the extent to which people normally
moved around the area on foot, the position of the coal and iron
masters in the society and the attitude towards them — these, and
similar impressions, can be built up by assembling the mass of small
and fragmentary pieces of information which can be gleaned from the
courts.

Finally, by the 1850s, a crime rate which would have been regarded
as frighteningly high in 1800 had become accepted as a normal and
inevitable feature of industrial society. By the early 1850s, in the
Black Country figures, committals per 100,000 of population for

larceny alone were at a higher level than the total committals for all indictable offences per 100,000 in 1835; the 1835 total figures per 100,000 of population had, in turn, been more than three times as high as those for 1805. Yet commentators in the 1850s do not show that same urgency of tone about 'increasing crime' which had marked those of the 1830s and 1840s. 'Crime' was no longer seen as linked to political subversion, rebellion, social breakdown, but as a social problem which, like disease, bad housing or the poor would be 'always with us'. The police forces, the apparatus of the courts, the prisons (and later other penal and remedial agencies) were increased in size and scope in preparation for, and expectation of, a regular large annual number of cases and offenders to be dealt with. This has continued to be the case to the present day: crime rates have never returned to the position before the Industrial Revolution, but have shown (on the whole) a continuous secular increase. In modern industrial society, crime has become 'normalised', and most people have adapted their lives to living with a higher crime rate.[2] Fears of a societal breakdown seem to be produced not by high crime rates alone, but only when the crime rates are linked with other factors, such as serious social and political discontent, riotous activity, and a high level of homicides. One finds such fears being expressed today about the situations in Northern Ireland, in the Black ghettoes of the American cities, or in the Black townships of South Africa. In England, this sort of fear has not been widely or seriously expressed for the past century and a quarter; this fear was exorcised, and crime became 'normalised' in English industrial society, at some point in the period between 1830 and 1860.

Notes

1. Rudé, The *Crowd in History,* pp.7-10, 198-203; Hobsbawm and Rudé, *Captain Swing,* pp.201-11; E.J. Hobsbawm and E.P. Thompson, Abstracts of papers delivered to Society for the Study of Labour History, in *Bulletin of the Society for the Study of Labour History,* 25 (autumn 1972), pp.5-6, 9-11; Thompson, *Making of English Working Class,* pp.75-7.
2. See S. Cohen, 'Living with crime', *New Society,* 26 (November 1973), pp.330-3.

APPENDIX I   SOURCES AND COMPILATION OF THE COMMITTALS FIGURES

The information on the committals to trial for indictable offences, which forms the quantitative core of this work, is drawn from the records of the Quarter Sessions and Assizes which dealt with criminal cases from the Black Country for the years 1835-1860 inclusive. Below are set out: (1) the sources from which this information is drawn; (2) the nature of the material obtained from these sources, and how it has been used; (3) the problems of supplementing the Quarter Sessions and Assize material, where changes in criminal procedure by legislation made it necessary.

(1) The Sources

Since the Black Country as an area cut across some county and municipal boundaries, it included, in the period 1835-60, four judicial authorities competent to try offences on indictment:

(a) Staffordshire County (i) their Quarter Sessions had jurisdiction over all the Staffordshire areas of the Black Country, with the exception of the Borough of Walsall; (ii) Staffordshire County Assizes tried the more serious indictable offences for *all* the Staffordshire areas of the Black Country, including Walsall.

(b) Walsall Borough Walsall was incorporated as a borough by the Municipal Corporations Act of 1835, and given the right to hold its own Quarter Sessions; their first criminal trials were held in May 1836, and they continued from then until the end of this period to try indictable offences at their Borough Quarter Sessions, though the more serious indictable offences went to the Staffordshire Assizes.

(c) Worcestershire County (i) their Quarter Sessions had jurisdiction over all the Worcestershire areas of the Black Country; (ii) their Assizes similarly had jurisdiction over all the more serious indictable offences for the Worcestershire areas. The only temporary exception to this was (d) below.

(d) Shropshire County The parish of Halesowen (including the towns

290

of Halesowen and Oldbury) formed, until 1844, a detached portion
of the county of Shropshire. Its indictable offences were tried at the
Shropshire County Quarter Sessions and Assizes for the period 1835-44;
in 1844, the parish was transferred to Worcestershire, and thereafter it
came under the jurisdiction of the Worcestershire Quarter Sessions and
Assizes.

Information gathered from all these four jurisdictions was compiled
for the years 1835-60. The chief sources used were the Indictment
Rolls and the printed Calendars of Prisoners for Trial for both Quarter
Sessions and Assizes; wherever possible, the Calendars were preferred,
since they are easier to use, and they contain all the information which
is contained in the Indictment Rolls plus other information which is
not. Where the Calendars were not available, the Indictment Rolls, and
material in the Public Record Office and contemporary newspapers,
were used.

(a) Staffordshire County This was by far the most important of the
four jurisdictions for the Black Country as it dealt with 68 per cent of
the total committals over this whole period.

(i) Staffordshire Quarter Sessions All the Calendars of Prisoners for
Trial for 1840-60 are available in the Staffordshire County Record
Office (SRO) in a bound volume (SRO Q/SPcl). For 1835-9, the
separate Quarter Sessions Bundles (SRO Q/SB1) for the sessions of
each year were used; almost all of these contain printed Calendars;
where they do not, the Indictment Rolls were used.

(ii) Staffordshire Assizes All the Assize Calendars for 1835-60 are
available in the William Salt Library, Stafford (WSL), with the
exception of spring 1837, summer 1845, summer and winter 1858,
and all three Assizes for 1859. The Calendar for summer 1845, and
Indictment Rolls for the other Assizes were found in the Public
Record Office (PRO Assizes 5).

(b) Walsall Borough No Calendars or Indictment Rolls at all were
available for the Walsall Quarter Sessions, which make up 7.4 per cent
of the total committals for the period; but Quarter Sessions record
books which record essentially the same information as the Indictment
Rolls survive in the possession of the Walsall Clerk of the Peace and
these were used.

(c) Worcestershire County Committals from here (with the Halesowen
cases heard in Shropshire until 1844) made up 24.6 per cent of the

total committals.

(i) Worcestershire Quarter Sessions All the Calendars for 1841-60 are available in bound volumes in the Worcestershire County Record Office (WRO). For 1835-40, the separate Quarter Sessions bundles for the sessions of each year were used; these bundles supply Calendars for all the Sessions of 1839, and all those of 1840 with the exception of the Easter Session; no Calendars are available for any of the Sessions of 1835-7, and for 1838 a Calendar is available for only one Session of that year. In these latter cases, the Indictment Rolls were used.

(ii) Worcestershire Assizes No Assize material was held by the Worcestershire Record Office; Assize material in the Public Record Office (PRO Assizes 5) was used, in which Calendars are available for about two-thirds of the Assizes, and Indictment Rolls for the remainder.

(d) Shropshire County

(i) Shropshire Quarter Sessions All the Calendars for 1835-44 are available and were used in the Shropshire County Record Office (Sal. RO).

(ii) Shropshire Assizes Like the Worcestershire Assize records, the Shropshire Assize records for 1835-44 were found and were used in the Public Record Office (PRO Assizes 5) Most of them had Calendars available; in the few cases where they were not available, Indictment Rolls were used.

(2) The Material Obtained

The standard entry in a Calendar gives the name of the person tried; his or her age, degree of education and occupation; the place where the alleged offence was committed; details of the offence; the verdict and sentence and previous convictions, if any; the name of the magistrate or magistrates who committed the defendant for trial is also given in most Calendars. The Indictment Rolls give only the name, place, offence and (usually) the verdict and sentence. (The occupation is theoretically given on Indictment Rolls, but in an unhelpful form — the word 'labourer' is used without differentiation to describe every sort of manual worker.)

The Calendar entry was taken as the basis of compilation of data. The name of each person tried was taken down and their age, degree of education (on the five-point scale used on the Calendars, ranging from 'Neither read nor write' to 'Superior education'), occupation, place, offence(s), verdict, sentence and previous convictions, were coded and placed on computer cards. In all, 20,232 such cases were

collected and coded, covering all trials for indictable offences in the
Black Country for the years 1835-60.

Not all these data were immediately available. Where the Calendar
was not available, the age, degree of education and occupation could
not be obtained. Such cases could be partially supplemented by use
of the Criminal Registers in the Public Record Office (PRO HO 27),
which recorded annually the name and some details of each person
tried on indictment in England and Wales, for the years 1805-92. As
they listed the people by their area of jurisdiction (e.g. Staffordshire
County, Walsall Borough, etc.) and grouped them into the Quarter
Sessions for each year, it is a simple matter to look up and obtain
details on names which have been taken from an Indictment Roll.
Until 1848, the Registers gave the age and degree of education but *not*
occupation of each person listed there; from 1849, however, these
were no longer given. Newspaper accounts of Sessions and Assizes
often, but not always, supply the ages, but they never give the degree
of education, and seldom supply the occupation; generally, their
information is not sufficiently regular to constitute a reliable
supplement for a whole year or series of years.

The Criminal Registers were used satisfactorily, up to 1848, to
supply the age and education of all the Walsall offenders, and to
supplement those Staffordshire and Worcestershire years or Sessions
where the Calendars were not available. But this supplementary
information is not available after 1848, so all the Walsall cases after
1848 are without age and education, as are those few post-1848
Worcestershire Sessions for which the Calendars are missing. The
information on *occupation* is also not complete for the whole period,
since the Staffordshire Calendars only started giving the occupation of
the accused from 1854; the Worcestershire and Shropshire Calendars,
however, gave the occupation throughout; while no information at all
is available on the occupations of those tried at the Walsall Borough
Sessions.

The table on the following page sets out the variables which have
been compiled, and the areas in which they are deficient.

Information on the occupation of those charged with offences is
available for the whole period only for the Worcestershire towns (in
fact, this is actually from 1839 to 1860, because the Worcestershire
Calendars are not available for 1835-8); information on the occupation
of the bulk of those charged, from Staffordshire, is available only for
1854-60; and there is no record of the occupation of those tried in
Walsall at all. The only other deficiencies are in the age and education

Variables	Periods for Which They are Available			
	Staffs. QS & Ass.	Worcs. QS & Ass.	Salop* QS & Ass.	Walsall QS
Name and Sex	1835-60	1835-60	1835-44	1835-60
Place	1835-60	1835-60	1835-44	1835-60
Offence	1835-60	1835-60	1835-44	1835-60
Verdict	1835-60	1835-60	1835-44	1835-60
Sentence	1835-60	1835-60	1835-44	1835-60
Age	1835-60	1835-60	1835-44	1835-60
Education	1835-60	1835-60	1835-44	1835-48
Occupation	1854-60	1839-60	1835-44	NA
		Together		
% of Total Committals	68.0	24.6		7.4

NA = Not Available

* The Salop. Figures are relevant only until 1844, after which they are included
  in Worcs.

figures for Walsall from 1848 to 1860.

These variables, coded for computer and tabulated, give totals and
trends for the offences and offenders tried. In order to get a fuller
picture of the sorts of offences, the behaviour of offenders and the
workings of the machinery of law enforcement, two sample years out
of these twenty-six were investigated in depth by looking at the facts
of each case brought to trial in those two years. The two years selected
were 1836 (a year of prosperity with full employment with a low total
of offences tried) and 1842 (a year of severe depression and
unemployment, with a very high total of offences tried). The
circumstances of all the cases in those years were investigated through
use of the sworn depositions of witnesses (found in the Quarter
Sessions Bundles of the Staffordshire Record Office) and the very full
reports of the Quarter Sessions and Assizes in the newspapers. Sample
Sessions and Assizes were also studied in detail from the newspaper
reports for 1847, 1848, 1851, 1855 and 1858; and depositions and
newspaper reports have been used, though not systematically, for
information on cases in other years in this period. Systematic use was
also made, for sample years, of the recognisances to prosecute and give
evidence at Quarter Sessions, which give the occupation of the
prosecutor and witnesses; they were used for Staffordshire for 1836,

1842 and Epiphany Quarter Sessions 1847 (the Staffordshire recognisances have not survived for any time after 1847), and for Worcestershire for 1836, 1839, 1842 and 1851. No recognisances or depositions have survived for the Walsall Sessions; nor have any recognisances survived from the Staffordshire or Worcestershire Assizes.

(3) Supplements to Quarter Sessions and Assize Material

This study deals with indictable committals to trial only, but there is one area in which the material taken from the Quarter Sessions and Assizes needs to be supplemented by information on offences tried summarily (see Appendix II for this distinction). Three Acts of Parliament, passed during the period under consideration, allowed larcenies hitherto triable only on indictment to be tried summarily. These were: the Juvenile Offenders Acts (JOA) of 1847 (10 and 11 Vict. c. 82) and 1850 (13 and 14 Vict. c. 37), by which simple larcenies by juveniles under sixteen (under fourteen by the 1847 Act — raised to under sixteen by the 1850 Act) could be tried summarily; and the Criminal Justice Act (CJA) 1855 (18 and 19 Vict. c. 126), which allowed summary trial for a larceny of under the value of five shillings if the accused agreed to it, and for a larceny of five shillings or over if the accused pleaded guilty. These three Acts, and in particular the CJA, resulted in a very large number of larcenies which had previously been triable only on indictment being tried summarily; the result was that the number of larcenies, and the total number of offences, tried at Quarter Sessions and Assizes fell markedly. However, this was not a real fall in the number of larcenies being committed to trial but merely a transfer of a large number to a different sphere of jurisdiction — for the year 1857 already, there were more Black Country larcenies dealt with under the CJA alone than the total Black Country number of committals to trial at Quarter Sessions and Assizes. Investigation of the offences tried under these three Acts shows that they are of the sort which, up to 1847, were tried only at Quarter Sessions and Assizes. If, therefore, one leaves out of account the offences tried under these Acts after 1847, the result would be to distort greatly any comparisons over time of the numbers of larcenies and total indictable offences being tried.[1] It is therefore necessary, for the years 1847-60, to add to the totals of larcenies and of all committals to trial, the numbers of those tried under the JOA and CJA.

Records of convictions registered under these Acts are available for Staffordshire — for the JOA for 1847-60 (SRO Q/RCj) and for the CJA for 1855-60 (SRO Q/RCr/a and Q/RCc/a). These are records of *convictions* under the Acts, and not of total committals, so the figures will slightly understate the total numbers of people committed to trial for these years — but the understatement will be slight because the vast majority of these summary convictions are under the CJA, and most of these are people pleading guilty to larcenies, so there would be a very small number of people committed under the CJA who were not convicted. The records of these convictions give the name, place, offence and sentence of the people tried under them. No information on occupation or degree of education is given, nor do the CJA records give the age of the person convicted; the JOA records fairly often give the precise age of the person convicted and, in any event, it can be deduced that the JOA offender must always be aged fourteen or under, until 1850, and thereafter sixteen or under.

These records of JOA and CJA convictions are not available for Worcestershire and Walsall. The absence of figures for these convictions would obviously affect the totals of committals for larceny and of all committals for the period 1847 (when the JOA first comes into effect) to 1860, and will thus affect the accuracy of the totals of all committals and of all larceny committals for the whole period 1835-60. To remedy this, an attempt has been made to *estimate* the number of Black Country CJA and JOA committals for Walsall and Worcestershire for 1847-60.[2] All the committals under these Acts are less serious larcenies which, before the passing of the Acts, were tried on indictment at Quarter Sessions. Looking at the Black Country committals to trial for larceny for 1835-46 shows that the proportion of these tried by the Staffordshire Quarter Sessions remains constant at about 69 per cent. Taking the larcenies tried at Quarter Sessions only, for 1847-60, shows the Staffordshire proportion still almost identical. Over the whole period 1835-60, the proportion of all the larcenies tried at Quarter Sessions which were tried at Staffordshire Quarter Sessions is 68.2 per cent. One can then conclude that larceny committals for Staffordshire for 1847-60 continued to occupy roughly this proportion (68.2 per cent) of all Black Country larceny committals under the CJA and JOA. Since we have the Staffordshire CJA and JOA totals, we can estimate the missing CJA and JOA totals for Worcestershire and Walsall for 1847-60, on the basis that the Staffordshire totals constituted 68.2 per cent and the Worcestershire and Walsall figures made up 31.8 per cent of the total Black Country CJA and JOA committals. This would only be seriously incorrect if the relative proportions of total larcenies committed to trial at Staffordshire and at Walsall and Worcestershire changed over this period; the evidence suggests that this did not happen — the proportion remains steady up to 1846; and after 1846 the proportion of Quarter Sessions larceny committals remains steady, suggesting that the same proportion of larcenies was being transferred to summary trial from Walsall and Worcestershire as happened in Staffordshire.

The estimated figures for Walsall and Worcestershire CJA and JOA convictions for 1847-60, added to the totals already compiled from Quarter Sessions and Assize figures and Staffordshire CJA and JOA figures, give us the total Black Country indictable committals and the total larceny committals, for each of those years and for the whole period. In all, for 1847-60 there are 3,950 CJA and JOA convictions from Staffordshire and another 1,842 estimated convictions for Walsall and Worcestershire. Of course, as far as the estimated figures are concerned, they can only be used in order to make up crude totals, to be used for comparisons over time or calculation of percentages; one cannot further estimate how the estimated totals break down as regards sex, age, type of larceny, etc. But being able to make this estimate with confidence does give reliable totals for the years 1847-60, and for the overall period 1835-60.

It is from these sources and estimates and for the range of data outlined above, that the material has been compiled on which the quantitative analyses of chapters 5-8, and parts of some of the other chapters, are based.

Notes

1. This error was made by Macnab in an otherwise impressive work. He talks of a rapid decrease in crime in 1855 and 1856, and a continuous fall to 1860, whereas this simply reflects the transfer of a large number of indictable larcenies from trial on indictment to summary trial. (Macnab, 'Social Aspects', p.342.)
2. I am grateful to Clive Payne, of the Research Services Unit of Nuffield College, Oxford, for assistance on this point.

APPENDIX II   LEGAL DISTINCTIONS

(a) Indictable and Summary Offences

Indictable offences were offences for which an offender had to be tried on a bill of indictment before a judge or Bench of magistrates, sitting with a petty jury; the jury decided on the verdict, and the judge or magistrates formulated and pronounced the sentence. Summary offences were tried summarily by two or three magistrates, sitting without a jury at Petty Sessions; both verdict and sentence were pronounced by the magistrates.

Trials on indictment were heard either at Quarter Sessions (before magistrates) or at Assizes (before a judge). An Act of 1842 (5 and 6 Vict. c. 38) laid down the limits of their respective jurisdictions: Assizes could try any indictable offence; Quarter Sessions could try any indictable offence except (1) those for which the death penalty could be imposed (including treason and murder), (2) those for which a first offender could be sentenced to transportation for life, (3) certain specified offences, including blasphemy, perjury, forgery, bigamy, libel and bribery. This Act merely made explicit what had been the practice for two centuries — that Quarter Sessions did not try capital cases or their equivalent in degree of seriousness. Quarter Sessions tried far more of the indictable offences than Assizes did. Assizes tended to try only the more serious of the indictable offences — murder, homicides, burglary, rape, robberies with violence, assaults accompanied by wounding; Quarter Sessions tried the less serious and more common of the indictable offences — larcenies, housebreaking, assaults, robberies not accompanied with serious violence, frauds.

Indictable offences generally tended to be the more serious offences, summary offences to be the less serious offences. There was a great extension of the magistrates' powers of summary jurisdiction in the early nineteenth century, especially in the 1820s. The Summary Jurisdiction Act of 1848 (11 and 12 Vict. c. 43) consolidated and improved the holding of Petty Sessions, which had been held to try cases summarily for a considerable time before that. On the whole, those offences which were tried summarily were the less serious ones — common assaults, breaches of the peace, minor riots and affrays, drunk and disorderly conduct, vagrancy, breaches of licensing laws or of local bylaws, etc. But this distinction was not absolutely observed —

poaching, for instance, was tried summarily, but the theft of an article of the tiniest value continued to be an indictable offence. Some offences could be tried either summarily or on indictment, depending on the seriousness of the particular act in question – thus, for assaults or riot offences, the magistrate at the preliminary examination could choose either to try the accused summarily directly, or commit him for trial at Quarter Sessions or Assizes; if the latter was chosen, then the accused, if found guilty, was likely to receive a heavier sentence than from a summary trial. In examining men for participation in the same fight or riot, the magistrate could choose to commit some of them for trial on indictment (because he felt their conduct constituted a more serious offence) and try the others summarily.

Basically, all serious offences were indictable offences, though not all indictable offences were necessarily serious offences. So Quarter Sessions and Assizes handled all serious offences plus a large number which were not so serious.

As the century progressed, and the need to deal with the mounting number of prosecutions grew, summary jurisdiction was further increased. The instances which concern this study are the Juvenile Offenders Acts of 1847 and 1850, and the Criminal Justice Act of 1855, which allowed minor larcenies, under certain conditions, to be tried summarily; but the offences themselves remained *indictable offences;* it is simply that there was now the option of having them *summarily tried.*

(b) Felonies and Misdemeanours

The distinction between felonies and misdemeanours dates back to the Middle Ages, when felonies were the crimes for which men could forfeit their lives and goods, while misdemeanours were minor offences. By the 1830s, the legal distinction still existed, and technically, a felony was a more serious offence, though this distinction had been eroded in fact. It is true that any capital offence such as murder, was a felony; but so too was theft of 6d worth of goods; while a serious assault, obtaining goods by false pretences, and perjury, were all misdemeanours. So, by the period covered by this study, the distinction of felony and misdemeanour had no longer any clear-cut validity as regards the seriousness of an offence – most serious offences were felonies, but some were misdemeanours. The distinction could still affect the question of punishment (only felonies could be capital), legal procedure (different provisions for felonies and misdemeanours as regards the payment of the expenses of prosecution, and the right of an accused's counsel to address the jury), and the means employed to arrest a suspect (to arrest a suspected felon, force could be used; to apprehend a suspected misdemeanant, 'reasonable means' only could be employed; this had relevance particularly in the handling of riots which could be felonies or misdemeanours, depending on the action of the authorities).

It is important to note that these two distinctions of indictable and summary offences, and felony and misdemeanour, do not coincide. All felonies were indictable offences and could only be tried on indictment, except where statute expressly permitted their summary trial; but a number of misdemeanours were also indictable offences, and many assaults, riots, cases of obtaining by false pretences, perjury, etc. were tried on indictment.

References

E. Melling (ed.), Introduction to *Kentish Sources, vol. VI, Crime and Punishment;* Maitland, *Justice and Police,* p.16; Abel-Smith and Stevens, *Lawyers and the Courts,* p.31; Radzinowicz, *History,* vols.1, 2 and 4.

APPENDIX III   POPULATION OF THE BLACK COUNTRY TOWNS AND PARISHES, 1831-61

Town or Parish	Population			
	1831	1841	1851	1861
Wolverhampton	24,732	36,382	49,985	60,860
Dudley	23,430	31,232	37,962	44,951
West Bromwich	15,327	26,121	34,591	41,795
Walsall	14,420	19,857	25,680	37,760
Bilston	14,492	20,181	23,527	24,364
Sedgley parish	20,577	24,819	29,447	36,637
Kingswinford parish	15,156	22,221	27,301	34,257
Tipton	14,951	18,891	24,872	28,870
Halesowen parish	9,355	13,018	18,286	23,381
Wednesbury	8,437	11,625	14,281	21,968
Rowley Regis parish	7,438	11,111	14,249	19,785
Darlaston	6,647	8,244	10,590	12,884
Oldswinford and The Lye	6,490	8,493	9,858	11,562
Stourbridge	6,148	7,481	8,327	8,783
Willenhall	5,834	8,695	11,931	17,256
Smethwick and Harborne	4,227	6,657	10,729	16,996
Handsworth	4,944	6,138	7,879	11,459
Cradley	2,022	2,686	3,383	4,075
Wednesfield	1,879	3,168	4,858	8,553
Tettenhall	2,618	3,143	3,396	3,716
Amblecote	1,236	1,623	2,053	2,613
Great Barr	859	1,087	1,001	1,075
Bentley	104	428	380	346
TOTAL	211,323	293,301	374,566	473,946

Notes: 'Walsall' is the Parliamentary Borough of Walsall, which comprised the Borough of Walsall, Foreign of Walsall, and Bloxwich. 'Kingswinford parish' includes Wordsley and Brierley Hill, both originally part of Kingswinford parish, but created as separate parishes in their own right, by the 1850s. Adjacent areas, falling into the same parish, for which the population figures were usually given jointly, are given jointly — Halesowen parish includes Oldbury; Smethwick and Harborne, and Oldswinford and the Lye, are listed jointly.

Sources: Census 1831, 1841, 1851, 1861.

BIBLIOGRAPHY

(A) Manuscript Sources

(1) Staffordshire County Record Office

Q/SPc 1 Quarter Sessions Calendars of Prisoners for Trial (bound) 1840-60.

Q/SB Quarter Sessions Bundles 1835-60.

Q/RCj Numbers 1-1,250 Records of convictions under the Juvenile Offenders Acts 1847 and 1850, for 1847-61.

Q/RCr/1 and Q/RCc/1 Register and Bundles of Convictions under the Criminal Justice Act of 1855, for 1855-61.

Q/SBm Miscellaneous Quarter Sessions material.

C/PC Deposited material on the Staffordshire County Police Force.

Q/APr Lists, reports, and regulations relating to the parish constables and the police force for the Southern Division of the Hundred of Offlow South.

Q/ACp Correspondence, committee minutes and reports, and other material relating to the early Staffordshire County Police Force.

Q/SOp Quarter Sessions Order Book 1833-60.

D 260/M/F/5 Hatherton correspondence.

D 649/10 Letter Book of Earl Talbot 1822-42.

D/590/741 Minutes of the Chillington Association for the Prosecution of Felons.

(2) William Salt Library, Stafford

Calendars of Prisoners for Trial at Staffordshire Assizes 1835-60.

(3) Worcestershire Record Office

Quarter Sessions Calendars of Prisoners for Trial 1841-60.

Quarter Sessions Bundles (including Calendars, Indictment Rolls, Recognisances, Police material, Miscellaneous material) 1835-60.

(4) Shropshire Record Office

Quarter Sessions Calendars of Prisoners for Trial 1835-44.

(5) Office of Clerk of the Peace, Walsall

Walsall Borough Quarter Sessions Record Books 1836-60.

(6) Wolverhampton Central Library

Watch Committee Minutes 1853-60.
L 3522/1408 Outline of Duties and General Instructions of
    Wolverhampton Police contained in a Report to the Watch
    Committee of that Borough 1863.

(7) Dudley Central Library

LD 352.1 Town Commissioners' Minutes 1830-53.

(8) Public Record Office

Assizes 5 Oxford Circuit Assize Indictments, 1835-60.
HO 27 Criminal Registers, Series II, 1835-60.
HO 41 Disturbances Entry Books (Out-letters) 1835-60.
HO 40 Disturbances In-letters 1835-40.
HO 45, Old Series Disturbances In-letters 1840-60.
HO 43 Out-letters, domestic 1835-42.
HO 52 Counties; Correspondence 1835-50.
HO 63 Police Returns 1858-60.
HO 65 Police, Series I, Out-letters Boroughs 1856-60.

(B) Printed Sources

(1) Parliamentary Papers

(a) Reports (in date order)

Second Report from the Select Committee on the State of the Police
    of the Metropolis. P.P. 1817, VII (484), pp.321-562.
Report from the Select Committee on Criminal Laws. P.P. 1819,
    VIII (585), pp.3-270.
Second Report from the Select Committee on Criminal Commitments
    and Convictions. P.P. 1828, VI (545), p.419.
Report from the Select Committee on the Police of the Metropolis.
    P.P. 1828, VI (533), pp.3-417.
Report of the Commissioners for Inquiring into County Rates.
    P.P. 1836, XXVII (no number) pp. 1-383.
First Report of the Commissioners appointed to inquire as to the Best
    Means of establishing an efficient Constabulary Force in the Counties
    of England and Wales. P.P. 1839, XIX (169).
Appendix to First Report of Children's Employment Commission
    (Mines). P.P. 1842, XVI (381) pp.1-88.

First Report of the Midland Mining Commission (S. Staffs.). P.P. 1843, XIII (508), pp.1-303.

Appendix to the Second Report of the Children's Employment Commission (Manufactures). P.P. 1843, XV (431), pp.561-738.

Report of the Commissioner relating to the alleged Ill-treatment of Eliza Price by Members of the Staffordshire Constabulary. P.P. 1845, XXVII (658), pp.249-56.

First and Second Reports from the Select Committee on Police, with the Minutes of Evidence. First Report, P.P. 1852-53, XXXVI (603), pp.1-159; Second Report, P.P. 1852-3, XXXVI (715), pp.161-343.

Select Committee on Public Prosecutors. First Report, August 1855, P.P. 1854-5, XII, pp.3-309; Second Report, May 1856, P.P. 1856, VII, pp.347-84.

(b) Accounts and Papers (in date order)

Annual Reports of Registrar-General 1839-60.

Copy of Letter from the Secretary of State for the Home Department to Lords-Lieutenant of certain Counties, respecting Arming and Training. P.P. 1839, XXXVIII (179), p.1.

Copies of the Letter of Lord John Russell to Lords-Lieutenant of certain Counties, suggesting the formation of Associations for the protection of Life and Property, etc. P.P. 1839, XXXVIII (299) p.3.

Copy of a Letter from Her Majesty's Secretary of State for the Home Department to Colonel Rolleston. . .etc. P.P. 1839, XXXVIII (448), p.7.

A Return of all Associations formed and armed for the Protection of Life and Property. . .etc. P.P. 1839, XXXVIII (559), p.13.

Copy of a Circular Letter addressed by direction of Lord John Russell to the Chairmen of the Quarter Sessions of all Counties (except Lancaster and Salop) in England and Wales. P.P. 1839, XLVII (259), p.517.

A return of the Number of Troops, or Corps, or Regiments of Effective Yeomanry in Great Britain and Ireland, according to the last Muster Roll. P.P. 1840, XXX (488), p.265.

Return to House of Commons of Counties, or Divisions of Counties, which have adopted the County Constabulary Acts. . . P.P. 1841, XX (121), pp.297-301.

Returns of Police established in each County or Division of a County in England and Wales under the Acts 3 Vict. c. 93 and 3 and 4 Vict. c. 88. P.P. 1842, XXXII (345), pp.649-75.

Return of the Several Cities and Boroughs of Great Britain, their

Population respectively, the Number of Police, and the list of the same in each, in each year from their Establishment. . .P.P. 1854, LIII (345), p.509.

Return setting forth the Expense and Cost of Maintenance of the Police Force in the Year 1852 in the following cities and towns. . .P.P. 1854, LIII (22), pp.597-617.

Return of the several Counties in England and Wales, their Population, the number of Rural Police appointed under the Acts 2 and 3 Vict. c. 93, and 3 and 4 Vict. c. 88, in each County. . .P.P. 1854, LIII (211), pp.617-31.

Return of the Number of Justices in the Commission of the Peace for each County in England and Wales, in each of the years 1852, 1853 and 1854. . .P.P. 1856, L (110), pp.161-512.

A Return of the Names and Salaries of all the Stipendiary Magistrates in England and Wales. . .P.P. 1856, L. (371), pp.513-18.

Return of the Number of Persons Summarily Convicted and Committed to Prison in the several Counties of England and Ireland, for Breach of Contract in neglecting work or leaving Service, during each of the years 1854 and 1855. P.P. 1856, L (441), pp.633-7.

Return of the Number of Rural Police in each County in England and Wales, appointed under the Acts 2 and 3 Vict. c. 93 and 3 and 4 Vict. c. 88. . .P.P. 1856, L (186), pp.665-79.

(2) Newspapers

Staffordshire Advertiser, 1835-60.
Wolverhampton Chronicle, 1835-60.
Worcester Herald, 1835-60.
Worcester Chronicle, 1838-60.
Northern Star, 1839-40.
Morning Chronicle, 1849-50.
Occasional issues of: *Staffordshire Examiner, Berrow's Worcester Journal, Walsall Guardian and Midland Counties Advertiser.*

(3) Journals

Journal of the Statistical Society of London vols. 1-23 (1838-60).

(4) Directories (in date order)

W. White, *History, Gazetteer and Directory of Staffordshire* (Sheffield 1834).
Robson's Birmingham and Sheffield Directory (London 1839).
Bentley's History and Guide to Dudley, Dudley Castle, and the Castle

Hill, and Alphabetical and Classified Directory of the Borough of Dudley (Birmingham, n.d., ? 1840).

Bentley's History and Guide to Dudley (Birmingham 1841).

Bentley's History, Directory and Statistics of Worcestershire, 7 vols., (Birmingham 1840-42), vols. I, V, VII.

Pigot & Co's Royal National and Commercial Directory and Topography of the Counties of Derbyshire, Herefordshire, Nottinghamshire, Shropshire, Staffordshire, Warwickshire, Worcestershire and Yorkshire (London 1842).

Wolverhampton Post Office Directory for 1847 (Wolverhampton 1847).

Melville & Co's Directory of Wolverhampton (Worcester 1851).

Directory of Dudley and the Mining District (Worcester 1852).

General and Commercial Directory and Topography of the Borough of Birmingham. . .with Wolverhampton. . .in South Staffordshire; and Dudley and Oldbury in Worcestershire (Sheffield 1855).

M. Billings' Directory and Gazetteer of the County of Worcester (Birmingham 1855).

Directory and Gazetteer of Staffordshire with Dudley in Worcestershire (Harrison, Harrod & Co 1861).

The Wolverhampton and South Staffordshire Almanack and Municipal Directory for 1861 (Wolverhampton 1861).

(5) Contemporary Books, Pamphlets and Articles

[Alison, A.] 'Causes of the Increase of Crime', *Blackwood's Edinburgh Magazine,* LVI (1844), pp.1-14.

[Anon.] *A Catechism Relating to Clerical Magistrates and the Anti-Truck Act* (Bilston, n.d., ? early 1830s).

[Anon.] 'Cautionary Hints to Speculators on the Increase of Crime', *Blackwood's Edinburgh Magazine,* III (1818), pp.176-8.

[Anon.] 'The Black Country', *Edinburgh Review,* 117 (1863), pp.406-43.

[Anon.] *The Towns of the Black Country* (n.d., ?1865 Wolverhampton Central Library).

Archbold's Quarter Sessions (4th edn., 1885).

Bailey, D. *The Truck System – A Book for Masters and Workmen* (London 1859).

Burritt, E. *Walks in the Black Country and its Green Borderland* (London 1868).

Clark, C.F.G. *The Curiosities of Dudley and the Black Country from 1800 to 1860* (Birmingham 1881).

Cobbett, W. *Rural Rides* (Everyman edn., 2 vols. London 1941).

[Denman, T.] 'Police of the Metropolis; Causes and Prevention of Crime', *Edinburgh Review,* 48 (1828), pp.411-22.

Derrincourt, W. *Old Convict Days* (London 1889; Penguin facsimile reprint, Harmondsworth 1975).

Dyott, W. *Dyott's Diary 1781-1845,* ed. Jeffrey, R.W., 2 vols. (London 1907).

Engels, F. *The Condition of the Working Class in England* (1844), trans. and ed. Henderson, W.O. and Chaloner, W.H. (Oxford 1958).

Faucher, L. *Etudes sur l'Angleterre* (Brussels 1845).

Glew, E.L. *History of the Borough and Foreign of Walsall* (Walsall 1856).

Griffiths, S. *Guide to the Iron Trade of Great Britain* (London 1873).

Hawkes Smith, W. *Birmingham and its Vicinity as Manufacturing and Commercial District* (London 1836).

Hill, M.D. *Suggestions for the Repression of Crime Contained in Charges Delivered to Grand Juries of Birmingham* (London 1857).

Lawley, G.T. *Bibliography of Wolverhampton* (Bilston 1890).

Lawley, G.T. *A History of Bilston* (Bilston 1893).

Maitland, F.W. *Justice and Police* (London 1885).

Mayhew, H. *London Labour and the London Poor,* 4 vols. (1861-2; reprinted New York 1968), vol.4.

Morrison, W.D. *Crime and its Causes* (London 1891).

Owen, Rev. J.B. *Lectures and Sermons; with a Brief Memoir of his Life by his Son, Edward Annesley Owen* (London 1873).

Owen, Rev. J.B. *A Memoir of the Late G.B. Thorneycroft, Esq.* (London 1856).

Plowden, A.C. *Grain or Chaff? The Autobiography of a Police Magistrate* (London 1903).

Porter, G.R. *The Progress of the Nation* (3 vols., London 1836-43; revised edn. 1847).

Pratt, A.C. *Black Country Methodism* (London 1825).

Robinson, W. *The Magistrate's Pocket-Book* (London 1891).

Scrivenor, H. *History of the Iron Trade* (London 1854).

[Shaw, C.] *When I was a Child, by an Old Potter,* with an Introduction by Robert Spence Watson (London 1903).

Stephen, J.F. *A History of the Criminal Law in England,* 3 vols. (London 1883; reprinted Burt Franklin, New York, n.d.).

Stone, J. *The Practice of the Petty Sessions,* 5th edn. (London 1844). *The Thorneycrofts' Patents and Inventions. . .and a Biographical Sketch* (1891; privately printed scrapbook, in WCL L 92/T512).

Tocqueville, Alexis de, *Journeys to England and Ireland* (1835), trans.

Lawrence, G. and Mayer, K.P., ed. Mayer, J.P. (London 1958).

Vance, Rev. W.F. *A Voice from the Mines and Furnaces* (Wolverhampton and London 1853).

Von Raumer, F. *England in 1835*, trans. Austin, S. (London 1836).

Wade, J. *History and Political Philosophy of the Middle and Working Classes* (Edinburgh 1842).

White, W. *All Round the Wrekin* (London 1860).

Willmore, F.W. *A History of Walsall and its Neighbourhood* (London 1887).

(6) Modern Books and Articles

Abel-Smith, B. and Stevens, R. *Lawyers and the Courts* (London 1967).

Allen, G.C. *The Industrial Development of Birmingham and the Black Country 1860-1927* (London 1929).

Armstrong, W.A. 'The Use of Information about Occupation', in Wrigley, E.A. (ed.), *Nineteenth Century Society: essays in the use of quantitative methods for the study of social data* (Cambridge 1972), pp.191-310.

Arnstein, W. 'The Murphy Riots: a Victorian Dilemma', *Victorian Studies*, XIX (1975).

Ashton, T.S. *An Economic History of England: The Eighteenth Century* (London 1955).

Banton, M. *The Policeman in the Community* (London 1954).

Barnsby, G.J. *Dictatorship of the Bourgeoisie: Social Control in the Nineteenth Century Black Country* (Communist Party History Group, Pamphlet 55, Summer 1972).

Barnsby, G.J. *The Dudley Working Class Movement 1832 to 1860* (Dudley 1970).

Barnsby, G.J. 'The Standard of Living in the Black Country during the 19th Century', *Economic History Review*, 2nd series XXIV (1971), pp.220-39.

Becker, H.S. *Outsiders: Studies in the Sociology of Deviance* (New York 1963).

Becker, H.S. (ed.),*The Other Side: Perspectives on Deviance* (New York 1964).

Best, G. 'Popular Protestantism', in Robson, R. (ed.), *Ideas and Institutions of Victorian Britain* (London 1967).

Brennan, T. *Midland City: Wolverhampton Social and Industrial Survey* (London 1948).

British Association for the Advancement of Science *Birmingham and Its Regional Setting* (Birmingham 1950).

Broeker, G. *Rural Disorder and Police Reform in Ireland 1812-36* (London 1970).

Burn, W.L. *The Age of Equipoise* (London 1964).

Carson, W.G. and Wiles, P. (ed.) *Crime and Delinquency in Britain* (London 1971).

Chandler, G. and Hannah, I.C. *Dudley as It Was and As It Is Today* (London 1949).

Chesney, K. *The Victorian Underworld* (London 1970).

Chitham, E. *The Black Country* (London 1972).

Church, R.A. *Kenricks in Hardware* (Newton Abbot 1969).

Cicourel, A. *The Social Organisation of Juvenile Justice* (New York 1968).

Cicourel, A. and Kitsuse, J.I. 'A Note on the Uses of Official Statistics', *Social Problems,* 11 (autumn 1963), pp.131-9.

Cohen, S. (ed.) *Images of Deviance* (Harmondsworth 1971).

Coleman, T. *The Railway Navvies* (London 1965).

Collins, J.H.A. *History of the former Walsall Borough Police Force* (Brierley Hill 1967).

Collins, P. *Dickens and Crime* (London 1965).

Cornish, W.R. *The Jury* (Harmondsworth 1971).

Court, W.H.B. *The Rise of the Midland Industries 1600-1838* (London 1953).

Critchley, T.A. *A History of Police in England and Wales 900-1966* (London 1967).

Critchley, T.A. *The Conquest of Disorder* (London 1969).

Cross, R. and Jones, P.A. *An Introduction to Criminal Law,* 6th edn. (London 1968).

Cullen, M.J. *The Statistical Movement in Early Victorian Britain* (Hassocks, Sussex 1975).

Davies, V.L. and Hyde, H. *Dudley and the Black Country 1760 to 1860* (Dudley 1970).

Devlin, P. *The Criminal Prosecution in England* (London 1966).

Devlin, P. *The Enforcement of Morals* (London 1965).

Downes, D.M. 'Perks v. The Criminal Statistics', *Criminal Law Review* (1965), pp.12-18.

Drabble, P. *Black Country* (London 1952).

Ede, J.F. *History of Wednesbury* (Birmingham 1962).

Elwell, C.J.L. *The Iron Elwells* (Ilfracombe 1964).

Erikson, Kai T. *Wayward Puritans. A Study in the Sociology of Deviance* (New York 1966).

Finer, S.E. *The Life and Times of Sir Edwin Chadwick* (London 1952;

repr. New York 1970).

Freeman, J. *Black Country Stories and Sketches* (Bilston 1930).

Gash, N. *Mr. Secretary Peel* (London 1961).

Gatrell, V.A.C. and Hadden, T.B. 'Criminal Statistics and their Interpretation', in Wrigley, E.A. (ed.), *Nineteenth Century Society: essays in the use of quantitative methods for the study of social data* (Cambridge 1972), pp.336-96.

Gibbs, Jack P. 'Conceptions of Deviant Behaviour: The Old and the New', *Pacific Sociological Review* (1966), pp.9-14.

Hackwood, F.W. *The Story of the Black Country* (Wolverhampton n.d. ?1900).

Haden, H.J. *The 'Stourbridge Glass' Industry in the Nineteenth Century* (Halesowen 1971).

Hair, P.E.H. 'Mortality from Violence in British Coal Mines 1800-1850', *Economic History Review,* 2nd series XXI (1968), pp.545-61.

Hall, J. *Theft, Law and Society* (New York 1952).

Hanson, H. *The Canal Boatmen, 1760-1914* (Manchester 1975).

Harding, A. *A Social History of English Law* (London 1966).

Harper, F. *Joseph Capper* (London 1962).

Harrison, B. *Drink and the Victorians* (London 1971).

Hart, J. *The British Police* (London 1951).

Hart, J. 'Reform of the Borough Police 1835-56', *English Historical Review,* 70 (1955), pp.411-27.

Hart, J. 'The County and Borough Police Act, 1856', *Public Administration,* XXXIV (1956), p.405.

Hay, D., Linebaugh, P. and Thompson, E.P. (ed.). *Albion's Fatal Tree: Crime and Society in Eighteenth Century England* (London 1975).

Heidensohn, F. 'The Deviance of Women: a Critique and an Enquiry', *British Journal of Sociology* (1969), pp.160-75.

Henriques, U. 'The Rise and Decline of the Separate System of Prison Discipline', *Past and Present,* 54 (1972), pp.61-93.

Hilton, R.W. *The Truck System* (Cambridge 1960).

Hobsbawm, E.J. *Labouring Men* (London 1968).

Homeshaw, E.J. *The Corporation of the Borough and Foreign of Walsall* (Walsall 1960).

Homeshaw, E.J. *The Story of Bloxwich* (Walsall 1955).

Hood, R. and Sparks, R. *Key Issues in Criminology* (London 1970).

Jackson, R.M. *Enforcing the Law* (Harmondsworth 1971).

Jackson, R.M. *The Machinery of Justice in England,* 4th edn. (Cambridge 1964).

Jones, H. *Crime in a Changing Society* (Harmondsworth 1969).

Jones, J. Wilson *The History of the Black Country* (Birmingham 1950).

Jones, W.H. *Story of the Municipal Life of Wolverhampton* (London 1903).

Kenrick, W.B. (ed.) *Chronicles of a Nonconformist Family* (Birmingham 1932).

Lane, R. 'Urbanization and Criminal Violence in the Nineteenth Century: Massachusetts as a Test Case', in Graham, H.D. and Gurr, T.R. (ed.), *The History of Violence in America* (London 1969), pp.468-84.

Langley, S.J. 'The Wednesbury Tube Trade', *Univ. of Birmingham Historical Journal* (1949-50), pp.163-77.

Laski, H.J., Jennings, W.I. and Robson, W.A. (ed.) *A Century of Municipal Progress 1835-1935* (London 1935).

Lee, J.M. 'Parliament and the Appointment of Magistrates', *Parliamentary Affairs*, 13 (1959-60), pp.85-94.

Lemert, E.M. *Human Deviance, Social Problems, and Social Control* (Englewood Cliffs, N.J., 1967).

Lewis, B. *Coal Mining in the Eighteenth and Nineteenth Centuries* (London 1971).

MacDonagh, O. 'Coal Mines Regulation: the First Decade 1842-1852', in Robson, R. (ed.), *Ideas and Institutions of Victorian Britain* (London 1967).

MacLeod, R.M. 'Social Policy and the "Floating Population" 1877-1899', *Past and Present*, 35 (1966), pp.101-32.

Malcolmson, R.W. *Popular Recreations in English Society 1700-1850* (Cambridge 1973).

Mander, G.P. and Tildesley, N.W. *A History of Wolverhampton to the Early Nineteenth Century* (Wolverhampton 1960).

Mannheim, H. *Comparative Criminology*, 2 vols. (London 1965).

Martin, J.P. *Offenders as Employees* (London 1962).

Mather, F.C. *Public Order in the Age of the Chartists* (Manchester 1959).

Matza, D. *Delinquency and Drift* (New York 1954).

Melling, E. (ed.) *Kentish Sources*, vol.6; *Crime and Punishment* (Maidstone 1969).

Midwinter, E. *Social Administration in Lancashire 1830-1860: Poor Law, Public Health, Police* (Manchester 1969).

Moir, E. *The Justice of the Peace* (Harmondsworth 1969).

Morris, T. 'The Social Toleration of Crime', in Klare, H.J. (ed.), *Changing Concepts of Crime and its Treatment* (Oxford 1966).

Palfrey, H.E. *Foleys of Stourbridge* (Worcester 1945).

Palmer, R. and Raven, J. (eds.) *The Rigs of the Fair* (Cambridge 1976).

Parris, H. 'The Home Office and the Provincial Police in England and Wales 1856-1870', *Public Law* (1961), pp.230-55.

Perks, W. (Chairman) *Report of the Departmental Committee on Criminal Statistics* (HMSO, cmnd. 3448, 1967).

Phillipson, M. *Sociological Aspects of Crime and Delinquency* (London 1971).

Pollard, S. *The Genesis of Modern Management* (Harmondsworth 1968).

Powell, E.H. 'Crime as a Function of Anomie', *Journal of Criminal Law, Criminology and Police Science', 57 (1966), pp.161-71.

Price, J.M. *The Story of Bilston* (Bilston 1951).

Radzinowicz, L. *A History of English Criminal Law and its Administration,* 4 vols. (London 1948-68).

Raven, M. and J. (ed.) *Folklore and Songs of the Black Country,* 2 vols. (Wolverhampton 1965-6).

Raybould, T.J. 'The Development and Organization of Lord Dudley's Estates 1774-1845', *Economic History Review,* 2nd series XXI (1968), pp.529-44.

Raybould, T.J. *The Economic Emergence of the Black Country* (Newton Abbot 1973).

Reith, C. *A New Study of Police History* (Edinburgh 1956).

Reith, C. *British Police and the Democratic Ideal* (London 1943).

Reith, C. *Police Principles and the Problem of War* (London 1940).

Reith, C. *The Blind Eye of History* (London 1952).

Reith, C. *The Police Idea* (London 1938).

Robson, L.L. *The Convict Settlers of Australia* (Melbourne 1965).

Roper, J.S. *History of Coseley* (Coseley 1962).

Rubington, E. and Weinberg, M. (ed.) *Deviance: The Interactionist Perspective* (New York 1968).

Rudé, G. *The Crowd in History 1730-1848* (New York 1966).

Sellin, T. 'The Significance of Records of Crime', *Law Quarterly Review,* 67 (1951), pp.489-504.

Sellin, T. and Wolfgang, M. *The Measurement of Delinquency* (New York 1964).

Seth, R. *The Specials: The Story of the Special Constabulary in England, Wales and Scotland* (London 1961).

Shaw, A.G.L. *Convicts and the Colonies* (London 1971).

Silver, A. 'The Demand for Order in Civil Society: a review of some themes in the history of urban crime, police and riot', in Bordua, D. (ed.) *The Police: Six Sociological Essays* (New York 1967), pp.1-24.

Simon, D. 'Master and Servant', in Saville, J. (ed.) *Democracy and the*

Labour Movement (London 1954), pp.160-200.

Skolnick, J.H. *Justice Without Trial: Law Enforcement in Democratic Society* (New York 1966).

Smith, W.A. 'The Town Commissioners in Wolverhampton', *Journal of West Midlands Regional Studies* 1 (1967), pp.26-47.

Steer, D. *Police Cautions – a Study in the Exercise of Police Discretion* (Oxford 1970).

Stevenson, J. and Quinault, R. (ed.) *Popular Protest and Public Order* (London 1974).

Sutherland, E.H. and Cressey, D.R. *Criminology,* 8th edn. (New York 1970).

Thomas, D. *Social Aspects of the Business Cycle* (London 1925).

Thompson, E.P. ' "Rough Music": Le Charivari Anglais', *Annales: Economies Sociétés, Civilisations* (mars-avril 1972), pp.285-312.

Thompson, E.P. *The Making of the English Working Class* (Harmondsworth 1968).

Thompson, E.P. 'Time, Work-Discipline, and Industrial Capitalism', *Past and Present,* 38 (1967), pp.56-97.

Thompson, F.M.L. *English Landed Society in the Nineteenth Century* (London 1971).

Thorley, A. *The History of the Former Wolverhampton Borough Police Force* (Brierley Hill 1967).

Tildesley, N.W. *A History of Willenhall* (Willenhall 1951).

Tobias, J.J. *Crime and Industrial Society in the Nineteenth Century* (1967; Harmondsworth 1972).

Turk, A.T. *Criminality and Legal Order* (Chicago 1969).
Victoria County History of Staffordshire, vol.I (London 1908), vol.II (London 1967).

Walker, N. *Crime and Punishment in Britain* (Edinburgh 1965).

Walker, N. *Crimes, courts and figures – an introduction to criminal statistics* (Harmondsworth 1971).

Ward, J.T. and Wilson, R.G. (eds.) *Land and Industry – The Landed Estate and the Industrial Revolution* (Newton Abbot 1971).

Webb, R.K. *The British Working Class Reader 1790-1848* (London 1955).

West Midland Group *Conurbation: a Survey of Birmingham and the Black Country* (London 1948).

Whitbread, J.R. *The Railway Policeman* (London 1961).

Wilson, P. *Murderess* (London 1971).

Wolfgang, M., Savitz, L. and Johnston, N. (eds.) *The Sociology of Crime and Delinquency* (New York 1970).

Wootton, B. *Crime and the Criminal Law* (London 1963).

Wootton, B. *Social Science and Social Pathology* (London 1959).

Worcestershire Constabulary: History of the Force (Hindlip 1951).

Zangerl, C.H.E. 'The Social Composition of the County Magistracy in England and Wales, 1831-1887', *Journal of British Studies,* XI (1971), pp.113-25.

(7) Unpublished Theses

Barnsby, G.J. 'Social Conditions in the Black Country in the Nineteenth Century', Birmingham University Ph.D thesis 1969.

Barnsby, G.J. 'The Working-Class Movement in the Black Country', Birmingham University MA thesis 1965.

Cockroft, W.R. 'The Rise and Growth of the Liverpool Police Force in the Nineteenth Century', University of Wales MA thesis 1969.

Cumberland, A.G. 'Protestant Nonconformity in the Black Country 1662-1851', Birmingham University MA thesis 1951.

Eade, S. 'The Reclaimers: A Study of the Reformatory Movement in England and Wales, 1846-1893', Australian National University Ph.D thesis 1976.

Fereday, R.P. 'The Career of Richard Smith', Keele University MA thesis 1969.

Foster, D.O. 'Public Opinion and the Police in Lancashire 1839-42', Sheffield University MA thesis 1964.

Huffer, D.B.M. 'The Economic Development of Wolverhampton 1750-1850', London University MA thesis 1957.

Jones, J.D. 'The History of the Caernarvonshire Police Force 1856-1856-1900', University of Wales MA thesis 1956.

Lawton, R. 'Population Migration into and out of Staffordshire and Warwickshire 1841-1901', Liverpool University MA thesis 1951.

Macnab, K.K. 'Aspects of the History of Crime in England and Wales between 1805-1860', Sussex University D.Phil thesis 1965.

Westcott, R.A. 'Shoplifting and Law Enforcement: A Consideration of Social Factors affecting both Shoplifting and the Initiation of Legal Proceedings consequent to the Offence', London University M.Phil thesis 1971-2.

INDEX

accused, rights of during trial 106-8
acquittals 107-8
Addenbrook, Smith and Pidcock
    (Ironmasters) 193
Alison, Sir Archibald 13, 14, 15,
    284
Allen, G.C. 28
army 55, 57, 64, 71, 76-7, 271
assault 128, 262-3; aggravated 263-6;
    incidence of 22-3, 238, 262, 266,
    283; sentences for 173, 267-8;
    specific cases cited 262-5; upon
    police 86, 264-5, 266, 273; with
    weapons 265-6
Assizes 36, 50, 97, 98-9, 105-6,
    109, 111, 298-9; see also
    Committals to trial
Associations for the Prosecution of
    Felons, 119-23, 202, 206

Badger, Thomas and Isaac
    (Ironmasters) 193
Bagnall, John and Sons (Ironmasters)
    193
Baker, T.B.L. (magistrate) 19-20, 70
Barker, John (Ironmaster) 193, 194-5
Barrows and Hall (Ironmasters) 193
Bentley, Joseph 154-5
Bilston 25, 29, 30, 31, 32, 36, 55,
    301
Binny, John 228, 231, 232
Black Country, area and people
    24-37, 159-60, 164, 166;
    see also under entries for specific
    towns and parishes; Staffordshire;
    Worcestershire
Blackwell, Samuel Holden
    (Ironmaster) 193
Bloxwich 25
Bradley, John and Co (Ironmasters)
    193
Bramwell, Baron 258, 277
breaking and entering 126, 238-43;
    sentences for 173, 241, 243, 244;
    specific cases cited 239-40, 241-2,
    243-4
Brougham, Lord 118-19
buggery 259-70
burglary see breaking and entering
Burritt, Elihu 24-5
Byles, Mr Justice 277

canal boatmen 153, 165-8
Carpenter, Mary 19

Casey, Inspector 80
Chadwick, Edwin 20
chainmakers 29, 165-7, 251, 276-7
Chance Brothers, (glassmakers)
    193
Chartism 57, 77, 271, 274
Chillington 120-2, 206
Chillington Iron Co 193
Cicourel, A. 45
Clay, Rev. John (chaplain
    Preston gaol) 19-20
Clay, Rev W.L. (prison chaplain)
    19-20
Cobbett, William 201-2, 203
committals to trial 15, 44, 45-6,
    86-7, 97-9, 131, 133, 135-6,
    141-6; see also Quarter Sessions;
    Assizes
constables, parish 49, 54, 59-63, 64,
    75, 78-9, 81, 85, 87, 89 (n 19)
    90 (n 38), 113-14; background
    62-3; relations with New Police
    79-81
constables, special 55
counsel, legal, use of 103-5
courts, see Assizes; Quarter Sessions;
    committals to trial
Cradley 29, 30, 301
Cresswell, Mr Justice 184
crime: contemporary attitudes
    towards 13-15, 17-18, 20, 34,
    44, 83, 149-50, 154-8, 161.
    184-91, 202, 207, 238, 250, 283,
    284-5, 288-9; definition of 16,
    17-18, 20-21, 41-6, 238; and
    drunkenness 18, 22-3, 157,
    see also public order;
    drunkenness; and economic
    conditions 15, 18, 20, 22-3,
    145-7, 149, 163-4, 201, 203-4.
    186; and education, 17, 154-61;
    and industrial disputes 243-5,
    286-7, see also political crimes;
    public order; riots; strikes;
    juvenile 18, 19, 20, 161-4;
    see also Juvenile Offenders Acts;
    offenders, age of; and law
    enforcement 41-7, 48-50, see also
    police; prosecution system;
    prosecutors; measurement of
    incidence 16-24, 41-50, 142,
    144-7, 174 (n 7), 257, 283, 284;
    'official crime' 43-5, 49, 147;
    official statistics of 14-24, 43-50,

INDEX OF VICTIMS, PROSECUTORS AND ACCUSED IN CASES CITED